Motivated Resumes and LinkedIn Profiles!

(Including Cover Letters and Other Important Job Search Topics)

Insight, advice, and resume samples provided by some of the most credentialed, experienced, and award-winning resume writers in the industry!

Brian E. Howard, JD, CCMC, CJSS, CPRW
Certified Career Management Coach
Certified Job Search Strategist
Certified Professional Resume Writer

Virginia

Published in the United States by WriteLife Publishing
(An imprint of Boutique of Quality Books Publishing Company)
www.writelife.com

Printed in the United States of America

978-1-60808-183-7 (p)
978-1-60808-184-4 (e)

Library of Congress Control Number: 2017942563

Book design by Robin Krauss, www.bookformatters.com
Cover design by Ellis Dixon, ellisdixon.com
Editor: Michelle Booth

Other Books by Brian E. Howard

The Motivated Job Search
The Motivated Networker
Over 50 and Motivated!
The Motivated Job Search Workbook

In Appreciation

I would like to express my appreciation to Natalie Keylon for putting this project in motion. Without her initiative and project management skills, this book would likely still be on the drawing board rather than a reality.

I would also like to express my gratitude to each resume writer who donated their work, time, and insight to the creation of this book. The advice and samples you provided will inspire a lot of job seekers and touch their careers and lives for years to come. You have my deepest appreciation.

Message From the Author

Over the course of my career as an executive recruiter I have viewed thousands of resumes. The majority are terrible! They have a poor appearance, are badly formatted, or the content is utterly unpersuasive (the resume "tells" rather than "sells"). A bad resume reflects poorly upon the job seeker and hurts their chances in landing a job. An impactful resume is imperative to a successful job search!

The same can also be said for many LinkedIn profiles. Most are not complete, optimized (so that you can be discoverable by a LinkedIn word search), or compelling. A poor LinkedIn profile also hurts job seekers' chances of being discovered for career opportunities. It can also leave a less-than-favorable first impression when viewed by a HR recruiter or hiring executive.

This book was written for all career-minded professionals who want to improve the effectiveness of their job search by creating an impactful resume, LinkedIn profile, and other job-search communication and marketing materials. This book contains numerous samples written from some of the most experienced, credentialed, and award-winning resume writers in the industry. Each resume writer was profiled for experience, credentials, and quality of work. They have graciously donated their work for your benefit.

To make this book as instructive and informative for you as possible, each resume writer who participated in this project was provided a questionnaire about a host of resume writing, LinkedIn, and cover letter topics. Their responses formed the basis for "What the Pros Say." Their insight is invaluable.

Many of the resume writers provided detailed responses that were too lengthy for inclusion in the instructional part of this book. However, they are rich with insight and tips! Check out the Appendix, More of What the Pros Say, at the end of the book for additional information.

Brian E. Howard

Table of Contents

Part I

Some Things to Know about Your Job Search

There isn't a ruler, a yard stick or a measuring tape in the entire world long enough to compute the strength and capabilities inside you.

— Paul Meyer[1]

As you begin to think about your resume, LinkedIn profile, cover letters, and other job-search marketing materials, it is important to have a solid grasp of some fundamental elements of your job search and how they will affect the writing and creation of these important materials. This part of the book will help you understand and leverage the power of branding, understanding the employer's mindset, transferable skills, and professional qualities. Understanding these concepts and weaving them into your resume, a LinkedIn profile, and your other job-search marketing materials will increase their persuasiveness and lead to more interviews and job offers. Let's start with branding.

---

1 "Unleashing Your Genius," Quotes from the Masters, http://finsecurity.com/finsecurity/quotes/qm121.html (accessed February 4, 2017).

Branding

Always remember: a brand is the most valuable piece of real estate in the world; a corner of someone's mind.

— John Hegarty[2]

For a job search, your brand is a statement of who you are as a professional. It identifies you and works to differentiate you from other job seekers. It is imperative that you craft a professional brand for use on your resume and LinkedIn profile. A professional brand announces your distinct talents and what you represent to the marketplace. In essence, what do you want to be known for or found for (especially on LinkedIn)?

The process of branding is discovering who you are, what you are, what your unique abilities are, and communicating them through your resume, LinkedIn profile, and other job search marketing materials.

There are numerous benefits of creating an impactful brand, including:

1. You will differentiate yourself from other job seekers, and gain a huge advantage.

2. You create the initial impression the employer has of you.

3. You can convey your value to the employer more quickly.

4. You can match your skills and value proposition to the employer's needs more easily.

5. You can better determine which opportunities to pursue.[3]

The drawback of not having a professional brand is simple: You become a commodity. There is no perceived differentiation from other job seekers. You cannot command a premium and you have reduced leverage when it comes to compensation. Perhaps worse, employers will determine for themselves what they want to see in you. They will cast you in a light based on their own conclusions, which may not be the message you want to communicate.[4] This situation can be hazardous during a job search. Having a succinct brand immediately directs the hiring executive's thinking toward what you can do for them.

---

2 "10 Ways You're Building a Fantastic Brand," *Design Aglow* (blog), February 3, 2015, http://designaglow.com/blogs/design-aglow/16728432-10-ways-youre-building-a-fantastic-brand (accessed May 28, 2015).

3 Whitcomb, *Job Search Magic*, p. 122.

4 Ibid.

Perhaps the biggest benefit of creating a professional brand is the self-awareness of your unique skills and experience, and recognition of how they work together to create an impact. You will project the value of your abilities more clearly, resulting in a job that's a good match for your skill set. Branding can also help you set your sights on what you want your future career to be.

Additionally, when your networking contacts know your brand, they are much more likely to advance it for you through referrals, recommendations, and so on. When the right opportunities come along, you become top of mind (because of your brand).

The professional branding process requires introspection and thoughtful reflection. In some cases, thinking through your branding can be both an emotional and a professionally enlightening event.

Think of it this way: Your goal is to connect with employers both intellectually (you can do the job) and emotionally (you're a good fit). Having a well-crafted, professional brand helps on both levels. You must be perceived as the right candidate; and through branding, you are better able to align yourself to an open job position.

Keep in mind that the effectiveness of your brand is determined by the connection that exists between what the brand claims and what it can actually deliver. In other words, you must be able to prove and quantify your professional brand (through experience and accomplishments). Failing to do so will have disastrous results. Don't oversell your brand and capabilities.

Create a succinct brand. Think of it, in analogous terms, as a tagline or a theme that will be the foundation of your job search.

To help determine your brand, ask yourself some questions:

1. What am I good at or an expert in?

2. What have I been recognized for?

3. What is my reputation with others (subordinates, peers, senior management)?

4. What have been my strong points in past job reviews, including notable and consistent comments (if applicable)?

5. What differentiates me from others with the same job?

6. What professional qualities do I have that make me good at my job?

7. What are the professional achievements I am most proud of?[5]

The answers to these questions and the thoughts they provoke are essential to forming your brand. Now, synthesize the answers and thoughts into single words or short phrases

---

5 Ibid., Chapter 5, "Communicate Your Value Via a Career Brand."

that capture the concept of your responses. A convenient formula that seems to work for many job seekers is this:

[Job function or title] + [A bridge phrase, e.g., "with experience in," or "specializing in." Or, use of an action verb e.g., "applying," "focusing," etc.] + [reference to products, services, skills, industry, professional qualities, etc.]

For example:

Sales
Award-winning Sales Executive with Experience in Workers' Compensation, Pain Management, Consistently Exceeding Sales Goals.

Operations Management
Operations executive dedicated to improving operational efficiency through effective leadership.

Account Management
Client-focused account manager focused on client satisfaction and retention.

ERISA[6] Lawyer
Experienced Attorney Protecting ERISA fiduciaries from the Department of Labor.

A branding statement could also be a few separate descriptive words or phrases:

Process Improvement • Lean Six Sigma[7] • Turnaround Specialist
Marketing • Advertising • Public Relations

Your branding statement or branding keywords must appear with prominence on your resume, LinkedIn profile, and other job search marketing materials. It announces to the market what you want to be known for or found for.

---

6 Employee Retirement Income Security Act; see "Frequently Asked Questions About Retirement Plans and ERISA," US Department of Labor, http://www.dol.gov/ebsa/faqs/faq_consumer_pension.html (accessed July 8, 2015).

7 A process that resolves problems while reducing costs; see "What is Lean Six Sigma?" Go Lean Six Sigma, https://goleansixsigma.com/what-is-lean-six-sigma/ (accessed July 8, 2015).

What the Pros Say:

In your opinion, is it important to have a brand (either a branding statement or branding words) on a resume?

I think it's essential to have a branding statement. To me, it's your personal selling proposition. It is what will capture the attention of the hiring manager or recruiter in those six to ten seconds they read your resume. Every person is unique, and in order to stand out from others with similar qualifications, you must have your personal brand embedded in the document.

Michelle Robin, NCRW, CPRW

A strong, brief branding statement is crucial for an effective resume: it highlights the job seeker's unique value proposition, and gives the reader an immediate understanding of who the candidate is and what he/she can accomplish.

Nelly Grinfeld, MBA, NCRW, CEIC

Understanding the Employer's Mindset

There are a variety of motivations that prompt an employer in the commercial market to hire. However, the true essence underlying each motivation comes down to two reasons: to make or save the company money.[8]

Your career experience tells you that the sole reason a job exists in a company is to contribute to the profitability of the company.[9] The level of your performance in your job must add value. Depending upon the job, you can help an employer's bottom line by:

1. **Making the company money (generating new revenue)**—This can be achieved through sales, client retention, product development, and so on. You make money for the company by generating new revenue and keeping the revenue the company has.

---

8 Whitcomb, *Job Search Magic*, p. 274.

9 See also, Yate, *Knock 'em Dead*, p. 17.

2. Saving the company money (productivity improvements)—This is achieved by increasing productivity, increasing or creating operational efficiency, saving time, making others' jobs easier (more efficient or effective), and so on.

Having these concepts in mind when you write a resume, create a LinkedIn profile, and a cover letter (all of your marketing materials) is very important. When your marketing materials speak to these motivations, you will be getting and holding the hiring executive's attention.

There are many ways to generate revenue or save money for a company. Revealing them to an employer establishes or increases your value (ROI—Return on Investment) for hiring you. Here is a short list to get you thinking:

- Your duties and responsibilities from previous positions and how they translate to this position's ROI.

- Implement an improvement that saves time, improves efficiency, and/or streamlines workflow.

- Improve company image and branding.

- Open new sales-distribution channels.

- Improve a current product, or develop a new one.

- Expand business/sales through existing accounts.

- Enhance competitiveness through best practices, innovation, and so on.

- Improve client retention.

- Improve company culture, morale, and/or employee retention.

Whatever value you bring to the table will be directly related to your professional brand, skillset, and value proposition. These must be apparent in all of your job search marketing materials.

What the Pros Say:

What do you have your client think about to give you information to formulate the brand?

Their history of impacts, the things they do differently than their peers, the things they have been applauded for or complimented on. Their influence on sales, profits, efficiency, productivity, and cost-cutting. Their unique experiences, credentials, and pedigree elements.

Cheryl Lynch Simpson, CMRW, ACRW, COPNS

Knowing What an Employer Wants in an Open Position

Since an employer's purpose when hiring is to make or save money, how can you get inside an employer's mind and determine what he or she is looking for in the position (or position types) you want? The answer is simple, but you'll need to do a little research, as follows:

1. **Gather Job Postings.** Go online and collect some well-written job postings for a job you are qualified for and would enjoy. Websites such as http://www.indeed.com and http://www.simplyhired.com are rich resources.

2. **Create Your Own Master Job Description.** Call the document your "Master Job Description" (or anything else creative you want, i.e., "My Dream Job"). The purpose of your Master Job Description is to give you a road map inside the thinking of employers so you can better determine what they are looking for in filling a position (or position types).

a. **Title.** What words do employers use? These titles will likely reflect jobs you target when you search. The key is to use these same words—or very similar—on your resume, business cards, LinkedIn profile, cover letters, in your elevator speech, and so on.

b. **Skills, Duties, and Responsibilities.** Examine the job postings for skills, duties, and responsibilities that are common or frequently mentioned and note how often they are used.

    c. Match. Tie these skills to your experience. The more you use the keywords from the skills and titles in your written and verbal communications (including your resume), the higher your chances are of getting noticed because you make yourself directly relevant to an open job position.[10]

Once it's done, familiarize yourself with your Master Job Description. Think about it. What would you look for to fill this position if you were the hiring executive? Think both technical skills and transferable and "soft" skills (more on that in a moment). Congratulations—you are thinking like an employer!

With the understanding of how an employer thinks about an opening, relate or match how you have generated or saved money with former employers, while keeping your Master Job Description in mind. This is a crucial step, because you'll be tying an executive's hiring needs to your own experience and accomplishments. As you go along, refer to these insights you've discovered as you create your resume, LinkedIn profile, cover letters, emails, and so on.

Matching Experience and "Word Clouds"

There is a very clever way to match your experience with what an employer is looking for in a position(s). "Word clouds" are images made out of large words interspersed with smaller ones (you may have seen them). Some websites that can create them include www.wordle. net, www.tagcrowd.com, and www.worditout.com. Here's how you use this concept to your advantage:

Take the cursor on your computer and copy the job description electronically, go on one of these sites, and put the copied description into the space provided. Give it a second and "Voila," you have a word cloud. Pay particular attention to the larger words. Those are the words that are mentioned most frequently or the programming has selected as more important. List those words and make sure they appear in your resume, LinkedIn profile, and other communications. For example, let's say you see terms like "customer experience," or "client success" in the word cloud. You read the full description and conclude that these terms mean account management (to you). Therefore, you need to change your terminology on your resume perhaps to match the language employers are using (at least for that employer).

This technique works especially well when you have an actual job description for a position you are pursuing so you can alter your resume to use the terminology of the employer.

---

10 Ibid., p. 32.

Transferable Job Skills and Professional Qualities

Start by doing what's necessary, then what's possible, and suddenly you are doing the impossible.

— St. Francis of Assisi[11]

Transferable job skills come in two forms. First are the technical skills (expertise or ability) of your profession. If you are an engineer, you know engineering concepts. An accountant has skills related to accounting, and so on. These are your "hard" skills.

Hard skills can be transferable by convincing an employer that your skills can be easily repurposed and still be valuable to the employer. An oversimplified example is an accountant using math skills in a new role.

The second type of transferable job skills used in most professional level positions is "soft" skills. They are in addition to your technical expertise.

Here is a list of some sought-after, soft transferable job skills (not listed in any order of preference):

- Communication Skills (writing, listening, and speaking)—This is the most frequently mentioned skill employers desire.[12]

- Analytical Ability (problem solving)—This is your ability to view a situation, identify issues, evaluate relevant information, and implement a plan.

- Time Management (prioritizing)—This is your ability to prioritize and devote the appropriate amount of time to a task.

- Innovation (out-of-the-box thinking)—This involves harnessing creativity, reasoning skill, and what you've learned in life to solve problems.

- Collaboration (teamwork)—This means working with others toward a shared goal.[13]

- Management (people leadership)—This is your ability to gain buy-in or respect from a team, lead by defining goals and methods, and manage and guide a group toward shared goals or production targets.

11 "Doing What's Necessary, What's Possible, and What Seems to be Impossible," *The Recovery Ranch*, http://www.recoveryranch.com/articles/necessary-possible-impossible/ (accessed May 27, 2015).

12 Hansen, Randall S., PhD, and Katharine Hansen, PhD. "What Do Employers *Really* Want? Top Skills and Values Employers Seek from Job-Seekers," *Quintessential Careers*, http://www.quintcareers.com/job_skills_values.html (accessed May 27, 2015).

13 Ibid.

- Customer Focus (customer service)—This is your understanding that your employer must please and serve customers to be successful.

- Business Understanding (business acumen)—This is your ability to understand the business realities and the influences in the market and how they affect your employer.[14]

Since these skills are important and sought-after by employers, it is advantageous to mention transferable skills that apply to you on your resume and LinkedIn profile.

What the Pros Say:

What is your resume-writing philosophy about listing or mentioning transferable skills (e.g., communication skills, time management, etc.) on a resume?

I always have a Skills (transferable skills) section listed right after the summary statement. Ideally, the skills should match the skills required for the job being applied for.

Bob Janitz, NCRW

Closely aligned with the concept of transferable job skills are Professional Qualities. These can be viewed as your professional character traits. Here is a non-exclusive list of professional qualities (character traits) sought after by employers:

- Honesty—This is the foundation of every employment relationship. An employer must be able to trust you and respect you as a professional for the employment relationship to last and flourish.[15]

- Positive Attitude—Make no mistake—this is a big deal. Employers gravitate to people who show enthusiasm, energy, and a positive outlook.[16] Displaying a positive attitude will give you a competitive advantage in interviews and is a career management strategy. A positive attitude is that important.

---

14 Grant Tilus, "Top 10 Human Resources Job Skills Employers Want to See," (blog), *Rasmussen College*, July 29, 2013, http://www.rasmussen.edu/degrees/business/blog/human-resources-job-skills-employers-want-to-see/ (accessed July 10, 2015).

15 Hansen and Hansen, "What Do Employers *Really* Want?"

16 Victoria Andrew, "The Power of a Positive Attitude," (blog), Kavaliro Employment Agency, May 23, 2013, http://www.kavaliro.com/the-power-of-a-positive-attitude (accessed June 8, 2015).

- Interpersonal Relationships—Employers want employees who can get along with other coworkers. They avoid those who "rock the boat" and do not fit the culture.

- Work Ethic—Employers seek employees who put forth their best effort at all times. They seek employees who are motivated and internally driven. They want employees who are persistent and passionate about their jobs.[17]

- Dependable—Employers seek employees who will show up on time. They want to rest assured you will "be there" for the company. If you are a remote employee, they want to know you are working even though you are out of sight.

- Willingness to Learn—This is your intellectual flexibility, curiosity, and your ability not to get stuck in your own way of thinking. As you well know, markets change. Business changes. Your industry changes. You must be open and pursue opportunities to learn and change.[18]

- Other transferable skills and professional qualities include: Accountability, accuracy, ambition, assertiveness, autonomy, competitive, consensus building, decision making, enthusiasm, goal oriented, initiative, motivation, organized, presentation skills, quality management/improvement, tactful, working under pressure, among many others.

Just like transferable skills, mentioning professional qualities on your resume, LinkedIn profile, and other communications can be persuasive to a hiring executive. They can differentiate you from other job seekers that fail to include them.

What the Pros Say:

Can you, as a resume writer, create a level of differentiation by mentioning professional qualities on a resume (e.g., work ethic, honesty, etc.)?

Yes. These sorts of details are core to a person's brand—so if it is central to the client's sense of self, then I include, but also ground them with some details if possible to help the reader differentiate this candidate from a sea of others.

Virginia Franco, NCRW, CPRW

---

17 Hansen and Hansen, "What Do Employers *Really* Want?"

18 Ibid.

My style is usually to include three professional traits at the outset of a resume (methodical, tenacious, and pragmatic being a few of my favorites). This allows me to personalize the resume with traits that the client accurately possesses.

Wendi Weiner, JD, NCRW, CPRW, CCTC, CCM

Some job seekers have difficulty identifying transferable skills and professional qualities because they have not had to think about them for a long time. They've been doing their jobs not thinking of the skills they've been using to succeed. That's normal. There are a couple of ideas that can help expand upon your transferable skills (and perhaps your professional qualities). Think about your last position or two. What skills did you use? Now, think how you can break down those skills into smaller elements. For example, let's say you were in sales. What does that skill really entail? What's really going on there? Plenty!

Research on target industries	Identifying decision makers
Cold calling	Email marketing
Persuasive verbal skills	Articulation of value proposition
Presentation skills	Overcoming objections
Closing	Negotiating
Follow-up	And so much more . . .

By identifying these skills you can open yourself to other opportunities and employers who are searching for job seekers with these skills.

Once you have identified your transferable job skills and professional qualities, there are several things you can do with this valuable information:

- Weave them into your resume and LinkedIn profile.

- Make them a component of your branding message.

- Use them in cover letters and emails.

- Use them to write success stories.

- Use them as a part of your elevator speech.

- Use them in networking conversations.

- Use them in interviews.

The key to using these skills on the resume, LinkedIn profile and other written communications is to convey those skills and your unique professional qualities as valuable and match them to solving an employer's need. For the most impact, use your accomplishments as evidence of your transferable skills and professional qualities. Provide success stories of the skills and qualities in action. Making this connection is crucial when you are changing career paths.

Transferable skills and professional qualities cut across industry lines. For example, an employer will always value an employee with a strong work ethic whether they are an accountant or a zookeeper.

The Sum Total

Here is the magic formula for becoming a sought-after job seeker:

Your Technical Skills (your ability)

+ Your Transferrable Job Skills/Professional Qualities

+ Your Track Record of Success

= A Qualified Candidate!

Predominately, it is your resume and LinkedIn profile that are the marketing tools used to educate an employer that you are a Qualified Candidate. Once you are a Qualified Candidate, you must then differentiate yourself from other qualified candidates.

Part II

Impactful Resumes

Great works are performed, not by strength, but by perseverance.

—Prince Imlac,
character from Samuel Johnson's Rasselas[19]

During a job search, having an impactful resume is imperative. It sells your abilities, accomplishments, professional abilities, and establishes the match between you and the open position. Properly written and creatively presented, it will differentiate you from other job seekers and create a positive mental impression of you in the mind of the HR recruiter or hiring executive.

Do Job Seekers Need a Resume AND a LinkedIn Profile?

With the worldwide acceptance of LinkedIn, many job seekers ask whether there is still a need for a traditional resume. Has the LinkedIn profile replaced it? The simple answer is no. You must still have a well-written resume in your job-search arsenal. A LinkedIn profile does not replace your need for a resume.

Some writers have pushed the notion that a LinkedIn profile has made the traditional resume obsolete.[20] Nothing could be further from the truth. Understand that each serves separate and distinct roles in a job search.

Purpose of a LinkedIn Profile. Discoverability and Confirmation of Information. Your LinkedIn profile is your ever-present online resume. It is your digital presence and footprint. When complete, optimized, and compelling, its function is to get you noticed and

---

19 "Quotes on Perseverance," *The Samuel Johnson Sound Bite Page*, http://www.samueljohnson.com/persever.html (accessed June 2, 2015); "Rasselas: A Word of Caution," *The Samuel Johnson Sound Bite Page*, http://www.samueljohnson.com/rasselas.html (accessed June 2, 2015).

20 Some of these writers seem to have limited (discernable) experience in the staffing or employment industries, in either an HR or recruiting capacity. They are consultants in the media, marketing, and management arenas, or have a financial interest in promoting the idea that traditional resumes are passé or outdated.

discovered by a hiring executive or recruiter. It also functions to confirm and supplement information about your professional background. However, it has limitations. A LinkedIn profile is a one-size-fits-all template. Although the content differs from person to person, the format remains the same. LinkedIn has features that allow for customization such as attaching media, links, Slideshare presentations, and so on. This can heighten the interest of a hiring executive or HR recruiter, if they should take the time to look at them. This is all good. But, the purpose is to get you noticed and create interest; the resume has a different function.

The Tactical Uses of a Resume. A resume is a completely customizable document. It can, and should be, tailored to specific positions and for particular companies. It allows you to present yourself in a creative way apart from the format limitations of a LinkedIn profile. You can create your resume to showcase your achievements, skills, knowledge, and competencies that appeals to one hiring executive offering one position. When done properly, a customized resume can be used more easily by the hiring executive as a guide for the interview. This is a tactical advantage. Your customized resume plays to your strengths because you designed the format and strategically placed the information to differentiate you from other job seekers. You should feel comfortable about how it represents you.

Resumes Still Required. Most employers, either by direct request of the hiring executive or through the HR department, still require job seekers to submit resumes, via online applications or by email, as a required and accepted business practice. If resumes are passé, why are they still a requirement in the application and interview process? The truth is they are not passé. This is not to say that there could be pockets in some industries that are moving away from using resumes. However, for the majority of industries, and for most positions within those industries, the need for a well-written resume lives on.

What the Pros Say:

Do you still need a resume if you have a LinkedIn profile?

The resume is not dead and never will be. When LinkedIn first became relevant in the job market, employers would receive a resume and then seek to verify and clarify details by going to LinkedIn as part of the vetting process. Things have shifted somewhat. This still happens, but more frequently now we find the employer seeking out candidates using LinkedIn first. So, the employer's first introduction to the candidate is their LinkedIn profile. If they like what they see they will contact the candidate and ask to see a resume before inviting them for an interview. The order has changed, but both are still highly essential.

Michelle Dumas, NCRW, CPRW

Yes, because the two documents serve different purposes. A LinkedIn profile is a quick overview of your candidacy but doesn't convey all that you bring to the table. Hence a resume can do a better job of showcasing your career brand and achievements. In addition, there are many details in a resume such as numbers, client names, and the like, which shouldn't be made public on LinkedIn.

Cheryl Lynch Simpson, CMRW, ACRW, COPNS

What Is a Resume?

Let's start by defining what a resume is and is not. A resume is a unique form of written communication designed to quickly gain the attention of the hiring executive, inform them about you, sell you as a qualified candidate, and differentiate you from other job seekers. You have complete control of the appearance and content, and you should feel comfortable about how it represents you.

You are not writing an autobiography! Many job seekers put too much historical information into a resume. It's easy to do. You start writing and remembering and all of a sudden you have a resume that is a blizzard of words. Hiring executives simply will not read resumes like that. It's too much work. A resume must be informative, but it is really a marketing piece. It must be easy on the eyes and have adequate white space. The job market can be tough enough; don't create a self-inflicted obstacle by having a poorly formatted and poorly written resume.

Occasionally, job seekers will use personal pronouns ("I", "we") in their resumes. Don't do this. Although there are some differences of opinion by commentators, it is the prevailing view that a resume should not contain personal pronouns. Who else would you be talking about if not yourself?[21]

---

21 Messner, Max, "5 Tips for Better Resume Writing", http://www.dummies.com/careers/find-a-job/resumes/5-tips-for-better-resume-writing/ (accessed February 5,2017), Greenberg, Carrie, "Oops! Common Resume Mistakes," http://www.fastweb.com/career-planning/articles/oops-common-resume-mistakes (accessed February 5, 2017).

When you write your resume, the rules of proper sentence structure and punctuation are relaxed. However, it is essential that you convey complete thoughts with good use of action verbs.

What the Pros Say:

As a resume writer, what is your definition of a resume?

A resume is a sales pitch, a marketing document, part of a strategic multimedia communication plan, and a brand messaging piece rolled into one that defines a person's unique brand distinguishing it from competitors' through a strategic combination of visual (format, color and word placement), verbal (keywords and power phrases) and emotional attributes (qualitative soft skills and quantitative successes).

Cheryl Minnick, M.Ed., Ed.D, CCMC, NCRW

A resume is a marketing document that is targeted toward a specific audience and presents enough features and benefits to tell the reader that the candidate is a solution to a hiring problem. It is not an obituary of one's career!

Norine Dagliano, BA, NCRW, CFRW/CC

Time Is of the Essence

Most hiring executives generally spend between five and twenty seconds when first looking at a resume. So assume yours will not have much time to make an impression. If you're perceived as valuable to the company, you're in! If not, you're out! An employer must be able to quickly determine your potential value.

How can you make the most of those precious seconds? Showcase your most impactful qualifications and accomplishments on the upper half of the first page of your resume. The title of your resume, branding words/phrases/statement, the first sentence of your summary, and the first bullet point or two of your first showcase section create the biggest impact. By then, time's up! (More on showcase sections in a moment.) If these grab the interest of the employer, you get the next few seconds and perhaps more. This is another reason to use the word cloud technique—keywords and phrases will appear on your resume and "speak" to the hiring executive. Use this technique to capture any buzzwords that employer uses. Titling, branding, and a showcase resume have become important and popular for their ability to keep your resume in the executive's hands even longer. Once you have created initial interest, then the hiring executive will generally look at your current/previous employer, your position/function, length of employment, and successes.

What the Pros Say:

Studies have repeatedly shown that employers spend between five to twenty seconds when first looking at a resume. As a resume writer, how do you create a resume to capitalize on such a brief period of time?

First, it needs to be visually appealing and easy to read: plenty of white space, font size not too small or too large, font enhancements (bold, caps, color etc.). More to the point, the resume should immediately answer the following questions on every employer's mind: Who are you? What do you do? What can you do for me?

    This is accomplished by formatting the client's name as the predominate bit of information on the resume, following this with a headline that identifies the client's occupation/occupational focus, and then a branding statement that states what problems the client is best at solving.

Norine Dagliano, BA, NCRW, CFRW/CC

Putting the most compelling elements that substantiate a person's qualifications for the targeted job in the top one-third of the resume will help to pass that initial five- to twenty-second first review. Using a headline, short bullets, list of keywords or brief paragraphs will help to keep the eye moving along this section and, because of that content, persuade the reader to read the entire document with the ultimate goal of having the job seeker called for an interview.

Beate Hait, CPRW, NCRW

Your Resume Is Your Marketing Brochure

Your resume is frequently the first formal presentation of your professional credentials to a hiring executive. Think of it as your marketing brochure. It must have an impressive appearance (easy on the eyes), be well formatted (layout of how and where information is presented), and have persuasive content. Take the time to write a resume that appears professional. In order for your resume to provide that positive first impression, make sure that it:

- Has a clean, professional appearance. Develop a document with plain, simple language. Also be sure that the use of font size, bold print, lines, headings, spacing, bullet points, and so on, is consistent throughout. Any graphics and shading must be readable. Your resume must have a "wow" factor.

- Has a title. This will announce the professional qualifications to follow in the body of the resume.

- Has branding words or a branding statement. Either of these will help present your value proposition.

- Contains accurate contact information. Be sure your contact information is up to date.

- Features a concise, professional summary. This should highlight your background and give information to support your professional value proposition.

- Lists core competencies or qualifications. Showcase your strongest skills, abilities, experience, education, and special knowledge.

- Lists achievements. State what separates you from the pack.

- Is written for easy reading. Keep paragraphs short and use subheadings to break apart information.

- Could include charts, graphs, and pictures. To create distinction and visual appeal, use charts and graphs to show your accomplishments. Pictures that align with your industry, if well used, can be unique and draw the attention of the reader. As the saying goes, "a picture is worth a thousand words."

- Honestly represents your background. It is estimated that "more than 80 percent of resumes contain some stretch of the truth."[22] Be honest with your background and achievements. If an embellishment is discovered, you lose your integrity and

---

22 Bucknell Career Development Center, "Creating an Effective Resume," Bucknell University, http://www.bucknell.edu/documents/ CDC/Creating_An_Effective_Resume.pdf (accessed February 19, 2016).

credibility, and they will be extremely difficult to regain. Your employer won't trust you. And if others find out you embellished, that will make it harder still on your reputation.

It is perfectly acceptable, and encouraged, to write a generic form of your resume. You can modify it for specific opportunities that you pursue. Just remember what form of your resume you use with specific employers!

What the Pros Say:

Should a resume be written or revised for each position a job seeker pursues?

If a job seeker hopes to have a fighting chance—100 percent YES! Employers are looking for experts (specialists) and NOT generalists. The more you can make small customizations to your resume to show that you're the best fit for the company, company culture, the industry, and the position the higher your resume response rate will be from potential employers.

Jessica Hernandez, Certified Social Branding Analyst

Yes, as a gift should be carefully selected, thoughtfully assembled and individually wrapped for each person on your Christmas list. One size does NOT fit all in a world of diversified talent, compartmentalized jobs and ATS [Applicant Tracking Systems].

Cheryl Minnick, M.Ed., Ed.D, CCMC, NCRW

Use of Keywords

Keywords are specific words or phrases that reflect your experiences and abilities, and are frequently buzzwords, or terms-of-art. You are undoubtedly familiar with the keywords of your industry and your abilities. Make sure they appear prominently on your resume. Examples include "P & L" and "ROI" for commerce. Others include "pull-through strategies" for sales and marketing, or are specific to a particular industry (like a professional designation). Your resume must contain certain keywords to get the employer's attention and communicate that you are qualified for a particular position. The importance of keywords on your resume cannot be overstated.

Keywords can include the following:

- Position title
- Industries
- Professional designation
- Skills, knowledge, core competencies
- Industry terms-of-art (and abbreviations)
- Employer names (past or present)
- Licenses, certifications
- Location (city, state)
- Software and technologies you're familiar with
- Education (school names and degrees)

It can be impactful to connect a keyword to an accomplishment, whenever possible. For example, Client Retention—maintained a client retention rate of 94 percent for the last four years.

When pursuing a particular opening, use the word cloud technique to capture buzzwords used by that employer.

What the Pros Say:

The use of keywords is important on a resume. What would you consider are the more important kinds of information that lead to keywords?

If you want a resume that will pass resume scanning programs, attract the hiring manager's attention, and get you interviews, you need to tailor the resume to the specific job you're seeking. You need to closely read the job posting to find key words and phrases in order to match what the employer is seeking with what you've done.

Write your resume to highlight your accomplishments, then weave in some keywords from the job posting while staying honest. State your accomplishments and contributions in order to position yourself to interview effectively.

Nelly Grinfeld, MBA, NCRW, CEIC

Reading job postings and job descriptions will provide a wealth of information on the keywords to include in the resume. O*Net OnLine (www.onetonline. org) offers information on job roles in all industries and is a great tool to research the types of jobs available.

Beate Hait, CPRW, NCRW

Resume Formats

The three fundamental variations of resumes are: Chronological, Functional, and Showcase.

The Chronological format is the most traditionally used resume format. A job seeker's experience in the work world is listed in reverse chronological order. This format emphasizes duties and responsibilities with accomplishments listed under each employer. Jobs, as well as managerial and other responsibilities, are grouped by title and company, with dates of employment. This is a common format frequently used by tenured professionals with consistent work experience in one field or position type.[23]

What the Pros Say:

What is your opinion regarding the use of a reverse Chronological resume?

It's the best plan 99 percent of the time. It's the easiest to read and the format that most hiring managers and recruiters expect to see.

Amy Adler, MBA, MA, CMRW, CCMC

---

23 Yate, *Knock 'em Dead*, p. 45–46.

I always use a chronological format. A client's most recent job and accomplishments usually carry the most weight to the reader.

Bob Janitz, NCRW

The Functional format emphasizes skills and qualifications to strategically sell experience that may align to the needs of the employer. A job seeker's experience is divided into a skill-based section that demonstrates qualifications, training, education, and specific accomplishments, and a reverse chronological listing of employment including company name, title, and dates (toward the end of the resume). This format works well for those with gaps in employment and those whose career has involved several employers.[24] Most job seekers should be careful when considering the Functional format since employers strongly favor a Chronological or Showcase resume.

What the Pros Say:

What is your opinion regarding the use of a Functional resume?

Don't do it! The functional resume typically is the kiss of death to a candidate— it's all about what someone "could" do in some context rather than about what the person has done and is likely to do in in their next role. When in doubt, go with the traditional reverse-chronological resume, as it's easily digestible by the candidate's audience, whether that person is a recruiter or a hiring manager.

Amy Adler, MBA, MA, CMRW, CCMC

In ninety-nine percent (99%) of cases it is best to stay away from a functional resume format. Recruiters and hiring managers get confused by this ambiguous format that does not associate your experience with any specific job, so the resume ends up in the trash. It is almost always best to write the resume in reverse chronological format, with the current or most recent position listed first.

Nelly Grinfeld, MBA, NCRW, CEIC

---

24 Ibid., p. 46.

The Showcase resume is a growing trend that has developed over the last several years and combines the best features of the Chronological and Functional formats. For most experienced professionals and executives (whether they have a more diverse employment background or not), this format is worth serious consideration. The concept is to showcase your best professional selling points—qualifications, industry knowledge, and achievements—immediately in the top half or top two-thirds of the resume's first page. Work and education is then listed in reverse chronological order just like a traditional chronological resume. Using this format, you are allowed to be selectively repetitive. Some of your showcase items can appear again in the chronological section of your resume. This way, the hiring executive knows where and when you learned or achieved your showcase qualifications.

What the Pros say:

What is your opinion regarding the use of a Showcase resume? (a.k.a. Combination resume)

This is an extremely successful format if the job seeker is showcasing functions and successes within each employment.

Cheryl Minnick, M.Ed., Ed.D, CCMC, NCRW

To me this is the best of both worlds. It allows the candidate to highlight older experience that may be more relevant, up front in a summary section. Then you still have a professional experience section that shows when you did what. Sometimes I even turn the experience section into a more functional format by listing a skill and then supporting that with an accomplishment underneath each job.

Michelle Robin, NCRW, CPRW

The Dateless Resume

A dateless resume can be any of the resume formats just mentioned, and is void of any dates . . . employment, education, volunteer work, everything. Listing information this way is not recommended because a hiring executive will immediately notice and probably think "Oh my goodness, he [or she] must be ancient!" Raising red flags or emphasizing age biases is not the first impression you want to make. However, there is one viable alternative.

Provide dates going back only fifteen to twenty years, and leave off other dates. This concept can be used with any resume format. You can also group employment beyond your chosen time frame as a subsection to your experience section without dates. There's a risk the hiring executive may still conclude you are a "tenured" professional. But it is a middle ground if you want to omit some dates from your resume.

What the Pros Say:

What is your opinion regarding the use of a Dateless resume?

Fatal mistake. It appears that employment gaps are being hidden.

Bob Janitz, NCRW

Haven't written one in thirty years in the business; cannot imagine that I ever will. This wouldn't be acceptable to 99.99999 percent of employers out there.

Cheryl Lynch Simpson, CMRW, ACRW, COPNS

Parts of a Resume

No matter what form of resume you choose, each has certain parts in common that appear in the same places, or serve the same function. These are:

Identification/Contact Information

This section appears at the top of your resume and includes your name (with notable professional designations), telephone numbers (home and/or cell phone), and email address. Including your LinkedIn profile address is optional. A new trend is omitting your residence address. This is acceptable, but still include city and state. Make sure your name stands out with larger font, bolding of the letters, or another technique.

No photos should appear on your resume (unless it is required in your industry). If they want to know what you look like they can look at your LinkedIn profile.

Email Address

Your email address must be professional. Some advocate that you create an email account tailored for your job search and the email address should be supportive of your branding, i.e., engineeringexpert@xyz.net. Avoid this. Many hiring executives view this "technique" with chagrin.

Make sure your email address does not contain any reference to your age or year of birth, e.g., Johnsmith1961, or shelia57.

There are several professional formats you can use:

- jsmith@xyz.com

- john.smith@xyz.com

- smithj@xyz.com

- john@xyz.com

- johns@xyz.com

- johnsmith@xyz.com

If you need to, add your lucky number, area code, zip code, or other number prior to the @ symbol.

Title

By titling your resume, it announces what the resume is going to describe so the reader doesn't have to scan the entire resume to determine your professional background. Be reasonably specific with your title. For example, "Senior Healthcare Sales Representative," "Casualty Field Claims Professional," "Vice President of Operations."

The title of your resume should align with your LinkedIn profile and the business card type(s) you choose to use.

What the Pros Say:

Is it important to have a title on a resume?

Yes, it provides clarity to the person who is doing the initial resume scan and deciding whether to consider a candidate further. Leaving off a title can also create confusion over which position you're interested in applying for with larger companies.

Jessica Hernandez, Certified Social Branding Analyst

Yes. It is the equivalent to a headline on a newspaper article. Would you ever read an article that was missing a headline?

Virginia Franco, NCRW, CPRW

Branding Statement

Your branding statement should appear under your resume's title. This could be either a statement or a few descriptive words that relate to or support your brand. Some examples include:

Dedicated to improving sales through effective leadership.

Process Improvement • Manufacturing Efficiency • Strategy

Objective Statement

The objective statement has fallen out of favor for seasoned professionals and should not be used except for special circumstances (a significant change in career path, industry sabbaticals, and so on).

If you choose to use an Objective Statement, ensure it clearly states your purpose for pursuing a position with the employer. The content of the resume must support the Objective Statement.

Using an objective statement properly means keeping it short. Avoid such nebulous phrases as:

- "Opportunity for advancement" or "Advance my career"
- "Challenging opportunity"
- "Utilizing my experience"
- "Professional growth"
- "Increase in compensation"

State the benefits you can bring to the employer—not the benefits you want from the employer.

What the Pros Say:

What is your opinion regarding the use of an Objective Statement?

RUN AWAY! Employers couldn't care less about your objective. They naturally assume that your objective is to secure employment with them. Opt for a position title, personal branding statement and career snapshot that show the employer how you can meet a bleeding need and be a benefit to their company.

Your resume is not the place to talk about what you want, it's the place to convince employers that they're going to lose out on all the great success you'll bring with you if they choose someone else.

Jessica Hernandez, Certified Social Branding Analyst

Summary

The summary brings together the experiences of your career into the present. It is a recommended section for seasoned professionals and should be a short paragraph with an overview of your most important job experience, technical or professional proficiencies, traits, and accomplishments.[25] It can also be formatted as a series of bullet point statements.

For some tenured job seekers, there is a fine line to walk when writing your summary. You want to communicate your experience without coming across as old. Here you have

---

25 Ibid., p. 47.

some judgment calls to make. Let's say you have over twenty-five years of experience. You could summarize that as "over fifteen years of experience." It is a true statement that communicates experience without coming across as older. Or, perhaps you have thirty-five years of experience. You could represent that you have "over twenty years of experience." The choice is ultimately yours. The concept is this: it is permissible to generalize your tenure in the summary section of your resume.

A summary section can have several different names, including:

- Career Description
- Career Summary
- Professional Qualifications
- Profile
- Qualifications
- Summary of Qualifications

The summary could contain some of the following information: level of responsibility, skills and responsibilities, potential contributions (as seen from the employer's perspective), and highlights of top strengths and accomplishments. It emphasizes key information detailed later in the resume. Be sure to mention languages, special degrees, and other noteworthy skills. The summary acts much like an executive summary section of a long document or white paper. A simple three-part formula to help you create an impactful summary is:

1. A statement regarding your function or title, possibly including a reference to tenure.

2. A statement identifying your technical abilities and qualifications. Accomplishments can be included here as well.

3. A statement regarding your transferable job skills and/or professional traits.

For example:

Position: Senior Accountant

Statement regarding function or title: A detail-oriented CPA with over fifteen years of experience.

Statement regarding technical ability or qualifications: Proven ability in financial forecasting and analysis, audit, reconciliation, tax law, and evaluating and consulting with clients regarding business investments and opportunities.

Statement regarding transferable job skills/professional qualities: Conscientious, self-motivated, and service-oriented professional who enjoys client interaction.

Complete Summary: A detailed-oriented CPA with over fifteen years of experience. Proven ability in financial forecasting and analysis, audit, reconciliation, tax law, and evaluating and consulting with clients regarding business investments and opportunities. Conscientious, self-motivated, and service-oriented professional who enjoys client interaction.

After you have this foundation in place, you can add to it as your discretion dictates. An effective summary section should be concise. Many professionals make the mistake of making a summary too long. By using this three-part formula you will be crafting a solid, impactful summary.

What the Pros Say:

As a resume writer, what do you want to achieve with a Summary section?

Besides answering the three burning questions on every employer's mind (Who are you?, What do you do?, What can you do for me?), I view the Summary section much the same as a movie trailer or the blurb on a book jacket. A good Summary will grab attention, pique interest, and create desire by presenting "the coming attractions." Just like a movie trailer, we want the "viewer" to feel "this is one I've got to see" so he/she will set it aside to dive into later.

Norine Dagliano, BA, NCRW, CFRW/CC

This is the most important part of your resume. It should highlight what you are most proud of in your career that is relevant to where you're going, and any common threads of your career.

If someone found the top third of your resume, which contains your header and summary, lying on the ground, they should be able to tell who you are, what is unique about you, and the value you bring to an employer. Not only that, but it should make them look around on the ground for the rest of your resume because they want to read more. That is what I aim to achieve with every summary I write.

Michelle Robin, NCRW, CPRW

Core Competencies

Almost all resumes for experienced professionals and executives should have a Core Competencies section. Although there are likely hundreds of competencies and skills that could be listed, as a rule keep it to no more than three columns of five, totaling fifteen.

Your competencies should fall into one of the following major areas: technical ability (what you are good at), communication skills, leadership, analytical thinking, teamwork, and time management. These tend to be the broad skills most employers seek.[26]

This section can have other titles, such as:

- Abilities
- Core Strengths and Expertise
- Key Skills
- Skills
- Signature Strengths

What the Pros Say:

Do you find it important, as a resume writer, to list Core Competencies/ Skills somewhere on a resume?

It is essential to include Core Competencies/Skills/Areas of Expertise somewhere within the resume since these terms often constitute the search criteria that a company uses in an applicant tracking system to identify candidates for initial consideration. We want that resume to land in the

---

26 Ibid., p. 48.

"active candidate pool" file. I often also include a list of those keywords to make it easy for the hiring authority to immediately note these essential skills in the job seeker's resume.

Beate Hait, CPRW, NCRW

Showcase Section(s)

If you elect to use a showcase-style resume, the next section (or two, depending on your circumstances) can be your Showcase section. Although you have a lot of discretion on titling and content, the key is to make this section substantive and impressive. Use lists and bullet points to make the information easier to read.

Possible titles for Showcase section(s) include:

- Achievement Summaries
- High-Impact Contributions
- Notable Performance Highlights
- Distribution or Vendor Partners
- Expertise
- Languages (Foreign or IT)
- Marquee Clients
- Product Knowledge
- Recommendations
- Sales Awards

Employment History

The Employment History section covers work experience for the last fifteen years or so. List employers in reverse chronological order. Work experience beyond fifteen years can be listed at the end with single sentences or as a grouping of employer names.

Begin with details on the most important items: current company/employer's name, your title(s), and dates (in years). List what the company's official name is now, even if it was purchased or merged after you began work there, e.g., "GlobalOutlook (formerly Global SpyGlass)." Many company names or initials could make it hard to figure out what the company is or does. Therefore, use a sentence that encapsulates the company's position, earnings, products, and/or other unique qualifiers. As an example: NAME OF COMPANY: *"A worldwide manufacturer of high-end personal-care products with $134M in annual sales."*

Most times, be sure to list the company name first, and only once. This reduces the likelihood employers will think you have job-hopped when you have not.

Next, follow the company name with your title. If this title is in-house and hard to understand, include a translation or generic job title. For example, you can substitute "Purchasing Agent" with "Product Specialist/Purchasing Representative" if that makes things easier for those who aren't a part of your industry or company. Providing a functional title educates the hiring executive about your actual function and role. If you held multiple titles with the same employer, mention a date next to each to show promotions or advancement within an organization.

Job Scope Description

For each position, write a four- to six-sentence description of your duties and responsibilities (what you did). This could include information regarding the dimension and scope of the position, function, staff size, geographical reach, budget, reporting relationships, departments, and so on. Here's an example:

Professional Experience

GlobalOutlook (formerly Global SpyGlass), Anytown, Anywhere 20XX–Present

Regional Sales Executive

Promoted to revitalize underperforming Northeast sales territory. Developed new business channels on a regional and national basis. Reestablished relationships with client base. Products included enrollment technology, analytics, and predictive modeling, among others.

This section can have other titles, such as:

- Career Experience
- Employment Background
- Experience
- Professional Experience
- Relevant Experience

- Work Experience
- Career Narrative

What the Pros Say:

When you create the employment history section of a resume, what is your approach? What are you thinking?

I aim to summarize their tenure and the context of their achievements in a brief two- to three-line position description. I reserve the bulk of each position's space for three to six hard-hitting achievements. I place these in order of importance or relevance and keep each bullet to one to two lines if at all possible. The higher the level of position the person is pursuing the more I emphasize their impact on strategic planning versus tactical execution.

Cheryl Lynch Simpson, CMRW, ACRW, COPNS

In the employment history section, rather than simply listing tasks performed, I look to tell the story of how well the job seeker performed the job and in doing so helped the employer save time, save money, make money, be more productive, increase market share, reduce expenses, etc. Including metrics in those statements makes these bullet points stronger.

Beate Hait, CPRW, NCRW

Accomplishments

An accomplishment is a detailed account of success regarding the duties and responsibilities of your job. Make sure your specific successes are crystal clear to the hiring executive.

Accomplishments are vitally important to your job search. It has been said that qualifications often get you an interview, but accomplishments and rapport are what get you the job[27]. Identify and quantify your accomplishments, and use bullet points for easy reading.

---

27 Guest Author (Bob Bozorgi), "Qualifications Will Get You an Interview, But They Won't Get You Hired," *The Undercover Recruiter* (blog), http://theundercoverrecruiter.com/qualifications-will-get-interview-wont-get-hired/ (accessed February 19, 2016).

Accomplishments:

• Clearly demonstrate your ability to improve a company's efficiency or bottom line.

• Emphasize positive work outcomes with dates, percentages, numbers, and so on.

• Display why an organization will find you effective.

• Translate your value by showing your performance in similar circumstances.

Accomplishments focus on quantities, improvements, and results from an organization's perspective. How did you make or save the employer money?[28] Or how did your actions lead to a beneficial result?[29] Highlight accomplishments with $, %, or # as applicable to enhance credibility.

Accomplishments can be a separate Showcase section on your resume. Or, especially for chronological resumes, they can be a subsection to each position you have held.

What Accomplishments Get Employers' Attention?

Remember that employers generally hire with two main goals: to make or save money.[30] The more obvious your accomplishments appear to achieve either goal, the more powerful the accomplishment is. The following list of accomplishments can help spark ideas as you contemplate your own (refer back to Understanding the Employer's Mindset):

1. Increased revenues

2. Awards, rankings against your peers, or production numbers

3. Process improvement that saves money or time, increases efficiency, or makes work easier

4. Improved company image, branding

5. Opened new distribution channels for sales

6. Product improvements, product development

7. Expanded business/sales through existing accounts

8. Anything that enhances competitiveness

9. Improved client retention

10. Improved company culture, morale, employee retention

---

28 Whitcomb, *Job Search Magic*, p. 274.

29 See also, Safani, "Tell a Story."

30 Whitcomb, *Job Search Magic*, p. 274.

The following is a list of positions. Under each are ideas from which accomplishment statements can be created. Although a particular position type may not apply to you, adopt this mindset when considering your accomplishments.

ACCOUNTING
- Design and implementation of cost controls and quantifiable results
- Optimization of business output through software or other technology
- Application of tax laws

ACCOUNT MANAGEMENT
- Client retention
- Contribution to sales growth (upselling)
- Key account responsibilities

ENGINEERING
- Financial outcomes from new designs or products
- Patents awarded or pending
- Projects managed and financial results

EXECUTIVE-LEVEL MANAGEMENT
- Measurable increases in revenues, profits, EBITDA[31], and ROI
- Leadership regarding strategic planning, long-term business development
- Mergers, acquisitions, joint ventures

HEALTH CARE
- Increase in quality of patient care, with detailed results
- Increased impact of outreach services, with their results
- Attainment and maintenance of stringent regulatory requirements
- Reduction in re-admittance

HUMAN RESOURCES
- Success in recruiting personnel
- Employee retention
- Improvements in employee benefits and cost reduction

---

31 "Earnings before interest, taxes, depreciation, and amortization"; see Arline, Katherine. "What Is EBITDA?" Business News Daily, February 25, 2015, http://www.businessnewsdaily.com/4461-ebitda-formula-definition.html (accessed February 19, 2016).

MANUFACTURING
- Increases in production and worker productivity
- Improvements in safety
- Reductions in operating costs and overhead expenses

RETAIL
- Increases in gross revenues, profit margins, and market impact
- Improvements in inventory turnover, speed to market
- Reductions in inventory, operating, and personnel costs

SALES
- Sales honors, awards, percentages over quota, rankings against peers
- Increases in revenues, profits, and market share
- Sold new national accounts
- Expansion into previously undeveloped territories and markets

TECHNOLOGY
- Development of new technologies and their financial results
- Detailed results of implementation (e.g., revenue increases, cost reductions)
- Patents awarded
- Timely systems conversion, integration

What the Pros Say:

How important is it to quantify accomplishments on a resume?

Very! In today's times, the readers of resumes want to see what differentiates one candidate from another. Job tasks and responsibilities will not vary much. However, the key accomplishments and achievements allow the job seeker to stand out more.

Wendi Weiner, JD, NCRW, CPRW, CCTC, CCM

Absolutely imperative! Without quantified achievements a resume is no more than a list of jobs and cannot position a candidate to compete in a tight job market.

Cheryl Lynch Simpson, CMRW, ACRW, COPNS

Education

Provide educational background starting with your most advanced degree or major, and the university or college name. Abbreviations are fine: BS, BA, MS, MBA, and PhD. Use the same fonts for school and company names. If you do not have a full degree, include those details by mentioning what degree you pursued and the amount of years or semesters attended (or percentage completed, if available). Include your education at the bottom unless you feel there are grounds to move it up or if it is customary in your industry to have it appear early on a resume.

What the Pros Say:

Do you have any unique techniques in writing the Education section?

I will ensure either the degree or the name of the institution stands out—depending on which one is more powerful and/or relevant to the job search. For instance, a degree from Harvard stands out regardless of the focus of study, as does a master's in information systems for someone gunning for a CIO role.

Virginia Franco, NCRW, CPRW

When writing the Education section, the focus can be either on the degree, the major area of study, or the college/university—whichever piece would best support the job seeker's target. If the Education piece is the job seeker's main qualification—such as a recent college graduate or someone who is changing careers and has earned new credentials—the Education section should be listed under the Summary section rather than at the end of the resume.

Beate Hait, CPRW, NCRW

Other Credentials

The following sections can add depth to your resume. You may not need every section below—just those representing strong qualifications for you.

1. Affiliations/Associations
Affiliations and associations can be impactful on a resume by indicating your involvement in your industry and the community. Include groups of which you are a member. An Affiliations section may look like this:

> American Marketing Association
>
> Society for Human Resource Management
>
> Health Care Administrators Association
>
> American Red Cross

2. Appointments
Appointments are a list of offices you held (generally in the last five years) and demonstrate involvement in both professional and civic organizations. Include only professional or significant charitable organizations. An Appointments section may look like this:

> Chairperson, American Management Association, 20XX–20XX
>
> Paul Harris Fellow, Rotary International, 20XX–20XX
>
> Regional Director—Rapid Response, American Red Cross, 20XX–20XX

3. Awards/Honors
This section reveals achievements, awards, and honors not connected to your career. Include accolades from college activities, professional service organizations, volunteer work, and so on. Examples include:

> Team Captain, Central Minnesota University Softball Team
>
> Up and Comer Award, Rotary International
>
> Volunteer of the Year, American Red Cross

4. Languages
The world is getting smaller. Being fluent or proficient in a foreign language can be

a significant differentiator, depending on the kind of positions you are pursuing. A Language section generally appears this way:

Fluent in Portuguese

Proficient in Italian

5. Licenses
List all licenses relevant or required in your industry or the job description for your desired position. Don't list a real estate license if you aren't seeking a position in that industry.

6. Professional Training and Designations
Continuing education in your chosen field is important. It's a clear indication to future employers that you stay current and are improving your skills and knowledge. List noteworthy workshops, seminars, and other continuing education you have completed in the last five years. List only those seminars that pertain to the type of position you are looking for. A typical professional training section will look like this:

Dale Carnegie Corporate Strategy—20XX

Managing for Excellence, sponsored by the American Management Association—20XX

Selling!, a five-day program sponsored by Kaufman and Gentry Sales Training—20XX

If you've attended more than five courses, just note the types along with who sponsored them, such as:

Completed sales, management, and computer skills trainings sponsored by the American Management Association—20XX

7. Technical
Understanding technology is becoming indispensable in today's world. Include your proficiencies with technology here. A Technical section generally appears this way:

C++, Cisco UCS, Commvault, VMWare, Windows Servers, Microsoft Active Directory, WordPerfect, PowerPoint, Microsoft Office, Microsoft Outlook, Adobe Acrobat

What the Pros Say:

There is a variety of additional information that can be included on a resume, such as: affiliations/associations, memberships, appointments (appointed positions), non-career related awards and honors, languages, and licenses, among others. How do you treat this information on a resume?

I present this information briefly. It's part of the personal brand, and you never know when you'll run into a hiring manager who was also an Eagle Scout or sits on the board of your nonprofit. A note on nonprofits, volunteerism is becoming increasingly important to put on a resume as companies are more and more concerned with corporate citizenship.

Kimberly Robb Baker, NCRW, CJSS, CMRW

It depends on what it is and how relevant it is to where my client is going in their career. Most often I regulate these types of things to a Volunteerism or Of Note section at the end of a resume. However, there are certain awards that are more impressive and may need to be featured earlier in the resume. I had a client once who was a top 36 under 36, a volunteer of the year, and was accepted into a special mentor program. While some of these were not career related, showing them all together up front made more sense.

Michelle Robin, NCRW, CPRW

Use of Recommendations on a Resume

When properly used, recommendations, testimonials, and endorsements appearing on a resume can be impactful. Due to a resume's limited space, a statement of recommendation must be short, relevant, and direct. Consider putting recommendations in quotes, italics (for effect), or both. Testimonials and endorsements from others are more powerful than what you say about yourself.[32] Some recommendations can double as accomplishments (as in the first example).

---

32 See also, Matt, "Brag Book."

For the recommendation to be effective, the person providing it must be identified by name and title. Get permission from this individual prior to including their recommendation on your resume.

Examples:

"Increased average profit on special orders by 17 percent, resulting in thousands of dollars in new revenue."

Letter of Appreciation from Elizabeth Jones, VP of Accounting

"Bonnie is a valued member of our team. Her expertise in cost-accounting strategies positively impacted our bottom line."

Elizabeth Jones, VP of Accounting

You can also close a resume with an impactful recommendation:

"Katy was clearly the most client-focused account manager we had on our team!"

Bob Johnson, Vice President of Account Management

What the Pros Say:

What is your opinion about including recommendations on a resume?

Short quips from positive performance reviews, letters of recommendation or appreciation serve brilliantly on resumes as testimonials and are quite successful if used strategically. A testimonial should speak to job tasks of the future job and to the candidate's past accomplishments that would add value to the future company. OR, the testimonial could be from a powerful player in the industry, whose voice holds power (the mayor, a senator, a senior VP).

Cheryl Minnick, M.Ed., Ed.D, CCMC, NCRW

I like to include brief quotes. You can let others say laudatory things about you that would have a false or boastful ring if you stated them in the first person. Brief is the keyword, though. Most recommendations are long-winded. Quote selectively from them so they can be consumed and understood quickly.

Kimberly Robb Baker, NCRW, CJSS, CMRW

Information NOT to be Included on a Resume

- Never put "References Upon Request" on a resume. It is naturally assumed that you will furnish references if asked.

- Never give reasons why you've left any of your previous jobs.

- Never list your career's salary progression on a resume.[33]

- Avoid putting personal or legally protected characteristics on your resume. This would include age, marital status, length of marriage, ages of children, race, state of health, social security number, height, weight, and so forth.

Testing the Impact of Your Resume

After your resume is complete, see if it makes the initial impression or impact you want. Give your resume to two or three objective colleagues who you can trust. Ideally, you want colleagues from the business world who hire as part of their job. Ask them to take ten to fifteen seconds to look at your resume. What do they remember?

If the "impact" points of your resume are not what you want them to remember, you may need to revise it. On the other hand, if your review group remembers what you want to communicate with your resume, it's ready for use! Have your "quality control" group do the same for your other job-search documents or online profiles.

QR Codes

You can add a QR code to your resume (a QR code is a static-like barcode found on many contemporary advertisements). They can add a unique visual appearance to your resume and be a differentiator. They have faded in popularity, but can be effectively used in some industries (e.g., marketing, advertising, etc.) Generally speaking, QR codes tend to appear on a resume either in the upper right hand corner of the front page or bottom of the second page, but there is no placement rule. Use discretion and make sure the code does not distract from your resume's overall appearance.

---

33 Yate, *Knock 'em Dead*, p. 48.

What the Pros Say:

What is your opinion about adding a QR code on a resume?

I think they are a bit of a fad. Personally, I have never put one on a resume. I could maybe see a case to put one on for someone in marketing because they want to demonstrate their knowledge of digital marketing. I will say that if you do include one, the site you lead the reader to better be impressive.

Michelle Robin, NCRW, CPRW

Dealing with Employment Gaps on a Resume

Employment gaps on a resume can create anxiety. Fortunately, most employers understand the difficulties of the job market, the negative employment dynamics of a particular industry, or have experienced a gap in employment themselves.

Judgments regarding employment gaps have eased. According to a study conducted by CareerBuilder, 85 percent of hiring executives and human resource professionals are more understanding of employment gaps than they once were.[34] While there is an understanding that bad things can happen to good people, there are limits. If your gap is reasonably short and you have been productive in some way using or enhancing your skills, the gap is generally overlooked. But the longer the gap, the more negatively an employer views that gap.

Studies indicate that once your employment gap exceeds six months, your job search can become precipitously more difficult.[35] The unstated reasoning is if you have been unemployed for over six months nobody wants to hire you (especially when you have been actively looking for a job).

So, how can you get around this potential judgment and frightening statistic? Take comfort—there are ways:

---

34 CareerBuilder, "Employers Share Encouraging Perspectives and Tips for the Unemployed in New CareerBuilder Survey," news release, March 21, 2012, http://www.careerbuilder.com/share/aboutus/pressreleasesdetail.aspx?id=pr684&sd=3/21/2012&ed=12/31/2012&siteid=cbpr&sc_cmp1=cb_pr684_ (accessed May 29, 2015).

35 O'Brien, Matthew. "The Terrifying Reality of Long-Term Unemployment," *The Atlantic*, April 13, 2013, http://www.theatlantic.com/business/archive/2013/04/the-terrifying-reality-of-long-term-unemployment/274957/ (accessed May 29, 2015).

- On your resume, list your dates of employment in years only, not month and year. It is honest and can cover your gap. However, if asked about actual dates of employment, be forthright with your answer.

- Use a Showcase resume. Do what you can to emphasize your strongest selling points up front on your resume. Hopefully, this will focus the employer on your skills, knowledge, and achievements and not on the employment gap.

- Become a consultant. You obviously have ability, so try to secure some paid opportunities to advise and consult with companies in your areas of expertise. The key is to show that you have remained active and are using your skills.

- Volunteer to offer your services for a worthy cause or association. It may not be complicated work, but it is using your skills in some capacity. Examples: As an accountant, do the bookkeeping for a nonprofit which you are passionate about. As a sales professional, volunteer to do fund-raising.

- Continue your education. This does not necessarily mean getting an MBA (although, clearly, that would be advantageous), but begin working toward a substantive industry designation.

- Be very cautious of the word "sabbatical" on a resume. It is an unusual word to the commercial private business sector. It raises the suspicion of long-term unemployment.

- Depending upon the circumstances, briefly address the employment gap in your cover letter. It could be that you chose not to look for a job, but you must have a very good reason. This information would come under the "Additional Information" section. (See Cover Letters and Other Written Communications.) Keep it brief.

- As a last resort, use the Functional resume format.

- Above all, never sacrifice your integrity.

What the Pros Say:

How do you deal with employment gaps on a resume?

I don't try to hide them or pretend they don't exist, but I also try to not have them jump off the page. Depending on the reason for the gap and how long of a gap, I may employ one of the following strategies:

Only list the beginning and ending years of all jobs (not the month and year).

Place the dates somewhere other than the right margin (possibly near the job title or the company name).

Press the client for details about what he/she was doing during this gap. Maybe I can fill the gap by including that the client was volunteering somewhere or taking a class (or traveling the world).

If the gap was due to something out of the client's control—such as a RIF (reduction in force) — I'd work language into the job description/job scope section for the position the client was in prior to the layoff. (For example, "Led the installation and launch of new customer relationship management platform that minimized need for telephone follow-up and ultimately led to closure of the customer service call center and elimination of my position.")

Norine Dagliano, BA, NCRW, CFRW/CC

That's a big question, and the answer is that "it depends."

In the case of a short-term gap in the candidate's deep history, I usually don't do anything, as most hiring managers will not take these sorts of things into account.

If the gap is short, then I use years of employment rather than months/years.

If the gap is longer, then it might be worthwhile to fill in the gap with something relevant, e.g., full-time school, relevant volunteerism, self-education programs, personal caregiving, and so on, in a single line item.

In any case, the candidate has to own his or her history, which they cannot change at this point. So they have to be prepared with a good story to tell about any gaps in their history.

Amy Adler, MBA, MA, CMRW, CCMC

Be honest. If you were out of work to raise your children or care for an ailing relative, I list it. There may be skills used or developed that are relevant to your career!

Bob Janitz, NCRW

Infographic Resume

An infographic resume is a colorful, high-resolution document that visually presents your background and accomplishments by using pie charts, bar graphs, time lines and other graphics in creative ways. They can be particularly impactful to display notable achievements, high-level recommendations, and patterns of success, among other things.

The impact of an infographic resume comes from the fact that readers are drawn to colorful images. It grabs their attention, which is precisely the differentiation you want in a competitive job market.[36] There's a tendency to remember things better when they are presented with images.

What the Pros Say:

For a job seeker, what could be the strategic advantages of using an infographic resume?

1. Candidate can stand out from the thousands of drab, mundane, and generic resumes.

2. Candidate becomes memorable due to being innovative and personally branded.

3. Interviewer catches a glimpse into the personality of the candidate and can determine if there is a culture fit with the organization.

4. Infographic resume tells a story in images, which sends a positive message to the interviewer. Images, when crafted appropriately, trigger an emotional and intellectual reaction. Images are embedded in our brains and when positive stories are told through infographic resumes, positive results can occur.

Tina Kashlak Nicolai, PHR, CPBA, CARW
Lominger Certified (Interview Architect)

---

36 Pamela Skillings, "The Ultimate Infographic Resume Guide," *Big Interview* (blog), June 18, 2013, http://biginterview.com/blog/2013/06/infographic-resumes.html (accessed February 17, 2016).

An infographic resume can, in limited circumstances, replace the traditional resume. This is most often the case in the creative fields like design, marketing, advertising, digital media, and so on.

However, for most, an infographic resume should be used as a supplement or differentiation tactic in conjunction with a traditional resume. Even then, its use is better suited for some positions (sales, for example) than others.[37] With these caveats, an infographic resume can be a persuasive tool in your job-search arsenal.

What the Pros Say:

Can an infographic resume replace the need of a traditional resume?

For industries that are more creative, progressive, and appreciate the innovation of the visual resume, infographic resumes can replace the need of a traditional resume. The other option is to use the infographic resume in lieu of a cover letter and entice the interviewer to ask for a supplemental document listing more detailed achievements.

Some infographic resumes have a comment stating, "Want a traditional resume? Call or email me and I'll send one to you!" This can lead to a better experience for the hiring leaders and the candidate because engagement has occurred.

Generally speaking, conservative companies and traditional organizations are not the place to submit an infographic resume. It's interesting, some people think that infographic resumes are strictly for creative industries, however it's not the industry that determines when to submit an infographic resume, rather it's the company and the culture.

Tina Kashlak Nicolai, PHR, CPBA, CARW
Lominger Certified (Interview Architect)

There are advantages, disadvantages, and considerations for using an infographic resume in a job search. Let's start with a few advantages:

---

37 See also, ibid.

Differentiation. An infographic resume is clearly a differentiation tactic. Although the idea of an infographic resume has been around for a while, they are not widely used and therefore seldom seen by hiring executives in most industries. A well-thought-out, well-prepared, and well-presented infographic resume can make you stand out compared to other job seekers.[38]

A Networking Tool. Instead of, or used in conjunction with, your traditional resume and business cards, an infographic resume can be shared at networking functions.

One unique approach would be selecting your most persuasive achievements and creating an infographic "handbill." Create a four-inch-by-six-inch infographic handbill and put it on thicker paper or treat it as a large business card. This is truly unique and seldom seen. It will create conversation.[39]

Insight into Your Thinking and Presentation Skills. One interesting advantage to an infographic resume is it opens the door of insight into how you think and creatively present ideas and concepts. This can be very persuasive if the position(s) you are pursuing require presentation skills.[40]

Vividly Presents Your Professional Background. Infographic resumes are colorful, high-resolution documents. Unlike your LinkedIn profile (which is an online template) and your resume (which has expected and accepted sections), an infographic resume is a blank canvass. It is a platform to creatively present your professional background and accomplishments. You can present yourself in any way you choose using color and graphics.

Although the advantages of an infographic resume are attractive, there are also disadvantages to consider.

How Will It Be Received by Hiring Executives? This is a serious consideration. An infographic resume is a creative idea and can be very intriguing. It can open your mind to all sorts of creative thoughts on how to present your information. This is especially true once you start viewing examples. However, it is not the right or most impactful strategy for every industry or position.[41] Only you can gauge the receptiveness and persuasive influence an infographic resume would have on hiring executives in your job search.

It Must Contain Impactful Information. If an infographic resume does not have persuasive appeal, it will hurt your job search. It can be a distraction on your candidacy for the job or eliminate you from contention for the position.

---

38 Ibid.

39 See also, ibid.

40 Ibid.

41 Ibid.

It Must Look Great! Not just "good." Your final product must have a "holy cow, this is really cool" factor. Otherwise, it will not have the differentiating effect you are looking for. One interesting concept you could explore is creating an "Infographic" section to your traditional resume. This would be a form of a Showcase resume using color and graphics as your Showcase section. Then, traditional resume information would follow.

What the Pros Say:

Are some colors and graphic design concepts more impactful in creating an infographic resume than others?

Crisp lines coupled with contrasting textures and fonts are the key to creating a compelling infographic resume. There is not one color better than another. What makes a difference is how the colors are put together. Some infographics are very powerful with a lot of white space, while others are hugely compelling by using the entire canvas and filling in all of the white space with images, words, arrows, color, etc.

Tina Kashlak Nicolai, PHR, CPBA, CARW
Lominger Certified (Interview Architect)

A few final thoughts. It is highly recommended that you speak to professionals who create these documents. Seek their opinion as to whether you have the caliber of career information and accomplishments to have an impactful infographic resume (with the understanding that they will have the incentive to persuade you to buy their services). Seek out and evaluate examples of other infographic resumes from people with similar backgrounds to yours (if possible). Since creating the document on your own can take countless hours, consider hiring a professional.

If you create an infographic resume (or have one created for you), use it! One easy thing to do is attach it to your LinkedIn profile. Obviously you want to have it to hand out during networking events and as a supplement to interviews. Since you put in the time, effort, thought, and money into this tactic, look for ways to leverage it in your job-search activities.

What the Pros Say:

What is your opinion about the use of an infographic resume?

Infographic resumes are useful in some circles, for example if you are a social media professional. For the most part, I believe they don't work well with the applicant tracking systems recruiters and HR teams have in place to keep track of candidates. However, visuals are very powerful, and if an infographic resume truly adds to your case as a candidate, you might consider linking to it on your resume and/or bringing a printed version to interviews as a discussion tool or leave-behind.

Kimberly Robb Baker, NCRW, CJSS, CMRW

More and more frequently, I am including charts, graphs, graphics, and callout boxes on the traditional resume, to help call attention to and convey key points. In this way, the traditional resume is trending more toward what many may think of as an infographic resume. However, I still provide a graphic-intensive, one-page summary document that I have named an "infographic value profile." The purpose of this document is different than a resume. It is meant as a complement to the resume. I would never advocate its use as a stand-alone substitute for the resume for most industries.

Michelle Dumas, NCRW, CPRW

Part III

LinkedIn

Active participation on LinkedIn is the best way to say, 'Look at me!' without saying 'Look at me!'

— Bobby Darnell[42]

Please Note: LinkedIn changes its format, features, appearance, and functionality regularly. These changes enhance the LinkedIn experience as well as restrict some of its functionality. This topic on LinkedIn was current at the time of writing.

LinkedIn is the most used and effective professional networking website on the planet, with more than 467 million members in two hundred countries and growing.[43] In the United States alone there are more than 128 million members. At present, LinkedIn adds "more than two new members every second."[44] "Over 25 million profiles are viewed on LinkedIn daily."[45]

In today's job market, it is imperative to your job search to have a complete LinkedIn profile. In a recent survey of HR professionals and recruiters, 65 percent cite a lack of skilled candidates in the market as the largest obstacle to hiring.[46] Human talent is the lifeblood for every company, but there is a war for talent in the market due to the lack of well-qualified candidates.

Being in a candidate-driven job market is a good environment when you are looking

42 Knyszweski, Jerome. "How to Use LinkedIn as a Student—And Nail That Dream Job," *LinkedIn Pulse*, April 28, 2015, https://www.linkedin.com/pulse/how-use-linkedin-student-nail-dream-job-jerome-knyszewski (accessed May 28, 2015).

43 Smith, Craig. "133 Amazing LinkedIn Statistics." Last updated November 17, 2016, http://expandedramblings.com/index.php/by-the-numbers-a-few-important-linkedin-stats/. (accessed November 28, 2016). *See also*, Smith, Craig, DMR, "200+ Amazing LinkedIn Stats" (Last Checked/Updated October 2016) http://expandedramblings.com/index.php/by-the-numbers-a-few-important-linkedin-stats/ (downloaded November 28, 2016).

44 "About LinkedIn," *LinkedIn Newsroom*, https://press.linkedin.com/about-linkedin (accessed May 29, 2015).

45 Geoff, "Top LinkedIn Facts and Stats [Infographic]," (blog), *We Are Social Media*, July 25, 2014, http://wersm.com/top-linkedin-facts-and-stats-infographic/ (accessed May 29, 2015).

46 Jobvite 2016 Recruiter National Survey www.jobvite.com (accessed November 17, 2016).

for a job (should you be fortunate enough to be in that environment when searching for a job). But how can you maximize being discovered for open opportunities? Answer: your LinkedIn profile. LinkedIn is the overwhelming resource (87 percent) most frequently used by HR recruiters to identify and evaluate candidates.[47] By having a complete and robust LinkedIn profile, you significantly increase your chances of being contacted by a HR recruiter. In fact, "Users with complete profiles are forty times more likely to receive opportunities through LinkedIn."[48]

Having a complete LinkedIn profile is **imperative** to your job search.

What makes your profile complete? Generally speaking, your profile is complete when it has the following:

- Your location and industry
- A current position (with a description)
- Two past positions
- Your education
- Your skills (minimum of three)
- A profile photo
- At least fifty connections[49]

If your profile is incomplete, it won't register as high in searches as those that are more robust.[50] It cannot be overemphasized. LinkedIn should be your primary online professional networking and job-search tool.

In many cases, your LinkedIn profile could be the first impression a hiring executive has of you. A strong profile is a must. It gives you credibility.

Before we begin discussions on specific LinkedIn topics, and if you already have a profile, it is recommended that you turn off the network notification function of your profile until you have completed making all changes to your profile. Here's how: Go to your Profile page. Click on the "Me" icon at the top and from the drop down, select "Settings and Privacy."

---

47 Ibid. *See also*, Smith, Craig, DMR, "200+ Amazing LinkedIn Stats" (Last Checked/Updated October 2016) http://expandedramblings.com/index.php/by-the-numbers-a-few-important-linkedin-stats/ (downloaded November 28, 2016). This source indicates that 94 percent of recruiters use LinkedIn to vet candidates.

48 Foote, Andy, Why You Should Complete Your LinkedIn Profile, (December 7, 2015). https://www.linkedinsights.com/why-you-should-complete-your-linkedin-profile/ (accessed November 22, 2016).

49 Ibid.

50 Reynolds, Marci. "How to Be Found More Easily in LinkedIn (LinkedIn SEO)," Job-Hunt.org, http://www.job-hunt.org/social-networking/be-found-on-linkedin.shtml (accessed June 4, 2015).

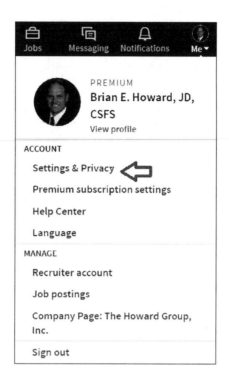

Then, select the Privacy option.

Scroll down and click on the "Sharing Profile Edits." Turn off your network announcements.

By doing this, your network will not be alerted regarding changes you may be making. You can reactivate the announcements later if you choose.

Use of Keywords

It is estimated that there are more than a billion searches annually on LinkedIn.[51] Companies and recruiters search keywords to find candidates (in addition to people who search for a particular company or person).

Let's take a quick review of keywords. As you know, keywords are specific words or phrases that reflect your experiences and abilities, and are frequently buzzwords, or terms-of-art that are applicable to you professionally. Like your resume, your profile must contain certain keywords to get attention and communicate that you are qualified for a particular position.

Keywords can include the following:

- Position title

- Industries

- Professional designation

- Skills, knowledge, core competencies

- Industry terms-of-art (and abbreviations)

- Employer names (past or present)

- Licenses, certifications

- Location (state, city)

- Software and technologies you're familiar with

- Education (school names and degrees)

We will have an extended discussion about the use of keywords when we talk about optimization.

Your LinkedIn Profile - Sections

Before we begin our discussion on building an impactful profile ("optimization"), let's briefly introduce the major components of your profile.

---

51 Stephanie Frasco, "11 Tips To Help Optimize Your LinkedIn Profile For Maximum Exposure and Engagement," Convert with Content (blog), https://www.convertwithcontent.com/11-tips-optimize-linkedin-profile-maximum-exposure-engagement/ (accessed June 10, 2015).

1. Photo

Your photo is important. It shows that you are a real person. Since LinkedIn has a professional focus—and you are looking for a job—it is recommended to have a photo taken at a studio by a professional or, at a minimum, a close-up photograph of you professionally dressed. According to experts, "profiles with a photo are fourteen times more likely to be viewed."[52] Moreover, having a photo makes you thirty-six times more likely to receive a message on LinkedIn.[53]

Here are some Dos and Don'ts when it comes to your LinkedIn photo. Many of these have been cited in a study by PhotoFeeler[54], while others should be common sense considering that LinkedIn is a professional networking site.

Do:

Be professionally dressed
The photo should be of your head and shoulders
Look directly into the camera; make eye contact
Smile

Don't:

No sunglasses (clear eyeglasses are fine)
No fish
No pets
No golf course photos
No family portraits
No kids or grandchildren
No shopping mall Glamour Shots

It is highly recommended that your LinkedIn profile photo be professionally taken.

2. Name

Use the name you commonly go by. If your given name is Richard, but you go by Rich, use Rich. It is permissible to put both your given name and the name you use in quotation marks or parentheses. If you have a common name, you may want to add your middle initial.

---

52 Smith, Jacquelyn. "The Complete Guide To Crafting A Perfect LinkedIn Profile," *Business Insider*, January 21, 2015, http://www.businessinsider.com/guide-to-perfect-linkedin-profile-2015-1 (accessed June 4, 2015).

53 Smith, Craig, DMR, "200+ Amazing LinkedIn Stats" (Last Checked/Updated October 2016) http://expandedramblings.com/index.php/by-the-numbers-a-few-important-linkedin-stats/ (downloaded November 28, 2016).

54 PhotoFeeler."New Research Study Breaks Down The Perfect Profile Photo, PhotoFeeler, May 13, 2014 https://blog.photofeeler.com/perfect-photo/ (accessed November 7, 2016).

What the Pros Say:

What is your opinion about the name a client should use on their LinkedIn profile? Should they use their birth name, the name they go by, or their birth name with the name they go by in quotation marks?

Most often, the name they go by. But distinction is important. For example, there are many Kim Bakers, so even though that's the name I go by, I use my full name Kimberly Robb Baker so that there is only one of me on LinkedIn and other online platforms.

Kimberly Robb Baker, NCRW, CJSS, CMRW

I recommend that the name used on a LinkedIn profile should match how the individual is known in the workplace so the profile is easily found when doing a search. For consistency, that form of the name is also the one that should be used on the resume.

Beate Hait, CPRW, NCRW

Professional designations appearing in the name field. There is a difference of opinion among commentators on this topic.[55] However, it can be to your advantage to put one (maybe two) notable professional designations behind your name. Designations should be significant to your industry, add to your credibility, or create a competitive advantage in the job market. Using one notable designation could increase the odds of having your profile viewed.

---

55 Isaacson, Nate. "Professional Designations Are Great But They Are Not A Part of Your Name," *LinkedIn Pulse*, April 14, 2014, https://www.linkedin.com/pulse/20140414223601-23236063-professional-designations-are-great-but-they-are-not-a-part-of-your-name (accessed July 16, 2015); Hanson, Arik. "Should You Put MBA Behind Your Name on Your LinkedIn Profile?" *LinkedIn Pulse*, May 29, 2014, https://www.linkedin.com/pulse/20140529131058-18098999-should-you-put-mba-behind-your-name-on-your-linkedin-profile (accessed July 17, 2015).

What the Pros Say:

What is your opinion about including one or two professional designations in the last name box of a LinkedIn profile?

For job seekers who have industry-specific designations that align with their job search goals, it is imperative to include them in the name and/or headline sections of their profile, since these two locations are prime real estate on LinkedIn.

Cheryl Lynch Simpson, CMRW, ACRW, COPNS

I recommend listing a law degree (JD), relevant master's, MBA, or doctorate after the last name. You want those professional designations to stand out. They can also be used strategically to position yourself in certain industries. For example, someone may have a JD but may not actively practice law. However, a JD is a very valuable educational tool that can position someone in business consulting or management work. So, definitely stand proud of your educational achievements and don't be afraid to boast about them in your LinkedIn profile.

Wendi Weiner, JD, NCRW, CPRW, CCTC, CCM

3. Headline

Under your name is your Headline area. It is the first thing someone reads about you.

You have 120 character spaces in your headline. Make it impactful (which will increase the number of views you receive) by describing yourself with keywords or short phrases that best describe your function. "What do you want to be known for?"[56] Or found for? Avoid superlatives or flamboyant adjectives in your headline (e.g., The Industry's Best Sales Representative on the Planet).

The headline ultimately attracts viewers with the intention that they continue to read your profile and be impressed with your experience, skills, and accomplishments. When we discuss optimization, we will delve much deeper into the strategic use of your headline.

What the Pros Say:

How do you view the Headline section? What is your thinking when you formulate the Headline?

The headline under your name should make it very clear what you do, by using keywords and job titles your target audience will associate with. Make sure you use the keywords, industry phrases, and terms your reader will understand.

Nelly Grinfeld, MBA, NCRW, CEIC

---

56 Whitcomb, *Job Search Magic*, p. 68.

Your headline should act like teaser copy to get people to click on your full profile. I take one of two approaches when writing headlines. One, I go with a lot of keywords that will help my client get found faster. Two, I go with a value statement or personal branding type statement.

Michelle Robin, NCRW, CPRW

The headline section should be keyword rich and convey some sense of who the job seeker is and what they offer, while providing an enticing reason to click through on the profile and read more.

Michelle Dumas, NCRW, CPRW

4. Location and Industry

The Location section appears below your Headline.

LinkedIn lists every significant metropolitan city in the country (more than 280 geographical location phrases at last count). Your location (or one very close) is likely listed.

It is important to put an accurate metropolitan city location on your profile. When employers and recruiters conduct searches, they often look for profiles of individuals who live in a particular city or region. Listing no location or a generic "United States" makes you almost invisible to employers and recruiters who may need a qualified candidate in a particular location.

When selecting a city, use a major metropolitan area instead of a suburb. This increases your odds that a HR recruiter will find you.

Be accurate when choosing an industry specialty. LinkedIn lists 145 industry phrases (at last count), so choose the one that best fits you. Your industry specialty is only viewable to HR recruiters that use advanced platforms of LinkedIn. When employers and recruiters conduct searches, they may look for profiles from particular industries—ones from which they have made successful hires in the past.

Including an industry on your profile has the potential to get you fifteen times the amount of views than those who do not list an industry.[57]

To access your Location and Industry, click "Me" at the top of the LinkedIn page. From the drop down, select Settings and Privacy. Scroll down and select Name, location, and industry.

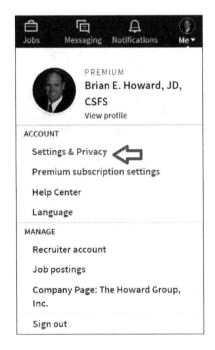

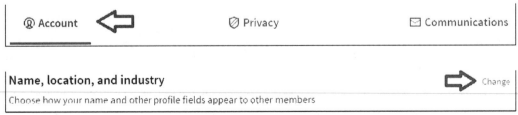

57 "10 Tips for the Perfect LinkedIn Profile," LinkHumans, Slideshare, published July 1, 2014, http://www.slideshare.net/linkedin/10-tips-for-the-perfect-linkedin-profile (accessed November 11, 2015).

5. Contact and Personal Information

LinkedIn allows you to provide contact information. Your Contact and Personal Information is located down the right side of your profile. It looks like this:

Click "show more" and you're in. This is a good place to put your personal email address and your cell phone number.

6. Summary Section

The Summary section is an area where you can write a narrative of your background, experience, and achievements. This is a biographical description of your career, so keep the content professionally relevant and use keywords. It appears directly below your name and location.

To edit or create a Summary, click on the pencil icon in the upper right-hand corner of your profile.

There is a difference of opinion regarding how the content of this section should be presented. Some advocate that it is an opportunity for you to write in the first person and show personality.[58] Others contend that it should be written in the third-person narrative. The choice is yours; however, make your decision based on how it will be best perceived by a potential hiring executive for your level of position.

Your Summary section has a significant impact on optimizing your LinkedIn profile and will be discussed at length in the pages that follow.

What the Pros Say:

How do you approach or what strategy do you use when writing the Summary section to a LinkedIn profile? And, how does it differ from the Summary section of a resume?

I tell clients to think of their summary section as an open cover letter. You need to address what your target audience is looking for and have a call to action. You should never dump your resume summary into the summary section of LinkedIn. First off, your resume summary is likely pretty short. Second it's not written in normal conversational language. Your summary on LinkedIn should be written in first person unless you are in a pretty traditional field like finance or are a high-level executive.

Michelle Robin, NCRW, CPRW

We have the ability to do so much more with a LinkedIn profile summary than we ever can with a resume summary! Resume summaries need to be quick snapshots of your career history written specifically for a particular position, industry, and company. LinkedIn summaries can be in a narrative format where you make a connection with your audience, share your story, and target your specific audience.

Jessica Hernandez, Certified Social Branding Analyst

---

7. Experience

This is reasonably straightforward. Think resume. Use relevant keywords. Remember

---

58 Smith, Jacquelyn. "Here's What To Say In Your LinkedIn 'Summary' Statement," Business Insider, December 19, 2014, http://www.businessinsider.com/what-to-say-in-your-linkedin-summary-statement-2014-12 (accessed July 9, 2015).

that your LinkedIn profile and your resume must match in general content. According to LinkedIn, "add[ing] your two most recent work positions . . . can increase your profile views by twelve times."[59] Strategic use of the Experience section will be discussed with optimization.

What the Pros Say:

What is your strategy and approach when drafting the Job Experience section?

I try to complement the resume when writing the experience section on LinkedIn. You usually have more room in LinkedIn so it's easy to expand on your accomplishments to add more context. I also use first person in the description of the job to tell the story of the person's career.

Specific advice for those in between jobs is to have what I call a "transition position." This is a current position that lists the type of role you desire (see Robin Green sample resume in my resume portfolio section). The reason to do this is LinkedIn surfaces people that have a current job higher in the search results. It also gives you an additional opportunity to sell yourself and add information you didn't put in your summary.

Michelle Robin, NCRW, CPRW

In the experience section, I believe that the most overlooked component is the job title. There is no rule that says your job title must be written exactly as it is on your resume. For example, if you are a teacher, you can create this job title: Science Teacher – Mentor – Team Leader. By including relevant descriptive keywords and providing more detail, the job title field becomes a great marketing tool for the job seeker.

Nelly Grinfeld, MBA, NCRW, CEIC

---

59 Daniel Ayele, "Land Your Dream Job in 2015 with These Data-Proven LinkedIn Tips," *LinkedIn Blog*, January 29, 2015, http://blog.linkedin.com/2015/01/29/jobseeking-tips/ (accessed June 9, 2015).

8. Education

Your education should align directly with your resume. Start with your highest degree and work backward in reverse chronological order. If you are a tenured job seeker, determine whether you want to include dates. Review the Education section of the Impactful Resumes portion of this book. LinkedIn users "who have an education on their profile receive an average of ten times more profile views than those who don't."[60]

Additional sections of your profile. LinkedIn has additional sections to further customize your profile. Depending on the HR recruiter or hiring executive, these areas may have an impact on their impression of you. To find these additional sections on your profile, look for a large blue box titled "Add a new profile section" that appears along the right side of your profile.

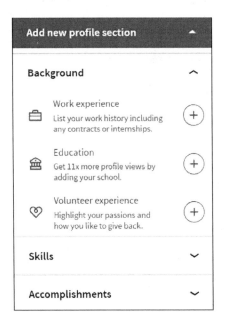

Click it and you will see an option regarding Background which will allow you to add information regarding your work experience, education, and volunteer experience. You will also see an option where you can add Skills. The last option is Accomplishments. This will give you a drop-down list that includes publications, certifications, courses, projects, honors and awards, patents, test scores, languages, and organizations. We'll discuss some of these additional sections later in this book.

---

60 LinkHumans, "10 Tips." *See also*, Smith, Craig, DMR, "200+ Amazing LinkedIn Stats" (last Checked/Updated October 2016) http://expandedramblings.com/index.php/by-the-numbers-a-few-important-linkedin-stats/ (downloaded November 28, 2016). This source indicates that 65 percent of job postings on LinkedIn require a bachelor's degree.

9. Volunteer Experience

Many employers look favorably upon profiles of those who volunteer or are involved in civic causes—it speaks to matching the culture of the company. "In fact, according to LinkedIn, 42 percent of hiring managers surveyed said they view volunteer experience equal to formal work experience."[61]

10. Skills (and Endorsements)

LinkedIn allows you to list fifty skills. Be reasonably specific and don't use all fifty. You don't want a HR recruiter or hiring executive to view you as a "jack of all trades and a master of none." You may appear desperate if you list too many skills. How many skills are too many? When you feel you are starting to stretch to include a skill, you have likely reached the end. According to LinkedIn, listing five or more skills in your profile will get you up to seventeen times more profile views.[62]

Endorsements are a nice LinkedIn feature. They add credibility and a compelling nature to your profile as others agree with the skills you have listed (they can add others).

Endorse others. Remember, LinkedIn is a networking mechanism and a two-way street. The more you engage with others, the more they will engage with you.

11. Certifications

Listing certifications can enhance your value as a viable candidate for a position. Frequently a professional certification or designation is a significant differentiator from other job seekers.

12. Honors and Awards

List all notable honors and awards you have received, signaling to an employer that others have recognized you for your performance.

13. Organizations

Listing your memberships in professional associations can have an influence on employers because it reflects that you are in touch with and following the industry. It can also be a source of networking and education.[63]

---

61 Dougherty, Lisa. "16 Tips to Optimize Your LinkedIn Profile and Your Personal Brand," LinkedIn Pulse, July 8, 2014, https://www.linkedin.com/pulse/20140708162049-7239647-16-tips-to-optimize-your-linkedin-profile-and-enhance-your-personal-brand (accessed November 11, 2015).

62 Smith, Craig, DMR, "200+ Amazing LinkedIn Stats" (Last Checked/Updated October 2016) http://expandedramblings.com/index.php/by-the-numbers-a-few-important-linkedin-stats/ (downloaded November 28, 2016).

63 Yate, *Knock 'em Dead*, p. 86.

14. Ask for Recommendations

Remember that having others say good things about you is better than you promoting yourself.[64] "Recommendations are mini testimonials that people give you who have worked with you. You can request them via LinkedIn. It's another way to build credibility [for] you and your work. As appropriate, remember to return the favor when someone gives you a recommendation."[65]

Many recruiters review recommendations as part of their evaluation protocols. As a minimum goal, get at least three recommendations posted on your profile from former bosses, colleagues, customers, or vendors you've interacted with.

15. Groups

LinkedIn groups are valuable, give you a platform to be an expert in an industry or topic, and help you gain insight and knowledge. "Your profile is five times more likely to be viewed if you join and are active in groups."[66]

HR recruiters and hiring executives search LinkedIn, and they also interact in LinkedIn groups.[67] With more than two million groups on LinkedIn,[68] there is no excuse not to join a group relevant to your industry or location. Eighty-one percent of users surveyed were in at least one LinkedIn group,[69] meaning hiring executives and recruiters—maybe even the one who will give you your dream job—are likely already members of, and might even be active in, a group. In a survey of LinkedIn users who found a job within three months of focused searching, 82 percent interacted with a group on LinkedIn.[70]

LinkedIn allows you to join one hundred groups, but only join those pertinent to your background, industry, and location. Determine a group's membership—larger ones offer more exposure. You will need to request membership to join a group.

Once you join a group, it is much easier to relate to people. You have something in common. Common ground is a good thing when starting a networking communication.

---

64 Matt, "Brag Book."

65 Frasco, "11 Tips."

66 LinkHumans, "10 Tips."

67 Lindsey Pollak, "How to Attract Employers' Attention on LinkedIn," *LinkedIn Blog*, December 2, 2010, http://blog.linkedin.com/2010/12/02/find-jobs-on-linkedin/ (accessed June 4, 2015).

68 Arruda, William. "Is LinkedIn Poised To Be The Next Media Giant?" Forbes, March 8, 2015, http://www.forbes.com/sites/williamarruda/2015/03/08/is-linkedin-poised-to-be-the-next-media-giant/ (accessed June 5, 2015).

69 Pamela Vaughan, "81% of LinkedIn Users Belong to a LinkedIn Group [Data]," Hubspot Blogs, August 11, 2011, http://blog.hubspot.com/blog/tabid/6307/bid/22364/81-of-LinkedIn-Users-Belong-to-a-LinkedIn-Group-Data.aspx (accessed June 8, 2015).

70 Shreya Oswal, "7 Smart Habits of Successful Job Seekers [INFOGRAPHIC]," LinkedIn Blog, March 19, 2014, http://blog.linkedin.com/2014/03/19/7-smart-habits-of-successful-job-seekers-infographic/ (accessed June 9, 2015).

16. Other Enhancements

You can also use a variety of media to showcase your skills (video presentations including Slideshare, pictures or screenshots, and text documents). These are optional and not required to get you found by a HR recruiter or hiring executive. However, they can add credibility to your experience on the job. Upload a video if you do public speaking. If you're skilled in graphic design, showcase your portfolio. If you write, add an article or a chapter of your book. Consider adding anything unique or impactful to prove and reinforce your skills, experience, or achievements.

Introducing LinkedIn Optimization

Optimization is taking full advantage of how the LinkedIn algorithms and programming work to be discovered for what you want to be professionally known for or found for. It means effective use of your keywords, putting those keywords in the correct areas of your profile, proper use of repeating those keywords, profile completeness, adequate number of connections, and making your profile compelling. All of these elements, pulled together, optimize your LinkedIn profile for maximum effectiveness. An optimized LinkedIn profile makes you more discoverable and more desirable when a HR recruiter uses LinkedIn to find a professional with your skills and background. Since 87 percent of HR recruiters use LinkedIn to identify and recruit candidates[71], having an optimized LinkedIn profile could lead you to your next career opportunity.

How Does It Work . . . How Does a HR Recruiter Use LinkedIn to Find Candidates?

There are numerous ways a HR recruiter can use LinkedIn to locate candidates. To illustrate one method, go to your LinkedIn home page or profile. Along the top, next to the LinkedIn logo, is a Search box with a spyglass.

Put the following words in that space just as written: insurance AND sales. Click the spyglass. Your results will be millions of profiles appearing on the page (and potentially a couple of job openings). The example terms used were overly broad but it gives you a

71 Jobvite 2016 Recruiter National Survey www.jobvite.com (accessed February 4, 2017).

concept of how a recruiter uses LinkedIn by refining search terms (keywords) to identify candidates. The purpose of this section is to teach you how to optimize your LinkedIn profile so you are one of those top candidates!

The Goal of Optimization

Now that you have a general understanding of the functionality of the LinkedIn algorithms and programming, you need to know what you are striving for by optimizing your LinkedIn profile. Your goals, in descending order are: (1) to be listed (ranked) as the number one profile on the first page (the ultimate achievement), (2) to be on the first page, and (3) to be on the first three pages.

These goals can be achieved provided you have adequate career achievements and information and you follow the instructions for optimization. Depending upon your professional circumstances, you may need to evaluate your ranking by limiting it to your city or metropolitan area.

Keyword Location

Where your keywords appear on your profile does matter. The sections listed below are the primary areas where the algorithms and programming look to match keywords.

1. Headline
2. Summary
3. Job title
4. Experience/employment descriptions
5. Skills

There are advanced platforms that can be purchased from LinkedIn that could expand this list, but these are the primary sections where the algorithms and programming match keywords.

Headline

You have 120 character spaces available to you in your headline, which is actually a lot of room. Since we know that this is a section where the algorithms and programming go to match keywords, make sure they appear here.

The headline section provides an excellent opportunity for you to create a branding statement describing yourself. What do you want to be known for or found for?[72]

A convenient formula that works well for many job seekers is:

[Job function or title] + [A bridge phrase or action verb (e.g., "with experience in," "with expertise in," "specializing in," or "utilizing")] + [keywords: reference to products, services, skills, industry, and so on]

For example:

"Senior Sales Executive with Experience in Workers' Compensation, Pain Management, Leadership."

Or:

"Product Development Professional Applying Behavioral Research to Health Care Technology."

Here are some real examples from LinkedIn profiles:

Sr. Sales Executive Specializing in Executive Leadership, Referenced Based Pricing, Stop Loss

Health Care Leader Skilled in Key Account Growth, Sales, Strategy, Analytics, Problem-solving, and Partnership Optimization.

When choosing keywords for your headline, use those that are skills, knowledge, products, and services you have experience with. Most HR recruiters will use keywords that are skills- or knowledge-based to identify candidates on LinkedIn. Then, during the screening process, they explore and evaluate soft skills (e.g., work ethic, communications skills, etc.). We'll mention your soft skills in just a moment in the Summary section.

This raises an interesting concept that you need to be aware of. As you build your LinkedIn profile, you occasionally need to think like a HR recruiter. What keywords would a HR recruiter or hiring executive use to find a professional like you? More often than not, the keywords you use will align with those used by a HR recruiter. However, that is not always the case. For example, some companies use the title Business Development to mean "sales." Other companies use that same title to mean marketing, branding, public

---

72 See, Whitcomb, Susan Britton. *Job Search Magic: Insider Secrets from America's Career and Life Coach.* (Indianapolis, IN: JIST Works, 2006), p. 68.

relations, and so on. If you happen to have one of those titles that is not generally accepted or representative of your function, you will want to use terminology on your LinkedIn profile that is more accepted and used by a HR recruiter. The point is to double check your thinking along the way.

Summary

You have two thousand character spaces available to you for your summary[73], which is a ton of room. Do not get "long winded" when writing your summary. Your summary is just that . . . a summary of your career, not an autobiography. Think of your summary as the executive summary of a white paper.[74]

An effective technique is to start your summary by restating your headline, word-for-word, and then expanding upon it to include other keywords that would not fit or were of secondary importance in your headline (perhaps your soft skills). Below are the "banner statements" contained in the Summary of the two Headline profile examples:

Senior Sales Executive Specializing in Executive Leadership, Referenced-Based Pricing, Stop Loss, Self-Funding, Product Distribution

Effective Health Care leader skilled in strategy, key account growth, sales, analytics, partnership optimization, team mentorship, and problem solving.

Remember, LinkedIn is looking to match keywords and tracking the number of times they appear when ranking you against other similar profiles. By restating your headline you create an introductory statement (banner) running along the top of your summary. The HR recruiter does not think twice about it but you have taken advantage of the programming by stating keywords twice between your headline and your introductory banner statement in your summary.

After your introductory banner statement, write one to three (maybe four) paragraphs that summarize your career experience so far. This will include duties, responsibilities, and your keywords. As you write, be aware that this paragraph(s) must read smoothly. A good approach is to write the paragraph(s), then insert keywords as appropriate. It's also a good technique to write your summary paragraph(s)—and other sections—in a Word document and then copy and paste it into the appropriate section. This way misspellings and grammar

73 Foote, Andy, Maximum LinkedIn Character Counts for 2016, December 10, 2016 https://www.linkedin.com/pulse/maximum-linkedin-char-acter-counts-2016-andy-foote (accessed November 22, 2016).

74 See, Kolowich, Lindsay, What is a White Paper, June 27, 2014 http://blog.hubspot.com/marketing/what-is-whitepaper-faqs#sm.0000lbm5cb-9ke7e11nu1h1l4e63aj (accessed November 22, 2016).

errors will be caught. This is important. A survey conducted by Jobvite indicated that 72 percent of HR recruiters view typos negatively on social media.[75]

The next component of your Summary, following your career summary paragraphs, is your career accomplishments. These are your achievements you are most proud of. Start with, "Career Accomplishments Include:", then list your top three or four. If you are not sure whether to include a particular achievement, hedge toward not including it. You want these achievements to be your best ones.

This discussion on accomplishments fits directly into one of the tenets for optimizing your LinkedIn profile—Compelling. The concept of "compelling" will be woven throughout the rest of this discussion as we address other topics and strategies.

Once you have your accomplishments listed in your Summary section, either use the programming on your computer or go to the Internet and copy and paste an icon and place it in front of each of your accomplishments. When choosing an icon, choose something dark, like a bullet-point ● or a black diamond ◆. These dark icons draw the eye of HR recruiters and highlight your achievements in their minds. Whatever icon you select, use it consistently throughout your profile. Using different icons makes your profile look jumbled or gaudy. Here are a couple of examples that appear in the Summary section of some profiles:

Career Achievements include:

● Implemented cost-saving strategies throughout a variety of initiatives resulting in a cost savings over $1 million.

Career Achievements include:

● Recipient of 20XX Female Executives Award.

● Developed and executed business development, marketing and sales plan that yielded 30 percent year-over-year growth.

● Marketed and sold new business to large employers, generating 30 percent of the overall company revenue.

● One of six senior managers who re-engineered corporate-wide business practices resulting in savings of more than $13 million.

75 Jobvite 2016 Recruiter National Survey www.jobvite.com (accessed November 17, 2016).

Finally, at the end of your summary, provide your personal email address and cell phone number. This is a good strategy because people that are not connected to you cannot see your Contact and Personal Information.[76] You want to make it as easy as possible for a HR recruiter to contact you. Providing this information at the end of your Summary makes it easy to do so.

Job Title

The Job Title area of your employment background is where LinkedIn looks for matching keywords. You have one hundred character spaces for your title.[77] If you have a title that is unique to your company, make sure to also include a more descriptive terminology so the HR recruiter can determine your actual function.

Experience

This is your employment history and it is a section where you should use your keywords heavily. For each employer, write one or two paragraphs describing your duties, responsibilities, product knowledge, distribution, territories, target markets, and so on. Use your keywords. Beneath the paragraph(s), put: "Achievements" or "Accomplishments" then, like you did in your Summary, list the important accomplishments you achieved in that position. This approach informs the HR recruiter of what your duties and responsibilities were and that you were successful in the role.

INCREASED SALES:

- 141 percent in 2016 over prior year

- 197 percent in 2015 over prior year

- 179 percent in 2014 over prior year

Follow this formula for each employment going back fifteen to twenty years. In your Experience section, your career-level accomplishments listed in your Summary will appear again under the employment from which they occurred. This is fine. It is recommended to put your dark icon in front of each accomplishment like you did in your Summary.

Skills

List your keywords as skills, when appropriate. According to LinkedIn, the number

76 Pearcemarch, Kyle, SEO for LinkedIn: How to Optimize Your LinkedIn Profile for Search (March 19, 2015) https://www.diygenius.com/how-to-optimize-your-linkedin-profile-for-search/ (accessed November 22, 2016).

77 Foote, Andy, Maximum LinkedIn Character Counts for 2016, December 10, 2016 https://www.linkedin.com/pulse/maximum-linkedin-character-counts-2016-andy-foote (accessed November 22, 2016).

of times you are endorsed for a skill has no weight on how many times the algorithms and programming recognize that particular keyword. In other words, having thirty people endorse you for a skill (keyword) does not mean the algorithms sees that keyword appearing thirty times on your profile. We will discuss an advanced technique using your Skills section in a moment.

Keyword Stuffing

Keyword stuffing is abusively overusing your keywords throughout your profile to increase your ranking.[78] It's a strategy designed to game the system. Sadly, this is a strategy too often suggested by some LinkedIn profile writers and career coaches. According to discussions with LinkedIn customer service, the algorithms and programming are now designed to detect this strategy and can reduce your ranking.

The better approach (and the one promoted in this book), is to construct a profile using accepted and common-sense optimization strategies that present your professional background and experience in a sincere manner to make the most positive impression possible on the HR recruiter.

This finishes the discussion regarding the first tenet of optimizing your LinkedIn profile regarding keywords. We will now move the discussion to the next tenet of optimization—Completeness.

Completeness

The more complete your LinkedIn profile is, the higher it will rank compared to other profiles. According to LinkedIn, "Only 50.5 percent of people have a 100 percent completed LinkedIn profile."[79] Consequently, by having a complete profile you can outrank many other competing profiles.

Profile completeness is important. The LinkedIn algorithms and programming display search results (how you rank compared to other profiles) based on the following:

1. Profile completeness
2. The number of shared connections

---

78 See, Practices to Avoid When Optimizing Your Profile For LinkedIn Search. https://www.linkedin.com/help/linkedin/answer/51499/practices-to-avoid-when-optimizing-your-profile-for-linkedin-search?lang=en (accessed November 23, 2016).

79 Foote, Andy, Why You Should Complete Your LinkedIn Profile, (December 7, 2015). https://www.linkedinsights.com/why-you-should-complete-your-linkedin-profile/ (accessed November 22, 2016).

3. Connections by degree (1st, 2nd, and so on)

4. Groups in common

Profile completeness is the "trump card" with the LinkedIn algorithms and programming.[80] The other factors of ranking do not matter if your profile is not complete. If you need a refresher on what constitutes a complete profile, here are the components:

- Your location (and industry)
- A current position (with a description)
- Two past positions
- Your education
- Your skills (minimum of three)
- A profile photo
- At least fifty connections[81]

You are already well down the road to completeness as you work on your profile using keywords. However, LinkedIn has additional sections that can be added to your profile beyond those that are most commonly used. They include:

- Volunteering Experience
- Publications
- Certifications (Professional Designations)
- Courses
- Projects
- Honors and Awards
- Patents
- Test Scores
- Language
- Contact and Personal Information

---

80 Ibid. ("Profile Completeness is a trump card in the search engine.")

81 Ibid.

- Organizations (Professional Associations and Affiliations)
- Posts

Volunteering Experience, Organizations

There are a couple of considerations regarding these sections. First, volunteering experience is favorably viewed by employers, but it must be substantive. Standing behind the card table selling brownies at the Cub Scout meeting doesn't count. However, being a volunteer Red Cross first responder does. Second, avoid referencing any organization or cause that could be viewed as controversial. This generally means anything regarding politics, religion, race, and so on. Of course there are exceptions if your career is in politics, religion, and race relations.

Honors and Awards

It is perfectly acceptable to restate your accomplishments and achievements in the Honors and Awards section. This is especially true if the achievement resulted in an award. Repetition of your achievements affirms in the mind of the HR recruiter that you are a well-qualified job seeker.

Language

If you live in the United States and English is your native language, do not list it. It is assumed that you are fluent. This section is used for foreign languages.

Personal Details

Avoid providing any personal information that would be inappropriate for a HR recruiter to ask about in an interview. Marital status and year of birth are two notable ones.

Connections

The more connections you have, the better the probability you will rank higher than other profiles.[82] Your ranking is, in part, influenced by how closely connected you are to a HR recruiter (or anyone else looking). The difficult part is you have no idea who could be looking on LinkedIn and how closely connected you are to them.

The best strategy to combat against or take advantage of this connection factor is to increase your connections and join industry-relevant groups. Try to get connected to as

---

82 Pearcemarch, Kyle, SEO for LinkedIn: How to Optimize Your LinkedIn Profile for Search (March 19, 2015) https://www.diygenius.com/how-to-optimize-your-linkedin-profile-for-search/ (accessed November 22, 2016).

many professionally relevant people as possible. These are professionals that can hire you or help you. This includes colleagues and peers at other organizations such as clients, vendors, competitors, and so on. If you want to work for a particular company, seek connections within that company. Strive to get a minimum of five hundred connections (possibly more depending upon your professional circumstances). The more connections you have, the higher the probability that you will be more closely connected to the HR recruiter who is searching on LinkedIn. The closer the connection, the higher you will appear in the ranking of profiles.

You are allowed to join up to one hundred groups on LinkedIn.[83] Since your ranking is influenced by the number of common groups you have with a HR recruiter, it is very important to join relevant and well-populated groups.

Fully appreciate that your network has value and is an area of evaluation when a hiring executive or HR recruiter looks at your profile. An evaluation of the number of contacts in and the quality of your network creates a "Network Value Score." By analogy, it's like your credit score when applying for a mortgage. The higher your Network Value Score, the more valuable you become as a quality candidate for the position.

If you are new to LinkedIn or have been inactive, work to get five hundred connections. The number of connections you have appears on your profile until you exceed five hundred. After that, it appears as "500+." You want HR recruiters and hiring executives viewing your profile to conclude that you have a network of professional colleagues. It can add to your professional value as a candidate. If you're staying within your field, some hiring executives will see how many common connections you have—the more the better. Some hiring executives will reach out to these connections and inquire about you. Hence this is another good reason to stay active with your network.

Compelling

A profile is compelling when it intellectually or emotionally moves the HR recruiter to contact you. There are several factors that can make a profile compelling. They include: your knowledge and skills, accomplishments, endorsements, recommendations, the overall appearance and completeness of your profile, and anything else that makes you unique in the eyes of the HR recruiter.

Your profile can be compelling based on your knowledge and skills. You know things or have done things in your career that a HR recruiter is looking for or is impressed by. You

83 General Limits for LinkedIn Groups, https://www.linkedin.com/help/linkedin/answer/190/general-limits-for-linkedin-groups?lang=en (accessed November 23, 2016).

have experience and a skillset in need by the HR recruiter. This can range from knowing and having experience with a particular software program to having Profit and Loss (P&L) experience with a large organization. There are thousands if not millions of qualifications a HR recruiter could look for that are knowledge- or skill-based.

Documented accomplishments are clearly compelling. The most influential accomplishments are those that can be quantified with numbers, percentages, dollars signs, savings (in time and money), and the list goes on. Accomplishments can heavily influence a HR recruiter to contact you. Your accomplishments communicate that you are good at what you do.

The number of endorsements you have for a sought-after skill can influence the compelling nature of your profile. If a HR recruiter finds a profile with 99+ endorsements for a sought-after skill or experience, it is a clear indication that the professional could be a qualified candidate.

An advanced technique is to list one professional character trait you possess as a skill. Examples are work ethic, perseverance, honesty, and so on. Then, get as many connections to endorse you for that character trait as possible. Having a professional character trait listed as a skill and an adequate number of endorsements for it is a differentiator from other profiles and will get noticed by a HR recruiter. Endorsements for a sought-after character trait open the door to what kind of person/professional you are as seen through the eyes of others.

Recommendations can also make your profile compelling. Once your profile is identified as a "probable" qualified candidate by a HR recruiter, the number and content of the recommendations can influence the HR recruiter to contact you. As a general rule of thumb, try to get three positive recommendations for each employer going back to at least two to three employers.

And finally, the overall completeness and appearance of your profile can be a compelling factor. There are millions of well-qualified job seekers who fail to appreciate the career-enhancing power of a LinkedIn profile. Potentially life-changing opportunities pass those people by through their failure to have a complete and professionally appearing LinkedIn profile. However, to your benefit, you will have a complete, professional, and compelling profile that will open your career to opportunities that others will not have (or ever know about).

Put It to the Test

After you have revised your profile and optimized it, put it to the test. Get on LinkedIn and run a search for yourself. Put in one keyword or phrase that you are using in your profile along with your title in the Search field at the top of your profile.

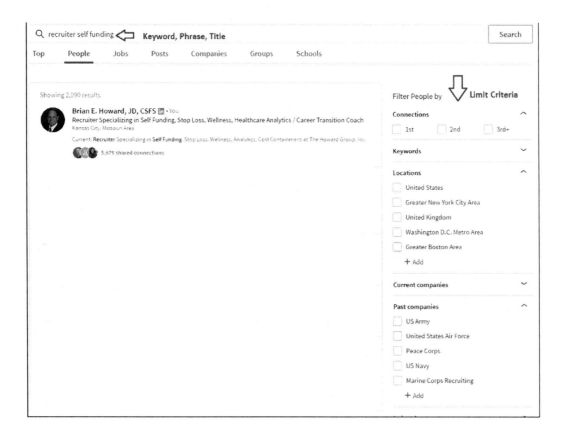

You may need to further limit the criteria by location. For example, "Regional Sales Director" AND Telemedicine AND Dallas. How did you rank? Did you appear on the first page? On the first two or three pages? Try another one of your keywords. How did that one work? If you are not coming up on the first three pages, double check to make sure you have all of the elements of a complete profile. Then, look at the profiles that appeared ahead of yours and see if you can make improvements based on what those candidates put on their profiles. Selective borrowing is permitted. Make revisions and try it again. Do what you can to improve your ranking to appear on the first page or the first three pages, if possible.

Understand that regardless of the revisions you make and the optimizing strategies you use, you may only be able to improve your ranking so much. Don't get frustrated. You can only do what you can with the algorithms based on the information in your profile. But, whatever you do, don't go overboard! Your profile must still appear professional and informative. Optimizing is a great strategy and it will improve your ranking, but creating an awkward-looking profile for ranking purposes defeats the ultimate objective . . . impressing a HR recruiter or hiring executive.

What the Pros Say:

In your opinion, what strategies do you use to make a LinkedIn profile compelling or persuasive?

The primary tool for doing so is to make sure the profile is achievement-driven. A profile that is rich in achievements will communicate value to recruiters and hiring managers. In addition, I focus on writing short, impactful content and using the limited formatting elements LinkedIn allows to optimize visual branding.

Cheryl Lynch Simpson, CMRW, ACRW, COPNS

While a resume shows the reader who you are, LinkedIn is an opportunity for the reader to hear your voice. Therefore I work to capture the client's personality relevant to the industry they are targeting.

Virginia Franco, NCRW, CPRW

Strategies for Your LinkedIn Profile When You are Unemployed

If you are unemployed, what do you put on your LinkedIn Profile? Do you announce your availability or would doing so reduce your attractiveness as a candidate? Fortunately, you have several strategic options.

As you consider the options that follow, the primary consideration is this: How would a HR recruiter or hiring executive react to the strategy you use for the level of position you are seeking? After we discuss the strategic options, we'll discuss factors that could influence your decision on which strategic approach to take.

Put an End Date on Your Last Employment. Your first option is to list an end date on your current employment. It's honest and your profile is up-to-date. HR recruiters will draw the conclusion that you are currently unemployed.

Announce Your Unemployment in Your Headline. As you know, the headline is the area immediately below your name. It is acceptable to use your headline as an advertisement of your availability: "Currently Seeking New Opportunities," or "In Transition," among others.

However, there is a more effective approach since the LinkedIn algorithms and programming searches the Headline for keywords. Create your Headline with your keywords and include "Seeking New Opportunities." For example, "Banking Professional Specializing in Commercial Lending, Seeking New Opportunities." This strategy capitalizes on your keywords and announces your availability.

Announce Your Availability as a Statement in Your Summary Section. Another option is to include a statement of your availability early in your Summary section. Your statement could be as simple as "Actively Seeking New Employment."

As you recall, your Summary section is also an area where the LinkedIn programming and algorithms look to match keywords. There is a strategic advantage of adding a sentence or two with keywords about position types, industries, and types of companies that would interest you. For example, "Actively seeking a new opportunity as an account manager in the employee benefits industry." This can help tighten your search but be aware that it can also reduce potential opportunities. After you make this statement, continue with the rest of the Summary in a traditional fashion.

List Your Availability as Your Current Employment. The LinkedIn programming and algorithms look at position titles and position descriptions for matching keywords. So simply putting "Open to Opportunities" as your title does not take advantage of the programming. A better approach is stating an actual title or job function followed by "Seeking New Position." For example, "Sales Operations Professional Specializing in Health Care Seeking New Position." You have one hundred character spaces in the title area which should give you ample room to use this strategy. You could reword your headline and put it here as well.

For the Company Name, you can put "Unemployed." But, that sometimes can carry a negative stigma—though the weight of that stigma has faded in recent years. Instead, consider a more positive approach, such as putting "Exploring a Career Move," "Seeking New Position," or "In Transition" as your current employer.

Your position description provides some unique opportunities. If you resigned from your previous employment, the first sentence of your description could read something like this:

"Currently seeking a new position after voluntarily leaving [Past Employer] in good standing with recommendations."

Or,

"Actively looking for a new job in event planning after resigning my position at [Past Employer] with strong job performance evaluations."

If you were laid off, you could state the description something like this:

"Was subject to a company-wide layoff affecting [XX number employees, the entire marketing department, X number of departments]. Release was not performance-related."

If you were terminated for performance, it's probably best to leave that unspoken and use the position description space for other strategies.

For the rest of the job description space, create the messaging that puts you in the best light. According to LinkedIn, there is now a two-hundred-character minimum and a two-thousand-character maximum in the position description area.[84]

The content of the position description could be a brief statement of your abilities and knowledge, using keywords. It could function as an abbreviated cover letter. You could also rework your elevator speech (if you use one as part of your overall job search) and put it here. The key consideration is to use the space wisely, not be lengthy, and consider how a HR recruiter would react to what you write. When pulled together, it could look something like this:

---

84 Foote, Andy, Maximum LinkedIn Character Counts for 2016, December 10, 2016 https://www.linkedin.com/pulse/maximum-linkedin-character-counts-2016-andy-foote (accessed November 22, 2016).

Title: Account Manager Seeking Opportunities in Employee Benefits

Company: Exploring A Career Move

Description: Was subject to a company-wide layoff affecting over one hundred employees at [Past Employer]. Release was not performance-related.

Seeking an account management position to benefit an insurance organization with proven skills in client service, ACA compliance, implementation, renewals, and claim resolution. (Then customize the content based on your best judgment.)

Be a Consultant. You can list your current employment as consulting and your title as a consultant. Taking this approach is accepted "code" that you are unemployed but doing consulting projects to stay active and engaged.

The key to this strategy is the use of your keywords. Knowing that the LinkedIn programming and algorithms look at position titles, describe your title using keywords. For example:

"Security Technology Consultant"

Or,

"Workers' Compensation Cost-Containment Consultant"

You can also shorten and manipulate the wording of your headline (you have one hundred character spaces).

For company name, many use their last name or initials followed by "Consulting." You have a lot of latitude for the name of your consulting practice, just be professional in the naming.

Your professional description should contain your keywords, as previously discussed. This will help you when a HR recruiter or hiring executive searches for you.

Do Nothing At All. The final option is do nothing at all and if asked about your profile, go with "I forgot." This is not ideal, but the option is available to you.

Which Strategy Would Be Best for You?

The correct strategy(ies) depends on your unique professional circumstances. You may choose a select combination of approaches.

If you work in an industry where it is common to hire on a project basis, contractor-to-hire, or consulting basis, announcing your availability using these strategies makes sense.

The level of your position or positioning on the corporate organizational chart for the position you are pursuing also has an influence on your strategy. Generally, these "announcement" strategies may be more acceptable to lower- to mid-range sales and management roles rather than true senior management or C-Level positions. The size of the organization you are targeting could be a consideration as well. Smaller, more entrepreneurial organizations may be more receptive to the announcement strategies. Exercise your professional judgment as to whether or which strategy(ies) to use. Your strategy hinges on how you believe a HR recruiter or hiring executive for your desired position could respond.

The Open Candidates Feature on LinkedIn

LinkedIn has a feature where you can signal recruiters that you are open to new opportunities. This feature is called "Open Candidates."

How to Access the Open Candidates Feature. To access this feature, click the "Jobs" option at the top of your LinkedIn profile.

From there you will see "Jobs you may be interested in." Close to that will be a link entitled "Update preferences." Click it.

Jobs you may be interested in
Any location · Training to Director level · Any industry · 50 to 10,000- employees ... Update preferences ⇐

Scroll down and begin answering the questions about location, experience, industries (LinkedIn may offer suggestions), company size, and availability. When you activate the feature you are also given an Introductory section with three hundred character spaces.

Finally, let recruiters know you're open by activating the feature to "On."

Who Can See Your Open Candidate Profile? Only recruiters who have paid for and use LinkedIn's premium "Recruiter's Platform" (prices begin at around $8,000 per license) can see that you have filled out the Open Candidates questionnaire.[85] Your current employer, and its affiliates should not be able to view your Open Candidates profile. However, LinkedIn provides this disclaimer: "We take steps to not show your current company that you're open, but can't guarantee that we can identify every recruiter affiliated with your company."

Naturally, if you are unemployed, there is no risk. Even if you are employed, the risk of discovery is reasonably small. Besides, it is not illegal, immoral, or unethical to be open to a new job that can enhance your career experience. Most employers know that the job market is a free-agency market. Employees, especially today, look to maximize their career experience and that can mean pursuing new jobs when the time is right (this includes your boss and other senior executives of your current and former employers).

Strategies for Using the Open Candidate Feature. For most job seekers, using the Open Candidates feature is a good idea. Recruiters can screen potential candidates not only based on qualifications, but to those that are open to new opportunities. This shortens their work and can place you toward the top of their contact list! According to LinkedIn, "open candidates" are more likely to be contacted by recruiters[86]. Use the Introductory section of the questionnaire to emphasize skills/background and accomplishments. Remember, you only have three hundred character spaces so you have to be succinct. For example:

"Account management professional seeking a position with a health insurance organization with proven skills in client service, ACA compliance, implementation, renewals, and claim resolution. Promoted three times, 95 percent client retention, recognized with client services award, have client recommendations."

If you are unemployed, there is virtually no reason for not using this feature. The only rare consideration (employed or unemployed) would be perception based on the level of position you are seeking. Would a senior-level hiring executive, board of director, or possibly a retainer-only search firm pause to reach out to you because you are an Open Candidate on LinkedIn? Very unlikely (hopefully), but it is worth a moment of thought.

---

85 Uzialko, Adam, LinkedIn's Open Candidates: How to Search for a New Job, Quietly, October 6, 2016, http://www.businessnewsdaily.com/9468-linkedin-open-candidates.html (accessed November 25, 2016).

86 Bell, Karissa, LinkedIn will now help you secretly tell recruiters you want a new job , October 6, 2016, http://mashable.com/2016/10/06/linkedin-tell-recruiters-you-want-a-new-job.amp (accessed November 7, 2016).

Measuring the Effectiveness of Your LinkedIn Profile

Having a complete profile, implementing optimization strategies, and making your profile compelling are necessary steps to maximizing the use of your LinkedIn profile in your job search. But the true effectiveness of your profile is the number of views it gets. If you are in a full-blown, active job search utilizing all the tools at your disposal, one measure of success is getting a minimum of twenty profile views a week. This is not a scientific number but rather a minimum threshold number to use as a benchmark for the effectiveness of your LinkedIn profile.

You can track the number of views from your profile page—look for "Who's viewed your profile" that appears on your Profile page.

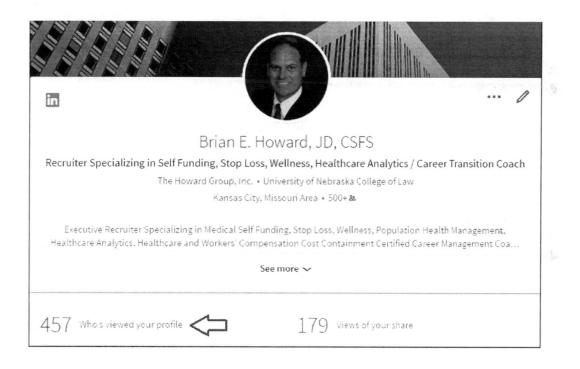

What Do You Do with Your LinkedIn Profile after You Get a New Job?

Once you land a new job, you have a couple of choices with your LinkedIn profile. First, you can create your Experience section in the same fashion as previously instructed.

There is another approach to consider. Understand the construction of your profile has been focused on you. It has been written to showcase you as a professional with the purpose of a job search. When you get a new job, you may want to shift that focus to your new employer. This is achieved by putting a paragraph in your current employment section that describes the company, its products, services, value proposition, etc. You can often get this information from the company website or company LinkedIn page.

After you insert the company description, follow the same advice as previously instructed with a paragraph about your duties and responsibilities. Remember to list your accomplishments as they occur.

Keep Your Profile Current

Update your information and keep it current so it doesn't appear stale. According to LinkedIn, keeping your positions up to date on your profile makes you eighteen times more likely to be found in searches by recruiters and other members.[87]

LinkedIn is a dynamic site that changes frequently, adding some features and functionality and taking others away. Be aware of the programming changes and their possible implications for your profile use.

Sample of an Optimized LinkedIn Profile

Once you have implemented all of the optimization strategies, your LinkedIn profile should look similar to the sample profile that follows.

87 Smith, Craig, DMR, "200+ Amazing LinkedIn Stats" (Last Checked/Updated October 2016) http://expandedramblings.com/index.php/by-the-numbers-a-few-important-linkedin-stats/ (downloaded November 28, 2016).

Nancy Brock

Sales Executive Specializing in Healthcare Benefits Administration/SaaS, Wellness and Women's Health

Ovia Health • Washington University in St. Louis

Washington D.C. Metro Area • 500+ 👥

Sales and Business Development Executive Specializing in Healthcare, Benefits Administration/SaaS Technology, Women's Health, Wellness, Consumerism, Work Ethic, Integrity.

Leadership Roles in Health Care Start-Ups, Early Stage Companies, and Insurance

Nancy has over 20 years of sales, business development, and client management leadership experience spanning employee benefits, wellness, population health, consumer-driven health, behavioral health and Employee Assistance Programs. Nancy has managed sales, account management, marketing, and product management teams and has worked with Fortune 500 employers, mid-size employers, payers and benefits brokers and consultants.

Nancy's expertise includes sales and marketing, strategic planning, distribution partner development & management, business plan development, account management, product management, project management, market research and intelligence, and P & L in wellness, population health, consumer-driven health and benefits administration.

Career Achievements include:

● Recipient of 2014 Top Female Executives
● Developed and executed business development, marketing and sales plan that yielded 30% year-over-year growth
● Marketed and sold new business to large employers, generating 30% of the overall company revenue
● One of six senior managers who re-engineered corporate-wide business practices resulting in overall savings of more than $13 million

nancy.brock@gmail.com
703-555-5555

Experience

Regional Sales Manager

Ovia Health

Nov 2016 – Present • 5 mos • Potomac Falls, Virginia

Ovia Health is the leading digital health platform for women and families. Trusted and loved by millions, Ovia Health's mobile apps for fertility, pregnancy, and parenting have empowered over 5 million women to take control of their healthcare and start families with confidence. We are passionate about helping women and families understand their reproductive health and using technology to make it easier for them to do so.

Accountable for managing the full sales cycle of new enterprise opportunities in the Maryland South Atlantic region.

See less ∧

Sales & Business Development Consulting

Independent Wellness Consulting

Sep 2016 – Oct 2016 • 2 mos • Potomac Falls, VA

Provide sales consulting services to wellness companies to help them demonstrate the value of solving their clients' problems, the cost of inaction, and the urgent need for change. Assist with the development of sales presentations and case studies.

See less ∧

Vice President, Sales

bswift

2014 – 2016 • 2 yrs • Chicago, IL/Computer Software

Accountability for managing the full sales cycle of new business opportunities initially in the Mid-Atlantic region and then for the Eastern region. Sold benefits administration/exchange technology and services to employers with 1,000+ employees.

Achievements include:
• Top 5 in pipeline generation
• 2015 sold highest total contract value
• Hand picked by CEO to manage new vertical

See less ∧

Vice President/Senior Consultant

Willis of Virginia, Inc.

2012 – 2014 • 2 yrs • Reston VA

Identify, secure and manage new business development opportunities. Partner with employers to solve human capital and benefit challenges. Develop comprehensive and tailored Total Rewards strategies and programs in collaboration with Willis Human Capital team. Conduct analysis, prepare strategic recommendations and coordinate review of documents to ensure compliance. Developed and coordinated conference on Innovative Next Practices for a Healthy and Productive Workforce.

Education

 Washington University in St. Louis
MSW, Social Work

Graduated with an MSW from the George Warren Brown School of Social Work

See less ∧

 University of Michigan
BA, Psychology
Activities and Societies: Delta Gamma, William J. Branstrom Freshman Prize

Graduated from the University of Michigan School of Literature, Science, and the Arts, Ann Arbor

See less ∧

Volunteering Experience & Causes

 Participant
March of Dimes

March for Babies Annual Walk

See less ∧

 Fundraiser
Make-A-Wish Foundation of Greater Virginia
May 2013 · 1 mo
Children

Featured Skills & Endorsements   Add a new skill ✎

View 1 pending endorsement

Leadership · 90   Shelly Slebrch and 89 connections have given endorsements for this skill

Sales · 27   Brad Hemmingsen and 26 connections have given endorsements for this skill

Business Develop... · 29   Lisa M. Holland, RN, MBA and 28 connections have given endorsements for this skill

Nancy is also good at…

Strategy · 85	Wellness · 15	Employee Benefits · 56
Health Insurance · 37	Start-ups · 17	Managed Care · 47
Program Manage... · 36	Strategic Partners... · 48	Work Ethic · 10
Tenacious Work Et... · 6	Human Resources · 17	Disease Managem... · 11
Health Policy · 16	Management · 34	Healthcare Manag... · 13
CRM · 20	EAP · 7	Strategic Planning · 43
Consumer-Driven ... · 5	Healthcare Inform... · 10	Health Care Reform · 6
Training · 9	Account Managem... · 8	Customer Relatio... · 6

Adjust endorsement settings

See less ∧

Recommendations   Ask to be recommended ✎

Received (33)   Given (27)

Tara Lathrop
Account Executive at
OneSource Virtual
November 3, 2016, Nancy worked
with Tara in the same group

Nancy and I were colleagues at bswift. She has a passion for health and benefits technology, is a strategic and creative problem solver, and is a collaborative team player. From her first week on the job, Nancy was eager to learn, and she took the initiative to successfully bring together a group of sales colleagues for a series of ongoing training and development activities, which added significant value and was universally well received.

One situation really stood out to me during our time together. Nancy won a very large new account for the company within just a few weeks on the job. She put together a very compelling and creative strategic business plan and presentation when the employer came to our office for a site visit. Later, this employer shared that this effort had differentiated Nancy and the company from the other vendors that they were considering. Nancy is a sales executive that I would highly recommend to any company.

Kelly Challenger
Senior Director, Marketing
June 20, 2016. Kelly worked with Nancy in different groups

I worked alongside Nancy for a year executing lead generation campaigns in support of her region and the Public & Labor sector and she is by far one of the best sales executives I've ever had the pleasure of working with.

Nancy was always incredibly well organized, managed her accounts with the utmost professionalism while at the same time valued the relationships she had developed – both internally and externally – and handled them with the utmost care.

I was particularly impressed by Nancy's knowledge of the industry and her ability to get the job done. Whether it was executing a regional event in her area, or supporting an appointment setting campaign for her particular vertical, Nancy always gave 100% and was completely invested in its success. I've spent my entire career working with and supporting sales and Nancy is by far one of the best Account Executives I've ever had the pleasure of working with.

View 31 more recommendations ⌄

Accomplishments   +

6 **Honors & Awards**   ✎

   2014 Top Female Executives

   Recognized for Outstanding Professionalism, Excellence, and Dedication

   Feb 2014

   Top Female Executives

Dedication, Leadership and Excellence

Recognized for demonstrating dedication, leadership and excellence

http://halloffame.cambridgewhoswho.com/HOF/2013/Q1/P4.html?I=14

Jan 2013

Cambridge Who's Who

Professional of the Year, Health Care Support Services

http://www.worldwidebranding.com/Members/VA/Nancy-Brock-1309800.html

2013

Worlwide Who's Who

Professional of the Year, Health Care Support Services

http://www.worldwidebranding.com/Members/VA/Nancy-Brock-1309800.html

2012

Worldwide Who's Who

Elite American Executives, Certificate of Recognition

http://eliteamericanexecutives.com/2014/01/10/nancy-brock/

Aug 2011

Elite American Executives

William J. Branstrom Freshman Prize

Awarded to first-term freshmen who rank in the upper five percent of their class within their school or college at The University of Michigan.

1981

University of Michigan

See fewer honors ∧

4 **Organizations** ✎

Society of Human Resource Management

WTPF, The Business Forum for HR Professionals

March of Dimes Maryland-National Capitol Chapter, National Capitol Chapter

2011 – 2014

Northern Virginia Technology Council

Sep 2015 – Present

See fewer organizations ⌃

2 **Publications** ✎

Interview by Jean Chatzky, "Protect Your Health," December 2006 | See publication |
Interview on being a savvy healthcare consumer.

Harpo Productions, Inc.
Dec 4, 2006

Authors

The Road to Health Consumerism | See publication |
Evolution of consumer-driven health plans and UnitedHealth Group's CDHP results.

VAHU News
Jun 2008

Authors

See fewer publications ⌃

1 **Certification** ✎

Identify Sales Growth Opportunities | See certificate |
Sep 2016 – Present

in LinkedIn

See fewer certifications ⌃

Part IV

Cover Letters and Other Written Communications

Dost thou love life? Then do not squander time, for that is the stuff life is made of.

— Benjamin Franklin[88]

Some employers focus on a cover letter, while others will bypass it and go straight to the resume. If the resume is strong, some employers will then go back and read the cover letter or cover email. Regardless of how an employer treats the letter, make sure you invest an appropriate amount of time writing a well-thought-out cover letter. A well-written cover letter immediately begins to differentiate you from other job seekers by highlighting strong points in your background and provides a sample of your writing ability. A well-written letter can also serve as a customizable template for different job opportunities.[89]

Types of Cover Letters

In general, cover letters fall under three categories:

A **letter of application** is used to match a specific employment position.

A **letter of inquiry** is written (frequently to HR) when you are exploring whether the employer may have a possible open position within the company.

A **marketing letter (or email)** is written to quickly grab the hiring executive's attention. The goal of this "attack" strategy is to showcase your qualifications and create enough interest so the hiring executive reads your resume and engages you in conversation. You are proactively marketing yourself directly to a potential hiring executive who could likely hire you for the position you seek.

---

88 Franklin, Benjamin [Richard Saunders, Poor Richard, pseud.]. *The Way to Wealth.* July 7, 1757, *American Literature Research and Analysis*, http://itech.fgcu.edu/faculty/wohlpart/alra/franklin.htm (accessed May 27, 2015).

89 Claycomb and Dinse, *Career Pathways*, Part 4.

The Cover Letter Success Formula

The kind of cover letter doesn't matter: getting your cover letter read increases the odds that your resume will be read. Be concise. With your cover letter (as well as all your written communications), proofreading is mandatory. Executives are reading not only for content, but for sentence structure and how you express your thoughts. Spelling or grammar errors broadcast that you don't pay attention to detail, or are careless. Have someone who's unfamiliar with your letter read it. You could also let your writing sit overnight. Some claim that reading it backward helps. And when it comes time to send your letters, don't send the same one to every executive. Having a template is fine, but customize each one. And don't mention salary, compensation, or benefits in a cover letter.

To maximize your effectiveness when writing cover letters, use the following approach, which has proven effective over the course of time:

- Create interest (first sentence)

- Match

- Showcase an accomplishment/qualification

- Provide additional information

- Close

Here's an in-depth look at how to do this:

Create interest

You must quickly get the attention and interest of the employer. Personalizing the letter with their name (found by searching LinkedIn or the company website, or calling the company) will go a long way. Adding a "RE:" line (meaning "regarding") lets the executive know what your letter is about and the position you're interested in. Generating interest increases the time the executive will spend on your letter. All too often, people do the opposite by beginning their letters with something similar to:

I am writing you today regarding any potential need you may have for a director of operations. I believe I have the qualifications you are looking for.

This type of opening sentence is ineffective. Some better examples are:

- **Mention a personal or professional referral.** *Our mutual friend, Peter Huggins, suggested that I reach out to you.* Mentioning a common acquaintance is one of the most effective ways to capture a reader's attention.

- **Come out swinging with one of your top achievements.** *For the last four years I have been ranked as one of my company's top ten sales representatives for overall sales production.*

- **Identify yourself by a unique or highly sought-after skill or knowledge base.** *I am a software engineer with a Microsoft Master's Certificate and five CCIEs from Cisco.*

- **Refer to a statistic.** *According to the most recent polling, 43 percent of small businesses will explore private healthcare exchanges for their company's health insurance needs, up from 21 percent just a year ago.*

- **Offer to solve a business problem.** *If you need to decrease your company's operating expenses by 20 percent, without layoffs, I have a track record of doing just that.*

- **Ask a relevant business question.** *Have you found it difficult to increase company revenues during this economic downturn? If so, that is my specialty.*

- **Mention a recent company event or a news release that is significant.** *Congratulations on your acquisition of Plate Co., Inc. I understand this could increase your market share significantly.*

- **Use a quotation.** *Jeremy Johnson of the American Marketing Association recently found that redefining target markets can increase effectiveness by almost double.*

- **Cite a relevant industry trend.** *It is a well-known fact that health care reform is causing a silent exodus of tenured physicians from private practice. I have a track record of recruiting these doctors to onsite clinics.*

What the Pros Say:

What technique do you use to quickly capture the attention of the reader of a cover letter?

I don't have any set formula or strategy. Every letter is different. However, some of my favorite openings have been to start the letter with a quote: either a famous quote that encapsulates my client's brand or a quote taken from a referral letter that a peer or former boss has written. I will also often start with a particularly compelling story from the client's past that I know will pique the interest of the reader. Or, another of my favorite openings is to use some compelling piece of research that clearly reflects the most compelling "problem" of the relevant industry, then immediately shift to a focus on how the client is the most qualified person to solve that problem.

Michelle Dumas, NCRW, CPRW

Match

After you have the hiring executive's attention, hold it by briefly identifying your function, which must match one the company already has, even using their exact wording, if possible. Consider using the word cloud technique discussed earlier. "Matching" makes you relevant and encourages the hiring executive to read on. Here are a couple of example phrases:

As an industrial engineer with over fifteen years of manufacturing experience . . .

I am a senior-level account management professional with a specialty in wellness and care management . . .

Depending on your writing style, this matching statement could be placed at the end of the "create interest" paragraph, added as the first sentence of the "showcase" paragraph, or be a short paragraph by itself.

Showcase an accomplishment/qualification

The accomplishment paragraph is even more important after interest is created and you have matched a known company role. Make this paragraph noticeable by using bold lettering (use it sparingly) to focus the executive on key points, but do not repeat your resume. Make your accomplishments relevant by identifying the position's most important requirements, link your qualifications to them, and then show your accomplishments in each or most of the job functions. In other words, tell a prospective employer you can do the job and you have a track record of doing it well. These "showcase" techniques can also help to get your resume read.

If you want to pursue job opportunities as a director of operations (just as an illustration), start with your Master Job Description, combined with research on similar open positions (or a job description from the employer). You may find a job description like this:

Director of Operations

Candidate must have at least ten years' experience managing multisite locations. Individual will have experience with the following: process management systems, personnel management, performance improvement, and emergency response plans.

So, when writing your cover letter, use the exact wording to demonstrate your skills in the listed job requirements. This paragraph of your cover letter could look like this (important portions in bold for clarification):

*In the last fifteen years, I have worked as a **director of operations** for three manufacturers in the plastics industry. During my most recent position at See Through Plastics, LLC, I had success in the following areas:*

- *__Managed four manufacturing facilities in four separate regions of the country.__ Exceeded production and profit goals for the last five consecutive years.*

- *Designed and implemented a **process management system** that resulted in **improved production efficiency** by 32 percent and increased product output by 20 percent.*

- *Created a workplace accountability matrix with floor supervisors that decreased absenteeism of workers by 15 percent while **improving productivity per worker** by 21 percent.*

- *Worked with company auditor to develop an auditing system that revealed resource and time inefficiencies. **Program saved 12 percent on resource orders** in the first year and reduced fulfillment time by over 20 percent.*

- *Worked with safety consulting firm to create and **implement a state-of-the-art emergency response plan for catastrophic events** and business interruption. Plan has been duplicated by other manufacturers.*

To keep your letter concise, only use bulleted items that address the position's most important requirements. In the above example, the job seeker may only use two or three of the five accomplishments.

Occasionally (although rare), there will be unique situations where accomplishments can be less important. This occurs when you may be one of relatively few in your field or area with a certain skill, certification, or knowledge that becomes an important element of your candidacy. Showcase your unique qualification in this paragraph.

What the Pros Say:

What makes a cover letter persuasive or impactful?

Clearly indicating the qualities and talents that the job seeker will bring to the position to benefit the employer—mentioning that additional qualifications will be found in the resume—and having a call to action in the closing paragraph makes a cover letter persuasive and impactful.

Beate Hait, CPRW, NCRW

As with the resume, when writing a letter, you have to understand your audience and write to very clearly and succinctly address their concerns. Additionally, the letter should be personal and let the reader know that you are writing specifically to them, not just sending some template letter that you have sent to one hundred others.

Michelle Dumas, NCRW, CPRW

Provide additional information

In the following paragraphs of the letter, elaborate on your experience, skills, background, and achievements. This is where you have a fair amount of latitude on what you want to showcase. Choose those topics you feel are the most relevant or impressive to the employer. Once again, inform the employer what you did, in addition to how this produced positive results.[90]

> *I am a motivated sales professional with a positive track record of opening new territories. At Ins. Company, I took over a three-state, virgin territory with no sales or business contacts. I researched and identified broker-dealers, set appointments, traveled, and made sales presentations. Within the first year, I generated over $1.2M in product and exceeded sales goals by over 300 percent.*

Another approach is to add a strong recommendation. This paragraph should be indented and single-spaced. To realize this technique's full impact, identify the person providing the recommendation by name and title. Here's an example:

> *My supervisor, Susan J. Smith, Director of Operations, Cyban, Inc. states:*
> *Sandra has a strong work ethic. She is organized, resourceful, and can work successfully without supervision. She is flexible and will roll up her sleeves to get the job done!*

Remember, it is always more influential when others speak well of you than when you promote yourself.[91]

Another technique you can use in this section is to reveal a professional insight about yourself to personalize the letter. It must be something relevant or important to the employer. This paragraph can start with a phrase such as: "I am passionate about . . . ", "I am professionally rewarded when . . . ", "I continue to be intrigued by . . . ", and so on. For example:

> *I am passionate about wellness. I get a great deal of satisfaction knowing that the wellness services I promote to clients will have a personal impact on the health and well-being of that employer's employees.*

You may choose to add some information about your personal life that could have relevance to the job. Some hiring executives occasionally want to know about you as a person as well as a professional.

---

90 See also, Safani, "Tell a Story."

91 Matt, "Brag Book."

I am competitive professionally as well as in my personal life. In fact, I routinely compete in local tennis tournaments . . . successfully I might add!

Use these paragraphs to inform the employer about any other piece of information relevant to your job search, such as relocation.

I will relocate to Portland in the next sixty days as a result of my wife's promotion.

Close

Conclude your letter by using a brief closing statement, followed by your intention to follow up:

Based on my track record of successful operational efficiency, I believe I have the qualifications and accomplishments to make a positive impact on ABC Inc. I look forward to discussing this opportunity with you and I will contact your office next week.

Cover Letters and Career Transition Job Seekers

For job seekers making a transition from one career focus to another or possibly changing industries, consider adding a paragraph informing the employer exactly how your skills translate or are directly transferable to the job opportunity. This explanation of transferability must be succinct. If it isn't, the employer may conclude that you are struggling to draw the analogy between your skills and the job. In that case, you lose. This information about your transferability of skills should be a part of the third or fourth paragraph. For example:

- "There is a strong correlation of my skills as a . . . and your open position for a . . . "
- "My skills and experience as an employee benefits account manager are directly transferable to your need of an internal benefits human resource specialist. (Now explain why) . . . "

Cover Letters and Recruiters

When contacted by a recruiter for a specific opportunity, the following technique can differentiate you from other job seekers since you will be competing against other well-qualified candidates.

Here's the scenario and how to gain a potential edge:

You have been contacted by a recruiter regarding a specific opportunity. You are interested and qualified and the recruiter is willing to submit your credentials to the employer. Ask the recruiter if there is a job description or job posting. If so, get it and read it. In the same conversation or a follow-up call, tell the recruiter that you are going to send a brief cover letter (by email) regarding the position. Most, if not all, recruiters will accept the letter. Ask the recruiter, at his or her discretion, to include the cover letter as a part of your submission to the employer. Here's why: Many recruited candidates don't bother with cover letters because they think a recruiter's involvement makes a cover letter unnecessary. Differentiate yourself from your competition and showcase your accomplishments and qualifications by writing a cover letter (remember the word cloud technique, which could help). Employers will note that you took the time and effort to write the letter, and draw the conclusion that you must be more interested than some of the other candidates who did not. And when the letter gets read, you have differentiated yourself even more.

Marketing Emails—Proactively Marketing Your Professional Credentials

Proactively marketing your professional credentials by email directly to hiring executives is an effective job-search technique that drives straight to the heart of the hidden job market. With reference to the Cover Letter Success Formula, write a compelling email cover letter.

Marketing emails essentially follow the identical formula for content as any other letter with some distinct differences that should be observed to increase effectiveness. These differences include:

Subject Line. Good use of the subject line is vital. It must be short and attention-getting. A poor subject line would read: "Accountant looking for work." A good subject line would read: "#1 Provider Technology Sales Representative."

A very good approach is using your Headline from your LinkedIn profile, and then modifying it as needed using your professional judgment.

Inside Address. This is a communication sent by email, not by the US Postal Service. Do not put an inside address in the email. A date is unnecessary as well.

Attaching a Resume. Here you have to make some decisions. Some companies have servers with robust firewalls that screen out all unfamiliar emails with an attachment. You can either send an attached resume or not. If your email that had a resume attached is returned with an undeliverable kickback, try again without the resume attached. Another consideration is your current employment status. If you are unemployed, it is recommended that you attach a copy of your resume. If you are currently employed, think through whether you want to provide a copy of your resume. You may decide to be selective and send a copy to some companies and not to others.

When it comes to attaching a resume, customize the name of the document. It should at least be your first and last name with a space between them e.g., John Smith.docx. A better approach would be your name plus a branding statement e.g., John Smith Lean Six Sigma. docx. Or, add a position type or function e.g., John Smith Senior Engineer.docx.

Close. Your close should be different due to the "reply" function with emails. It is recommended that you ask the recipient to act in response to the email. An example of a good close would be:

"If you have an interest or a need for a proven account manager with a documented track record of success, please reply or call me."

Telephone Number. Always put your telephone number in your marketing emails. The hiring executive may want to bypass the reply button and speak to you directly. Give them a way to do so.

What the Pros Say:

What advice would you give a job seeker that wants to send a cover letter by email?

Absolutely do it!

- Keep it very brief.
- Don't attach it, put it in the body of the email.
- Address the person by name.
- Do not be vague! Specifically address how your experience can benefit the company.
- Include all your contact information; phone, email, LinkedIn profile URL, professional website—give them ways to find out more about you quickly and easily.

Jessica Hernandez, Certified Social Branding Analyst

I coach my clients to include the cover letter in the body of the email. People are reluctant to open attachments from people they don't know and especially when they arrive with a blank or almost blank message. Including your cover letter in the body of the email, with the resume attached, gives you the chance to establish some trust, credibility, and rapport with the recipient, piquing their interest and making them feel comfortable enough to open the attachment to learn more.

Michelle Dumas, NCRW, CPRW

Thank-You Letters

The primary purposes of thank-you letters are to express your appreciation, reiterate your relevant background, qualifications, and successes, and differentiate you from other job seekers. Most hiring executives appreciate a thank-you correspondence after an interview.[92] And "some employers may expect a job interview thank-you card."[93] However, it has been said that only 20 percent of all job seekers take the time to write a thank-you note.[94] If so, writing a thank-you note can differentiate you from other job seekers. And not sending a thank-you note may reflect negatively on your candidacy.[95]

An important secondary purpose is to make sure the hiring executive remembers you. In a survey by The Ladders, a combined 76 percent said a thank-you note was "somewhat important" or "very important" to their hiring decision.[96] That's three out of every four! Therefore, capitalize on this opportunity to reinforce your skills and accomplishments. Write a thank-you note after every interview. And keep it short. This is a thank-you letter, not an interview transcript.

To maximize the impact of your thank-you letter, use the following approach:

1. Express your appreciation

2. Match

92 Accountemps, "Farewell to the Handwritten Thank-You Note? Survey Reveals Email, Phone Call Are Preferred Methods for Post-Interview Follow-Up," news release, June 14, 2012, http://accountemps.rhi.mediaroom.com/thank-you (accessed July 9, 2015).

93 "Do Employers Expect a Job Interview Thank-You Card?" CVTips, http://www.cvtips.com/interview/do-employers-expect-a-job-interview-thank-you-card.html (accessed July 10, 2015).

94 Helmrich, Brittney. "Thanks! 20 Job Interview Thank You Note Tips," *Business News Daily*, June 23, 2015, http://www.businessnewsdaily.com/7134-thank-you-note-tips.html (accessed July 9, 2015).

95 "Thank-You Note Etiquette," CareerBuilder, http://www.careerbuilder.com/JobPoster/Resources/page.aspx?pagever=ThankYouNoteEtiquette (accessed July 9, 2015).

96 "Give Thanks or Your Chance For That Job Could be Cooked," *TheLadders*, http://cdn.theladders.net/static/images/basicSite/PR/pdfs/TheLaddersGiveThanks.pdf (accessed June 5, 2015).

3. Emphasize past achievements

4. Close

Let's look at each step in more detail:

Express your appreciation

Thank the hiring executive for their time. Then, build rapport, depending upon the circumstances. Your first paragraph could look something like this:

I appreciate you taking time to meet with me regarding your implementation consultant position. I enjoyed learning how you derived the concept behind your state-of-the-art system. As we discussed, my knowledge in this area could assist your department with the challenges it will face in the coming months.

Or, perhaps like this:

Thank you for meeting me on Tuesday regarding the regional sales position. I appreciate your time. And, by the way, good luck to your son during tryouts for the starting quarterback position!

Match

Because you were interviewed, you should know what the hiring executive is looking for in the position. Briefly restate and match your qualifications to the need.

During our plant tour last week, I was impressed with your use of robotics in the manufacturing process. I can honestly say I have never seen such an efficient after-market manufacturing plant! With over fifteen years as an industrial engineer from near identical manufacturing environments I am well-suited for the challenges of this position.

Emphasize past achievements

Express your interest in the position, and link two or three job requirements with your accomplishments. For maximum impact, try to make them relevant to company needs, a position's special qualifications, or topics mentioned in the interview. Your paragraph could look something like this:

I am interested in joining your company in an engineering operations capacity. As we discussed, my recent accomplishments include:

- *Implemented a manufacturing process improvement system resulting in an $800,000 savings.*
- *Designed and implemented an inventory auditing system that increased turnaround time by 30 percent and reduced spending by 12 percent.*
- *Developed and implemented a "Visions" business plan that forecast budgets for a variety of business operations including equipment and technology upgrades, new facility construction, and reduced operating expenses.*

Close

Here, express your continued interest and outline your plan to contact the hiring executive. Here's an example of this final paragraph:

What I achieved for Sinc Company, I can do for you. I will follow up with you in ten days, as you requested, to discuss additional steps.

What the Pros Say:

What suggestions would you pass along about writing a post interview thank-you letter?

After an interview is your vital moment to continue selling your unique skills, qualifications, accomplishments, and credentials. Most candidates don't bother sending a thank-you letter, so you will already stand out by actually sending one.

What should you include in the thank-you letter?

1. Address your candidacy: If, during an interview, there was a specific objection raised as to your appropriateness as a candidate, use your thank-you letter to respond to and overcome those concerns.
2. Meet their needs and challenges: If, during an interview, the company communicated their specific needs and challenges, use the thank-you letter to clearly demonstrate how you can meet those needs and eliminate those challenges.
3. Reiterate qualifications: If, during an interview, the company communicated

their ideal qualifications for a candidate, use the thank-you letter to outline how you meet and exceed each of those qualifications.

Even if you feel you are repeating yourself by reiterating what was already discussed in the interview, I assure you that there is nothing more effective than repeating those things to the interviewer. Of course most of us would prefer to email a thank-you letter, but I encourage you to mail a handwritten note if you have the chance, for the precise reason that almost nobody does this anymore.

Nelly Grinfeld, MBA, NCRW, CEIC

The thank-you letter is the perfect summary of your interview performance. It's your chance to underscore an important answer or say something more about a subject you feel you didn't quite say enough about the first time around. It's also your opportunity to repeat why you're the right person for the job and what you can do on the job that another candidate cannot.

I also believe strongly that email-only thank-you letters, while convenient, are impersonal. I urge my clients to send handwritten notes or cards as thank yous whenever possible—I can just about guarantee this will make their candidacy stand out.

Cheryl Lynch Simpson, CMRW, ACRW, COPNS

Thank-You Letters When You Are Not Selected for the Job

This letter builds bridges for the future and is a very strong networking technique. It will differentiate you from others and create a favorable impression with the hiring executive. There are two good reasons for doing this. First, it can leave the door open for future opportunities with the company. It is not uncommon for employers to revisit previous candidates when new opportunities become available.

Additionally, since professionals within an industry often run in the same circles of influence, the letter distinguishes you and could lead to other business relationships with the hiring executive. Writing a professional correspondence after a decision not to hire shows the hiring executive your character and professionalism. You don't know where, when, and in what way your paths may cross again. The letter helps ensure the next engagement is positive—be it business or personal.

Some Final Words about Written Communications

As you know, communication is a sought-after skill (written, verbal, and listening).[97] Being able to write effectively and persuasively is important in your job search and it will be evaluated. What you write about, how you communicate it, sentence structure, word choice, grammar, punctuation, and proofreading are evaluated against other job seekers. By following the Cover Letter Success Formula and proper thank-you letter writing techniques, you can feel confident that your written communications will differentiate you from other job seekers, grab the attention of the employer, and result in a higher success rate.

Proofread everything and have someone unfamiliar with the documents review them. Using an effective writing formula will be rendered useless if there is spelling, grammatical, or punctuation errors.

---

97 Hanson and Hanson, "What Do Employers *Really* Want?"

Part V

Business Cards

High expectations are the key to everything.

— Sam Walton[98]

Having a business card during a job search is a necessity. Circumstances will present themselves where providing a resume is awkward or inappropriate.

There are four different approaches to the standard three-and-a-half inch by two-inch business card for a job search: traditional business cards, networking business cards, resume business cards, and infographic business cards (handbill).

To determine the best business card approach for your needs, consider this key factor: Which would be best received by a networking contact or the hiring executive for your level of position?

It's easy to get sidetracked when creating business cards, especially networking, resume, and infographic versions. Resist that urge. Don't overanalyze. Just remember: The messaging behind your brand and the information on your resume and LinkedIn profile must match the message and information on your card.

A solid case can be made for getting two sets of cards to use in different settings: traditional for truly social events, and a networking or resume card for job networking events.

Here are examples for each kind of job search business card:

Traditional Business Cards

This business card is simple in design. It contains only your name, city of residence, (street address is optional), telephone number(s), email address, and LinkedIn profile address. It is used for information exchange purposes only.

---

98 Bergdahl, Michael. *What I Learned From Sam Walton: How to Compete and Thrive in a Wal-Mart World.* (Hoboken, New Jersey: John Wiley & Sons, 2004), p. 39.

Bob Johnson, CSFS®

1340 Main Street	(816) 987-6543 (C)
Blue Springs, MO 64015	Bob.johnson1340@gmail.com
(816) 123-4567 (H)	www.linkedin.com/in/bobjohnson

Networking Business Cards

Networking business cards contain the same key contact information as a traditional card, except this variety also has a title and a concise statement regarding your career focus and unique value proposition or brand. Remember to keep the messaging consistent between your networking card, your resume, your LinkedIn profile, and so on. With some variations, the theme of these job-seeking tools must align.

Award-Winning, Population Health Management
Sales Professional

Bob Johnson, CSFS®

National Sales Executive

1340 Main Street	(816) 987-6543 (C)
Blue Springs, MO 64015	Bob.johnson1340@gmail.com
(816) 123-4567 (H)	www.linkedin.com/in/bobjohnson

Resume Business Cards

A resume business card takes the networking card one step further. Here you may expand descriptive information on the front of the card, and put key qualifications and accomplishments on the back. Focus on your top two or three strong achievements (or qualities), instead of responsibilities or titles.

This next point is optional, but leave a little white space at the bottom of the back of the card, allowing the recipient room to jot a note about you. Hopefully the note will read, "Need to call."

Bob Johnson, CSFS®

National Sales Executive

Award-winning, population health management
sales professional with 5+ years of consistent
goal achievement

1340 Main Street	(999) 473-5678 (C)
Blue Springs, MO 64015	bob.johnson1340@gmail.com
(999) 473-1234 (H)	www.linkedin.com/in/bobjohnson

Front

Qualifications Summary

• #1 Sales Producer last three years
• Presidents Club Qualifier 2009 to present
• Consistently produced over $4M annually

Back

It's fine to mix and match the concepts of the three forms of business cards. For example, you may determine that it would be best received by your target audience that the front of the card has a traditional look. But, on the back, you may choose to include a branding statement and a couple of achievements. That's fine. Exercise your best business judgment.

What the Pros Say:

As a resume writer, have you ever given advice to a job seeker about the design or use of a job-search business card? If so, what was your advice?

I have given advice on this. I recommend clients incorporate a personal branding statement, and not just say what they do. You want to be memorable. This was not a client of mine, but I met a woman who was a marketing executive. She had mini-business cards that were very simple, her name, Strategic Marketing Executive, phone and email (personally I would have added her LinkedIn URL) on one side. The other side of the card had a tag line, like Dynamic Leader, and each card had a different line. When she passed out cards in a group interview it became a talking point and people were comparing what each card said.

Michelle Robin, NCRW, CPRW

I suggest to my clients that their business card design should match the formatting, color, and tone of their resume and other career communications tools whenever possible. I also suggest using a networking title on the front of the card and including a short WhyBuyROI on the reverse side. This succinctly summarizes for the reader why a company should hire the person and what impact their tenure has made for past employers.

Cheryl Lynch Simpson, CMRW, ACRW, COPNS

A business card or a double-sized card (folded to the typical size) is easy to carry and hand to someone as part of a job seeker's networking and self-marketing process. It would include the job seeker's name, contact info, the target job, brief bullet points, LinkedIn profile URL, and the URL and/or QR code to access the full resume.

Beate Hait, CPRW, NCRW

Business cards can be printed at most office supply stores and are reasonably inexpensive for a few hundred cards. In addition, many online companies produce business cards inexpensively. And if you're technology savvy, you can print your cards using special paper and a template that is already loaded on most computers.

When creating your job-search business cards, keep the design simple. Use traditional fonts and conservative, business-appropriate color schemes. If you are pursuing jobs in advertising, media marketing, or other creative fields, you have more latitude with design and use of colors.

Infographic Business Card

An infographic business card is a very unique concept. It is not a "business card" in the traditional sense. Instead, it is more of a "networking handbill." In concept, an infographic business card is a colorful, high-resolution document containing persuasive background information and accomplishments presented through pie charts and bar graphs of creative design.

An infographic business card was briefly addressed in the Infographic Resume section of the book. It is larger than the standard three-and-a-half inch by two-inch business card. Although there is no rule, a four-by-six-inch card is a good size or starting point.

The infographic business card is ideal for networking events, especially for association gatherings and conventions. Printed on business-card grade paper, with colorful graphics, it is a clear differentiator. If not too large, it can still easily slip into an inside jacket pocket or portfolio of a networking contact or hiring executive.

If this infographic card idea appeals to you, it is highly recommended that you use the services of a professional with experience creating infographic resumes, as this experience translates well to infographic cards. Remember, networking cards, resume cards, and infographic cards do not replace your resume. They are designed as job-search marketing pieces. Always have these cards handy, regardless of which version or versions you decide to use. Who knows who you could meet, and if they'll contribute to your search? You never can tell.

Part VI

Sample Resumes and Other Great Resources

In the sections that follow, you are given the unique opportunity to view resumes and cover letters from some of the most experienced, credentialed, and award-winning resume writers in the country! They are the same pros that have been giving you advice throughout this book. They were selectively chosen and profiled for their experience, professional credentials, and quality of work. There was an attempt to provide you with writers that were geographically dispersed.

The resume writers have graciously donated their work. They did not receive any compensation to be included in this book. This book is unlike any other resume book they have participated in because it provides them with a platform to display their portfolio of work to you.

If you choose to have your resume professionally written, please consider contacting the writers in this book whose work appeals to you or perhaps are located closest to you.

Understand that resume writing is an art form. It takes time and focused concentration. What you may see may not completely align with the instructional section of this book. However, each sample resume was written with a specific job, strategy, or goal in mind. You have the wonderful advantage of having the education of the instructional part of this book. With the resume samples that follow, you can blend and create your own unique resume or decide that a professionally prepared resume is the way to go.

Each writer was given an introductory page followed by samples of their work. The introductory page provides information about the writer and contact information. They were asked to provide a diverse sampling of resumes and cover letters from different professional levels and different industries. They have attempted do so with the understanding that many specialize with certain levels and industries. All of the resumes have been fictionalized.

To further increase the use of this book, many of the resumes have been posted on themotivatedjobsearch.com website under the Resumes tab. There you can view the resumes in their original electronic form (with colors). The Resumes tab is password protected. The password is: BEMOTIVATED

Virginia Franco, NCRW, CPRW
Virginia Franco Resumes

Virginia Franco, NCRW, CPRW
Virginia Franco Resumes
100% Customized Resumes for Today's
    Readers that Garner Interviews in 60 Days
www.virginiafrancoresumes.com
VAFrancoResumes@gmail.com
704-771-8572

Virginia Franco is a Nationally Certified Resume Writer with several industry credentials, holds a master's in social work and a bachelor's in journalism.

She founded the Charlotte, NC-based Virginia Franco Resumes several years ago when recognizing her years of corporate communications and freelance web, newspaper and magazine writing offered her a unique understanding of how people read online, in print and when in a rush.

Virginia helps clients all over the world to get interviews in 60 days with career documents including resumes, cover letters and LinkedIn profiles that appeal to 21st century online, skim readers.

She shares her writing and job search insight regularly as a member of the Forbes Coaches Council and with readers of Ivy Exec, Business2Community.com, MedReps, Career Metis and BusinessGists 24/7 Business News.

CHRISTOPHER JONES

New York, NY 10022

555-555-5555 cjones@jmail.com
@cjones @cjones
linkedin.com/pub/chris-jones

INTEGRATED DIGITAL EXPERIENCE PRODUCTION EXECUTIVE
DIGITAL MEDIA, ADVERTISING & MARKETING STRATEGY FOR LEADING INDUSTRY BRANDS

Leads teams that spearhead $60K–$9M integrated content campaigns from pitch to implementation. Gains stake-holder buy-in for custom solutions that align with and inform business goals for Fortune 500s and nonprofits alike.

Mentors and motivates sales, marketing, creative, technical and account teams of 5 to 20 that collaborate with third-party and in-house development teams to build brand products for web, mobile, social, TV, print and real-time events.

Achieves client retention via meticulous, agile production management and a keen eye for aesthetic and craft; lever-ages expert knowledge of web/mobile-based technologies, digital/TV media planning, user experience and interface design.

AREAS OF EXPERTISE

Digital/Interactive Production • Presentations • Thought Leadership • Stakeholder Management
Cost Estimation SOWs • Contract Negotiations • Vendor/Partner Management
Budget Management • Digital Asset Man-agement

DIGITAL MARKETING LEADERSHIP

XYZ Agency | VP INTEGRATED PRODUCTION DIRECTOR | New York, NY   20XX–Present

> **SNAPSHOT: Led concept-to-execution collaborations that gave shape to the agency's agile, omni-media communica-tions platform key to guiding digital first experiences for diverse industry clients.**

- Lead mentor that structured fully integrated Strategy, Analytics, User Experience, Creative, Production, Account and Operations teams of 5-20 people.

- Instrumental in agency acquisition of $50K - $9M+ Digital and Social AOR business.

- Co-concepted and pioneered Newsdesk that serves today as a model for real-time listening and a brand insights engine; and Twitter co-administrator.

- Authored and presented Digital Boot Camp series; as chair and co-creator of XYZ-U that educated agency audienc-es on digital communications topics including emerging technologies, mobile, social and real-time marketing trends.

Continued

- **CLIENTS: P&G, Abbot, Nestle, TGI Fridays, UBS, AdCouncil,BACSnowglobe.com, SelfiForASienna. com, TriToyo-taDealers.com, BoostUp.org, Frigidaire, Lenscrafters, AngelSoft, Pepto-bismol.com.**

ABC Agency | EXPERIENCE DIRECTOR | New York, NY   20XX–20XX

SNAPSHOT: As brand experience lead, drove day-to-day development of a digitally capable, credentialed and inte-grated advertising capability via collaborative leadership spanning Creative, Production, Finance and Account Plan-ning.

- Developed and instituted department's first processes, implementation guidelines and document templates that introduced structure and optimized operational efficiency.

ABC Agency | EXPERIENCE DIRECTOR | New York, NY

- Led web production, technical and creative teams that executed development of all creative, technical and admin-istrative client deliverables.
- **CLIENTS: Delta Airlines, Cadbury Adams, Smirnoff, Rolex, Johnson & Johnson, Smith Barney.**

123 Agency | EXECUTIVE PRODUCER | New York, NY   20XX–20XX

SNAPSHOT: Replaced ad-hoc with structure via implementation of development processes, implementation guide-lines and document templates key to seamless concept-to-case study delivery of all interactive advertising.

- Drove resolution of all financial issues including contract negotiations for $60K projects to multimillion-dollar retain-ers.
- Spearheaded interactive advertising leadership of all creative, web production and production teams including third-party resources.
- Ensured timely completion of all technical and administrative deliverables including client and internal estimates, schedules, SOWs and reconciliations.
- Oversaw development of all creative, technical, and administrative internal and client deliverables including esti-mates, schedules, SOWs and reconciliations.
- **CLIENTS: Johnnie Walker, Levis, Mentos, eSpeed (Cantor Fitzgerald), Match.com, theaxeeffect. com, game-killers.com, orderoftheserpentine.com, esuvee.com, toastgomez.com.**

Ocuvise | EXECUTIVE PRODUCER/SENIOR PROJECT MANAGER | New York, NY   20XX–20XX

SNAPSHOT: Pitch-through-launch interactive production and development leadership; mentored production, tech-nical and creative teams; oversaw creative, technical and administrative client deliverables for Deutsche Bank.

Razorline| SENIOR PROJECT MANAGER | New York, NY   20XX–20XX

SNAPSHOT: End-to-end website development for Forenkla client; supervised process mapping, task and deliverable matching and schedule templating; created and maintained proposals, estimates, schedules, budgets and reconcilia-tion.

Continued

ADDITIONAL EXPERIENCE

Grass Roots Online | SENIOR PROJECT MANAGER | PROJECTS: Global Sports, Fathom, Chase
Circus Tent Interactive Advertising | PRODUCER| PROJECTS: BB&T, Hearst, Ford, GMC
Digital City | ASSISTANT PRODUCER | PROJECTS: The New Yorker
Coastal Living Magazine | ADVERTISING DIRECTOR

TECHNOLOGY SKILLS

• Keynote • Ad Serving Platforms • Adobe CS6 • HTML • CSS • Flash • JIRA • MAC OS/iOS
• Windows   • MS Office

EDUCATION

University of Vermont | B.A., COMMUNICATIONS

John Doe

704-555-5555 • JOHNDOE

MARKETING, PR & COMMUNICATIONS

SPECIAL EVENTS • FUNDRAISING • MEMBERSHIP GROWTH

MARKETING & COMMUNICATIONS: Produce sompelling, branded messaging and marketing disseminated across traditional, digital and social media channels.

STRATEGY INNOVATION: Outside-the-box strategist perseveres and advocates; helps causes and candidates overcome obstacles to reach goals and drive change.

RECORD FUNDRAISING/EVENT MANAGEMENT: Launches events; rallies celebrities and sponsors to the cause to raise awareness and funds.

OPERATIONS/ADMINISTRATION: Leads daily operations, vendors, staffs and budgets; trusted counsel, finance strategist, ground support, reporting and compliance expert.

AREAS OF EXPERITSE

Campaign Development
Speech Writing
Advocacy/Outreach/Solicitation
Media Relations/Trainnig
Research & Analysis
Budget Management
Public/Private Partnerships
Vendor/Venue management
Contract Negotiations

PROFESSIONAL EXPERIENCE

COMMUNICATION STRATEGIES, LLC   **20XX–Present**

EXECUTIVE DIRECTOR/PRINCIPAL | Annapolis, MD

SNAPSHOT: Founded special events, fundraising and campaign strategy firm with word-of-mouth reputation for out-side-the-box creativity, logistics execution excellence and huge, against-the-odds successes.

STRATEGY: Championed concept-to-execution events, innovative social and traditional media, marketing and fundrais-ing campaigns that adhered to budgets from $10K to $1M.

RESULTS: Broke fundraising records via memorable special events and overcame 40+ point gaps to win seats in coun-ty, state and national Legislative and Congressional elections.

FUNDRAISING

- Raised $800K via targeted donor identification strategy that contributed to reducing a 40-point deficit to four points in the State Representative race for vacant seat.

- Managed end-to-end logistics for the most lucrative event in the history of a state's county's political party.

- Secured national recording artists, television and entertainment personalities, and top Party speakers to promote, perform and give speeches at conventions, concerts and event fundraisers with 700+ in attendance.

John Doe continued   704-555-5555 • JOHNDOE

EVENT PLANNING

- Promoted public/private partnerships for joint/cooperative fundraising including a well-received Susan G. Komen Air Show that raised funds and awareness for breast health.

- Events featured innovative programming concepts and logistics coordination; secured diverse and nationally rec-ognized sponsors including the Heritage Foundation and Media Research Counsel.

PUBLIC RELATIONS, MEDIA, MARKETING & COMMUNICATIONS STRATEGY

- Creator of only PAC commercial that earned primetime national news coverage and went viral with 400K YouTube views during state Senatorial race.

- Collaborated with Univision to coordinate state's 2012 Hispanic Outreach Initiative.

- Pitched feature stories and interviews to local and national print, radio, TV and electronic media outlets in tough U.S. media markets; secured coverage in AP, Reuters, The Wall Street Journal, NY Times, LA Times and CBS News.

- Authored and produced dozens of direct mail/marketing collateral for nationwide clients representing Congres-sional PACs, special events and gubernatorial candidates.

- Advised candidates on public image, voter interaction, and brand enhancement resulting in "against all odds" close election races. Provided public policy training based on analysis of voting histories, polling data and surveys/polls.

- Oversaw TV commercial production and media buys from concept to broadcasting debut; relied on trusted net-work of contracted script writers, graphic designers, TV/Radio producers that produced consistent, on-brand mes-saging.

- Developed talking points for debates, speeches, forums, press releases and media inquiries. Created and main-tained social media presence and online content.

PREVIOUS EXPERIENCE

MEDIA GRAPHICS

FOUNDER | Alexandria, VA

- Grew revenues to $4M with a 4,000-square-foot warehouse and a team of six whose client base spanned ten states. Earned status as a preferred vendor representing leading architecture and engineering soft-ware/equipment brands.

EDUCATION

B.S., Business Administration   University of Maryland

ELIZABETH JONES, M.A.

Skeet Bay, PA 05555

555-555-9554 | elizabethjones@gmail.com

Elementary Vice Principal/Supervisor

"If a child can't learn the way we teach, maybe we should teach the way they learn" -Ignacio Estrada

NY Certified educator applies Education, Administration and Supervision graduate program acumen with Bank Street Professional development and learnings required to obtain PA Principal and Supervisor Eligibility Certifications.

Leverages 21st century instructional strategies and knowledge of core curriculum/common core standards gained during 15-years as a teacher, data coach, literacy tutor and assessment rater to catapult students to grade level and beyond.

Works collaboratively with families, administrative and teaching staff to share knowledge of educational trends, school curriculum, instructional and curriculum improvement processes.

Education

M.A., Education, Administration and Supervision, NEW YORK UNIVERSITY

- Collected and analyzed data to evaluate long-term K-8 student growth as part of Administrative Internship.

- Curriculum below aligns with Educational Leadership Constituent Council (ELCC) national standards and includes organizational management, technology management and data-driven decision-making courses:

Orientation to Administration & Supervision	*Equity, Diversity & Access in Education*
Action Research & Evaluation	*Leadership & Collaborative Processes*
School Improvement Processes	*HR Leadership & Management*
Professional Learning for Continuous Improvement	*Business & Facilities Management*
Engaging in Communities of Practice	*Special Programs Administration*
Organizational Management	*Social Media for Professional Learning*
Instructional Leadership	*Family, Community & Media Relations*
Supervision of Curriculum	*Facilitating Change*
Instruction & Assessment	*Mentoring & Coaching*
Professional Communications	*Cultural Competency*
School Policy & Law	*Assessment, Evaluation & Instructional Strategies*

B.A., English, UNIVERSITY OF RICHMOND

Certifications & Memberships

Principal Eligibility Certificate, PA DEPARTMENT OF EDUCATION

Supervisor Certificate, PA DEPARTMENT OF EDUCATION

Professional Development Instructor, AMERICAN FEDERATION OF TEACHERS FOR EDUCATIONAL RESEARCH & DISSEMINATION

Leadership Development Program Certificate of Achievement, WEST CHESTER COUNTY PUBLIC SCHOOLS

K-8 Elementary Certification, NY DEPARTMENT OF EDUCATION

Advanced Grant Proposal Writing, NEW YORK UNIVERSITY

ELIZABETH JONES, M.A.

555-555-9554 | elizabethjones@gmail.com | Page 2

Instructional Experience

Educational Assessment Rater, EDUCATIONAL TESTING SERVICE   Jan 20XX–Present

As member of educational administrator team, provide bias-free student and teacher leadership candidate assessments. To date, have evaluated candidates in NC, VA and MD.

Educator, WEST CHESTER PUBLIC SCHOOLS   Oct 20XX–Present

Tangibly improved reading scores with measurable growth during tenures at five area schools as a Literacy Tutor, Data Coach, K-3 and Grade 7 teacher. Student body of this Title I district encompassed ESL, inclusion and 80+ nationalities.

ADMINISTRATIVE ACHIEVEMENTS

- Analyzed score data and exam questions to identify optimal instructional strategies and recommendation for lesson scaffolding.

- Received advanced professional development in collaboration with Bank Street to serve as a member of school team that implemented cross–curricular mapping aimed at stemming double-digit school decline.

- Tapped by school administrator to develop and facilitate teacher training on data incorporation, formative assessments, tiered lesson planning, guided reading and cooperative learning/differentiated instruction.

- Leveraged grant writing certification talents to secure two online grants.

INSTRUCTIONAL ACHIEVEMENTS

- Catapulted 75% of below grade-level readers to grade-level and 25% to above grade-level via strategy of transparent communication and student and family engagement.

- Championed small group reading strategies key to success passing NJASK for students performing below-grade level.

- Entrusted to apply Bank School professional development learnings with years of teaching experience during class looping experience that contributed to standardized testing success for these first-time end-of-year test-takers.

- Instituted classroom order and structure that mitigated behavioral/disciplinary issues.

Educational Research & Development Instructor, NEWARK TEACHERS UNION   Dec 20XX–Apr 20XX

Facilitated educational training to Union members on diverse topics including *Interactive Direct Instruction, Effective Teaching Strategies for Media Specialists* and *The Learning Zone.*

Technology Skills

MS Word, MS Excel, MS PowerPoint, MS Publisher

ROBERT JONES, MBA, PMP

WASHINGTON, D.C. 20005 | 301-555-5555 | email@xyz.com | linkedin.com/pub/robert-smith

SENIOR TECHNOLOGY EXECUTIVE

Guides Defense, Intelligence, Military, Non-Profit and Corporate IT strategy and transformation from SOW to implementation and beyond • Dual capabilities in Technology and Business – M.S., IT and M.B.A. and 10 Technology Certifications • Balances thought leadership with lifelong pursuit of knowledge and commitment to coaching, mentorship and community service.

Lifelong history of leadership and concept-to-execution IT strategy as an Army Veteran, a Defense IT Project Manager and Enterprise Software Service Delivery Executive catapulting clients onto Cloud/SaaS platforms at Microsoft and Salesforce.

"Expert knowledge of the nuances of Public Sector and the Intelligence Community industries; project management techniques to keep projects on scope, on target and on budget." - Program Manager at xxx

"A go-to for wealth of IT knowledge and dedication." - Portfolio/Program Manager at xxx

Military Command/CXO Stakeholder Management | Project/Program Management | Compliance | Risk Management
Security | Disaster Recovery | Public Speaking | Presentations | Data Integrity | Web Development | Hardware/Software
Network Architecture Agile/Scrum/Waterfall | CRM | Reporting | SDLC | Budget Management | Vendor Management

IT LEADERSHIP OVERVIEW

XYZ | SUCCESS ENGAGEMENT DIRECTOR   **20XX–Present**

Spearheaded strategy and hands-on coaching that propelled not-for-profit client from four months behind schedule to milestone-ready and poised for a successful SaaS platform conversion.

- Completed Salesforce certification credentials 50% more quickly than peers; critical to ability to contribute to capture of $7M in one-year subscriptions in just nine months.

- Exceeded 48-hour annual volunteer service target with 400 hours in nine months earned on weekends and evenings— earning recognition at FY Sales kickoff.

- Drove best practice IT infrastructure and cloud platform guidance, training, adoption, governance, partner enablement and risk mitigation to 40+ U.S. Defense, Federal, State and local government "customer for life" clients.

ABC | SENIOR MANAGER/ INFRASTRUCTURE BUSINESS DEVELOPMENT LEAD   **20XX–20XX**

Created and launched roadmap for obtaining Federal Risk Assessment Program (FedRAMP) approval integral to growing a Unified Communications solution go-to-market strategy.

123 COMPANY   **20XX–20XX**

CLOUD DELIVERY EXECUTIVE (20XX)

Developed CXO and Executive-level relationships to ensure alignment with IT strategy key to full lifecycle oversight of Cloud Service Delivery Engagements for U.S. Private and Public Sector clients.

SENIOR PROJECT MANAGER (20XX–20XX)

Turned around Department of Homeland Security contract in jeopardy; applied Scrum methodology to rapidly deliver tangible results key to CXO satisfaction Private Cloud IaaS, PaaS and Saas project implementation.

ROBERT JONES, MBA, PMP   555.555.5555 | XYZ@GMAIL.COM | PAGE 2

123 COMPANY

SENIOR PROJECT MANAGER (CONTINUED)

- Led cradle-to-grave $2.5M global product stack deployment requiring communication and buy-in from worldwide Army Intelligence Command leadership.

SENIOR TECHNICAL ACCOUNT MANAGER (2007–2008)

Earned MVP Award for full lifecycle Service Agreement service delivery to Federal and Intelligence Community customers.

ABC COMPANY   20XX–20XX

CLIENT SITE MANAGER/ SENIOR PROJECT MANAGER (20XX–20XX)

Drove customer service turnaround that elevated satisfaction ratings 10 points to 95% year-over-year, doubled Department of Navy contract value to $85M and expanded resources 10X.

- Full ownership of two-thirds of project's task orders; garnered senior military commendation for exemplary service designing CENTCOM's network architecture at Andrews AFB.

Team Leader/Senior Systems Analyst (2000–2002)

Oversaw hardware installations and help desk operations as a consultant and IT SME to 500+ local and remote users.

IT ANALYSIS & ENGINEERING EXPERIENCE

BOEING | SPACECRAFT ANALYST   **INTERFACE & CONTROL SYSTEMS** | SENIOR SE

U.S. ARMY | NETWORK ADMINISTRATOR

EDUCATION

M.B.A. | UNIVERSITY OF VIRGINIA, *Darden School of Business*
M.S., INFORMATION TECHNOLOGY | UNIVERSITY OF MARYLAND UNIVERSITY COLLEGE
B.A., MATHEMATICS | CATHOLIC UNIVERSITY

Maintained 4.0 Graduate School GPA while working full-time and serving in community mentorship and support roles.

IT CERTIFICATIONS

CISCO: CCNP | CCNA   **MICROSOFT:** MCSA | MCSE   **PMI:** PMP
SALESFORCE: Certified Administrator | Certified Sales Cloud Consultant | Certified Service Cloud Consultant
AMAZON: Web Services Business Professional | Web Services Technical Professional

THOUGHT LEADERSHIP/COMMUNITY SUPPORT

THOUGHT LEADERSHIP
TECH FEST 20XX | Cloud Computing Panelist
U OF VA DARDEN SCHOOL OF BUSINESS | M.B.A. Student Mock-Interview Preparation & 20XX Industry Summit Participant

COMMUNITY SUPPORT

VIRGINIA DEMOLAY | ADVISOR/COACH/ADULT LEADER   **ROBERG FROST HIGH SCHOOL** | FOOTBALL VIDEOGRAPHER

ELIZABETH DUNCAN

Raleigh, NC 55555 | 444.555.1234 | elizabethduncan@gmail.com

PRACTICE ADMINISTRATOR

EXPERT CLAIM REVIEW | RAPID REVENUE GROWTH | EXPONENTIAL COLLECTIONS INCREASE

Bonded & Insured | HIPAA/FDCPA/CCPA Compliant | Data Safety & Security

VALUE PROPOSITION

Practice Director Veteran knows firsthand the challenges faced by small and large multi-site/multi-doctor practices; recognizes the reality of dentistry today means juggling increased payment scrutiny with fast-paced patient care.

Eradicates outstanding debt, eliminates write-offs, achieves 100% billing accuracy and increases practitioner time dedicated to patient care via a time-tested method for claims review, submission and debt collection.

Trusted by General, Specialty and Pediatric practices alike to tactfully achieve patient payment resolution.

TANGIBLE RESULTS

☑ Executed efficient, impeccable Accounts Receivable methodology that achieved a 99% collection rate and contributed to revenue growth from $600K to $1.3M.

☑ Reclaimed $425K in funds outstanding for a seven-year-old dental practice; recouped 100% of private insurance funds and achieved a 92% revenue increase in just five months.

☑ Reconciled out-of-date A/R records and implemented strategy that increased collections rate from <70% to 95% and increased revenues $1.5M in 18 months.

PRACTICE MANAGEMENT EXPERIENCE

XXX Dental, *Durham, NC* (Apr 20XX–Nov 20XX)
XXX Family Dentistry, *Raleigh, NC* (Oct 20XX–Apr 20XX)

ADDITIONAL EXPERIENCE

XXXX Healthcare, NATIONAL CORPORATE LIAISON, *Charlotte, NC*
XXXXX, D.D.S., OFFICE MANAGER, *Charlotte, NC* | **XXXXX, D.D.S.,** OFFICE MANAGER, *Charlotte, NC*

TECHNOLOGY PROFICIENCIES

Eaglesoft | Dentrix | CS SoftDent | Dexis | Emdeon Dental

AFFILIATIONS

Member, *American Association of Dental Office Managers*
Agency Contacts, *I.C. Systems & American Profit Collection Recovery Group*

EDUCATION

B.S., Business Administration, UNC GREENSBORO

CALL FOR REFERENCES AND TO DISCUSS HOURLY/CONTRACT RATES

Jessica Jordan

jessicajordan@gmail.com ○ 555.555.5555

Public Relations Strategist & Media Specialist
Inspired Health Communications

Jessica spearheads concept-to-execution million-dollar public relations campaigns for pharmaceutical, healthcare and medical device clients. For the past 12 years, clients have sought her out to create compelling and media-friendly messaging as a trusted advisor, passionate advocate, skilled strategist and savvy media relations coach.

FULL-SERVICE MEDIA OUTREACH WITH RESULTS

Jessica personally researches and crafts media-friendly stories and leverages an expansive network of media and press relations.

Placements speak volumes in the world of PR and Jessica's results include strategic print, web, radio and television placement in national, regional and local media outlets as well as targeted niche trade publications and local affiliates from Boston to Fargo, ND, Chicago to Little Rock, AK, Chicago to Charlotte, NC.

END-TO-END EXPERT STRATEGY

She works collaboratively to understand a client's unique needs, and to develop and implement a customized campaign plan. Clients trust her expert counsel and rely on her years of proactive advocacy to drive resolution to any issues that may arise.

AGENCY EXPERIENCE AT A CONSULTANT PRICE

Jessica maintains a low overhead and a lean team that eliminates the need for mark-ups. This allows her to pass savings along to her clients.

TRANSFORM SPECIALISTS AND SMEs INTO MEDIA-TRAINED SPOKESPERSONS

Jessica's clients remain poised, on-message and on-point whenever they are in the spotlight thanks to her one-on-one coaching, training and rehearsal.

Jessica earned a B.A. in economics at UNC Chapel Hill. She provides pro-bono PR support to the local chapter of the XXXXX Association and reviews novels for XXXXX.

MEDIA PLACEMENTS INCLUDE
New York Times ○ Associated Press ○ USAToday ○ HuffPost 50 ○ HealthDay
Doctor Radio ○ CBSnews.com

AREAS OF EXPERTISE SKILLS
Public Relations ○ Campaign Management ○ Media Relations/Strategy ○ Message Development
Collateral/Press Materials Development○ Advocacy○ Regulatory Milestones ○ Celebrity Campaigns
Ghost Writing ○ Data Publicity ○ Press Releases○ Event Planning ○ Research

SUSAN B. ANTHONY

Chicago, IL 44173 ❏ 555.555.5555 ❏ anthonysusan@gmail.com

FRACTIONAL CFO LEADERSHIP & CXO ADVISORY STRATEGY

LEADERSHIP COACHING | BUSINESS STRATEGY | COST & BUDGET MANAGEMENT | PRODUCTIVITY IMPROVEMENT

EARLY STAGE STARTUPS ❏ IPOS ❏ GLOBAL EXPANSION ❏ HIGH GROWTH ❏ ACQUISITIONS ❏ TURNAROUNDS

Helps Organizations and Executives Achieve Their Full Potential and Vision for Growth

Susan Anthony is a former CFO, trusted CEO advisor and core member of the Executive Leadership Teams of XXX and XXX. Sought after to guide, plan and execute business and finance strategies, she has guided CXOs whose companies reside in various stages of growth to catapult them to the next level.

From leadership coaching to business strategy and global expansion, financial infrastructure improvements to ROI case development, Sue has spent the last nine years helping diverse organizations become increasingly lean and efficient and poised them for growth. Clients include XXXX, XXXX and XXXX.

Throughout Sue's 12-year tenure with XXX, her CFO leadership was critical to its explosive growth and evolution from a 40-person startup into a $400M, 4500-associate publicly traded and former S&P 500 enterprise. Her judgment proved vital to survival throughout its IPO, six acquisitions and tribulations including the dot-com bust.

During Sue's meteoric three-year rise from accountant to CFO of software development firm XXX, her guidance was instrumental to its stabilization and turnaround within one year, solid growth within two and IPO shortly thereafter.

In 20XX, Sue lent her entrepreneurial expertise to launch XXXX & XXX whereas co-CEO, the company quickly raised operational funding, introduced eight products and acquired 1,500 customers.

Sue earned her financial chops as a Senior Accountant with XXXX, where she led audit engagements for profit and non-profit clients in diverse industry sectors including technology, retail and manufacturing.

She holds a B.S. in management with a concentration in accounting from *XXX College*.

JOHN SMITH

Dallas, TX 75205

PRODUCT MANAGEMENT EXECUTIVE

MARKETING & COMMUNICATIONS STRATEGIES | EDUCATION | BUSINESS INTELLIGENCE | DATA ANALYTICS

Groundbreaking Leadership & Strategies that Bring Game-Changing Technologies to Market

February 2, 20XX

«Contact_Name»
«Contact_Title»
«Company_Name»
«Address_1»
«City», «State» «ZIP»

RE: Chief Product Officer

Dear «Salutation» «Last_Name»,

From motivating creatives and analysts to partnering with sales to translating engineer speak to laymen's terms—I love the challenge of bringing industry-changing products to market via high-impact product marketing strategies.

I have motivated high-performance teams and spearheaded strategies grounded in data analytics, persuasive sales and product training, and full lifecycle product management including positioning, roadmaps, features and pricing for high-tech products and tools.

Recognizing that outcomes speak volumes, below are career highlights that showcase how I am uniquely qualified to lead ABC Tech's continued product innovation and expansion:

- **VERIZON:** Drove analysis, development and go-to-market launch for a revolutionary wireless network product embraced by industry leaders and startups alike.

- **TMOBILE:** Led global cross-functional teams that uncovered worldwide product opportunities, marketed mobile Internet/GUI applications, API software and network management solutions for telecom technology forerunners.

- **J&J:** As a trusted IT Wireless Engineering partner and VOC, collaborated to translate product complexities into go-to-market collateral for cutting-edge patient care wireless technology.

I am confident I can leverage successes from product management, R&D and Data/BI analytics leadership roles to further ABC Tech's strategy for bringing products to market that change how people interact with technology.

Thank you for your consideration!

Kind regards,
John Smith
(Enclosure)

Megan Jordan, M.Ed.

803.555.5555 meganjordan@gmail.com
linkedin.com/in/megan-jordans

1511 East Riverview Drive ○ Richmond, VA 44445

October 20, 20XX

«Contact_Name»
«Contact_Title»
«Company_Name»
«Address_1»
«City», «State» «ZIP»

RE: Title of Job Description

Dear «Salutation» «Last_Name»,

From educational curriculum to instruction and assessment—I love the challenge of impacting learning results to better serve students and teachers with innovative pilots, programs and initiatives.

As a fierce public school advocate and thought leader, I have spearheaded sustainable instructional, time, technology and staffing innovations quickly embraced as best practice.

Recognizing that outcomes speak volumes, below are career highlights that show my ideal fit for the name of organization's name of role position:

o **Chesterfield County School District:** Built a high-performance team from the ground up and spearheaded a sustainable infrastructure that drove regulatory compliance, student growth and increased funding for this rural Title I district.

o **VA Department of Education:** Transformed DOE reputation among districts from punitive to supportive by cultivating an atmosphere of transparency and collaboration. Established new programs that adhered to RIT and PBS frameworks.

o **Westhampton High School District:** Introduced co-teaching pilot emulated as gold standard across district's six campuses.

o **John Brown Elementary School:** Increased special education teacher/student interaction 4X via a full inclusion initiative quickly embraced as a best practice district-wide.

I am confident I can leverage lessons learned at the State, District and School level while pursuing my Ph.D. in education to champion educational initiatives that further advance the vision and mission of name of organization.

Kind regards,

Megan Jordan, M.Ed.

Michelle Dumas, NCRW, CPRW
Distinctive Career Services, LLC

Michelle Dumas, Founder and CEO
Distinctive Career Services, LLC
www.distinctiveweb.com
michelle@distinctivecareerservices.com
Office - 800-644-9494
Direct - 603-397-0222
Text - 603-928-7357

With more than 20 years of experience, Michelle Dumas is a widely recognized and sought out leader and international award-winning expert in the fields of professional resume writing and career marketing. Michelle's genuine caring, natural intuitiveness, and relaxed interpersonal style have been credited in helping her clients feel comfortable in opening up and sharing the details of their lives, their careers, and their dreams—details that are absolutely essential to the work of developing a resume and other career marketing documents. At the same time, her intense focus and goal orientation, strong strategic thinking abilities, and commitment to excellence in everything she does has made her work with executives and aspiring executives a natural fit for her talents.

Founded in 1996, Michelle's company Distinctive Career Services, LLC (www. distinctiveweb.com and www.executiveresumewriting.services) is one of the longest-standing leaders in the industry, an Internet pioneer respected for unmatched expertise, quality, and commitment to their clients' success.

Michelle has earned multiple certifications and credentials in the fields of resume writing, personal branding, and career coaching, and her impeccable and creative resumes have won numerous awards. She is a published author as well as a contributor to well over a dozen books on resume writing. Michelle is also very active in her industry through professional associations, providing volunteer training and mentoring, advisory services for one of the industry's most highly regarded certification programs, and serving on the Executive Board for the industry's largest nonprofit association for resume writers.

ALLEN T. MAIN

97 Loon Pond Road ◆ Concord, NH 34209

Home: (603) 555-1065 ◆ Cell: (603) 888-9587 ◆ allenmain@email.net ◆ www.linkedin.com/in/allenmain

---

SENIOR CORPORATE FINANCE EXECUTIVE
Transforming Finance into a Streamlined, Strategic Business Partner

MBA and CPA with more than 15 years of process and operationally focused global finance leadership across all facets of the organization, diverse industries, multiple continents, up- and down-markets, changes in technology, and numerous course corrections.

In every position became an indispensable member of the core management team—not just for SEC reporting, or SOX, or US GAAP—but as a true partner in using finance to deliver competitive, sustainable, and profitable outcomes. Unwilling to settle for average; seek to continuously improve productivity, efficiency, accuracy, and bottom-line financial results. Deliver:

- ☑ Transparent, understandable, productive connectivity between the business and finance organizations.
- ☑ Quantifiable ROI in the support of multimillions-of-dollars in revenue growth and cost savings.
- ☑ Bottom-line profits enabled by the strategic and executable vision within the finance organization.

CAREER SUMMARY

Vidal Information, Inc. ◆ *International, internet-based information solutions company.*   Concord, NH

VP, GLOBAL REVENUE AND NORTH AMERICAN CONTROLLER (20XX – Present)
GLOBAL REVENUE AND NORTH AMERICAN CONTROLLER (20XX – 20XX)
NORTH AMERICAN CONTROLLER (20XX – 20XX)
DIVISION CONTROLLER (20XX – 20XX)

Global responsibility ◆ 5 direct and 45 indirect staff ◆ $5 million budget ◆ Oracle, Hyperion, Assurenet

Recruited during period of growth and promoted rapidly, earning full accounting operations responsibility for North America and then for global revenue, including Europe and Asia. Major areas of oversight and leadership include:

☑ Global Revenue Recognition Policy & Process	☑ North American & China Accounting Operations
☑ Global Revenue Accounting Operations	☑ North American Accounts Receivable/Payable
☑ North American Payroll	☑ GAAP & SOX Compliance/SEC Reporting/External Audit

Spearheaded build-out of accounting infrastructure and operations that served as foundation enabling growth from $500 million to $1 billion at height. Then flexibly shifted focus to streamlining the business, cutting costs, and optimizing efficiency during historic economic downturn and subsequent industry downturn, ensuring company remained vital and positioned for future growth. Built bridges throughout the business and transformed accounting team to become a valued, sought out business partner.

SELECTED ACCOMPLISHMENTS:

- ▶ <u>Process Development & Implementation</u> - Devised global quarterly financial reporting package template utilized in quarterly financial review process. Developed financial processes, revenue recognition processes, and business processes that:
  - Enabled newspaper business segment to grow to 1,000+ partnerships generating $40 million revenue.
  - Used Oracle to automate North American revenue recognition then replicated the process in Europe. Implemented strong process and controls globally and ensured IFRS compliance.
  - Facilitated successful financial execution of $26 million contract in Europe with the U.K. Department of Labor.
  - Streamlined monthly closing process from 7 days to 5 while simultaneously eliminating errors.

- ▶ <u>Team Leadership & Management</u> - Saved $625,000+ annually by reducing headcount 65% and consolidating 3 teams to 1, continually refined team structure to better leverage talent and technology. Sustained morale despite cutbacks and consolidations.

- ▶ <u>Reorganization & Efficiency Improvement</u> - Played key role on leadership team that planned and executed multiple major organizational restructurings; successfully streamlined North American accounting operations to achieve optimal efficiency while improving quality of deliverables and support provided to the business.

- ▶ <u>Mergers & Acquisitions</u> - Participated in acquisitions and divestitures including financial process integration of 3 acquisitions with a combined value of $350 million, sale of China operations, and closure of Emerging Markets.

ALLEN T. MAIN

Fleet Leasing, Inc. ◆ *$1 billion fleet leasing and services business with 250,000 vehicles under management.*   Portland, OR

CORPORATE CONTROLLER (20XX – 20XX)

9 direct and 40 indirect staff ◆ $3.5 million budget ◆ Proprietary technology

Recruited for financial operational background to assist this privately held company reorganize, create, and implement financial process and reporting to support the functional business segments. Oversaw all internal and external financial reporting; accounting; budgeting; A/P; income, sales, and use tax; external audit team; and forecasting and annual financial planning.

> During a period in which the business was evolving and becoming increasingly complex, established relationships across all business segments, positioning accounting team as a partner to help managers fully understand, apply, and measure/analyze financial results. Standardized and streamlined processes and helped propel a paradigm shift and culture change in which there was far greater consideration of financial impact in business decision-making process.

SELECTED ACCOMPLISHMENTS:

▶ Accounting Infrastructure Development – Created an accounting infrastructure and related processes, much of which still remains in place today more than a decade later:

- Refined fully burdened cost model for each functional area to assist in establishing pricing.
- Developed activity-based P&L identifying revenue per program.
- Automated management reporting and developed quarterly reporting package for senior management team.
- Implemented budgeting and forecasting process.
- Restructured external audit process, reducing audit cycle 50% and maintaining audit fees.

▶ Continuous Improvement – Generated significant cost savings and efficiency improvements:

Annual Cost Savings	Volume Purchase Savings	Lowered Cost of Labor	Quarterly Reporting	Quarterly Audit Review	Reduced Reserve Requirements
$4 million	$5 million	$1.1 million	55% faster	67% faster	$1.7 million

▶ Debt Structure – Implemented accounting procedures for $2 billion in complex debt structure including commercial paper program, conduit securitizations, SWAPs, and 144A bonds in accordance with GAAP, FAS133, and FAS140.

Williams Building Technologies ◆ *$1 billion manufacturer, installer, and servicer of building control systems.*   Seattle, WA

CONTROLLER (19XX – 20XX)

7 direct and 20 indirect staff ◆ $2.5 million budget ◆ Accounting for 120 branch offices in the U.S. and Canada

Promoted multiple times culminating in controller role. Hired initially as finance manager for worldwide distribution, directing financial issues for domestic and international distribution channels, joint ventures, and Hong Kong office. Later served as finance manager for a start-up, $40 million facilities management division. Managed financial due diligence and integration of 3 U.S. and Puerto Rican acquisitions. Coordinated due diligence and final transaction for business unit's divestiture.

SELECTED ACCOMPLISHMENTS:

▶ Efficiency Improvements – Introduced web-based tools and other creative solutions that streamlined and improved budgeting, forecasting, and reporting processes.

- Reduced time required to process monthly financial reports 65+%, from 15 to 5 days.
- Halved semi-annual planning cycle time for 120 branch offices, reducing from 8 weeks to 4 weeks.
- Decreased days' sales outstanding (DSO) 45 days by creating new customer payment program.

EDUCATION	M.B.A., Finance – Keller Graduate School of Management, Chicago, IL B.S., Accounting – Northeastern Illinois University, Chicago, IL Certified Public Accountant ◆ Member, New Hampshire CPA Society

Served in several independent financial consulting assignments including interim corporate controller, and projects completing pre-acquisition due diligence and post-acquisition purchase accounting, 20XX-20XX.

Tina McCarthy

324 River Run Road, Atlanta, GA 00000 ~ 555-555-5555 ~ tinamccarthy@gmail.com

HUMAN RESOURCES MANAGER / DIRECTOR
Global Business Savvy ~ Accomplished in all HR Functions ~ Technically Sophisticated

High-energy HR professional with almost 14 years of proven leadership fueling organizational effectiveness and delivering undeniable results for companies and organizations of all types and sizes: multi-site, multinational, start-up ventures, turnarounds, small regional companies, mid-size, and large corporations. Key areas of contributions include:

- ☑ Leading change management and HR initiatives to drive greater profits and stronger competitive advantage
- ☑ Envisioning and implementing fresh new ideas and proactive HR solutions to complex business challenges
- ☑ Increasing competitive advantage by hiring, training, and retaining the "best and brightest" talent at all levels
- ☑ Reengineering processes and leveraging technology to drive down HR delivery costs while improving effectiveness
- ☑ Expanding companies globally and partnering with senior management to propel strategic goals forward

> **Repeatedly delivered value to employers in excess of 10X salary as measured by efficiency savings, cost cuts, and bottom-line improvements.**

PROFESSIONAL HIGHLIGHTS

Ellis and Main Management Healthcare Incorporated *(Health care services company)*   20XX – Present
HUMAN RESOURCES MANAGEMENT CONSULTANT

Recruited to revitalize this 30-year-old company with fresh ideas and HR best practices designed to restart business growth, optimize organizational effectiveness, and strengthen standing in a competitive market place. Masterminded and introduced HR strategies, programs, initiatives, tools, and systems that have differentiated the company while raising the bar on client satisfaction and coalescing 220 employees to work together under a unified mission and culture of continuous improvement.

CONTRIBUTIONS SNAPSHOT:	KEY RESULTS:
- **Built multi-channel recruiting resources:** Assessed company's long and short-term goals then pioneered cost-effective hiring solutions to propel achievement of business objectives.	▶ Slashed recruiting costs 65% while concurrently bringing in new talent to drive business growth.
- **Strengthened employee performance:** Optimized compensation and internal benefits and introduced company's first system for measuring and tracking employee performance, including a highly motivating performance-based rewards scorecard.	▶ Increased utilization of contracts 40% ($500,000 gain in cash flow) and delivered 2-fold improvement in customer satisfaction.
- **Overhauled HR processes to optimize results:** Reengineered fragmented HR processes, modified internal policies, and improved employee training.	▶ Improved team morale and saved $125,000 through changes to training.

Azavedo, Inc. *(Brand strategy consulting and design firm)*   20XX – 20XX
HUMAN RESOURCES DIRECTOR

Completely reorganized the HR office to support rapid business expansion, including stabilizing high employee turnover, clearing extensive backlog of work, and revamping outdated processes. In a dynamic, highly matrixed, international organization with offices in the U.S., U.K., Dubai, and Hong Kong, managed 14 direct reports and outsourcing relationships, including business continuity and disaster recovery programs. Rolled out HR deliverables across all offices to 130 employees, adopting culturally sensitive, country-specific models while ensuring consistency in company vision and goals.

CONTRIBUTIONS SNAPSHOT:	KEY RESULTS:
- **Transformed HR into a valued business partner:** Rejuvenated the HR department, modernizing systems and revamping out-of-date processes while integrating disparate business models and transitioning multinational groups to follow a unified corporate philosophy. Coached managers on leadership topics and mapped staff accountability to performance.	▶ Achieved 100% perfect audit review just months after hire, ensuring complete compliance with federal and state laws, Sarbanes-Oxley regulations, and company policy.

...Continued

Tina McCarthy   555-555-5555 ~ tinamccarthy@gmail.com ~ Page 2

- **Positioned companies for global growth:** Took recruiting and employee development to the next level, bringing in high-caliber new talent and reducing turnover 60%. Delivered cutting-edge HR initiatives to drive strategic business goals.	▶ Propelled company to achieve the #1 most profitable year on record while growing rapidly and expanding into new international regions.
- **Streamlined HR for maximum cost-efficiency:** Improved accuracy and response times by restructuring global core HR functions, automating processes as an HRIS expert, and bringing other previously outsourced functions in-house, including global recruitment.	▶ Lowered overall HR costs and saved 55% on recruiting expenses for 3 straight years by conducting recruiting without a search firm.
- **Brought in talent from around the globe:** Handled full-cycle of immigration issues and conducted regular surveys of compensation to ensure competitive and creatively negotiated offerings that attracted top talent.	▶ Attained 100% of workforce planning goals and filled 65% of company's top performers.

Bacon-Brook Corp *(Global paper and pulp products company)*   20XX – 20XX
SENIOR HUMAN RESOURCES MANAGER
Within an environment of extraordinary growth and repeated acquisitions and mergers, took the lead in this 2,600-employee company for managing North American HR with dotted-line reporting into Europe. Fulfilling a very hands-on role requiring excellent HR generalist skills, championed start-up of the U.S. office for North American operations. Controlled $1 million HR budget. Managed numerous large, multifaceted special projects from start to successful finish, including 5 office relocations.

CONTRIBUTIONS SNAPSHOT: KEY RESULTS:

- **Established full-scale HR organizations from scratch:** Wrote all HR plans, policies, and procedures, designed complex compensation packages, developed succession plans, championed organization design, and traveled extensively to implement. Amended overseas HR planning models.	▶ Built entire North American HR organization from the ground up and led multimillion-dollar rollout of SAP. Aligned HR globally.
- **Managed HR through numerous acquisitions and mergers:** Spearheaded HR integration during repeated acquisitions and mergers. Hired extensively and performed rightsizing as necessary. Traveled worldwide, educating teams on U.S. compliance and implementing new HR policies.	▶ Held voluntary turnover to 0% and attained 100% of business objectives. Reduced workforce 50% in 8 months with zero interruption to business.
- **Handled employee relations in a diverse, multi-cultural environment:** Conducted heavy employee relations and managed all employee communications made especially complex due to the global component and numerous mergers. Collaborated with attorneys on legal affairs and flawlessly managed high-volume expatriate program.	▶ Created 65% more positive workplace as measured by dramatically reduced employee complaints. Held litigation costs to $0 despite multi-cultural complexity.
- **Saved money through HR initiatives:** Managed company benefits and served as trustee, plan administrator, and fiduciary. Developed HR record retention system and managed SAP HRIS module implementation. Devised HR records retention system that complied with all regulations.	▶ Delivered $246,000 annual savings by consolidating benefits plans and drove $1 million savings through automation of processes.

Kallenburg, Inc. *(Public relations consulting services)*   19XX – 20XX
REGIONAL HUMAN RESOURCES MANAGER
Promoted just weeks after hire to regional HR manager with a 5-person staff. Expanded company into the U.K. during the dot-com growth period, playing a key role in improving profitability by positioning firm as an industry leader. Increased headcount 60% for 3 straight years, delivered training 35% under budget, cut turnover 70%, and delivered 3-fold improvement in efficiency through HRIS technology. Supported employees and families following the tragic 9/11 attacks.

Kant Incorporated *(Human resources services)*   19XX – 19XX
HUMAN RESOURCES AND PAYROLL ASSOCIATE
Managed full-cycle recruiting and more than tripled employee performance. Conducted training and mentoring programs. Completed conversion and merger, consolidating an HR department of 6,000 to 2,000 in 12 months. Collaborated with IT to implement HRIS. Streamlined and resolved HR and payroll inquiries, reducing complaints 50%.

EDUCATION: B.A., Human Resources ~ Boston College, Boston, MA (19XX)
Professional in Human Resources (PHR), in process

Wayne Grossman

23 Ribbons Street ▪ Annapolis, MD 55555
888-888-8888 ▪ waynegrossman@email.net ▪ www.linkedin.com/in/waynegrossman

SALES & MARKETING EXECUTIVE, LOGISTICS SERVICES OUTSOURCING
Driving Change and Growth to Achieve Sustainable Competitive Advantage and Lasting, Positive Financial Results

Nearly 20 years of leadership in globally focused companies ranging in size from startups to Fortune 100s. Deep expertise across all aspects of distribution and logistics combined with experience encompassing not just sales and marketing, but also finance, operations, HR, and IT. Extensive cross-cultural and international travel background worldwide. Energized by a challenge, combining sound strategy with tactical execution to deliver results.

> **Enhanced Team Performance** ▪ **Increased Revenue & Profitability** ▪ **Stronger Client Relationships & Retention**
> **Lifted Organizational Professionalism** ▪ **Streamlined Business Processes** ▪ **Improved Employee Morale**
> **Won New, Major Contracts** ▪ **Heightened Brand Recognition** ▪ **Turned Around Underperforming Organizations**

Known for strong executive presence in and out of the board room; high-energy and approachable leadership style; and proven ability to attract, hire, and inspire top performers. Played crucial leadership roles on the executive teams that ...

▸ Built a start-up JV organization from scratch to produce sales of $350 million.
▸ Transformed an entrepreneurial, seat-of-the-pants firm into a disciplined, organized, profitable, growing company.
▸ Opened international markets, reversing a 90% revenue decline into strong growth and superior client retention.
▸ Led change initiatives, turning around 10+ years of stagnation /decline and generating $200+ million new revenue.
▸ Trained and mentored more than 200 new hires in 2 years, enabling rapid corporate growth and expansion.

PROFESSIONAL HIGHLIGHTS

ACME SUPPLY CHAIN *(A world leading contract logistics provider.)* ....Annapolis, MD
   ▸ **Vice President of Business & Customer Development, Technology Sector – Americas** (20XX – Aug 20XX)

Rebuilt the Technology Sector's business and client development team for the Americas, significantly increasing competitiveness in the sector. Recruited, hired, and trained new talent; led 7 direct and 25 indirect reports spanning Canada to South America. Managed targeting and account development planning in the region, providing both strategic and tactical guidance. Defined and developed new product offerings aligned to the technology sector's needs.

> **SNAPSHOT:** Accomplished goals attempted unsuccessfully by 5 predecessors in the previous 10 years, turning around and restoring growth for Acme's Technology Sector business in the America's region. Following a decade-plus of struggle to gain a competitive foothold in the market, completely rejuvenated business development, establishing a new direction, reviving passion and talent, building a winning culture, and positioning the organization with a clear roadmap for success.

ACHIEVEMENTS:
▪ Propelled sales of more than $200 million in contract value, the first positive business gains to the sector in 4 years.
▪ Added new talent and invigorated the dispirited team, inspiring team energy to pursue growth and retention goals.
▪ Reversed a negative client retention trend and led the team to retain 98% of current business.
▪ Instilled a new sense of process discipline and performance accountability to the sales team.
▪ Influenced a fundamental shift in the way the sales team targeted and pursued potential business.

GUERETTE, INC. *(Global transportation and logistics company based in Switzerland.)* ....Boston, MA
   ▸ **Vice President of Business Development, Lead Logistics Services – North America** (20XX – 20XX)

Recruited to lead the strategic and tactical charge in North America to raise market awareness and build sales for the group's product line, with a focus on Lead Logistics, Transportation Management, Inventory Management, Critical Service Logistics, Supply Inventory Management, and Vendor-Managed Inventory. Hired, trained, coached, and led a team of 5 direct and 30+ indirect reports selling value-added logistics services to new and existing KN clients.

> **SNAPSHOT:** Following the devastating loss of 2 major clients and related, sudden 90% decline in revenue, for this company that was virtually unknown in North America outside of the air and ocean freight segments, opened and expanded the market for lead logistics services throughout the U.S., Canada, and Mexico. Rebuilt the depleted business development sales team, devised a new marketing and sales strategy, and drove 100s of millions of dollars in logistics services sales.

...Continued

ACHIEVEMENTS:
- Led team to close on and deliver more than $225 million sales in contractual value.
- Won sales with multiple Fortune 100 clients, personally generating $70+ million.
- Established and cultivated a close working relationship with the sales teams from sister divisions.
- Positioned the organization for sustained and profitable sales growth through strategic targeting.
- Solidified client relationships to ensure a high 90+% rate of successful contract renewals.
- Improved sales team's rigor and consistency through introduction of a sales process and performance reporting.

DRT GLOBAL LOGISTICS, INC. *(Global provider of critical service logistics.)* .... San Diego, CA
> **Senior Vice President of Global Sales & Marketing** (20XX – 20XX)

Recruited to build a new sales force and client development team targeting clients worldwide in high-tech, medical device, and telecommunications industries. Managed a team of 9 direct reports and led sales and marketing globally, including go-to-market strategy, marketing collateral, advertising, and public relations.

SNAPSHOT: For this equity-funded company that had been recently acquired, worked with a non-existent budget and almost no resources to create the global sales and marketing functions from the ground up. Brought order and process discipline to a very chaotic situation, increasing professionalism, halting extremely high customer attrition, and restarting growth.

ACHIEVEMENTS:
- Constructed a solid foundation and lifted the level of professionalism, enabling continuous and profitable growth.
- Created structure, processes, and procedures for sales and marketing that remain in place today.
- Heightened sales and client development performance by reorganizing teams to better align with individual talents.
- Updated out-of-date branding, redesigned website and marketing materials, and implemented Salesforce.com.

ABC, INC. *(Fortune 100 provider of information technology products and services worldwide.)* .... Jersey City, NJ
> **Partner, Business Consulting** Services (20XX – 20XX)

Sold and led large, global business process outsourcing (BPO) services engagements to Fortune 1000 clients, with opportunities ranging from $15 million to $1 billion. Prepared business cases and spun compelling value propositions, gaining broad knowledge across diverse business functions. Managed contract negotiations, controlled pursuit budgets, devised sales strategy, cultivated client relationships, assigned and oversaw teams in delivery of engagements.

SNAPSHOT: Leveraged outsourcing experience and executive background in growing the fledgling business process outsourcing (BPO) portion of the Price Waterhouse Coopers consulting business that IBM had acquired. Sold and managed BPO engagements to Fortune 1000 clients, raising awareness of services across industry sectors, and setting the stage to generate $300 million new revenue for IBM in addition to $50 million personally sold.

HALPERT CORPORATION *(Provider of logistics services to chemical companies around the world.)* .... Charlotte, NC
> **Vice President of Sales & Marketing/Corporate Officer** (20XX – 20XX)

Member of executive team that led the launch and growth of this start-up organization. Managed sales, marketing, product development, and pricing. Led the corporate business strategy team for the enterprise. Controlled $5 million budget, developed strategic and tactical marketing and sales plans, created product offerings, developed service delivery metrics, and designed sales incentive compensation plans. Selected and oversaw advertising, branding, and PR partners.

SNAPSHOT: Built the sales and marketing functions from scratch for this start-up joint venture/corporate spin off. Hired, developed, and led a 40-person team (12 direct reports) of A-list talent that produced $350 million new revenue

BNH SYSTEM, INC. *(Provider of commercial transportation, logistics, and supply chain management solutions.)* New York, NY
> **Vice President of New Business/Corporate Officer** (19XX – 20XX)

Early career included progressive positions with BNH System. As an individual sales leader, exceeded quota for 10 straight years, setting new revenue and account records, and winning multiple awards. Promoted to manage a national sales force in selling logistics services. Called upon by the COO to participate in strategizing and executing a major corporate reorganization and consolidation; promoted to VP of New Business managing 20 directors and 10 regional sales teams.

SNAPSHOT: Promoted into management at a young age and during one of the most challenging times in the corporation's history due to extremely rapid growth. Regularly exceeded sales goals as much as 30%, led the division with #1 sales for 3 years and trained 200+ employees in 2 years. Member of executive team that reorganized and streamlined the company.

EDUCATION: Bachelor of Science (B.S.), Political Science – Massachusetts State University, Salem (19XX)
Completed numerous professional development courses

Susan T. Ellis

387 Capital Street | Seattle, WA 55555 | 888.888.8888
susanellis@hotmail.com | www.linkedin.com/in/susanellis

DIRECTOR OF INVESTOR RELATIONS AND CORPORATE COMMUNICATIONS
Biotechnology Industry ◆ Small- to Mid-Cap Companies

Ten years of broad communications experience: Serve as a central resource and partner on all corporate communications and investor relations issues for biotech industry companies, including leadership of strategy around public and media relations. Serve as poised, intelligent, and articulate representative of the company to media, investors, and analysts.

Strategically and creatively produce high-level, time-sensitive communications: Skillfully handle requests for communications from c-level corporate officers, requiring multidisciplinary collaboration with financial, legal, regulatory, and clinical departments.

Bring IRCC functions in house, building fully-functioning, integrated programs and departments for multiple companies: Repeatedly successful building smooth-running, flexible, adaptable, and cost-efficient IRCC programs from the ground up. Develop and implement consistent, efficient processes and ensure delivery of a steady flow of timely, accurate, and reliable communications to shareholders, potential investors, analysts, and the press.

DELIVERING:
Enhanced Shareholder Relations | Stronger Company Profile | Broader Exposure to the Analyst Community
Heightened Reputation with the Street | Increased Media Coverage | Consistent, Efficient Processes & Systems

Career Highlights

GINKGO PHARMA, INC. ....*Seattle, WA*
Oncology-focused nanotechnology biotech company that makes nanoparticle-drug conjugates (NDCs). Lead indications in Phase 2 clinical development in RCC, ovarian and rectal cancers. (20XX – Dec 20XX)
> **MANAGER, BUSINESS DEVELOPMENT AND CORPORATE COMMUNICATIONS**

Built the investor relations and corporate communications function from the ground up, serving as the first and only in-house IRCC officer for this small-cap biotech. Maximized limited resources, assuming an unusual blend of responsibilities that included full-charge leadership of IRCC while providing business development support. Leveraged medical communications knowledge in hiring and overseeing PR agency that greatly improved recruitment of patients for clinical trials, enabling company to meet project milestones and deliver on promises to investors. Managed all:

- Communications strategy
- Corporate written communications
- Investor relations
- Competitive intelligence analysis
- SEC filings in collaboration with finance and legal teams
- Shareholder meetings and proxy solicitation
- Publications and medical meeting planning
- Meetings and calls with the Street (buy-side and sell-side)

Relied on to handle sensitive communications issues. Mitigated a public image challenge resulting from turnover of CEO shortly after initial IPO. Developed and executed IR and communications strategies to keep confidence in the company high, ultimately facilitating a $40 million secondary offering .

Selected Contributions:
- ✓ Created and executed on company's first 18-month strategic communication plan.
- ✓ Initiated outreach to 15 investment banks and pitched technology and value proposition to bankers and analysts.
- ✓ Saved $80,000 by negotiating contract with Business Wire for an IPO package.
- ✓ Strengthened company's profile throughout the investor community and more than doubled participation in banking conferences, increasing 120%.
- ✓ Increased analyst coverage 135% in less than 12 months.
- ✓ Managed $500,000 budget and devised budgeting and expense tracking systems.
- ✓ Project managed redesign of company website, refreshing content and user interface to better articulate value proposition and investment thesis.

Page 1 of 2

Susan T. Ellis

888.888.8888 | susanellis@hotmail.com

JESKA PHARMACEUTICALS, INC. .... *San Diego, CA*
Small-molecule, oncology-focused biopharmaceutical company with drug candidates in stages from preclinical to Phase 3. Key indications have included melanoma, non-small cell lung cancer and breast cancer. (20XX – 20XX)
  ➢ **INVESTOR RELATIONS AND CORPORATE COMMUNICATIONS MANAGER**
  ➢ **INVESTOR RELATIONS AND MEDIA RELATIONS ASSOCIATE**

Recruited shortly after IPO and reported directly to the executive committee, heading development and leadership of company's first formal investor relations program. Built program completely from scratch and participated in multiple fundraising campaigns. Promoted to manage all aspects of investor relations and collaborate with VP of IRCC in strategizing and executing corporate communications and media outreach activities. Managed IR-related budget, contracts, vendors, consultants, and communications.

Remain calm and focused in even the most stressful of situations. Smoothed and minimized impact to the company and shareholders when potentially devastating news was released regarding a Phase 3 trial. In a crisis situation and within just 7 hours, executed flawless delivery of well-received internal and external communications.

Selected Contributions:

✓ Built company's first-ever IR program, including development of all vendor relationships and departmental processes.
✓ Played key role in successful fundraising of $35 million as result of a smoothly executed Analyst Day meeting in Chicago with just 2 weeks' notice.
✓ Produced $35,000 savings while improving service provided by vendors as result of renegotiating and/or replacing key vendor contracts.
✓ Raised company's profile throughout the investor community and opened the door to meet new groups of investors through participation in key conferences.
✓ Saved $50,000, negotiating favorable terms with key vendors, such as Business Wire and NASDAQ.
✓ Created electronic review system for public disclosures that ensured detailed version control over documents.

KARPINSKI, PLC .... *San Francisco, CA*
Fully integrated, $5 billion global biopharmaceutical company providing treatments for major clinical conditions; specifically focused on central nervous system (CNS) disorders, such as schizophrenia, addiction and depression. (Feb – May 20XX)
  ➢ **CONTRACT ROLE: CORPORATE COMMUNICATIONS CONSULTANT**

Assumed temporary role in a planned move to shift career into the biotech space. Wrote news releases and Q&A documents, coordinated investor conference and roadshow details, prepared background and data packages for management, planned corporate functions, and developed content and design for monthly employee newsletter.

KINCAID ASSOCIATES .... *San Francisco, CA*
Full service investor relations and corporate communications agency. (20XX – 20XX)
  ➢ **INVESTOR RELATIONS ASSOCIATE**

Member of a team serving multiple small-cap companies with corporate communications and investor relations support. Assisted in developing new business pitches for delivery to prospective pre-IPO clients. Other contributions included:
  - Wrote press releases, conference call scripts, fact sheets, and other corporate collateral
  - Completed shareholder analysis and peer valuation
  - Coordinated quarterly conference call news release distribution
  - Scheduled call and webcast with vendors
  - Targeted new investors, maintained database, fielded phone calls, and sent out investor packets
  - Conducted market surveillance and prepared analyst report summaries

Education

M.S., Public Relations – California University College of Communication, San Francisco, CA
B.S., Psychology/Sociology – Oakland College, Oakland, CA

National Investor Relations Institute (NIRI)
Certificate in Investor Relations ♦ Member ♦ Board of Directors, Seattle Chapter

Kathleen T. Block

14 Adams Court
Key West, FL 00000
555-555-5555 · kathleenblock@gmail.com

Target: Management Executive – Healthcare/Medical Industry

> *"Perseverance is an essential element of success. In every challenge conquered and every obstacle overcome there is an opportunity to learn...grow...expand ...improve."*

Uncommon blend of business and healthcare/medical industry background and experience. Started career in nursing, moving quickly into supervisory and administrative roles before circumstances required the assumption of the top executive role in the family business.

Quickly learned a new industry and became decision-making member of executive team and inspiration behind a team-focused, positive company culture that enabled 2-fold organic and acquisitional expansion of company locations and 195+% growth of revenues to a height of $94 million. Built team of employees from original 80 to more than 250.

BUSINESS QUALIFICATIONS AND EXPERIENCE INCLUDES:

✓ Administrative Management	✓ Public Relations/Community Outreach
✓ Strategic Business Planning	✓ Employee Relations/HR Management
✓ P&L/Cash Flow Management	✓ Team Building & Teamwork
✓ Budgeting Review & Approval	✓ Vendor/Supplier Relationships
✓ Management Team Collaboration	✓ Multi-Site Operations Oversight

HEALTHCARE/MEDICAL INDUSTRY AND EXPERIENCE INCLUDES:

- ✓ Bachelor of Science in Nursing degree with an emphasis in emergency room care
- ✓ Nearly ten full years of nursing and nursing administrative experience in hospital settings
- ✓ Interest in holistic therapies; recent Holistic Health Practitioner certification

Executive Management Highlights

Block Lumber, Inc.   **Atlanta, GA**
CHIEF EXECUTIVE OFFICER/CEO (October 20XX – June 20XX)

Assumed executive leadership of the family business, a lumber company providing products and services to the professional builders' market throughout the southeastern U.S. Quickly learned the industry, serving as primary decision-maker and working in close collaboration with the management team to provide high-level oversight for multiple locations. Indirectly managed as many as 250 employees.

Adapted flexibly as the economy changed and the market demands shifted over the past 14 years, leading both growth and consolidation initiatives as called for in the business strategic plan. Beginning in January 2015, planned and orchestrated an orderly exit strategy and divestiture of company assets, including multiple locations, fleet of vehicles, inventory, machinery, and office supplies.

SELECTED ACHIEVEMENTS:

- ▸ **Spearheaded growth**, including a key acquisition that expanded company from 3 locations, 80 personnel, and $32 million sales to 5 locations and 250 employees producing $94 million revenue.
- ▸ **Created a positive company culture** that promoted the belief that challenges are opportunities and mistakes are opportunities to learn and grow. Personally visited locations to answer questions and build rapport with staff. Strengthened employee morale and held turnover to below-average levels.
- ▸ **Led business reorganization and streamlining initiatives**, including implementation of expense control programs to build a stronger and healthier company infrastructure.

...Continued

Kathleen T. Block

▸ **Enhanced efficiency and increased profitability** by unifying disparate branding, consolidating operations, and centralizing key departments and functions, including accounting and credit, customer service, pricing, purchasing, service, and outside sales.

▸ **Improved skills of management and outside sales staff**, providing training opportunities with an emphasis on leadership and consultative selling.

Healthcare/Medical Industry Highlights

New Bern Medical Center (19XX – 20XX)   **New Bern, NC**

Earned 3 promotions in 6 years, advancing through progressive nursing and administrative positions in this 300-bed acute care hospital. Served as co-chair of Hospital Fundraising Campaign. Contributed as member of multiple committees, including Physician Committee, Disaster Drill Committee, Emergency Department Committee of Community Agencies, Quality Assurance Committee, Nursing Department Committee, and Board of Trustees.

PATIENT REPRESENTATIVE

Took over a chaotic, reactive function and transformed it, changing it into a proactive role that successfully enhanced the patient experience and strengthened satisfaction among both patients and their families—ultimately increasing hospital revenues and minimizing complaints and lawsuits.

▸ **Implemented an open-door policy** and aggressively recruited hospital volunteer staff to assist in making personal contact with every new admission to the hospital.

▸ **Raised visibility throughout the hospital,** attending staff meetings on every floor, meeting with department heads and the Board of Trustees, participating in hospital functions, and creating/distributing "marketing" materials such as brochures, business cards, an in-hospital television promo, and bedside introduction cards.

NURSING CARE COORDINATOR – Emergency Room
ASSISTANT NURSING CARE COORDINATOR – Emergency Room
STAFF REGISTERED NURSE – Emergency Room

Hired initially as an RN performing direct patient care in the ER. Within several months, transitioned into supervisory position working as charge nurse, triaging incoming patients, and overseeing scheduling of hospital personnel to cover 24 hours/day, 365 days/year. Within 6 months, promoted again into administrative management charged with overseeing quality of patient care and equipment in the hospital's Emergency and Outpatient departments. Ensured quality and performed daily operational reviews. Hired and supervised staff.

▸ **Created environment that delivered safe and effective care of the highest quality and value** while ensuring 100% compliance with all medical hospital regulatory requirements, working in close cooperation with the NJ State Health Department and the Joint Commission/JCAHO.

▸ **Strengthened skills of hospital employees** through facilitation of various educational programs; became certified CPR and ACLS instructor and taught courses to hospital personnel and the public.

▸ **Enhanced public image of the hospital's ER,** conducting extensive community outreach and interfacing with local police and fire departments as well as volunteer ambulance services in surrounding towns.

St. Mary's Hospital (19XX – 19XX)   **Boston, MA**
STAFF REGISTERED NURSE – Intensive Care Unit
Began nursing career as a night nurse and rotated with counterpart on opposite weekends, overseeing 2 employees on a 6-bed intensive care unit as a charge nurse within a 200-bed acute care hospital. Volunteered in American Heart Association program that provided post-heart-attack services to patients and their families.

Education

Bachelor of Science, Nursing (BSN) · Boston University – Boston, MA (19XX)
▸ Additional business coursework includes training programs in leadership, sales, payroll law, human resources, workplace safety and OSHA compliance, and FMLA compliance.
▸ Certified Holistic Health Practitioner, Holistic Health Institute – May 20XX
▸ Recent coursework in Holistic Nutrition, Integrative Health, and Holistic Alternative Therapies – 20XX

TAMMY LAWSON

486 Wiggin Drive ▪ Austin, TX 39876
764.555.2098 ▪ t.lawson@gmail.com
www.linkedin.com/in/tlawson

SALES, MARKETING & TRAINING MANAGEMENT EXECUTIVE

"Tammy is one of the most dynamic leaders I have ever had the pleasure to work with. No matter what the challenge she faces, she attacks it with creative solutions that galvanize growth to record levels." – CEO, HJT Inc.

☑ Track record of sales leadership success in both small business and Fortune 500 corporate environments, including proven, repeated ability to quickly come up to speed and excel in new industries and situations. Managed organizations with 350+ employees and held P&L responsibility for $10+ million.

☑ Relentlessly pursue goals with a 'failure isn't an option' attitude. Futuristic thinker with a rare mix of analytical and financial skills from early accounting background combined with a true talent for solving business problems in creative ways that often break new ground and lead companies in pioneering new directions.

☑ Passion for training, speaking, and presenting. Created and delivered sales training programs that far exceeded goals and produced 200% increase in sales after just the first year. Co-developed and delivered educational sales seminars for customers that created a new multimillion-dollar revenue stream that lasted 10 years.

STRENGTHS:
- Key Account Management
- Sales Team Leadership
- Consultative Sales
- Sales Training
- Sales & Marketing Strategy
- New Business Development

REPRESENTATIVE ACHIEVEMENTS:
42.5% SALES GROWTH ⬆ 33% HIGHER GROSS MARGINS ⬆ #1 IN SALES FOR 5 STRAIGHT YEARS ⬆ 52 POINT GAIN IN MARKET SHARE ⬆ $6.2 MILLION NEW REVENUE ⬆

SALES LEADERSHIP HIGHLIGHTS

Frost Enterprises, LLC, a franchisee of Acme Foods .... Austin, TX
PRESIDENT of a $10 million, 9-unit Acme Foods franchise organization (20XX – 20XX)

IMPACT SUMMARY: Grew a multi-unit franchise business an average of 12% year-over-year for 10 straight years and increased base profits more than $1.1 million (48.8% growth). Built a family-friendly and flexible company culture that strived for excellence in the customer experience, strengthening employee morale and retention. Continuously improved processes and systems to enhance efficiency, drive down costs, and increase profitability. Negotiated and managed all aspects of profitable sale of company for a figure that was $2.9 million higher than expected by business brokers.

Negotiated acquisition of a 9-unit Acme Foods franchise organization that included 6 significantly underperforming stores, and with all 9 facing challenges associated with poorly performing employees, exceptionally high staff turnover, weak sales, theft, and operational inefficiencies. Replaced non-performers, rebuilt management team, and provided leadership for 5 direct and 9 indirect reports heading the 350-employee operation that grew to $10+ million annually.

KEY RESULTS:

- **Increased annual revenue 42.5%,** representing additional $3.1 million sales yearly. Grew gross margins 33% in same period.

- **Improved cost control 5+%** through process improvements and rigorous management of labor and inventory, producing regular increases in gross margin, EBITA, and flow-through profit.

- **Shaved off $2.3 million in debt,** an achievement that catapulted company to much higher levels of financial success.

- **Launched new training programs** tailored to the needs of the diverse workforce; curtailed problems with theft and turnover.

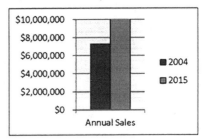

HJT Incorporated .... New York, NY
DIRECTOR OF NATIONAL ACCOUNTS (19XX – 20XX)

IMPACT SUMMARY: Led company to outpace the competition and win accounts against the entrenched competition, ultimately capturing 74% of the top 50 accounts nationwide, up from 36% in 1996. Relentlessly pursued and influenced extensive and necessary changes in customer service and product enhancements, better meeting target market needs and dramatically strengthening competitive edge in the top-tier marketplace.

Continued

Member of executive team charged with P&L responsibility for up to $9 million sales annually, managing 6 direct reports and 15 indirect reports selling a top-tier software package to the most prominent CPA firms nationwide, including all the Big 4 firms. Personally negotiated new and existing contracts for national and large key accounts. Collaborated on marketing team to develop strategies for customer acquisition and retention.

KEY RESULTS:

- **Strengthened exposure in the top-tier market** that was dominated by the competition in 19XX; listened to needs of customers and worked tirelessly to implement customer support program and 20 major product enhancements.

- **Built and cultivated relationships with all 50 top-tier accounts** in the market, landing lucrative new accounts. Won $3 million business from the competition, expanding from 18 of 50 accounts in 19XX to 37 of 50 in 20XX.

- **Set company records, driving 21% average annual account growth** and produced 96+% account renewal rate for 7 straight years. Recognized as #1 performer for 5 consecutive years.

- **Conceived and pioneered changes and improvements in processes** and programs that significantly shortened the sales cycle and attracted/onboarded new business more effectively.

> Record-breaking sales performance with benchmark-setting growth and renewal rates for 7 straight years and #1 top sales performer for 5 years.

SALES DIRECTOR, WESTERN REGION (19XX – 19XX)

IMPACT SUMMARY: Created and delivered sales training programs, marketing strategies, and sales tools that, in the first year alone drove a 200% increase in sales for new flagship product. Pioneered highly successful seminar program that generated $6.2 million in new revenue over a 2 year period; program was so successful that it remained in place, virtually unchanged and generating significant multimillion-dollar revenue stream for the next 10 years

Promoted to help transition the sales force to fully embrace and sell software offerings, providing training and a full battery of sales tools to drive the success of account managers. Created marketing strategies to educate CPAs—a traditionally conservative and change-averse market—to adopt new technologies and integrate into their practices.

KEY RESULTS:

- **Produced 2-fold increase in sales** of flagship product and received continually high accolades for developing and delivering excellent sales training programs and associated training materials.

- **Worked on strategic reorganization team** that optimized costs and revenues by re-engineering the sales organization; set target for 15% annual growth through combined acquisitional and organic strategies.

- **Collaborated on a 3-person team that developed educational seminars** delivered to CPAs; launched pilot program that produced sales 43% higher than target; expanded reach and continually increased revenue stream:

	# of locations	Average sales per location	Total sales
Pilot	15	$35,000	$525,000
Fall 1995	26	$52,000	$1.3 million
Spring 1996	30	$68,000	$2 million
Fall 1996	30	$85,000	$2.55 million

SALES ACCOUNT MANAGER (19XX – 19XX)

IMPACT SUMMARY: Helped propel the company into the future, selling their then-revolutionary in-house software systems to CPA firms, 95% of which were still using manual methods. Educated customers on anticipated future trends and the need to embrace new technologies.

Aggressively pursued and landed sales job with the largest tax and publishing company in the world, despite having no prior experience in sales. Sold in-house software systems to CPA firms.

- **Delivered #1 highest sales nationwide** for new in-house system and exceeded quota 181% in first year of tenure.
- **Tapped by upper management** to travel to division offices, helping to increase sales by training sales force.

Began career (19XX – 19XX) as a tax and accounting specialist in Thomas Mathews, a CPA firm.

EDUCATION: **B.S., Accounting and Marketing** – Washington State University, 19XX
Extensive training includes Miller Heiman Strategic Selling, Situational Leadership, The Power of Positive Relationships, Leadership Excellence, Effective Negotiating, and Selling Business Solutions, among others

ARTHUR ROBERTSON

67 River Road ◆ Santa Fe, NM 00000
555.555.5555 ◆ artobertson@gmail.com
www.linkedin.com/in/artrobinson

SENIOR IT MANAGEMENT EXECUTIVE
CTO – CIO – VP OF INFORMATION TECHNOLOGY

Masterful problem solver and creator of the technical foundations and innovations on which growing, thriving companies are built. Highly valued for bridging the gap between business needs and technology solutions. Key member of executive teams that have successfully navigated a diversity of challenging issues:

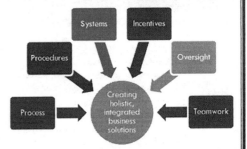

- ▸ **Early-Stage Growth:** Enabled explosive, profitable 10-fold growth to $20 million in 3 years
- ▸ **Startups:** Transformed $70,000 seed capital in 4 years into a $30 million, 300-employee, international firm
- ▸ **Turnarounds:** Built integrated, stable, flexible platform that empowered revitalization of a struggling company

Skillfully make the most of resources, dissecting complex business issues and crafting creative, cost-efficient IT and business process solutions that directly impact the bottom line. Excellent liaison between technical and non-technical audiences.

PROFESSIONAL HIGHLIGHTS

Business Solutions Applications, Inc. ◆ Santa Fe, NM ◆ 20XX – Present
Business process and software consulting services.

PRINCIPAL CONSULTANT

Launched and managed consulting firm that licensed and delivered business solutions using both SaaS and on-premises delivery models. Implemented solutions based on a proprietary meta data driven common software modelling framework which enabled no-code creation of web-based applications. Key clients include Castillo Associates, Findley Virtual Homes, Fox Direct, McCarthy Insurance Group, and Paiste Leaders.

Integrated Tech Marketing, LLC ◆ Santa Fe, NM ◆ 20XX – 20XX
Provider of integrated marketing services to major IT software hardware manufacturers/reseller partners.

CHIEF TECHNOLOGY OFFICER / EVP OF PRODUCT DEVELOPMENT

Strategic Impact:

Liberated company with the stable, flexible, adaptable technology platform and competent, talented IT team it required to pursue future business success unfettered by the technology problems and process bottlenecks that had dogged them for the prior decade.

Recruited by CEO to this recently acquired, private-equity-owned company that was struggling operationally, suppressed by a hodge-podge of 20+ disparate business systems that had evolved as fire-fighter solutions over the prior decade.

- ▸ Spearheaded redesign of ineffective, disconnected business processes, applying agile methodology in architecting and implementing a single integrated software systems infrastructure that became the hub that united company-wide business functions, producing significant operational improvements:
  - Provided stable, flexible platform that adapted to changing business needs
  - Delivered critical business functions within a single, unified platform
  - Slashed annual license fees 85% translating to $250,000+ savings per year
  - Integrated with external systems and eliminated previously manual processes
  - Enabled visibility into KPIs and provided holistic view into business performance
  - Improved ability to service customers and increased market competitiveness
- ▸ Overhauled financial modeling and reporting capabilities, providing ability for the company to accurately predict financial performance. Created comprehensive model that enabled ability for managers to quantify the financial impact of their decisions.

…Continued

ARTHUR ROBERTSON

Page 2 ◆ 555.555.5555 ◆ artrobinson@gmail.com

- ▶ Increased uptime of operational systems to 99.9%, eliminating recurring failures that were costing as much as $10,000 per hour of downtime. Upgraded network infrastructure, replaced end-of-life workstations, and outsourced hosting of critical business systems.

- ▶ Rebuilt and rightsized the IT team, reducing labor costs 28% annually. Recruited new IT talent, significantly improving team capabilities and restoring credibility of the group company-wide.

- ▶ Negotiated private-label deal for a large database of >24 million records at just 20% of the cost of existing data, ultimately driving down costs while simultaneously improving operational performance as much as 20%.

- ▶ Outsourced data acquisition process, eliminating 3 FT positions and 25 call center seats, significantly improving efficiency and saving as much as 40+% over previous costs. Eliminated additional 15+ hours in daily data selection tasks and freed account managers for more profit-intensive activities by creating an automated list selection tool.

Automark Software, Inc. ◆ Roswell, NM ◆ 20XX – 20XX
Developer of marketing automation software.

CHIEF TECHNOLOGY OFFICER

Transformed a vision and strong, marketable business idea into reality, providing technical leadership of this startup company. Within just 6 months, led creation of a highly reliable, flexible, and scalable software platform on which the company still delivers its services more than a decade later.

Johnson Communications, Inc. ◆ Clovis, NM ◆ 19XX – 20XX
Provider of marketing services to high tech companies.

CHIEF TECHNOLOGY OFFICER

Co-founded and partnered in executive leadership of this rapid-growth start up that achieved $4 million revenue by year 2 and $30 million by year 4, with 300 employees servicing numerous Fortune 100s and smaller technology startups from operational centers in Boston, San Jose, Brussels, and Munich, plus satellite operations in London, Paris, Stuttgart, and Istanbul. Managed team that developed marketing automation and sales lead management software solutions.

- ▶ Member of executive team that transformed $70,000 in seed capital into a growing, thriving $30 million international marketing services company.

- ▶ Drove growth through a mix of acquisitions and organic business development strategies. Participated in major sales calls, opened new offices, integrated acquisitions, and launched European operations.

- ▶ Recognized as the visionary and technology leader behind development of processes and easily customizable, scalable meta-driven applications that empowered the company's growth and success.

OTHER EXPERIENCE: Began career in software engineering, tapped quickly as a high-potential leader and promoted to director level, overseeing software development for Tillinghast, Inc, a marketing services firm. Developed and executed technical strategy that played pivotal role in propelling business unit (BU) revenue from $1.8 million to $20 million in just 3 years, ranking as the #1 fastest growing and #1 most profitable BU in the company. One of only 6 employees out of 3,000+ to receive annual achievement award.

EDUCATION

B.S.E.E., University of New Mexico, Roswell

Ali Morrison

888.888.8888 ▪ alimorrison@gmail.com ▪ www.linkedin.com/in/alimorrison

SENIOR MANAGEMENT EXECUTIVE
Catalyst for Business Change, Growth & Improvement

"Roll-up your-sleeves" executive with broad operating experience in companies of all sizes and a variety of industries, both domestic and international. MBA degree, Six Sigma MBB, and Lean Manufacturing expert. Passion for building high-performance teams. Differentiating talent for identifying and capitalizing on growth and improvement strategies overlooked by others, propelling change and driving companies to achieve higher levels of success:

"I truly enjoy seeing people and a team rise to achieve their highest potential. I always push myself to achieve more and encourage those around me to do the same by using their experience, trusting their intuition, thinking big, and 'swinging for the fences'."

Improved Quality ⬆ Higher Margins ⬆ Greater Productivity ⬆ Healthier Cash Flow ⬆ Increased Capacity

Enhanced Revenue Streams ⬆ Expanded Markets ⬆ Stronger Customer Relationships

EXECUTIVE CHRONOLOGY

PRESIDENT ▪ Ray Enterprises – Chicago, IL ▪ 20XX – Present
PARTNER ▪ Kahn-Welch – Chicago, IL ▪ 20XX – 20XX
SVP, BUSINESS IMPROVEMENT ▪ Acme and Staples ABC
Corporation – Chicago, IL ▪ 20XX – 20XX
DIRECTOR OF OPERATIONS ▪ Sears – Boston, MA ▪ 19XX – 20XX

Managed P&L up to $340 million and global teams with as many as 2,000 people. Repeatedly successful driving change, quickly identifying roadblocks, devising viable solutions to attain goals, and pioneering new strategic vision while persuasively gaining buy-in for changes...

- ✓ Implemented Lean and Six Sigma methodologies
- ✓ Led strategic acquisitions and integrations
- ✓ Coached and mentored teams to higher performance
- ✓ Created performance incentives and bonuses

- ✓ Drove down costs and instituted financial analysis
- ✓ Developed efficient business processes
- ✓ Established discipline and structure organization-wide
- ✓ Introduced customer-centric sales practices

REPRESENTATIVE ACHIEVEMENTS

Bolstered an entrepreneurial firm with 30+ years of flat performance, infusing it with new strategic vision, discipline, structure, and best practices—driving 17% top-line growth and a 100% increase in margins in 18 months.

Rejuvenated a $25 million manufacturing firm with Six Sigma and Lean methodologies, propelling EBITDA 46% higher before selling the company to a Fortune 500 acquirer for 12X EBITDA.

Shifted focus of a small, early-stage start up solar company, producing $10 million new revenue and positioning it as a thriving, global firm with customers worldwide before selling it for 7X EBITDA.

Leveraged Lean Manufacturing and Six Sigma expertise in a large corporate environment, delivering $150 million revenue growth, more than $110 million EBIT savings, and 10% increase in business unit profits.

Comprehensive Executive Résumé Available

Robert T. Fuller

(555) 555-5555 • Robert.fuller@gmail.com
www.linkedin.com/in/robertfuller

*Propelling Change, Creating New Businesses and Reinventing Existing Ones
at the Intersection of Strategy, Organizational Systems, and Leadership*

High-Performance Organizations

Great People Decisions + High-Performance Organization Systems + Hands-on Application of Strategy Disciplines & Execution = Acceleration of Strategic Change & High Impact Business Outcomes

Business Strategy
LEADERSHIP — ORGANIZATION
Human Capital
CULTURE
Behavioral & Organization Science

Strategy, leadership, and organization systems executive known as a solver of "wicked" problems who has been repeatedly successful designing, building, turning around, and reinventing organizations that work. 20+ years of distinctive, hands-on, global experience bridging strategy and the organization, diving into the whitespace with pioneering approaches that connect strategic problem-solving with insights into people and organizations.

Trusted advisor to boards of directors, investors, c-suite executives, and seasoned entrepreneurs with a focus on the intersection of strategy, organization systems, and leadership to drive desired business outcomes. Proven value creator (EBITDA improvement, top-line growth, M&A value creation, sales performance) for entrepreneurial and Fortune 100 companies, both privately held and public, spanning multiple industries, during periods of significant change:

- ✓ Rapid Growth
- ✓ Formation of Joint Ventures
- ✓ New Business Models
- ✓ Global Expansion
- ✓ Mergers & Acquisitions
- ✓ Turnarounds/Reorganizations
- ✓ Industry Convergence
- ✓ Start-Up Ventures
- ✓ New Distribution Channels

Real world experience solving the most complex strategic and management problems, complemented by deep expertise in human behavior and organization science drawn from track record of success in top-level strategy consulting, corporate leadership, and leadership consulting environments. Evidence-based, scientific approach, with expertise applying the most effective research-validated diagnostics and tools to help companies make great people decisions and achieve huge strategic shifts.

▸ CEO/ Executive Succession & Transition
▸ CEO Effectiveness & Impact
▸ Senior Team Construction & Effectiveness
▸ Executive Assessment/ Psychometrics
▸ CEO/Board/Executive Search
▸ Executive Leadership Development
▸ Corporate Governance
▸ Board/CEO & C-suite Team Interaction
▸ Business Strategy Formulation & Execution
▸ Business Model Innovation
▸ Innovation & Growth Strategy
▸ Culture Change/ Large Scale Transformation
▸ Executive & Organization Alignment
▸ Pre-Deal Due Dilligence/M&A Restructuring
▸ Crisis/ Turnaround Interventions
▸ Restructuring for Growth
▸ Organization Design
▸ Talent Management

PROFESSIONAL & EDUCATION CHRONOLOGY

SENIOR PARTNER, BOARD & CEO CONSULTING / MANAGING PRINCIPAL
Acme Consulting • 2012 – Present • New York, NY
Kratz Associates • 2011 – 2012 • New York, NY
Lambalot International • 2008 – 2011 • New York, NY
SVP, STRATEGY & INNOVATION EXECUTIVE
Bank of Citizens • 2006 – 2008 • New York, NY; Boston, MA
SENIOR MGR, STRATEGY & OPERATIONS / HEAD, INNOVATION & GROWTH CTR
Mair Consulting • 1995 – 2006 • New York, NY

YALE UNIVERSITY EXTENSION SCHOOL,
Boston ▪ Continuing Education –
Organizational Behavior, 2007
TEXAS STATE UNIVERSITY, Dallas ▪
M.S., Technology, 1995 and M.S., Risk
Management, 1994
UNIVERSITY OF Texas, Dallas ▪ B.B.A.,
Finance, 1990

Industry Expertise

| Private Equity |
| Healthcare |
| Life Sciences |
| Medical Devices |
| Pharmaceuticals |
| Technology |
| Consumer Marketing |
| Digital |
| Financial Services |

VALUE OFFERING

When solving questions of strategy and business transformation, strategy, organization, culture and people cannot be separated. Most failures and prolonged strategic change are not a result of poor strategy, but rather a misalignment with the many complex and interacting organization, culture, and leadership elements.

I bring a unique focus to the thorniest people and organization implications of business strategy, and bridge the gap between strategy, human behavior/psychology, leadership, and organization architecture to deliver against growth initiatives.

DAVID M. CORLISS

Chicago, IL 00000 ■ Available for travel/relocation
555.888.8888 ■ dcorliss@gmail.com
www.linkedin.com/in/davidcorliss

SENIOR MANAGEMENT EXECUTIVE- CEO/COO/SVP
Global Operations & Sales Leadership

BUILDING BUSINESSES FROM NICHE PLAYERS AND NEW ENTRANTS INTO MARKET LEADERS

WORLDWIDE BUSINESS EXPERIENCE

- ✓ P&L Management/Leadership of Industry-Dominating Businesses
- ✓ Growth-Focused Entrepreneurial Spirit
- ✓ Startups & Large, Multinational Corporations
- ✓ Public & Private Sector Background
- ✓ Valuable Regulatory Skill Set
- ✓ Financial Services Industry Expertise/Multi-Industry Skill Set

- ✓ Have traveled to and conducted business in a total of 72 different countries spanning 6 continents.
- ✓ Effectively lead global teams, skillfully navigating cultural, language, and time zone differences.
- ✓ Highly accustomed and comfortable liaising with regulators, governments, and agencies, in addition to the C-level leaders of the world's largest corporations, both domestically and internationally.

EDUCATION

M.B.A., focus on Finance and International Trade, Harvard University

B.A., with honors, Government & Legal Studies /Environmental Studies, Chicago College

CAREER AT A GLANCE

Citizens Investments– Chicago, IL (20XX – 20XX)
EXECUTIVE MANAGING DIRECTOR /MEMBER OF EXECUTIVE COMMITTEE – BGR Group
CHIEF EXECUTIVE OFFICER – Melton Research Associates; Taraman, LLC; BGR Research Solutions

Bank of Europe NV – Rotterdam, The Netherlands (19XX – 20XX)
MANAGING DIRECTOR, STRATEGY & CORPORATE DEVELOPMENT

The Bank of America – Boston, MA (19XX– 19XX)
SENIOR VICE PRESIDENT – International Marketing Division, The Bank of America (19XX – 1999)
VICE PRESIDENT – International Marketing Division, The Bank of America (1989 – 19XX)

Nationwide – Boston, MA (19XX – 19XX)
VICE PRESIDENT

Began career in the public sector on the Legislative and Campaign Staff of a Congressman and Senator, then in progressive positions of responsibility in the U.S.

Grew BGR Research Payments 460+% to $310 M

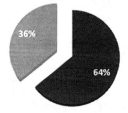

Propelled BGR Market Share from 5% to 25%

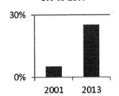

Drove Citizens to Dominate the DR Market With #1 Position

■ Citizens ■ Competitors

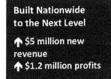

Built Nationwide to the Next Level
↑ $5 million new revenue
↑ $1.2 million profits

Quoted regularly as a thought leader in publications such as *The Wall Street Journal, The Financial Times, Los Angeles Times, Washington Post, San Francisco Chronicle*, and *Institutional Investor*, along with many trade publications.

...Comprehensive Résumé Available...

KAREN SPRIGGS

Karen.spriggs@gmail.com
www.linkedin.com/in/karenspriggs
555.555.5555

STRATEGY & BUSINESS DEVELOPMENT EXECUTIVE
Solar Industry Expertise | 10+ Years of Executive Accomplishment

Vision + Strategy + Execution =

Executive Leadership That Creates Thriving, Profitable, Sustainable Businesses with Optimal Triple-Bottom-Line Benefits

Accomplished executive with a passion for building streamlined, profitable, thriving organizations built on a value-based relational model, reflecting respect for the triple bottom line (profits, people, and the planet).

Solar Industry Highlights (5 Years)

SolarNow and ABC Solar

Influenced paradigm shift and culture change within the largest U.S. provider of solar energy, moving to a value-based relational selling model that has been highly successful in creating record-setting sustainable business ranking in the <u>top 1% of the company nationwide</u> and that quickly produced a <u>98% sales increase</u> in their flagship region.

Shifted region from 100% channel-dependent sales to generating 35% through referrals (compared to company-wide average of 10%), a figure that is steadily <u>growing at a double-digit percentage rate monthly.</u>

Set company records for personal sales achievement, including producing <u>the #1 highest number of referral sales</u> out of 4,000+ peers.

Closed deals with 240 new customers in just 14 months, producing approximately $6 million new sales annually ($500,000 monthly), a figure <u>4X higher than quota.</u>

Generated referrals from 79% of all customers and <u>maintained a 90% close ratio,</u> far exceeding 30% average of peers.

Year-Over-Year
Monthly Sales Growth

$3,000,000

$2,000,000

$1,000,000

$0

Sales Volume

■ Dec-14 ■ Dec-15

Executive Highlights (10+ Years)

Farrell, Inc. and Charity Today

Refined vision then created and executed strategies that transformed a small, regional cause marketing firm into a national leader that produced more than $52 million in value for partners within just 2 years.

Saved underperforming healthcare centers from failure, driving down costs, negotiating an 80% reduction in debt, increasing revenues and then leading positioning that resulted in sale of centers for 3X EBITDA.

Conceived, developed, and spearheaded numerous business ventures spanning North America and Europe, up to $50 million in size each and impacting 100s of employees. Provided executive leadership for a wide range of startup, turnaround, restructuring, and growth projects.

JEREMY T. KARASIK

Piloting beneficial business change, across-the-board results, and profitable growth through bold, inspirational leadership.

Repeatedly successful transforming underperforming businesses into customer-centric organizations with high-performance cultures that bring out the best in employees while leveraging cross-functional expertise to propel strategic and tactical execution and deliver extraordinary results.

CAREER AT A GLANCE

19XX – 19XX
- **COMMERCIAL DIRECTOR**
- Ashby, Inc.

19XX – 20XX
- **EXECUTIVE DIRECTOR**
- Acme, Inc.

20XX – 20XX
- **GLOBAL VICE PRESIDENT, SALES & MARKETING**
- Wingate Corp.

20XX – 20XX
- **GLOBAL COMMERCIAL VICE PRESIDENT**
- Kahn, Inc.

20XX – Present
- **PRESIDENT**
- Iglehart LLC

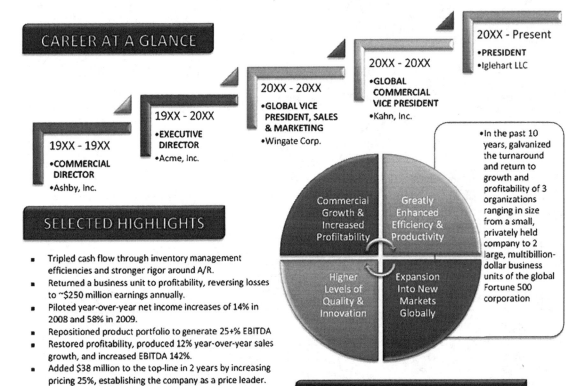

- Commercial Growth & Increased Profitability
- Greatly Enhanced Efficiency & Productivity
- Higher Levels of Quality & Innovation
- Expansion Into New Markets Globally

- In the past 10 years, galvanized the turnaround and return to growth and profitability of 3 organizations ranging in size from a small, privately held company to 2 large, multibillion-dollar business units of the global Fortune 500 corporation

SELECTED HIGHLIGHTS

- Tripled cash flow through inventory management efficiencies and stronger rigor around A/R.
- Returned a business unit to profitability, reversing losses to ~$250 million earnings annually.
- Piloted year-over-year net income increases of 14% in 2008 and 58% in 2009.
- Repositioned product portfolio to generate 25+% EBITDA
- Restored profitability, produced 12% year-over-year sales growth, and increased EBITDA 142%.
- Added $38 million to the top-line in 2 years by increasing pricing 25%, establishing the company as a price leader.
- Heightened market share 16% as a result of newly implemented market segmentation strategy.

CORE COMPETENCIES

Globally astute and accomplished senior executive with a long history of achievement piloting change and driving results as a P&L and commercial leader in companies of all sizes, from world-leading, multinational Fortune 100s to small, privately held firms. Key strengths in:

- Business Turnaround & Transformation
- Team Building & Leadership
- P&L / Operational Management
- Customer Service & Quality Improvement

EDUCATION & CREDENTIALS

MBA, Fordham University
BSBA, University of New Hampshire

- Twice chosen as a "Top-Achiever" for *JonesNet's Successguide Worldwide*, 20XX and 20XX
- Board of Directors, Operation JAIN
- Board of Directors, Detroit Cares, Big Brothers-Big Sisters
- Six-Sigma Green Belt
- Key leader and participant in cultural diversity programs at Acme and Kahn Adjunct Lecturer: Babson College and Harvard University Extension School
- Frequent speaker at industry conferences and events on topics of change management and leadership

THOMAS M. TUCKER

21 Cow Bell Lane ▪ Laramie, WY 00000
555-555-5555 ▪ tomtucker@me.com
www.linkedin.com/in/tomtucker ▪ about.me/tom_tucker

"Teamwork is the ability to work together toward a common vision. The ability to direct individual accomplishment toward organizational objectives. It is the fuel that allows common people to attain uncommon results."

-- Andrew Carnegie

Growing up in Wyoming, observing and emulating his parents who were both self-employed within the agricultural industry, Tom Tucker speaks of learning the importance of always having integrity and a strong work ethic. It wasn't until he had graduated from college and entered into a business partnership that he began to fully understand the importance of teamwork as well, and setting aside individual egos in order to fully capitalize on the power of a strong team to fuel business growth and success.

Now, with more than two decades of agribusiness leadership experience, Tom Tucker is known for his repeated success driving positive change, growth, and business achievements by building strong, cohesive, accountable team-oriented organizations that draw on individual talents while inspiring top performance. He has held P&L responsibility for up to $40 million annually, has managed more than 100 employees including those in geographically separated locations spanning multiple time zones, has successfully managed within a fast-paced corporate environment requiring ability to juggle often-competing priorities, and has provided leadership with equal success in entrepreneurial businesses requiring him to wear many different hats.

Most recently, at Acme Foods, a leading consumer packaged food and beverage company with domestic U.S. and international distribution, Tom served as the General Manager of Montana and Wyoming dairies, and as Director of Dairy Operations. While the situations and challenges faced at each dairy operation differed, they were each struggling and underperforming when Tom took over and the results of his transformational leadership were similar. Most significantly, he spearheaded turnaround of both operations, changing them into efficient, thriving operations, each ranking among the top three of the highest producing organic dairy operations in the nation, and in the top ten percent for quality.

Previously, as a Partner and General Manager in the launch, development, and growth of a startup dairy operation that was vertically integrated into a mature harvesting operation, Tom grew the company from a small, 300-unit startup to a 2,200+ unit operation generating $3 million revenue and six-figure net incomes annually with 25 employees in the diary complementing additional 120+ in the custom forage business.

Tom Tucker earned his B.B.A. from Wyoming State University and his M.B.A. with an emphasis on global business management from the University of Phoenix. He served on the Board of Directors for the Benn County Chamber of Commerce in Montana. Tom Tucker is the proud father of three children, two currently in college and the youngest college-bound after she completes her final year in high school.

After selling Acme Food's Wyoming dairy in a recently completed lucrative transaction, Tom is seeking his next career challenge and is especially interested in positions that will draw on the full scope of his agribusiness and organic experience, as well as his passion for and education in global business. Tom can be reached by phone 555-555-5555 or email TomTucker@me.com, and invites connections at www.linkedin.com/in/TomTucker.

Thomas Madbury

Address • City, XX • R: (555) 555-5555 • M: (888) 888-8888 • email@yahoo.com

Executive Biography

There is a relatively small segment of leaders in the business world; individuals who seem able to build relationships, trust, and rapport with almost anyone, and then are able to broker the relationships and make connections between people, creating partnerships and alliances, and motivating forward momentum to 'get things done.'

Thomas Madbury is one of those people, and 'getting things done' and driving results—through collaboration, partnerships, and relationships—as a senior manager in the healthcare industry, is what he is all about. With an enthusiastic and genuinely friendly attitude, Thomas radiates a sincere passion for delivering value and benefits to his customers.

A Registered Nurse (RN) by training, Thomas earned his B.S. in Nursing at Xxxxxx College in 19XX, and spent four years as a staff nurse at a 450-bed acute care hospital in Xxxx, Xxxxxxx, before making the life-changing decision that he could make a larger, positive impact on more people if he moved into administration and nursing management. After returning to school and earning his M.S. in Nursing Administration (*Magna cum Laude*) from Xxxxx University, Thomas's career quickly accelerated over the next 16 years to the executive level, and has expanded far beyond management of nursing and other direct care clinics to leadership in large, multi-state regions of a $22 billion alliance of 2,400 not-for-profit healthcare organizations (Xxxxxx.).

Promoted twice in his ten-year tenure with Xxxxxx, culminating in a VP position, Thomas's contributions centered on spearheading development and delivery of supply chain group purchasing services and clinical/operational programs and improvement activities. But more importantly, they focused on building long-lasting, loyal relationships within the C-suite of member hospitals, on developing programs to meet market demands and help deepen market penetration, and on coordinating teams of supply chain experts, strategic business partners, account executives, and clinical performance and member relations staff to deliver programs, services, and tailored customer solutions.

Prior to Xxxx, Thomas worked as a director of the 326-bed acute care Xxxxx Medical Center in the Xxxxx area. Promoted twice in four years at that company, in his final role he managed start-up and daily operations of 7 total primary and urgent care clinics generating aggregated annual revenue of $15 million and with leadership responsibility over a clinical and administrative staff of 55.

Throughout it all, Thomas has repeatedly proved his ability to lead through diverse and challenging situations. As a Six Sigma Black Belt Master, he is an excellent agent of change and has a documented track record of accomplishments that include the turnaround of chaotic and struggling operations; start-up and management of new healthcare facilities; creation and launch of new and improved educational, clinical, and operational programs; and growth and expansion of mature, established operations.

Today, Thomas resides on Xxxxx, across the Xxxxxx Sound from Xxxxx, with his wife and son. He is seeking his next opportunity and step in his executive career. As he has top-notch qualifications working across the entire healthcare continuum—providers, payers, and customers—it is challenging to put his skills in a "box." But what is absolutely clear, is that he has a great deal of value to offer the right company, and while the actual title may vary, it will almost certainly include some combination of strategic planning, operations, partnership and alliance building, account management and customer relations, marketing, and fundraising.

Thomas can be reach on his cell at 888.888.8888, in his home at 555.555.5555, or by email at email@yahoo.com.

Steven Dyer, CPA, MBA

43 Twitchell Drive
Charles, WV 55555
888.888.8888 ▪ steven@dyerfamily.com
www.linkedin.com/in/stevendyer ▪ about.me/steven_dyer

With a continuous drive for quality, results, and growth, as a senior corporate financial executive, Steven Dyer's leadership style is one of quiet influence. As an engaged observer and leader, Steven is respected on executive teams for his uncommonly strong ability to take in not just the details, but see them for their big picture, thoroughly analyze all the factors, come up with resourceful strategies to break through the barriers to growth and profitability, and then provide the facts, tools, processes, and financial foundation on which to execute.

In short, Steven Dyer is a financial leader who empowers companies with the analytical, strategic, transactional, and foundational leadership that propels improved financial performance and profitable business growth.

When Steven joined Amzy Services as a CPA and MBA with extensive experience across all spectrums of corporate finance and M&A transactions, the company was struggling with very high levels of debt and spending, weak cash flow, and poor profitability, and was further saddled by a completely ineffective and undisciplined finance department. His immediate contributions in leading the transformation of that department earned him two rapid promotions, and in less than two years he was appointed CFO. The groundwork that he laid in strengthening the department ultimately transformed the finance team into a highly valued strategic business partner that helped propel and facilitate the company's profitable growth and improved valuation as measured by virtually every key performance metric.

Steven's value in the corporate world is further enhanced by his early career working for Demby Insurance, one of the largest commercial lines insurers in the nation, where he was hired post-MBA as senior financial analyst and promoted twice in four years to serve as the director of mergers and acquisitions. During these years, he led multidisciplinary teams through the due diligence and M&A processes from both the buyer and seller perspectives, with targets that ranged in size from just $1.5 million to close to $2 billion.

Steven then transitioned this expertise into financial consulting with Adkins and MNT Consulting, providing transaction advisory services on numerous due diligence engagements across a wide diversity of industries for private equity clients. In total, throughout his career, he has successfully closed more than 20 M&A transactions and has spearheaded due diligence on countless other transactions, including joint ventures, development of new product lines and markets, bankruptcy restructuring, and more. Throughout his career, his credentials have been further enhanced by his work in orchestrating SEC and SOX compliance, public offerings, and NASDAQ listing processes. Additionally, Steven's career began in "Big Four" public accounting with Deloitte & Touche.

A member of the West Virginia Institute of Certified Public Accountants and Financial Executives International, Steven earned his BBA in Accounting from the University of West Virginia in 19XX and his MBA with a specialization in Finance from Tennessee University in 19XX.

Steven currently lives within commuting distance of Morgantown, West Virginia with his wife and their two children. In his spare time, he indulges his creative side, with a particular interest in all genres of music and forms of writing, and also enjoys weekly hikes. He is currently exploring his next career challenge and can be reached at 888.888.8888 or Steven@DyerFamily.com. He is active in social media and encourages connections at www.linkedin.com/in/StevenDyer.

Brianna West

Houston, TX 08347 ■ 623.555.8888
Brianna.west@yahoo.com ■ www.linkedin.com/in/briannawest

<Date>

Donald Smith, President
Boesiger, Inc.
500 Bouvier Drive
San Diego, CA 02907

Dear Mr. Smith:

I have been called on more times than I can count to do my "napkin math."

That's a term you may not be familiar with: It is the phrase that my colleagues have invented to describe the very unique value that I bring to the companies I work for. At Boyce Worldwide, a company that has gone through extreme growth phases and equally dramatic cutbacks during the time I have worked with them, this talent has earned me a trusted advisory spot at the table of the C-suite executives as they've hashed out and made nearly every strategic decision in the past eight years.

In brief, as a senior financial executive I offer unique value based on my exceptional ability to <u>uncover the story</u> that the numbers tell, to weave that story into easily <u>understandable terms</u> for the executives and managers who rely on those numbers, and then to take it a step further—to translate the stories into <u>robust metrics</u>, <u>data-driven strategies</u>, and <u>viable action plans</u> that produce results.

I am currently conducting a very confidential exploration of opportunities for the next step of my career. I was talking recently about my search with Michael Bohn, a mutual acquaintance of ours, and he suggested that I contact you. Although Mike wasn't certain you would know of a specific opportunity, he did suggest that you may have some advice for me or be able to discreetly point me in the direction of someone else I should talk with.

Mr. Smith, I offer excellent credentials as an MBA and experienced financial executive bringing more than 20 years of progressive experience to the table. But it is the results of my career that I am most proud of, and the results that are likely to be of the greatest interest to potential employers. Over the years, I have:

☑ Solved complicated business problems   ☑ Strengthened and streamlined business processes
☑ Modified and optimized business strategies and plans   ☑ Maximized top and bottom-line financial performance
☑ Increased sales and decreased expenses   ☑ Improved productivity and efficiency organization-wide

I'm absolutely passionate about my work and I'm confident I can produce similar results for my next employer.

As I am sure you are busy and I want to respect that, I promise not to take more than 15 minutes of your time. Whether you have advice or can point me in the direction of another person I should talk with, I will deeply appreciate it. I'll give you a call to follow up next week. In the meantime, I have enclosed my executive brief to familiarize you with my background.

Respectfully,

Brianna West

Enclosure

Brett T. Meserve
555.555.5555 ▪ brettmeserve@me.com ▪ www.linkedin.com/in/brettmeserve

<Date>

<First Name> <Last Name>, <Title>
<Company Name>
<Address>
<City, State Zip>

Dear <Name>:

I'm writing to you at the suggestion of <Name>, a mutual acquaintance. Allow me to briefly introduce myself as a seasoned management executive whose career has spanned leadership within large, multinational corporations and small, entrepreneurial companies. Armed with an MBA, expertise as a Six Sigma Master Black Belt, and close to a decade of leadership experience under my belt managing P&L up to $235 million and teams with as many as 1,500 people servicing customers worldwide, in 20XX I turned my attention to leveraging all of this experience to drive operational excellence and optimize revenue and profitability of small businesses. Just a few of my many accomplishments since then have included:

▶ Transforming an entrepreneurial firm with 30+ years of flat growth and profitability, infusing it with new strategic vision, discipline, structure, standardization, and best practices—driving 17% top-line growth and a 100% increase in profit margins in just 18 months.

▶ Rejuvenating a $25 million manufacturing firm with Six Sigma and Lean methodologies, propelling EBITDA 46% higher before selling the company to a Fortune 500 acquirer for 12X EBITDA.

▶ Shifting focus of a small, early-stage start up solar cell company, producing $10 million new revenue and positioning it as a thriving, global firm with customers worldwide before selling it to a publicly held company for 7X EBITDA.

As you can see, my value lies in partnering with the CEOs, founders, and Boards of Directors of these companies and serving as a catalyst for change. As Carl Bard said, *"Though no one can go back and make a brand new start, anyone can start from now and make a brand new ending."* That is what I help the companies I lead achieve. I have a talent for quickly being able to identify what is holding a company back from reaching their goals, devising viable solutions and strategies to overcome these challenges, then cultivating the team efforts that propel the companies forward to achieve the next level of success.

I'm presently exploring opportunities for my next challenge and was discussing these efforts with <Name>. <Name> suggested that it might be mutually beneficial for us to talk, and thought that even if you weren't aware of an immediate opportunity, that you might point me in the directions of others I should talk with.

Might we be able to meet for a brief discussion sometime in the near future? To better familiarize you with my background and capabilities, I have enclosed my résumé. I'll give you a call next week to follow up. Thank you!

Respectfully,

Brett T. Meserve

Kathleen T. Block

14 Adams Court
Key West, FL 00000
555-555-5555 · kathleenblock@gmail.com

<Date>

<First Name> <Last Name>
<Title>
<Firm Name>
<Address>
<City, State Zip>

Dear <Courtesy> <Last Name>:

From registered nurse to CEO...you've probably never met anyone with a career track and credentials quite like mine. But, while unusual, they also make me a stand-out within a competitive job market in which only those with truly differentiating and valuable offerings get noticed.

If you are working with a client company in the Miami-area and within the healthcare, medical, or other related industries (e.g., hospitals, managed care, pharmaceuticals) seeking to fill a management role that calls for a strong blend of business and medical industry credentials, I would be the perfect candidate for you to present to them.

My career could almost be a case study for solving business problems, hurdling what others might consider to be insurmountable challenges, and never giving up. What do I mean by that? After nearly a decade of experience in nursing and nursing administration, my next career move, 14 years ago, was when I had to unexpectedly take over as president and chief executive officer of the family business, a lumber and custom millwork company. When I stepped into this role I had no experience or knowledge of the industry, and while I had ascended into supervisory and administrative management roles at the hospital, I also had no executive experience. While my original plan was to sell the business almost immediately, I'm glad I changed my mind. What an amazing learning experience and journey this has been over the past decade-plus!

Working in close collaboration with my management team, we grew the three-location, 80-employee, $32 million company almost 200% through planned, strategic moves that included a key acquisition. At the height, the company was operating out of five locations, with 250 employees generating $94 million revenue.

Now, my goal is to combine this business experience with my early experience in the healthcare/medical industry. I would be a perfect choice for a company seeking a manager capable of...

▶ Streamlining operations and business processes to achieve maximum cost efficiency while improving quality
▶ Growing and expanding business to open new markets and increase cash flow
▶ Improving public outreach efforts and strengthening customer relationships
▶ Ensuring complete compliance within highly regulated environments
▶ Building a motivational and inspirational company culture and increasing employee morale

For your review, I've enclosed my résumé. Thank you for your consideration and please don't hesitate to contact me with any questions.

Sincerely,

Kathleen T. Block
Enclosure

MARC BRIER

marcbrier@comcast.net ▪ www.linkedin.com/in/marcbrier
Tampa, FL 00000 ▪ 555-555-5555

<Date>

<First Name> <Last Name>, <Title>
<Company Name>
<Address>
<City, State Zip>

Dear <Courtesy> <Last Name>:

I am writing to you at the suggestion of <Name>, a mutual acquaintance of ours. I was talking with <Name> yesterday regarding the recent acquisition and merger of the company I co-founded (Wolter, Inc) with a larger, complementary firm. With the integration now complete, it is time for me to move on to my next professional challenge, and I was discussing my options with <Name>. Although <Name> was unsure if you would know of any specific opportunities, he recommended that I reach out to you as you may be able to suggest others I should speak with.

Briefly, I am an innovative, strategic, and entrepreneurial-minded executive who offers a wealth of scientific, business, and management experience, especially as it relates to the delivery of pioneering software products to the pharmaceutical industry. In particular, my expertise in the areas of cGMP compliance, quality management systems, product development, pharma company operations and processes, and global enterprise software project management, position me as the ideal candidate for positions involving...

▶ Joining the executive team of a growth-focused, mid-stage pharmaceutical technology company which requires strong vision and leadership to bring it to the next level of growth and success.
▶ Developing and growing a streamlined, profitable professional services organization for a mature company that would benefit from my extensive expertise in the pharmaceutical market.

Just some of my many accomplishments include:

- Building a start-up company from $0 to $13M   - Driving success of 2 innovative product lines
- Negotiating a $35M acquisition   - Capturing more than 70% of the market
- Closing 99% of all competitive enterprise deals   - Passing 100% of customer software quality audits

And for customers (primarily pharmaceutical labs), we produced outstanding results as well:

- Cut pharma lab review costs more than 50%   - Reduced the time to validate more than 40%
- Delivered 25+% average overall cost savings   - Generated dramatic cGMP compliance improvements

I will give you a call next week to follow up. Should any opportunities come to mind, or if you know of someone it might be helpful for me to talk with, I will be deeply grateful for your introduction. Additionally, my résumé is enclosed. Please feel free to pass it along if you think it might be appropriate to do so. Thank you!

Sincerely,

Marc Brier

Katherine Griffin

Salt Lake City, UT 00000 ▪ 555-555-5555 ▪ kgriffin@gmail.com ▪ www.linkedin.com/in/kgriffin

<Date>

<First Name> <Last Name>
<Title>
<Firm Name>
<Address>
<City State Zip>

Dear <Courtesy> <Last Name>:

Over the course of my 20+ year career in the telecommunications industry, I have:

▸ Held full P&L responsibility, led teams of up to 80 people, and managed capital budgets up to $45 million
▸ Played a key role in an industry-transforming IPO, in mergers/integrations, and in growing a startup venture
▸ Managed operation of a telecom company's global IT infrastructure (data centers, servers, networks, applications, etc)
▸ Led transformation of backend telecom applications from internal facing to customer serving
▸ Helped develop products such as GTE Long Distance, CENTREX, VoIP, ATM, Frame Relay and wholesale services
▸ Headed major IT projects involving consolidations, process improvements, change management, and migrations
▸ Planned and executed the first successful full conversion to Cisco Unified Communications of a large Utah hospital

Most recently, I've worked on the consultancy side of the industry and have become widely respected as a Cisco UC expert, particularly in relation to leading large-scale conversions and deployments for customers, producing significant ROI through lower costs, improved efficiency, added functionality, and increased reliability.

But now, I'm ready to return to a corporate leadership role, building and leading a team of top-performers and holding P&L and budget responsibilities. As a leader of technology organizations, my goal is always to transform the organization to become a partner with the business they support and serve. I am an inventive, outside-the-box thinker and problem-solver, and I encourage the same of the people who work for me, creating an environment in which ROI is always a top concern and technologies are applied in a way that generates the greatest benefits possible.

Your advertisement for a <position title> at <Company Name> is exactly the type of opportunity I am interested in and I am confident I will be the ideal candidate to help you meet your goals for the position. I have enclosed my résumé and look forward to the opportunity to sit down with you and learn more about it.

Thank you. I hope to hear from you soon.

Sincerely,

Katherine Griffin
Enclosure: Résumé

JEAN BEDARD

San Francisco, CA 00000 / Available for Relocation
(555) 555-5555 ▪ jbedard@gmail.com ▪ www.linkedin.com/in/jeanbedard

<Date>

<First Name> <Last Name>, <Title>
<Company Name>
<Address>
<City, State Zip>

Dear <Name>:

I am an entrepreneurial leader who will not accept the status quo, nor will I accept the view that "it can't be done." I see opportunity where others see a void, solutions rather than problems, and, no matter how hard it gets, I persevere, learning and adapting quickly from lessons-learned along the way. I am genuinely excited by and passionate about opportunities to guide businesses to the next level of success, infusing the teams I lead with energy and focus, and helping them to navigate strategic challenges in order to chart new paths to growth.

If the above sounds like the type of leader you are seeking to fill the <PositionTitle> role at <Company Name> which I saw advertised at <website name>, please accept my enclosed résumé. I am certain that you will find I meet or exceed all your requirements:

▶ **Strong educational credentials:** MBA from California University and BA degree from Harvard University
▶ **Executive track record:** 15+ years of progressive leadership experience managing up to $120M P&Ls and 480-person teams
▶ **Globally savvy:** Emerging market expertise and a global mindset from working in NA, European, African, and Asian markets
▶ **Entrepreneurial:** Succeed in unstructured situations, creating strategy, structures, and systems from the ground up
▶ **Inspiring leader:** Demonstrated ability to lead teams to overcome significant challenges in order to achieve big goals
▶ **Business builder:** Leveraged deep commercial expertise to drive substantial top-line growth in each role
▶ **Change catalyst:** Have successfully grown mature businesses, turned around underperformers, and strengthened all

Throughout my career, my leadership has been tapped multiple times for a number of strategic initiatives. Most recently this has included:

- Building and leading the first standalone, internal Acme startup in 30 years which I grew into a thriving, global enterprise
- Spearheading turnaround and global growth of a business division that had been "left for dead"
- Transforming disparate, tired product offerings into a single, integrated offering that reinvigorated revenue growth

If results like these could be beneficial to <Company Name>, let's talk. I look forward to hearing from you to schedule an interview or to answer any questions that you may have.

Respectfully,

Jean Bedard

Norine Dagliano, BA, NCRW, CFRW/CC
ekm Inspirations

Norine Dagliano, BA, NCRW, CFRW/CC
ekm Inspirations
www.ekminspirations.com
www.linkedin.com/in/norinedagliano
norine@ekminspirations.com
Office – 301-766-2032

For more than 30 years, job seekers and professionals in career transition have relied on Norine Dagliano for expert advice, practical insight, inspiration, and support to help them get paid what they deserve doing work that they love.

Self-employed and operating as ekm Inspirations (in recognition of her children — her three greatest inspirations), Norine has continually honed her skills through ongoing training, which has earned her credentials as a Nationally Certified Résumé Writer (less than 50 professionals world-wide hold this credential) and Certified Federal Résumé Writer/Career Coach.

Taking a custom approach to each and every project, she excels in designing strategic and branded résumés and cover letters that capture attention, create desire, and move employers to reach out and connect. Through a personal approach, that includes an in-depth consultation and DISC Behavioral Style Assessment, Norine crafts documents that reflect each job seeker's unique personality and value proposition.

With a broad spectrum of knowledge and experience pertaining to hundreds of occupations and industries, as well as a vast network of colleagues she can tap for additional insight, Norine assists job seekers — from blue-collar and entry-level to executive — in distinguishing themselves from their competition. Her ideal clients recognize that an investment in professionally written documents is an investment in their careers.

Steve Arnone, Jr.

319 Bushnell Lane ~ Charles Town, WV 25414
Phone: 304-555-5478 ~ steve.arnone@gmail.com

Skilled Craftsman ~ Remodeler ~ Certified Lead Carpenter
Design/Build ~ Remodel and Repair ~ Residential and Commercial

Conscientious, accurate and intuitive professional with more than 18 years' experience evaluating, estimating, planning and delivering projects, on time and within budget. Well-versed and skilled in use of various methods, materials, tools and equipment; able to read an interpret blueprints, schematics, sketches, diagrams and manuals. Exceptional customer service, time-management and decision-making skills; equally effective working alone or managing a crew. Posses a natural ability to think outside the box and devise creative solutions to achieving desired results.

Professional Experience

HOME REPAIR SPECIALIST, Smith Design & Remodeling, Brunswick, MD   **20XX to 20XX**

Independently completed contracted residential projects, ranging in size from small household repairs to total room remodels (one as high as $45,000) on new as well as historic homes. Drove and maintained company truck and traveled extensively throughout the Metro-DC area and parts of Virginia and West Virginia to complete jobs.

Activities:
✓ Installed kitchen appliances, plumbing and bath fixtures
✓ Completed metal and wood framing, plaster work and dry wall
✓ Installed and repaired interior and exterior windows and doors, countertops and flooring
✓ Painted and completed finish work
✓ Specialized in finished carpentry, tile work and leak repair

- Tracked and maintained adequate materials and supplies. Followed up with vendors and company personnel to ensure projects were completed on time and within budget.
- Calculated time and materials and prepared final invoices.
- Professionally represented the company and built positive customer relations, which led to development of a loyal customer base and repeat business.
- Consistently earned customer satisfaction ratings of 3.6-3.7 on a 4.0 scale measuring skills, job knowledge, personal appearance, neatness, promptness and quality of work.

LEAD CARPENTER, Star Builders, Jefferson, MD   **2001 to 2004**

Performed interior demolitions, remodels and custom cabinetry work, primarily for small restaurants and major chains in Maryland and Metro-DC area. Laid out projects and directed crews comprised of plumbing and electrical subcontractors and as many as six carpenters. Completed all work after business hours and ensured work areas were cleaned and restored to previous standards prior to reopening and customer arrival.

Activities:
✓ Designed and built storage spaces
✓ Removed and installed new restaurant equipment and cabinets to upgrade food-prep and customer area
✓ Completed metal stud framing, dry wall, woodworking, ceramic tiling
✓ Applied stainless steel wall panels and stainless steel skins over existing countertops
✓ Worked with both laminates and veneers

Steve Arnone, Jr.   Phone: 304-555-5478 ~ steve.arnone@gmail.com   **Page 2**

Star Builders *(continued)*

Select Projects:
- Totally renovated front-counter line of a Dupont Circle Starbucks. Tore out existing cabinetry and custom cut and fit new cabinets for register counter, display cases and refrigeration unit. Overcame challenge of working around a small entranceway by removing and reinstalling a front window to bring in the refrigeration unit.
- Completed one of the first Ruby Tuesday's makeovers to reflect new corporate image. Changed all table and seating configurations and completed extensive painting and cosmetic work.
- Remodeled a Corner Bakery in Union Station to make it more customer friendly by updating the cabinetry in the cafeteria line and enclosing seating area for more restaurant-style service.

INDEPENDENT CONTRACTOR, Winchester Cabinetworks, Winchester, VA   **19XX to 20XX**

Founded and independently operated a residential repair and remodeling business. Managed marketing, project design and specifications, customer and vendor relations, record keeping and permits. Secured new business based on referral and reputation for doing quality work.

Activities:
✓ Completed electrical and plumbing (from rough-in through finish) including lighting design and installation. Installed kitchen appliances and bath fixtures
✓ Installed HVAC and duct work
✓ Completed design, layout and installation of ceramic-tile walls, floors and countertops; doors and windows; vinyl, laminate and hardwood floor
✓ Painted interior and exterior surfaces with latex, oil and texture

Select Projects:
- Converted a closet space into a wet bar, complete with lighting and mirrored panels.
- Custom built a display case with open shelving, mirrored panels and marble countertop for an antique doll collection.
- Demolished an old wood deck and built a screened-in porch from the ground up.
- Built an enclosed gazebo-style structure around an existing hot tub to create privacy.
- Refinished a basement with custom features, including built-in entertainment center and book shelves, bar and kitchenette with ceramic countertops and custom cabinets.

PRIOR CAREER EXPERIENCE: Acquired four years' experience as a maintenance mechanic for a biotech research firm and seven years' experience as a steel mechanic in the construction of large commercial buildings.

Education & Credentials

CERTIFIED LEAD CARPENTER (CLC)   **20XX**
National Association of the Remodeling Industry

COMPUTER AIDED DESIGN AND DRAFTING TECHNOLOGY   **20XX**

ASSOCIATE OF ARTS, MECHANICAL DESIGN TECHNOLOGY   **20XX**
James Rumsey Center, Martinsburg, WV

Patrick O'Malley

2335 Copperfield Lane • Nashville, Tennessee 37221
615.555.3587 • p.omalley@verizon.net

Professional Profile

I built my career around the culinary profession – as a corporate, fine dining & gourmet market chef...

And I discovered my passion in teaching ... where ever I go, it keeps calling me back

Multitalented and knowledgeable professional with more than 20 years of culinary experience. Trained on-the-job by some of Nashville's finest chefs and through formal instruction at The Culinary Institute of America. Demonstrate exceptional ability to balance diverse food preparation techniques with innate understanding and application of solid business management practices and principles. Possess strong public speaking and interpersonal skills – recognized for making learning fun while increasing student and employee confidence.

Business / Instructional / Culinary Expertise

- Employee Training & Cross-training
- On-the-Spot Customer Education
- Curriculum Development & Adult Education
- Menu Planning & Recipe Development
- Purchasing & Vendor Relations

- Menu Pricing & Food Cost Control
- Culinary Math & Budgeting
- Business Marketing Techniques
- Food Preparation & Presentation
- Wine Selection & Pairing

Professional Experience

Nashville, Tennessee

SEHRT SEAFOOD COMPANY
Assistant Manager/Chef

20XX–Present

Recruited by this independently owned an operated retail fish business to help manage expansion of in-house operations, diversification of menu items, and transition to an upscale, gourmet market. Develop recipes and prepare multiple gourmet dishes for carry-out. Supervise a full-time cook and a kitchen assistant. Oversee inventory and food costs; order all paper goods, packaging, and food prep supplies; look at ways to increase market visibility and sales.

- Learned all aspects of retail seafood operations; implemented costing of recipes to control food costs, and helped push fresh seafood sales to approximately 1000 pounds/week.
- Promote sustainable farming practices and higher food quality by selecting and using locally-grown produce for food preparation. Opened the door to selling fresh produce directly to customers.
- Developed prepared-foods side of the business and implemented various in-store tastings and sampling weekends — nearly tripled food sales.

GORDON'S MARKET & CATERING SERVICE
Executive Chef

2001–2006

Maintained total creative license in developing recipes and preparing dishes for gourmet grocery and catering business. Oversaw two assistant cooks. Heavily involved in inventory and ordering; held full responsibility for all wine selection and ordering.

- Demonstrated personal approach to meeting customer needs, recaptured lost customers, and forged new business relationships.
- Turned around negative profits and produced 45% increase in gross annual sales over four year period.

Culinary Instructor

UNIVERSITY OF TENNESSEE
School of Continuing Studies | 20XX–Present
- Teach core seafood and shellfish classes and several electives for the non-credit culinary arts program — 6 to 8 classes/semester; average of 16 students/class.

SUR LA TABLE | 20XX–Present
- As guest chef, provide hands-on cooking classes to groups of 16-20 adults. Help drive store business by promoting and nourishing appreciation for the culinary arts.

NASHVILLE STATE COMMUNITY COLLEGE – P.A.V.E. Program | 20XX to 20XX
- Taught basic cooking skills to students in the Program for Adults in Vocational Education — two semesters; 9 hours/week.

Culinary Chef Instructor

SALUD! COOKING SCHOOL | 20XX–20XX
- Selected menu themes, developed recipes, identified techniques to demonstrate, and facilitated students' hands-on experience — Instructed 2 to 3 hands-on classes/month; as many as 16 students/class.

Patrick O'Malley
615.555.3587 · p.omalley@verizon.net   **Page 2**

Restaurant Experience
Nashville, Tennessee

MIEL RESTAURANT   20XX–20XX
Garde Manger Chef

Expanded and diversified culinary experience and style by accepting position with Rob Jeter, one of *Food and Wine Magazine's Top Ten New Chefs of 20XX*. Developed and refined intricate presentation skills; learned creative dessert techniques.

SPERRY'S IN FRANKLIN SQUARE   19XX–19XX
Sous Chef

Studied with Chef Austin Morgan and learned innovative approaches to traditional cooking principles and importance of quality and freshness of ingredients. Supervised kitchen and menu preparations in Chef de Cuisine's absence. Maintained inventory, oversaw sanitation, and monitored costs.

- Managed Sperry's Bar Café. Accepted full responsibility for menu development and planning, food preparation, presentation techniques, and quality standards. Prepared all Café lunches and banquets for 20-60 guests.

STONY RIVER STEAKHOUSE & GRILLE   19XX–19XX
Regional Kitchen Manager/Kitchen Manager/Assistant Kitchen Manager/Line Cook

Rapidly progressed through higher levels of responsibility in recognition of industry knowledge, demonstrated management skill, and work performance. Managed all HR functions for kitchen staff of 25 to 30 employees. Served as principal representative to owner, troubleshooting and resolving any operational and personnel issues.

> Trained and supervised kitchen staff. Demonstrated ability to lead by example. Promoted atmosphere of teamwork and instilling "can-do" attitude in employees.

- Maintained entire food and equipment inventory, implementing more efficient use of computerized spreadsheets. Tracked numbers and percentages to effectively control costs and maximize profits.
- Developed and implemented policies and standards of quality for off-site catering; solicited and secured contracts; planned and executed menus for catering events for up to 200 guests.
- Charged with responsibility for establishing new Clarksville location, which included hiring, interviewing, and training kitchen staff and an on-site manager.
- Simultaneously oversaw day-to-day operation of Clarksville and Nashville restaurants to establish and maintain quality standards for menu development, food preparation, plate presentation, service, and staff/customer satisfaction.

Education

CULINARY INSTITUTE OF AMERICA   *Hyde Park, New York*
Servsafe Food Protection Manager Certification, National Restaurant Association

TENNESSEE STATE UNIVERSITY   *Nashville, Tennessee*
Bachelor of Arts—magna cum laude; Alfred Lund Award for Academic Excellence

DAVE JENKINS

1804 Market Street   ·   Frederick, MD 21702
djenkins@comcast.net   ·   240.555.5969

TECHNICAL SALES SPECIALIST

Field Sales · Business Development · Territory Management · Product Training
~ A trusted advisor who creates customized solutions ~

Competitive spirit, passion for setting and achieving performance-driven goals, consistent record of locking out the competition, and ability to quickly turn opportunities into orders—personal trademarks of a sales career spanning more than 15 years with a global provider of technology solutions for academic, research, and manufacturing sectors. Combine electrical engineering degree, prior hands-on experience, and exceptional interpersonal skills, to intuitively facilitate the sales process, from the technician level to executive decision makers. Skilled at technical probing and qualifying customers. Unwavering in overcoming obstacles and generating innovative ideas and solutions to close sales.

"Dave exceeding his overall annual quota year after year is a tribute to his ability to stay focused on results, a strong positive attitude, and exceptional work ethic. He prospects for opportunities to fill his funnel and then converts these opportunities to close the sale... Dave ranks amongst the strongest closers in the business." - District Manager

Sales Performance by Year

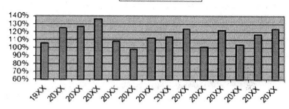

★ **Surpassed aggressive sales quotas 13 out of 15 years; overcame weak start in FY'04 and rallied 3rd and 4th quarters to secure $1.74M in sales with 11.5% year-end gain.**

PROFESSIONAL EXPERIENCE

FIELD SALES ENGINEER - Innovative Technologies, Rockville, MD   19xx–Present

Key contributor to Innovative Technologies' sustained reputation as world's leading supplier of electronic test and measurement equipment. As outside sales representative, bring technical and product expertise to identifying potential business opportunities, implementing strategies to capture competitors' market share, and grow existing accounts within assigned territories.

- Seamlessly transition through various business markets targeting telecommunications, manufacturing, research and academic sectors. Use perceptive listening and questioning to analyze customer challenges and assimilate information pertaining to customer buying practices, budget cycles, funding sources, and procurement processes. Identify and connect with key decision makers, overcome obstacles and objections, and persist in pinpointing creative solutions to close sales.

- Collaborate with internal and external business partners (distributors, online-sales organization, channel partners, field engineers, and program rental partners) to develop, refine and execute well thought-out reach plans that provide direction for forecasting monthly and quarterly sales performance, managing territories, and meeting quotas. Plan and facilitate various educational and promotional events aimed at improving customers' product knowledge and awareness of cutting-edge engineering design practices.

- Creatively implement innovative company programs and sales tools including customized financing; maintenance services and extended warranties; strategic and aggressive price discounts; direct mail and e-marketing campaigns; customer "lunch & learn" programs; and B2B promotional events.

"Dave is an excellent performer that I can always count on to exceed his goals, satisfy his customers and use solid judgment in all aspects of his job... a hard worker ...never satisfied with his own results and constantly searching for ways to improve." – Regional Sales Manager

Innovative Technologies *(continued)*

<u>**Key Assignments & Outcomes**</u>

Target Account Organization (current): ***<u>Territory</u>***: Maryland and Virginia; ***<u>Targets</u>***: Existing mix of high-volume, multimillion-dollar accounts and smaller strategic accounts with primary share-of-spend on competitors' products; ***<u>Challenge</u>***: Strategically grow accounts and weaken competitors' hold.

Geographic & Target Account Organization (2005–2009): ***<u>Territory</u>***: Large, geographically dispersed territory encompassing parts of Maryland and Virginia; ***<u>Targets</u>***: Competitive anchor accounts; existing key accounts with installed base and share-of-spend; current and potential distributors; ***<u>Challenge</u>***: Overcome landmark economic recession while continuing to grow and sustain business.

Educational Institutions Rep (2000–2002): ***<u>Territory</u>***: Maryland, Pennsylvania and Virginia; ***<u>Targets</u>***: Colleges and universities with engineering programs; key accounts included University of Maryland, Virginia Tech, Virginia Commonwealth University, Norfolk State University, Penn State, and Johns Hopkins University Applied Physics Lab; ***<u>Challenge</u>***: Position firm's products for inclusion in technical research proposals and permeate electrical, mechanical, and physics labs with test and measurement equipment.

New Business Team, Test & Measurement (1994–1999): ***<u>Territory</u>***: Multimillion-dollar territory comprised of 150+ emerging accounts; largest geographic territory of any field-sales engineer in the district; ***<u>Targets</u>***: Diverse market of wireless telecommunications, electronic manufacturing, fiber optics, and digital design firms; ***<u>Challenge</u>***: Prospect and mine new business by focusing sales efforts on market sectors with strongest potential for growth.

- **Aggressively penetrated Northern VA territory and shook competitors' stronghold**; in eight months, secured sales approaching $700K.
- **Persevered in hard-hitting battle with competitor that resulted in capturing key account** and unleashing stream with projected FY '09 revenues approaching $1.5M.
- **Triumphed over competitor's deep discounts and 40% lower price-point and prevailed** throughout lengthy sales cycle to ultimately secure $400K sale and exclusive installation in 52 labs of a major university.
- **Took immediate and collaborative action to salvage at-risk account** by engaging national and regional sales managers in resolving purchasing agent's concerns about firm's transition to Oracle and the fallout of problems and numerous obstacles impacting customers.
- **Disrupted competitor's control of account and gained loyal customer** by initiating collaborative cross-selling with internal business partner to offer customized product solution.
- **Made significant contributions to Mid-Atlantic Mega Team's six-month success** in producing $8.8M in new business revenue.
- **Trounced the competition and booked approximately $900K in business** from a contract manufacturer aimed at expanding to a new market channel.
- **Landed $280K deal with local division of a start-up wireless Internet provider that mushroomed** to a sole-supplier national account.
- **Pioneered operational restructuring models that shifted routine transactional sales activities** to internal departments and administrative personnel and equipped field sales engineers with more time for scouting complex "solution-oriented" opportunities.
- **Surpassed all other field-sales engineers for upfront sales of extended warranties** and calibration services.
- **Recorded district's highest customer attendance for annual product road show** by heavily marketing and promoting this one-week event through various repetitive outreach activities.

" Dave is exceptional at building and maintaining strong, positive working relationships resulting in unique competitive advantage because customers lose all interest in investigating other vendor options" - Sales Manager

---

EDUCATION & PROFESSIONAL DEVELOPMENT

Bachelor of Science, Electrical Engineering – Purdue University, Indianapolis, IN
**Basho Strategies Sales Training; Hewlett-Packard Sales Training I & II
Situational Sales Negotiations**

Jennifer M. Alvarez

109 18th Street, NW · Apt 413 · Charlottesville, VA 22903
Cell: 240.555.1746 · e-mail: jmalvarez@virginia.edu

Professional Profile

Analytical and intuitive 2010 graduate eager to secure paid internship or entry-level employment that will take full advantage of the following traits, skills, and real-world experience:

- Acute awareness of human rights, diplomacy, and political issues with desire to further education and experience in government, legal, and foreign affairs.
- Ability to balance creativity and intuition with a critical and systematic approach to information gathering, fact-finding, and problem solving.
- Proficiency in web-based research, Word, and PowerPoint; experience with Excel, graphic design, layout, and editing.
- Excellent writing, oral communication, and presentation skills; proficient conversational, reading, and writing Spanish language skills.
- International travel, residential, and academic experience; quickly adapt to people from diverse age groups, cultures, socio-economic, and educational levels.

Education & Extracurricular Experience

University of Virginia, Charlottesville, VA
Bachelor of Arts, Foreign Affairs and History (dual major)   May 20xx
- **University of Virginia Art Museum**, Charlottesville, VA (Sept 2007 to Present)
  As a Docent, lead tours for groups of elementary school students. Assist with facilitating "*Early Visions,*" an experiential learning and mentoring program aimed at giving youth exposure to the arts.
- **Migrant Aid Program, Tutor and Mentor**, Charlottesville, VA (Sept 2006 to May 2008)
  Provided one-on-one literacy tutoring for Spanish-speaking children and adults.

Saint James School, St. James, Maryland
High School Diploma
- **Yearbook Staff,** Co-Editor (senior year) and Layout Editor (junior year)
- **Co-Editor,** *The Syrinx,* a school literary magazine featuring art work, short stories, and prose.

Study Abroad

Universidad Iberoamericana, Mexico, D.F.   Aug to Dec 20xx
- Gained broader understanding of Mexican culture and history by residing with a host family and completing classes at the university. Studied basic Portuguese.

University of Virginia Hispanic Studies Program, Valencia, Spain   Jan to May 20xx
- Took part in a one-semester Spanish immersion experience that encompassed classes and residency with a Spanish-speaking host family.

London School of Economics, London, England   Jun to Aug 20xx
- Participated in a full-time academic program with students and professionals from around the world; studied international law, human rights theory and practices, and contemporary issues.

Practical Experience

Universidad Catolica, Valencia, Spain   Feb 20xx to Apr 20xx
- As intern with the International Relations Office, assisted the director by reading, analyzing, and preparing abstracts of pertinent journal articles to support his academic research project.

Frederick County Chamber of Commerce, Frederick, MD   Dec 20xx to Jan 20xx
- Completed one-month internship assisting with public outreach and administrative activities related to campaign for approval of home-rule charter.
- Conducted telephone solicitation to garner business support; created spreadsheets to track call activity; assembled information packets and helped plan and coordinate a business presentation.

Permanent Address: 642 Antietam Circle · Frederick, MD 21701

Nelly Grinfeld, MBA, NCRW, CEIC
Top of the Stack Resume

Nelly Grinfeld
Top of the Stack Resume
www.topofthestackresume.com
writer@topofthestackresume.com
Office – 513-328-8019

Nelly Grinfeld is a Nationally Certified Resume Writer whose 10+ years' experience is grounded in her Human Resources background and MBA education. With an insider's view of what hiring managers are looking for, Nelly knows the right questions to ask; she is able to highlight each client's strengths and accomplishments while meeting industry-specific demands. Her dedication to continuing education in the ever-changing arena of career marketing allows Nelly to consistently write concise, keyword-rich, attention-grabbing resumes and LinkedIn profiles that produce results for professionals at all levels.

As head writer and owner of Top of the Stack Resume, Nelly partners with motivated professionals to create powerful career documents that consistently land at the top of the stack and result in more interviews. Nelly provides a personalized service to clients in a variety of industries to bring out their strengths and expertly show their unique value to their next employer.

MICHAEL C. ADAMS

City, ST • 567.890.1234 • Michael_Adams@gmail.com • www.linkedin.com/in/MikeAdams

RESULTS-DRIVEN BUSINESS DEVELOPMENT EXPERT PROVEN TO MEET SALES, MARKETING, AND FINANCIAL OBJECTIVES

INSIDE/OUTSIDE SALES PROFESSIONAL AND MILITARY VETERAN with 15+ years experience in fitness, restaurant, and hospitality industries. Plan, develop, implement, and evaluate marketing plans and promotional programs within set budget and target market. BEAT INDUSTRY-AVERAGE CLIENT RETENTION RATES 288% (9 vs. 26 months) by evaluating competitors and optimizing product, service, and program knowledge to maximize profits and exceed sales goals.

WORK EXPERIENCE

SALES/MARKETING MANAGER, OWNER: TRAINING COMPANY NAME (City, ST)   **20XX–Present**
Lead team of 6 personal trainers in engaging, client-centered, fast-paced atmosphere with strong emphasis on growing online and in-person sales, increasing client retention, and running results-driven fitness studio. Reach financial objectives by carrying out strategic planning and programming initiatives while focusing on client service.

- Grow client base 258% by selling personal training and boot camp packages to target demographic.
- Increase monthly sales 214% ($7.8K to $16.7K) in 20XX by maximizing local business-to-business relationships.
- Retain 82% of existing clients and attract new business via social media promotion.

✓ EXECUTE SALES PLANS: Project $900/month sales growth and aggressively advertise/sell gym services to reach goals.

✓ MANAGE GROWTH: Prepare for major expansion to reach $28K monthly sales in 20XX by building outdoor facility, enhancing class schedules and offering, and promoting boot camp program to new/prospective clients.

✓ IMPLEMENT SYSTEM IMPROVEMENTS: Control program quality by training employees, writing workout routines, and observing via video recording to provide feedback. Run sales training meetings to teach client management skills.

✓ PROMOTE PROGRAMS AND SERVICES: Maximize client engagement and motivation by applying "Member of the Month" reward system and utilizing social media (Facebook, Google) to promote program via client results.

INDEPENDENT CONTRACTOR, PERSONAL TRAINER: FITNESS STUDIO (City, ST)   **20XX–20XX**
Maximized sales and referrals as contractor at gym facilities by selling and servicing personal training packages.

- Achieved 400% sales growth ($1.7K to $6.7K/month) by optimizing advertising and running referral contest.
- Initiated independent marketing programs and promotions through Facebook, online ads, and local networks.

PERSONAL TRAINER: ANY FITNESS (City, ST)   **20XX–20XX**
Supported club mission while maximizing internal client upgrades to influence recurring training session purchases.

- Sold $3K-$5K/month in training sessions by promoting wellness, developing effective plans, and implementing strategies to help clients reach weight loss and overall health goals. "Trainer of the Year" award recipient.

EARLY WORK HISTORY

SHIFT MANAGER, FAMILY BREAD (20XX–20XX) • DINING ROOM SUPERVISOR, DINING HALL (20XX–20XX)

EDUCATION

Community College–City, ST (19XX–19XX)
Extensive coursework taken towards Associate degrees: **Chef Technologies, Hotel/Restaurant Management**

MILITARY EXPERIENCE

Mustering Petty Officer Third Class / Physical Fitness Instructor–US Navy Reserve (20XX–20XX)
Deployed to Kuwait/Iraq in 20XX • **Navy Achievement Medal** recipient

EMILY BENSON

City, ST • 456.789.0123 • emilybenson@gmail.com • www.linkedin.com/in/emilybenson

Expert Writer and Driving Editorial Team Leader in Digital Publishing and Print Media Environments
Project Planning · Social Media · Research · Brand Promotion · Webcasting · Custom Content

Experienced writer, editor, and journalist with 9+ year reputation propelling projects in online and print production of financial, risk management, and insurance publications. Exceed projected readership goals by maximizing data use, optimizing sales copy, and promoting content, brand, and industry topics via social media channels. Industry thought leader with sponsored content expertise and ability to optimize media advertising, advise on corporate strategy, and lead teams to increase advertising revenue.

CAREER PATH

Company–City, ST   **20XX–Present**
Excel in roles of progressive responsibility influencing revenue growth for global leader in specialized business news and information serving the legal, real estate, consulting, insurance and investment advisory industries.

EDITOR IN CHIEF (20XX–Present)
Manage online and print content production of two business publications: *National Underwriter Life & Health* and *Retirement Advisor*. Maximize strategic content opportunities as thought leader and brand ambassador at company and external industry events. Create annual editorial calendar by collaborating with publisher to determine timeline, create quality topics, set budgets, and establish deadlines. Work with industry sponsors to research topics of interest: arrange readership surveys, organize data, and publish results. Interview, hire, and train new staff.

♦ **Manage online production projects**: Lead team of 5 editors/designers to develop daily website content for on-time digital production. Lead staff meetings, conduct performance evaluations, and meet all deadlines and page view goals without compromising quality.

♦ **Create custom content pieces**: Collaborate with marketing/advertising units to publish articles while promoting advertiser to maximize revenue. Represent publication during webcasts with subject matter expertise.

♦ **Produce monthly print publications**: Support 100K circulation of two publications by writing original news stories and integrating online content into compelling print layout while adhering to schedule and budget.

♦ **Analyze data via Google Analytics and Chartbeat**: Examine page views, top stories, and reader demographics to maximize user experience, suggest top-ranking story ideas, and discover hot topics to promote growth.

♦ **Utilize social media**: Maximize LinkedIn, Twitter, Facebook, and Google+ to grow brand recognition and stimulate discussion.

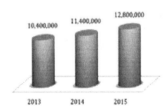

Website Page View Growth
▪ Annual Page Views

10,400,000   11,400,000   12,800,000
2013   2014   2015

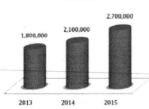

Website User Growth
▪ Annual Users

1,800,000   2,100,000   2,700,000
2013   2014   2015

Selected Achievements:

✓ Reach $30K advertising revenue from new Succession Initiative project by managing online publication to attract younger workforce to industry.

✓ Contribute to $2.2 MIL revenue as Markets Channel Editor for LifeHealthPro, leading online information source for insurance industry. Win Jesse H. Neal award with team as Executive Managing Editor on in-depth mental health series.

✓ Stay on top of trends at financial and insurance industry conferences; report on industry news for immediate online posting.

✓ Earn $70K in advertising and sponsorships by coordinating, researching, and publishing Athene fixed income annuities study.

Continued...

Emily Benson, page 2   **456.789.0123**

CAREER PATH, continued

Company experience, continued...
EXECUTIVE MANAGING EDITOR (20XX–20XX)

Managed online and print content production of National Underwriter Life & Health publication. Developed monthly and annual budgets for art, writing, professional development, supplies, and travel. Quickly promoted to Editor in Chief.

- Achieved rapid readership growth: 27% increase in online views, 7% rise in print subscriptions (from 60K to 64.2K).
- Led team of 4 writers and 4 freelancers to create unique content, editorial calendars, webcasts, and graphics. Maximized Content Management System use to edit/post news and incorporate infographics.
- Created meaningful content via interviews, case studies, and reported stories for broad industry readership.

Industry Magazine–City, ST   **20XX–20XX**
EDITOR (20XX–20XX), **ASSOCIATE EDITOR** (20XX–20XX)

Maximized effectiveness of print and online publishing to deliver information-packed industry publication and online resources to Risk Management Association members. Researched and wrote feature-length articles, case studies, and interviews and collaborated with editors and freelancers to develop editorial and art ideas with InDesign.

- Achieved #1 ranking for magazine as greatest association benefit as result of membership poll.
- Generated $47K revenue by managing daily WordPress blog with fresh content: articles, question/answer sessions, video clips, polls. Formed media partnerships across industry to cross-promote product.
- Represented company and brand at industry conferences; created timely, relevant stories and event news.
- Maximized social media use (Facebook, Twitter, LinkedIn) to develop voice, tone, and value of magazine.

PRIOR WORK HISTORY

Lifestyle Magazine–City, ST   **20XX**
CONTRIBUTING WRITER

Wrote editorial and advertorial articles about local events, people, and issues in the city area. Interviewed diverse business owners and groups and created compelling advertorial copy to maximize advertising revenue.

Independent Newspaper–City, ST   **20XX–20XX**
ASSISTANT EDITOR (20XX–20XX), **FREELANCE WRITER** (20XX)

Promoted from freelance to full-time position due to diligent, thorough, and timely coverage of local government, sports, community, education, and health topics. Developed exciting, original stories for bi-monthly publication.

Company–City, ST   **2005–2006**
TRADING ADMINISTRATOR

Executed fixed income securities trades for high net-worth clients and reconciled 300+ accounts to meet industry standards. Edited and proofread firm's publications, newsletters, and market commentaries. Earned Series 65 license.

EDUCATION / TRAINING

Master of Business Administration (MBA), City University (20XX)

Bachelor of Arts (BA) **English**, City University (20XX)

Bachelor of Science (BS) **Finance**, City University (20XX)

PROFESSIONAL ACTIVITIES

Writer, The Huffington Post (20XX–Present)

Member, Society of Professional Journalists (20XX–Present)

Member, Women in Insurance and Financial Services (20XX–Present)

Writer / Contributor, Honest Cooking (20XX–Present)

SARAH E. JONES

City, ST • 234.567.8901 • sjones@gmail.com • www.linkedin.com/in/sejones

Organizational Leader Skilled in Fundraising, Program Management, and Policy Development

Non-Profit Executive offers 15+ year reputation of providing leadership and guidance to regional start-up organizations. Propel agency expansion and strategic planning initiatives by collaborating with board of directors, establishing donor relationships, and ensuring proper use of funds. Facilitate board approval on program planning initiatives while managing agency risk, increasing community awareness, and prioritizing client satisfaction.

ACCOMPLISHMENT HIGHLIGHTS

✓ **Collaborate with executive board** to optimize programs by working with agencies to service regional clients. Guide executive meetings by preparing agenda, presenting financial statements, and resolving agency logistical and legal issues.

✓ **Advocate to improve family outcomes** by collaborating with agencies and investigators to streamline processes.

✓ **Write grant proposals** and narratives and develop custom agency policies for board approval and maximum financial impact. Implement aggressive grant strategies to manage contracts, budgets, and grant applications.

✓ **Meet client, region, and funding needs** by developing policies, guidelines, by-laws, and protocols. Expand program reach by presenting to stakeholders to maximize impact of annual fundraising appeals.

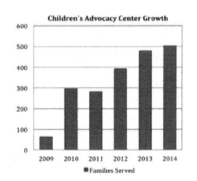

WORK EXPERIENCE

EXECUTIVE DIRECTOR   20XX–Present
Non-Profit–City, ST

Launch first-of-its-kind regional Non-Profit 501(c)(3) non-profit to provide forensic interview services according to National Children's Alliance and Indiana Department of Child Services standards. Work to reduce childhood trauma by offering collaborative approach to child abuse investigations. Partner with 23 law enforcement agencies, child services offices, and prosecutors to ensure safe, welcoming, and respectful process for families and children.

- **Propel 785% program growth** by researching other Non-Profits (**64 families served in 20XX to 503 in 20XX**).
- **Maximize $300K budget** and small team of 2 interviewers across 9 counties to service 500+ clients annually.
- Optimize business registration, 501(c)(3) application, tax-exempt status, and budget preparation processes to complement state criminal justice and welfare systems. Network with local elected officials to maximize support.
- Recruit and manage staff by streamlining interview process, preparing job descriptions, and conducting annual reviews.

Selected Achievements
- **Fundraising**: Raise $1.2MIL+ in local government and local/national foundation grants; administer grants, prepare reports, and manage budgets. Carry out innovative local fundraisers to raise $110K annually.
- **Board Development**: Recruit 8 board members for multidisciplinary roles while developing and promoting board contract, responsibilities, and requirements. Write initial board by-laws for start-up and amend board terms as needed.
- **Project Management**: Complete $526K building project by requesting and gaining HUD, foundation, and matching funds. Work with architects and contractors to design and remodel facility that meets program needs and budget constraints.
- **Program Implementation**: Reach program growth goals by reducing agencies' and social workers' resistance; increase perceived benefit of inter-agency collaboration.

Awards
- Congressional Record from Congressman S. James (20XX) for providing daily leadership and execution of goals.
- "Excellence in Victim Advocacy" awards (20XX–20XX) for perseverance, leadership, fortitude, and determination.

Continued...

Sarah E. Jones, page 2   234.567.8901

WORK EXPERIENCE, continued

FOUNDING PRESIDENT, INTERIM CO-DIRECTOR   19XX–20XX
Non-Profit–City, ST

Obtained $1MIL Lilly endowment gift to start comprehensive community center from scratch including by-laws, policies, and collaborations with area agencies and schools. Chaired new Board of Directors and led initiatives to develop new programs and maximize $2MIL+ capital, operational, and fundraising campaigns.

- **Reversed $100K funding block** by lobbying state and ICLU to reconsider funding restriction.
- **Oversaw $4MIL building project** for new 25,000 sq. ft. facility as Chair of building committee.
- Collaborated with lawyer on 501(c)(3) application; won grants and negotiated gifts from County and Corporations.
- Took initiative to maximize own learning opportunities in board building, agency standards, and program development.
- Received "**Distinguished Service**" award (20XX) from Johns County Chamber of Commerce.

ADDITIONAL EXPERIENCE

ADMINISTRATIVE DIRECTOR–Program (City, ST)   20XX–20XX
- Developed new summer art education program. Obtained local foundation funding to serve 30 children.

COURT INTERPRETER (City, ST)   19XX–20XX
- Created Spanish-English translation service company and expanded service to 4 Indiana counties.
- Supervised 3 translators by providing training, negotiating wages, and outlining responsibilities.

CO-FOUNDER, DIRECTOR–Program (City, ST)   19XX–20XX
- Wrote, won, and administered foundation and corporate grants for unique foreign language program.
- Maximized Safe Haven grant use to conduct safe, nurturing, and educational program for 80+ kids annually.

EDUCATION

Master of Public Affairs (expected 20XX)–Any University *City, ST*

Non-Profit Management, Graduate Certificate (20XX)–Any University *City, ST*

Bachelor of Arts (BA), Humanities (19XX)–Any University *City, ST*

TRAINING

Advanced Forensic Interview Training (20XX, 20XX) • Victim Advocacy Training (20XX)
Advanced Leadership Academy (20XX) • Family Advocate Training (20XX) • Preparing Successful Grant Proposals (20XX)
NX Level Business Start-Up (20XX) • YMCA Board Development ROI Training (20XX) • Fundraising Workshop (20XX)

BOARD INVOLVEMENT

Vice President: Nationwide Children's Alliance, State Chapter (20XX–Present)
Board Member: Northeastern State Regional Planning Commission (20XX–Present)
Governance Board Member: One Community, One Family (20XX–Present)

TECHNOLOGY

Microsoft Word, Excel, PowerPoint, Publisher

Jane Little

City, ST • 345.678.9012 • jane.little@gmail.com • www.linkedin.com/in/jane.little

LICENSED ATTORNEY: EXPERT IN RESEARCHING AND INTERPRETING LEGISLATION / ENSURING REGULATORY COMPLIANCE
Counsel to Financial Institutions • Corporate Entities • Government Agencies • Individuals

TOP-BILLING PRACTICING ATTORNEY in firm [collecting 96% of non-contingent fees billed] with 4+ years experience managing diverse projects and teams to interpret statutes, initiate legal proceedings, facilitate case disposition, and analyze data. Advisor to clients, staff, and attorneys focusing on minimizing risk exposure by evaluating case law, statutory/regulation changes, and compliance initiatives.

KEY STRENGTHS

RESEARCH AND WRITING: Create compelling written arguments to reach favorable results.

GUIDE CREATIVE SOLUTIONS TO REGULATORY AND LEGAL QUESTIONS via law research, review, and application.

MANAGE CASE BUDGETS AND PROJECTIONS: Complete feasibility studies with financial models and program analysis.

AUDIT TO MAINTAIN COMPLIANCE: Examine legislation, policies, and programs and evaluate stakeholder impact.

MAXIMIZE DATABASE USE: Ensure that firm is on track with investment clients' goals.

WORK EXPERIENCE

ASSOCIATE ATTORNEY   20XX–Present
LAW FIRM–City, ST

Manage 50+ concurrent civil litigation, tax collection, and employment law cases for full-service firm with 5 partners, 2 associates, and support team. Analyze complex problems by interpreting diverse regulations and presenting legal analysis to clients, paralegals, and attorneys. Maximize ethics and integrity of collection practice by ensuring compliance with third party tax lien purchaser statutes.

✓ CONDUCT RESEARCH: Write FLSA (Fair Labor Standards Act) exemption guide on wage and hour law. Research and draft favorable motion for disposition of malicious prosecution claim against government officials.

✓ GUIDE COMPLIANCE INITIATIVES: Conduct research to determine 1099c compliance requirements for financial institution and RESPA (Real Estate Settlement Practice Act) compliance for mortgage servicer client. Utilize research to advise clients on avoiding penalties by encouraging compliance with ongoing legislative changes.

✓ USE SOUND JUDGMENT TO PROPEL TAX COLLECTION CASES: Maximize profits by negotiating lump sum payments or arranging realistic payment plans. Successfully liquidate 76% of ~105 tax collection cases by securing payment, negotiating a settlement, or reaching resolution in the form of foreclosure sale or judgment lien.

✓ LEAD TEAMS BY PRIORITIZING ACCOUNTABILITY AND TRUST: Guide workload of 5 paralegals to propel casework, delegate assignments, and direct timely project completion. Train/evaluate paralegals to improve skill set.

✓ ANALYZE FINANCIAL POSITION: Advise partner on profitability of tax collection practice: Develop functional financial model that incorporates historical data on time spent vs. billed/collected fees. Communicate results firm-wide by preparing summaries and projections to increase profitability without overworking cases.

✓ DEVELOP, MANAGE, AND UPDATE BUDGETS: Create budget estimates for client approval. Evaluate progress, budget feasibility, profitability, and propose improvements.

"Jane is an exceptionally intelligent and talented individual... substantial experience in dealing with a vast array of legal issues... discussing complicated issues with competence and authority..." – Justice Daniel Smith

Continued...

Jane Little, page 2   **345.678.9012**

WORK EXPERIENCE, CONTINUED...

LAW CLERK   **20XX-20XX**
SUPREME COURT OF STATE-City, ST

Reviewed 27 civil and criminal cases with Justice Daniel Smith by evaluating statutes, examining legislative history and case law, and collaborating with decision makers. Set common law precedent by preparing 15 initial drafts of later published opinions. Capitalized on extensive legal/legislative knowledge to communicate case opinions to diverse audiences.

- Collaborated with Supreme Court Justices and court employees to research multiple areas of law and formulate reasonable solutions.

INTERNSHIPS

EXTERN
U.S. DISTRICT COURT, EASTERN DISTRICT OF STATE (20XX): Assisted in drafting Social Security benefits opinion.
ENERGY AND ENVIRONMENT CABINET (20XX): Researched mine workers' noncompliance with statutory regulations.

INTERN
NATURAL RESOURCES DEFENSE COUNCIL-City, ST (20XX)

Tackled non-profit program to input and evaluate scientific project data on effects of climate change on area plants and animals. Propelled public policy initiatives in Yellowstone National Park to educate diverse groups on impact to endangered species. Advocated to maintain Rocky Mountain Gray Wolf on endangered species list.

EDUCATION

Juris Doctor (JD), State University-City, ST (20XX)
Member, **Phi Alpha Delta** Law Fraternity
Bar Admission: State (20XX)

Bachelor of Science (BS), State University-City, ST (20XX)
Summa cum laude | Member, **Golden Key** International Honour Society

COMMUNITY ACTIVITIES

PROVISIONAL MEMBER, JUNIOR LEAGUE (20XX) | **VOLUNTEER**, STATE CENTER FOR LITERACY (20XX-Present)

BOARD MEMBER, CITIZEN FOSTER CARE REVIEW BOARD (20XX-Present)
- Review and advise on foster care cases. Summarize case information to aid judge's decision-making process.

PRESENTATIONS

VOLUNTEER TEACHER, CREDIT ABUSE RESISTANCE EDUCATION (20XX)
- Presented credit education seminar to high school students on proper credit use and abuse prevention.

PRESENTER, SUPREME COURT LAW UPDATE (20XX)
- Delivered update on Supreme Court decisions to 100 individuals during day-long educational seminar.

TECHNOLOGY

LEGAL RESEARCH TOOLS: Westlaw, Casemaker, LexisNexis • MS OFFICE: Word, Excel, PowerPoint, Outlook • PCLaw

ANNA SMITH

City, ST 22222 • 234.567.8901 • asmith@university.edu

PROFESSIONAL NURSING CANDIDATE: SKILLED IN TREATING CHILDREN AND ADULTS IN DIVERSE HOSPITAL SETTINGS
Family-Centered Care • Clinical Competence • Patient Diversity • Campus and Service Industry Leader

Graduating Registered Nurse focused on applying theoretical knowledge, clinical judgment, and communication skills to care for pediatric and adult patients. Balance coursework, rotations, and leadership/volunteer roles to maximize resources, provide excellent service, and work within established systems and procedures to ensure safety and regulatory compliance. Collaborate within units to solve problems, set priorities, and develop patient care goals.

EDUCATION

BACHELOR OF SCIENCE (B.S.) NURSING | 3.2 GPA Any University (City, ST)   **Expected May 20XX**
- EXCEL IN CLINICAL JUDGMENT COURSES: evaluate case studies and apply clinical knowledge to set treatment course.
- COMPLETE COMPREHENSIVE CARE PLAN each semester: evaluate symptoms, determine appropriate treatment.

MEMBER, Bachelor of Science Organization | **ELECTED ASSISTANT VP OF ACADEMICS**, Any Alpha Pi Sorority

CLINICAL ROTATIONS

MEDICAL SURGICAL | REHABILITATION, Any Medical Center (City, ST)   **01/20XX–Present**
Collaborate with preceptor nurse and assistants to provide nursing care to 6 patients per 12-hour shift. Treat wide variety of post-surgical, rehab, and general floor patients: start IVs, dispense medications, change wound dressings, anticipate needs, document care and data in charts. Observe care coordination with nurses, doctors, and providers.

LEADERSHIP AND COMMUNITY HEALTH, Any Health Systems (City, ST)   **10/20XX–12/20XX**
Shadowed nurse manager to gain insight on hospital management and operations. Participated in Joint Commission meetings to ensure documentation compliance for accreditation. Observed downsizing and purchasing decisions.

OBSTETRICS, Any Medical Center | **MEDICAL SURGICAL,** Any Memorial Hospital | **GERIATRIC,** Any Nursing Home

PEDIATRIC EXPERIENCE

PEDIATRIC ROTATION, Any Children's Hospital (City, ST)   **10/20XX–11/20XX**
- Provided age-specific, effective, and accurate care to infant, child, and adolescent patients and their parents.
- Evaluated developmental and cultural considerations when interacting with patients and families.
- Examined patient charts and conducted independent research on diagnoses and treatment options.

VOLUNTEER, Any Children's Hospital Medical Center(City, ST)   **20XX–20XX**
- Spent summers with pediatric patients to improve their experience in activity room, patient rooms, and ICU.

WORK EXPERIENCE

SERVER, Pizzeria | Waterside Music Center (City, ST)   **20XX–Present**
- Collaborate to prioritize client service and accommodate patron needs in fast-paced, diverse service environments.

STUDENT LEADER, Smith Dining Hall (City, ST)   **20XX–20XX**
- Promoted to leadership position in 20XX to train/supervise 100 student workers in delivering top-notch service.

COMMUNITY LEADERSHIP

ORGANIZER, RACE FOR THE CURE 20XX: Inaugural event with 1,000 participants: fundraising, planning, event management.

VOLUNTEER, BIG BROTHERS BIG SISTERS: Mentor at-risk children and youth to provide structure and stability.

John M. Wells

City, ST • 555.123.4567 • john.wells@gmail.com

Expert Trainer and Advisor in Commercial and Residential Lending, Bidding, Procurement, and Analysis

Leading commercial bidder who manages 200+ monthly appraisal orders while maintaining contract quality and efficiency. Build enduring relationships with managers, credit officers, and vendors while supporting appraisal and loan procurement process. Maximize software use to enable timely loan closing. Review environmental requests and residential form reports and identify, analyze, and dissect financials of real estate transactions. Advise on bidding, appraisal, and contract regulations.

ACCOMPLISHMENT HIGHLIGHTS

Conducted lender training seminar: Directed 30 Relationship Managers to complete request forms with proper documentation. Resulted in 100% accurate completion by stressing importance of following regulations in collateral risk management.

Coordinated Kick-Off Meeting calls: Orchestrated new communication system between RMs and appraisers to expedite $1MIL+ transactions by facilitating calls, setting ground rules, and coordinating schedules, resulting in bank-wide system implementation.

Handled 31 concurrent environmental loan requests: Educated Relationship Managers on timely due diligence for estimated commercial loan amounts while expediting requests to reach 92% adherence to tight deadlines.

Spearheaded efficiency-increasing efforts: Analyzed testing of Brilyint software to transition appraisal requests from Access.

• Recognized by Relationship Managers as recipient of **9 STAR awards** (20XX–20XX) •

CAREER PATH

ABC Bank–City, ST   **20XX–20XX, 20XX–Present**

APPRAISAL REVIEW ASSOCIATE I (20XX–Present)

Execute 81 concurrent commercial appraisal transactions to procure appraisal/environmental reports, review requests, and solicit bid requests to qualified appraisers. Minimize delays by proactively tracking transactions from start to finish. Align vendor qualifications with specific transaction requirements while analyzing proposals and offering competitive quotes to customers. Maintain 100% compliance with 8-business-hour turnaround requirement.

- **Manage 163% workload increase** due to staffing decrease and volume growth while achieving "Highly Effective" 92% success rate of identifying appropriate product types and qualified vendors. Train team members and new hires on Access.
- **Improve quality of appraisals and reduce delays** by facilitating Kick-Off Meeting Calls. Create email invites, spreadsheets, and daily/monthly reports to evaluate effectiveness, resulting in widespread implementation.
- **Ensure compliance and accuracy** of 6 Residential Form Appraisal Reports monthly by reviewing net/gross/line adjustments and comparables and recommending changes to fulfill all procurement plans and regulation requirements.
- **Optimize engagement letters** to outline requirements in price, turnaround time, and compliance with bank and government regulations. Navigate policies to determine reporting needs while considering various loan amounts and transaction types.
- **Offer expertise** to Relationship Managers to decode environmental policy requests by breaking down Matrix requirements.

CUSTOMER SERVICE REPRESENTATIVE (20XX–20XX)

Utilized Jack Henry/SilverLake software to complete customer requests accurately and on time. Balanced deposits and drawers and performed daily closing of bank branch. Handled complex transactions while serving customers by following proper policies.

OTHER WORK EXPERIENCE

SALES ASSISTANT–ABC Insurance (City, ST)   **20XX–20XX**

- Called 50 clients and prospects daily to offer financial advisor and insurance provider services. Organized community dinner seminars by mailing and tracking letters, analyzing prospect funds and cash flow, and compiling product packages.

EDUCATION

ASSOCIATE DEGREE, Business Administration (minor: Management) ABC Community College–City, ST (20XX)

TECHNICAL/SOFTWARE SKILLS

Microsoft Access, Word, Excel, PowerPoint, Outlook • MAC and PC • Jack Henry/SilverLake • Brilyint • type 50wpm

EMILY BENSON

City, ST • 456.789.0123 • emilybenson@gmail.com • www.linkedin.com/in/emilybenson

Expert Writer and Driving Editorial Team Leader in Digital Publishing and Print Media Environments
Project Planning • Social Media • Research • Brand Promotion • Webcasting • Custom Content

Date

Attention Line
Organization Name
Address Line 1
Address Line 2

Dear [name],

By propelling projects in online, print, sponsored content, social media, and advertising initiatives as Editor In Chief for Company, I have successfully influenced tremendous website user, page view, and revenue growth for the global news and information leader. As an accomplished writer, editor, and journalist, this is just one example of the kind of brand promotion and editorial leadership expertise that I would strive for in the role of [Position Name] with [Company Name].

With a solid background in digital publishing, print media, custom content, and data analysis, I am well-positioned to exceed projected readership goals to support [Company Name's] strategic objectives.

Consider the following:

- Lead team of 5 in online production projects while increasing website page views 23% (from 10.4M to 12.8M).

- Earn $30K advertising revenue and $70K in sponsorships by managing Succession Initiative project and researching/publishing industry study.

- Achieve 27% increase in insurance publication online views by leading 8 writers and freelancers: create unique content, direct editorial calendar, manage budgets, and adhere to deadlines.

- Expert in analyzing data and maximizing social media use to grow brand recognition and promote growth.

I would love to advance my career with [Company Name] and I welcome the opportunity to discuss this position with you. Please review my enclosed resume and reach me at your earliest convenience. Thank you in advance for your time and consideration.

Best Regards,

Emily Benson

Enclosure: Resume

SARAH E. JONES

City, ST • 234.567.8901 • sjones@gmail.com • www.linkedin.com/in/sejones

Organizational Leader Skilled in Fundraising, Program Management, and Policy Development

Date

Attention Line
Organization Name
Address Line 1
Address Line 2

Dear [name],

With a $300K budget for start-up Children's Advocacy Center (CAC), I have successfully grown program 785% to maximize the number of families served regionally by fundraising, developing executive board, and implementing all program aspects. As an accomplished leader of non-profits and start-up community organizations, this is just one example of the kind of strategic planning and expansion expertise that I would strive for in the role of [Position Name] with [Company Name].

With a solid background in fundraising, program management, and policy development, I am well-positioned to propel community programs while managing risk and optimizing growth initiatives for [Company Name].

Consider the following:

• Raise $1.2MIL+ in foundation grants and $110K in fundraisers while leading inter-agency partnership efforts to optimize regional program effectiveness and program reach.

• Collaborate with board of directors, establish donor relationships, and ensure proper use of funds.

• Oversee $4MIL YMCA building project and manage $526K CAC building project to meet program needs while working within budget and logistical constraints.

• Expertly start-up diverse non-profit agencies and programs to address community needs by maximizing endowment gifts, reversing funding blocks, and networking with community stakeholders.

I would love to advance my career with [Company Name] and I welcome the opportunity to discuss this position with you. Please review my enclosed resume and reach me at your earliest convenience. Thank you in advance for your time and consideration.

Best Regards,

Sarah E. Jones

Enclosure: Resume

Beate Hait, CPRW, NCRW
Resumes Plus

Beate Hait, Owner
Résumés Plus
508-429-1813
www.resumesplus.net
bea@resumesplus.net

Beate (Bea) Hait has been writing resumes for individuals in all industries and from entry level to executive since 1992. Bea is skilled at highlighting qualifications and accomplishments and puts them in a format that improves the chances of the candidate being called for an interview. Writing LinkedIn profiles and targeted cover letters—either for one particular job or for the general job target that the client can then customize for various postings—are additional services provided.

Having earned the credentials CPRW (Certified Professional Resume Writer) and NCRW (Nationally Certified Resume Writer) by completing a series of tests to demonstrate excellence in resume writing, Bea is one of only a handful of resume writers nationwide—and the only one in Massachusetts—to earn both credentials. By regularly attending professional resume writers' conferences sponsored by the National Resume Writers' Association (NRWA), Bea hones her skills and keeps current with career search process changes, such as the use of applicant tracking systems.

Based in the Boston, Massachusetts area, Bea works with clients in person or virtually by email and telephone. To date, her most long-distance client resided in Mongolia, and the consultation was done using Skype. Two measures indicate the effectiveness of the resumes she writes: the large number of referrals from satisfied clients and repeat clientele when the client is ready for an update to pursue that next career step.

THOMAS L. CRENSHAW

369 Main Street
Bloomfield, NJ 07003

www.linkedin/in/thomaslcrenshaw

555-308-4867
tlcrenshaw@yahoo.com

POWER PLANT OPERATOR

▶ 16+ years of experience **operating, designing, maintaining and repairing power plant equipment** to reliably deliver steam for various plant needs. Use multi-discipline skills to assess, evaluate and recommend utility plant and distribution system modifications to enhance performance.

▶ **Demonstrate progressive mechanical, electrical, instrument and control systems skills.** Prioritize and manage multiple tasks, project needs and reporting requirements. Ensure compliance with all local, state and federal regulations. Assess situations, make critical decisions and implement activity to ensure safety of equipment and personnel.

▶ Self-motivated to work independently; equally competent as team member/leader. Adept at recognizing/launching steps needed to attain objectives. Notable troubleshooter; calm even in stressful situations. **Earned reputation as "go to guy"** to overcome obstacles with solutions that are technically sound and financially feasible.

▶ **Oversee utility power plant operations and direct 12 to 50 staff.** Supervise boiler inspections, maintenance and repairs. Identify problems, diagnose causes and orchestrate corrective actions. Perform continuous emissions monitoring (CEM) to document compliance with environmental permit conditions. Initiate corrective action to maintain acceptable level output.

CORE COMPETENCIES

Control Room Protocols	Power Plant Systems	Equipment Rotation
Documentation/Reporting	Turbine/Boiler Operations	Preventive Maintenance
Instrument Controls	Low- and High-pressure Boilers	Analog/Digital Controls
Equipment Repair/Testing	Fuel Procurement Strategies	Piping/Valve Installation
Operating Procedures	Environmental Compliance	Machine Coupling
Fire Suppression	Diagnostic Equipment	Troubleshooting
Inspections/Audits	Oil/Gas/Solid Fuel-Fired Boilers	Safety Procedures
NERC Reliability Standards	Distributed Control System (DCS)	Steam/Gas Turbines
Air Quality Compliance	Turbosorp®	Budget Management

RECENT CAREER ACCOMPLISHMENTS

• Received **favorable audits that verified operational compliance** with North American Electric Reliability Corporation (NERC) standards. Collected evidence/data; submitted web-based reports.

• **Wrote and implemented operating procedures** for installing, commissioning and operating Turbosorp® Circulating Dry Fluid Bed Scrubber that removed acid gas constituents, including SO_2, SO_3, HCl, HF, mercury, and other trace pollutants from flue gas streams, making Edison coal plant one of the most environmentally friendly, coal-fired plants in the U.S.

• Managed and trained 8 shift supervisors with staff of 36 union personnel. Capably negotiated arbitration and discipline issues. **Facilitated achievement of production goals** through cross-training of personnel and securing, coordinating and overseeing work of outside contractors.

• **Attained record of 0 injuries and 0 lost time accidents** for six consecutive years. Continually reinforce safety procedures and use of personal protective equipment (PPE).

• Created and wrote new procedures for startup and shutdown as well as boiler chemical testing that **saved budget dollars and streamlined processes.** Saved $330,000 in fuel costs by spearheading initiatives for cleaning boilers and changing operating processes. Identified and implemented procedure that recycled 30–40 gallons of cooling water/minute to boilers, which resulted in $180,000 annual savings in operating expenses. Coordinated oil to natural gas fuel conversion and conversion of steam from high to low pressure.

• Directed maintenance manager in **planning and executing outages to facilitate scheduled maintenance.** Coordinated project to safely and efficiently decommission Tom River units 4, 5 and 6.

• Led transition from hard station to computerized workstations and **automated processes** in Plant Information (PI) Systems. Assisted in customizing design of screens to address companies' needs. Used Maximo and DataStream to track work orders, budget, NERC data and budgetary items.

EMPLOYMENT

OPERATIONS MANAGER, Highline Energy, Inc. – Newark, NJ   20XX–20XX

CHIEF ENGINEER, Wildwood Generating Corporation – Ocean Shores, NJ   19XX – 20XX

WATCH ENGINEER, Liberty Corporation Northeast – Trenton, NJ   19XX – 19XX

TRAINING

Recent workshops and coursework topics include the following:

Health & Safety Respirator	DEP Regulations	Fire Safety and Suppression
Boiler Operations	OSHA Guidelines	Confined Space Operations
Turbine Operations	Water Quality Testing	Piping Schemes
Best Practices Training	Controlling Emissions	Equipment Upgrades
HAZMAT Training	Lock Out/Tag Out Procedures	Health & Safety
SCR Operation	Chemical and Water Usage	Respirator
Turbosorp® Operation	Wastewater Treatment	Qualified Individual (QI)
Microsoft Excel Basics	Continuous Emissions Monitoring	Asbestos Abatement

LICENSURE

1st Class Engineer, New Jersey License #EN 1A 123456

EDUCATION

Rutgers School of Engineering – Piscataway, NJ
First Engineer | Second Engineer | Third Engineer | Second Fireman

WILLIAM F. FITZGERALD

Current Address
61 Main Street
Columbus, OH 43215

555-876-1234
williamffitzgerald@gmail.com
www.linkedin.com/in/williamffitzgerald

Arizona Address
1817 Summer Street
Scottsdale, AZ 85251

PROJECT MANAGER: CONSTRUCTION MANAGEMENT
Scheduling | Cost Management | Subcontractor Coordination | Quality Control

- Respected leader and manager with exceptional organization and communication skills. **Specialist in all aspects of commercial, institutional and manufacturing construction** ranging from small-scale to multi-million dollar projects. Earned reputation for superb estimating and scheduling savvy, consistently hitting project milestones, bringing in profitable projects on or ahead of schedule and on or under budget, and generating customer satisfaction.

- Promote collaborative working environment conducive to improving productivity, increasing efficiency, enhancing quality and strengthening financial results. **Combine construction expertise with business operations know-how** to readily establish rapport with owners, architects, engineers and other stakeholders. Capably prioritize, schedule and manage heavy workflow. Identify problems/needs and initiate effective solutions to satisfaction of all parties. Ensure proper documentation of change orders and submission of monthly payment requisitions.

- Savvy computer skills include Timberline; On-Screen Takeoff; Prolog Manager; BIM 360; Primavera P6; Primavera Contract Manager Expedition; Microsoft Word, Excel and PowerPoint.

CORE COMPETENCIES
Commercial Construction
Project Estimating
Contract Negotiation
Stakeholder Engagement
Scheduling Coordination
Cost Containment
Change Orders
Documentation
OSHA Regulations
Project Management
Operations Oversight
Sustainability
LEED Certification
Environmental Impact
Control Systems
Air Distribution Systems
Value Engineering
BOCA Codes

EMPLOYMENT

All-Right Construction Company, Inc. – Columbus, OH   20XX–Present
PROJECT MANAGER
As main point of contact between owner and architect, orchestrate construction projects for regional construction management and general contracting company that specializes in challenging projects and earns rave reviews from clients across market sectors that include colleges and universities, healthcare, life sciences and non-profit organizations. Plan, direct and coordinate project activities to ensure that goals are accomplished within prescribed timeframes and funding parameters. Lead team meetings, develop monthly progress reports and oversee document control procedures completed by project engineer. Perform cost reporting, schedule management and project closeout.

- Champion spirit of partnering among all stakeholders in construction projects. Facilitate collaboration among contractors, owners, architects and other stakeholders, which promotes innovation, best practices and achievement of mutual goals and objectives.

- Seen as subject matter project management expert for construction projects involving academic buildings, libraries and complex additions/renovations. Through analysis, innovation and decisive action, overcome challenges to keep projects moving forward. Examples include the following:

  - Conversion of 75,000 sq. ft. library into state-of-the-art science and research facility at Ohio State University; $48 million contract — Preserved historic exterior building features and materials while performing complete interior renovation on active campus. Prepared BIM 360 model of existing structural support of stone façade and performed analysis. Led detailed scheduling summit and organized schedule and sequence of demolition, rebar installer and shotcrete subcontractors, enabling project to remain on schedule. LEED Silver Certification.

  - Adaptive reuse of 4-story library with 40,000 sq. ft. renovation and 130,000 sq. ft. addition at Indiana University Bloomington; $60 million contract — Coordinated two distinctly separate project scopes and construction methods for renovation and new addition connected at a common wall. During survey phase, analyzed four original oversized chimneys, recommending two be replaced and two restored, which saved approximately $200,000. LEED Gold Certification.

All-Right Construction Company, Inc., *continued*

- Skilled in reviewing project proposals and determining scope of work, timeframes, scheduling, cost estimating, procedures for accomplishing projects, staffing requirements and allotments of available resources for phases of projects. Participate in bid presentation and pre-construction meetings with architect and owner. Work with architect on RFI; ensure materials meet specifications.

- Successfully incorporated intricate phasing on multiple school and campus renovation projects that allowed school to remain operational during construction while meeting project timelines and budgets. Adhered to all safety and air quality guidelines.

- Improved quality and customer satisfaction through key contributions to development of program that outlined procedures to be applied to every project regarding factors including the following: monthly cost reports, quality plan, safety plan, measurement, schedule and milestones, budget and labor production report (LPR), closeout procedures, subcontractor management, weekly updates, recruit-train-mentor-motivate (RTMM) and planning.

Engineering Specialists – Reynoldsburg, OH   19XX–20XX
PROJECT SUPERINTENDENT, PROJECT ENGINEER
Oversaw projects for company that provides engineering, procurement, construction, maintenance and project management to clients in diverse global industries such as chemicals and petrochemicals, commercial and institutional (C&I), life sciences, manufacturing, power, renewable energy and telecommunications. Delivered capital projects safely, on schedule, within budget, and with the quality expected by clients.

- Took leadership role in the field on construction projects for clean room, test labs and manufacturing facility (e.g., Ohio Biologicals, Inc. in Cincinnati – Phase 1 production facility featuring testing labs and cold storage).

- Oversaw 235 workers on $380 million, 680,000 SF new Class 1 Clean Room construction project in Bloomington, IN and related $80 million Ellettsville Project.

AWARDS

Marvin M. Black Excellence in Partnering Award, Associated General Contractors of America (AGC)
Grove City High School, Grove City, OH, new construction, 20XX
Lewis Recreation Center, Westerville, OH, renovation, 20XX

LICENSE / CERTIFICATION

Ohio Construction Supervisor License
OSHA 30-Hour Training Certification

EDUCATION

Business Management, ITT Technical Institute – Cincinnati, OH
Construction Management, Ivy Tech Community College – Richmond, OH

JESSICA MORTON

328 Major Avenue
Nashua, NH 03060   www.linkedin.com/in/jessicamorton   555-923-4567
jmorton@gmail.com

ENTRY-LEVEL LIBRARIAN
Resource Management | Customer Service | Project Management

▶ Dedicated employee embarking on career change that melds 16+ years of experience in facilitating projects, providing training, managing inventory and delivering exceptional customer service with passion for libraries, managing collections and maintaining positive patron and community relations.

▶ Pro-actively communicate with team members and leadership. Earned reputation for collaborative project management and solution development. Provide feedback to ensure quality and compliance with standards. Determine schedules and resources to meet goals and deadlines.

▶ Computer proficiency includes MS Word, Excel, PowerPoint; Microsoft Project; SharePoint, VMware. Conversant in Spanish.

Core Competencies
Program Management
Policy/Process Development
Budget Management
Presentations
Customer Relations
Inventory Management
Best Practices/SOPs
Team Building/Leadership
Technical Services
Information Systems
Data Entry/Reporting

EDUCATION

Master of Library and Information Science, University of Southern New Hampshire – Manchester, NH
Bachelor of Science, Computer Science and Mathematics, University of New Hampshire – Durham, NH

EXPERIENCE

Computer Systems Corporation – Concord, NH   19XX–Present

SOFTWARE INTEGRATION AND LAB COORDINATOR (20XX–Present)
SOFTWARE TASK MANAGER, OPERATIONS & MAINTENANCE (19XX–20XX)

Results-driven project manager with solid experience leading diverse teams, developing schedules and tracking resources to fulfill government contracts for software development. Design workflow planning/prioritization strategies that result in improved productivity, efficiency, inventory control and cost savings. Supervise up to 5 technicians in software testing lab and support up to 200 employees delivering secure communication projects. Attend meetings to gather information regarding project scope, equipment requirements and deadlines. Top Secret Security Clearance.

▶ Spearheaded budget savings and efficiency improvements by taking initiative to assume role of cross-functional group facilitator. Advised project teams regarding opportunities to share equipment and other resources, thus saving budget dollars.

▶ Improved productivity and efficiencies by influencing collaboration between systems and software departments working on similar projects.

▶ Assigned to new role, turned around poor audit outcomes and achieved consistent passing grades by conducting physical inventory to account for each piece of government-owned equipment.

▶ Customized trainings and informative presentations of high-level technical material based on makeup of target audience.

▶ Recipient of President's Award in recognition and appreciation of above-and-beyond performance.

Interest in reading, research and helping others led to volunteering in public libraries while attending high school and college.

A life-long passion for library services coupled with a graduate degree in library and information science supports the current career transition.

REBECCA SILVER

842 Main Avenue
Naperville, IL 60540   www.linkedin.com/in/rebeccasilver_operations   rebeccasilver@gmail.com   555-956-1453

OPERATIONS EXECUTIVE

*Make decisions based on analysis, judgment and the sincere desire to do what is
right for the company and its associates and customers.*

- Possess superior knowledge of organizational management initiatives that drive efficiencies, maximize financial benefits, slash budget costs, and contribute to strong and sustainable financial growth.

- Create and execute operational roadmap/strategies and establish framework, infrastructure and processes to support those strategies. Communicate vision and launch steps to attain goals. Work collaboratively and effectively with all levels of management and staff.

- Exceptional interpersonal and communication skills (network, collaborate, negotiate); readily establish rapport with wide range of people of various cultures and all professional levels. Build positive, effective business relationships with vendors and team members. Respected team leader with record of inspiring high morale and productivity.

- Proficient in use of computer technology such as Microsoft Word, Excel, PowerPoint, Access; Item Data Warehouse (IDW) and Computer Assisted Ordering (CAO).

CORE COMPETENCIES

Strategic Business Planning
Leadership
P&L Oversight
Business Finances
Systems Optimization
Communications/IT
Market Analysis
Project Management
Cost Controls/Budgeting
Contract Negotiations
Outsourced Services
Facilities Management
Construction/Remodel
Policy/Procedure Development
Human Resources
Team Building

BUSINESS OPERATIONS EXPERIENCE

Whole Foods Market – Naperville, IL   20XX–Present
STORE MANAGER
- Drive sales and gross profit, manage shrink control programs and oversee 170 staff development in 51,282-sq. ft. store, one of Chicago area's highest volume prototype locations.
  - Grew sales 6.3% in Deli, 3.8% in Meat Market and 12.2% in Produce departments in first year while controlling product losses to budgeted targets.
  - Spearheaded strategies that generated above-company averages in customer satisfaction metrics in categories of associate friendliness and overall store cleanliness.

Giant Food Stores – Hagerstown, MD   19XX – 20XX
MANAGER OF STORE SERVICES, Hagerstown, MD (20XX–20XX)
DISTRICT MANAGER, STORE OPERATIONS, Lancaster, PA (20XX–20XX)
STORE MANAGER, SUPERSTORE STARTUP, Harrisburg, PA (19XX–20XX)
RECRUITING COORDINATOR, SUPERSTORE EXPANSIONS, Carlisle, PA (19XX–19XX)

Through decisive and visionary leadership and mentorship in strategic planning, operations, communications and human resources, drove sales and profits for largest growing food retailer in Maryland and Pennsylvania. Earned reputation as go-to person to develop business teams that drive company programs, manage crisis situations and deliver results for corporate initiatives.

BUSINESS OPERATIONS LEADERSHIP / FACILITY MANAGEMENT
- Took initiative to attend WIC meetings to plan rollout of new USDA food package. Stores were prepared, associates were trained and WIC sales surpassed $100 million.
- Directed sales, inventory control and HR activities during corporate-leveraged buyout and two acquisitions that resulted in launch of successful new 13-store district. Expanded 5 stores, managed 7 new stores and fully staffed stores with 2150 employees in less than 8 weeks.
- Took 15 stores from construction through inventory stocking and staffing; managed $3.1 million budget per store. Within two years in multiple districts, increased annual sales to $208+ million and profits from $6 million to $14 million; grew sales 117% and propelled profits up 355%.

Giant Food Stores, continued

BUSINESS OPERATIONS LEADERSHIP / FACILITY MANAGEMENT, continued
- Masterminded realignment of metropolitan 95-store division that improved management efficiencies and cut overhead cost increases without changing existing infrastructure.
- Directed operations and $45 million expense budget for district with $305+ million annual sales. Grew division from 58 to 95 stores within 7 years and managed three districts, doubling square footage through extensive remodeling/expansion.

CORPORATE SOCIAL RESPONSIBILITY (CSR)
- Forged re-engineering of cardboard and plastic recycling program company-wide, which optimized sustainability goals. Negotiated with vendors and rolled out program that netted $3 million incremental income in one year.

CORPORATE COMMUNICATIONS/eCOMMERCE
- Collaborated with IT and directed creative and technical ideation for gatekeeper communication/ email protocols for 8000 corporate and store users. Quadrupled sales in business niche within 18 months while driving toward profitability.
- Revamped management and administration of state and federal licensing acquisition, renewal and tracking procedures. Consolidated oversight into central hub to keep 4600 licenses up-to-date and provided a single departmental point-of-contact, improving accountability and compliance.

HUMAN RESOURCES
- Pioneered buyout plan for long-term associates that freed positions for fresh talent, slashing $3 million in wages while leveraging down costs in a single department. Devised innovative labor package and HRIS that correlated employee utilization with sales.
- Managed 1700 employees and 58 senior managers for 16-store division. Resolved labor disputes and negotiated wages/conditions with union of 4000. Determined staffing for 28 stores in 4 districts; administered all HR, training, development and hiring functions.

STORE MANAGEMENT
- Orchestrated opening of 58,000-sq. ft. superstore in Harrisburg, PA, which became one of three most profitable stores in region. Earned numerous "Top 10 Profitability" awards.

EDUCATION / CONTINUING EDUCATION

Dale Carnegie Training: Design Toward Public Speaking

Master of Science, Business Management, Northwestern University – Evanston, IL

Bachelor of Science, Management, Loyola University – Chicago, IL

MICHAEL WHITSTONE

555-874-4523　mwhitstone@yahoo.com

43 River Road, Wethersfield, CT 06109　　www.linked.com/in/michaelwhitstone

ACCOUNTING MANAGER

- ► Respected, hands-on accounting professional with 18+ years of experience. Streamline operations to expedite the flow of information, enabling senior management to make informed decisions. Clearly communicate results of work orally and in writing. Possess clear understanding of GAAP.

- ► Meticulously manage daily accounting functions and meet deadlines. Competently analyze, compare and interpret facts and figures; make sound judgments based on this knowledge.

- ► Demonstrate high standard of quality, integrity, exemplary attention to detail and precise record keeping in compliance with corporate policies and procedures. Capable team member or team leader; equally effective working independently.

- ► Technical skills include Microsoft Excel and Word; CPSI integrated software; Kronos; ADP; Paycom; Patcom Billing System; Lawson Software; Peachtree; PeopleSoft.

CORE COMPETENCIES
General Ledger
Journal Entries
Bank Reconciliation
Cash Management
Financial Forecasts/Budgets
Online Accounting Systems
Monthly Financial Statements
Month-end Financial Close
Analytical/Statistical Reports
Wire/ACH Transactions
Accounts Receivable/Payable
Internal/External Audits
Automated Processes
Web-based Payroll Processing
State and Federal Regulations

EMPLOYMENT

Sonic Hospital Partners – Hartford, CT　　20XX–Present
SENIOR ACCOUNTANT
Perform accounting functions for healthcare facility with 3 inpatient and 3 outpatient sites generating $65 million gross revenue annually. On three separate occasions following purchase of company by new entity, selected as key member of accounting team to transition financial data to new systems and set up rules per policies and procedures. Train staff on CPSI integrated software. Prepare audit schedules for external auditors. Collaborate with HR and brokers to audit employee-related benefit programs, e.g., medical and dental, life insurance, vision and flexible spending plan.

- ► Meticulously maintain integrity of general ledger, including chart of accounts. Perform daily online review of deposit transactions to ensure accurate allocation (i.e., Medicare and remote deposits). Perform bank reconciliations for three accounts: operating, payroll and deposit. Interact with Conn. Rehabilitation Council regarding grants up to $750K; track grant revenues and expenditures.

- ► Initiated data collection and reporting procedures that slashed 4 hours from 5-day close process. Created schedule of data collection from cross-functional departments that resulted in expediting the audit process. Analyze monthly balance sheet accounts to prepare corporate reporting.

- ► Recouped $85,000 from electricity provider and $60,000 from gas utility after noticing a spike in usage and initiating an investigation that identified erroneous double billing and broken meter, respectively.

- ► Achieved <60 days outstanding for monthly $16K to $20K AR collections (i.e., physician leases, trainer contracts, etc.) by creating Excel spreadsheet to track status and being proactive with follow-up.

Master Developers, Inc. – Cheshire, CT　　20XX–20XX
MANAGER OF GENERAL ACCOUNTING
Compiled financial reports pertaining to cash receipts, expenditures and P&L for commercial and residential real estate development company with 15 entities. Prepared budgets; analyzed monthly variances; coordinated audits and audit workpapers. Hired, supervised and trained 3-person staff.

Waste Management Company – Portland, CT　　20XX–20XX
DISTRICT ACCOUNTING MANAGER
Facilitated monthly close procedures, created daily and weekly cash reports, reconciled discrepancies, prepared multistate sales and fuel-user tax returns, and oversaw collections for waste management company. Spearheaded shared-drive process that reduced audit review time.

EDUCATION

Bachelor of Science, Accounting, Roger Williams University – Bristol, RI

JENNIFER CHAMBERLAIN
68 Park Drive | Brockton, MA 02302 | 555-234-0752
jenchamb@comcast.net | www. linkedin.com/in/jenniferchamberlain

DATE

CONTACT
COMPANY
ADDRESS
CITY, STATE ZIP

Re: JOB POSTING TITLE AND/OR ID NUMBER

Dear CONTACT:

Building corporate value and delivering sustained revenue growth is my expertise. Whether challenged to launch the startup of a new business, orchestrate the successful turnaround of an underperforming company, or accelerate growth within an established corporation, I consistently delivered strong and sustainable results. Isn't that the type of individual you seek to fill your advertised position of POSITION?

As you review the attached resume, you will get an overview of achievements that are indicative of the quality, caliber and strength of my career. Let me share some specific achievements and how they relate to the requirements you established for this position.

Your Requirements	My Background
➢ Minimum ten years management experience in retail environment	✓ Possess combined 15+ years management experience in startup and established retail/hospitality organizations.
➢ Ensure sales team has proper support to achieve expected results	✓ I mentored the team to embrace corporate policies and procedures when making sales presentations as a way to strengthen the company's brand image. Subsequently, the store ranked as the 4th highest in sales of 250 stores nationwide.
➢ Ensure positive customer experience	✓ I spearheaded a revamp of customer service training. A recent survey indicated our customer base had a high percentage of repeat clientele, which is an indicator of satisfied customers receiving first-class service.

If my approach to business and my track record appeals to you, I am confident that given the opportunity I would soon be considered a valued addition to COMPANY's management team. I will follow up with your office next week to answer any preliminary questions you may have. Naturally, if you wish to contact me before then, I can be reached at 555-234-0752. Thank you for your attention and professional consideration; I look forward to our conversation.

Sincerely,

Jennifer Chamberlain

Attachment: resume

WILLIAM F. FITZGERALD

Current Address	555-876-1234	Arizona Address
61 Main Street	williamffitzgerald@gmail.com	1817 Summer Street
Columbus, OH 43215	www.linkedin.com/in/williamffitzgerald	Scottsdale, AZ 85251

DATE

CONTACT
COMPANY
ADDRESS
CITY, STATE ZIP

Re: POSTING ID NUMBER AND/OR JOB TITLE

Dear CONTACT:

Through a commitment to a high standard of results-oriented leadership and a keen aptitude for project estimating and scheduling that leads to customer satisfaction in the construction industry, I successfully contributed to the productivity, profitability and stellar reputation of each of my employers. With an imminent relocation to Scottsdale, I express interest in your advertised position of POSITION.

As you review the attached resume, I am confident you will determine that my qualifications match those established by you for this position. I take pride in orchestrating a construction project so project goals are accomplished within prescribed schedules and job cost parameters. By fostering a spirit of partnership among project leaders (e.g., owner, architect, supervisors, engineers) and spearheading regular communication of issues, events and progress of job site activities, steps can be taken to facilitate the most cost-effective solutions to problems that arise. Let me share what Dave Powers, my supervisor at All-Right Construction, reported about my project management performance:

> One of Bill's most recognized qualities is his ability to organize project teams according to their strengths, and how they can best benefit the owner. Another of his core strengths is his ability to maintain high levels of client involvement throughout the project. Beyond daily communication, Bill identifies ways to convey scheduling and cost data in a variety of formats.

> Bill shows real passion for what he is doing and gets along with all his fellow team members, including the client team. He is very trustworthy and dependable, and demonstrates a strong work ethic. Bill is able to completely schedule out a project and does a better job than most with regard to job cost reporting, billing and payable procedures. He always knows where he stands cost-wise and how to use the PM tools to his advantage.

> Bill always has a strong grasp of where he stands financially. He has thorough knowledge of contract language and, when entering a negotiation, he knows his end-game goal and keeps an open mind in search of a fair agreement.

In anticipation that you will have questions for me, I invite you to call 555-876-1234 to schedule a time for us to talk. Until then, thank you for your attention and professional consideration. I look forward to our conversation.

Sincerely,

William F. Fitzgerald

Attachments: resume, project list addendum

Michelle Robin, NCRW, CPRW
Brand Your Career

Michelle Robin, NCRW, CPRW
Chief Career Brand Officer, Brand Your Career
www.brandyourcareer.com
info@brandyoucareer.com
773-531-3457
www.linkedin.com/in/michellerobin
twitter.com/brandyourcareer

Does this sound like you?

√ Marketing or sales is in your DNA and you're currently at a director-level or higher role.

√ You realize you're too close to your career to look at it objectively.

√ You're a superstar when it comes to selling or promoting your company's products, but don't feel comfortable promoting yourself.

If you're ready to take charge and be the CEO of You, Inc., then Michelle Robin is your executive career consultant.

Passionate about direct marketing and helping people find jobs, Michelle has translated her extensive B-to-B marketing background into a career focused on her true love: creating powerful career marketing campaigns that lead to interviews at her clients' target organizations. As Chief Career Brand Officer at Brand Your Career, she primarily works with executive-level sales and marketing professionals across the U.S., and helps them discover their personal brand and fast track their job search.

Michelle was a recipient of the first-ever ROAR (Recognizing Outstanding Achievement in Résumés) award and is a dual-certified resume writer (NCRW and CPRW).

After working with Michelle you'll:

√ Get your phone to ring with calls from your ideal employer.

√ Increase your LinkedIn profile views.

√ Shorten your job search by a minimum of 3 weeks.

√ Have a strong career portfolio with a bulletproof search strategy.

√ Feel you can command the salary you deserve.

AMY GOLDBERG

773-531-3457 | amygoldberg@gmail.com | Chicago, IL 60615 | **Linked in**.

Corporate Finance Executive | Senior Finance Management Professional

Dynamic and resourceful problem solver who mitigates risk and addresses opportunities for profitable growth

> *"Amy is a fantastic team player and regularly shows team leader qualities wanting to ensure constant support to the business is maintained not only from her FP&S side, but also from the product control side."* – Nancy Smith, **managed Amy at Kawasaki**

> **Strategic about cost-savings:** Eliminated, averted or saved $3M+ during tenure at Kawasaki.

> **Adaptable to fast-paced changing environments:** Partnered with cross-functional team to create financial model to calculate weekly one-year cash liquidity position during financial crisis at Lehman Brothers.

> **Extensive finance and management skills:** Eliminated key man risk in department by creating cross coverage task list and initiating cross training of staff, allowing continuous workflow during absences.

> **Analytical approach to achieve results:** Led development of database to consolidate disparate data sources so bankers could have accurate real-time picture of expenses, saving time and money.

> **Global perspective:** Established the Asia Capital MIS and analytics platform while in Tokyo, Japan at Lehman Brothers, and reported P&L on international deals at Kawasaki.

PROFESSIONAL EXPERIENCE

KAWASAKI HOLDING AMERICA, INC., New York, NY and Chicago, IL   Jan. 20xx–Jul. 20xx
SENIOR FINANCE MANAGER, Americas Investment Banking Division

Scope: Led budget and forecasting process for $200M+ operating budget with 200+ bankers. Prepared data and developed presentations for senior management on business performance. Tracked international P&L, supporting bankers and partnered with CAOs and HR leads on strategy and 3-year plans. Managed offshore support team.

Drove down costs across the business

- Negotiated $400K annual savings by changing allocations methodology from head-count to time-spent driver.

- Saved $1.4M by eliminating a $900K SIPC insurance fee and recovering $500K in legal fees.

- Averted $2M compensation risk by reclassifying key hires in compensation budget from new initiative to baseline.

- Increased accuracy in vendor payments and expense recoveries from external clients after becoming sole resource for bankers, regional branches and vendors to funnel inquiries.

- Reached targeted spend and met year-end targets by centralizing month-end close.

Established efficiencies and enhanced accuracy in tracking revenue

- Developed new financial model to align budget vs. actuals and provide senior management an accurate view to evaluate profitability.

- Pioneered product profitability financial model to achieve accurate pre-tax income for primary product groups.

- Streamlined monthly executive management presentations by templating reports for banking and capital markets.

Monitored controls and identified deficiencies to improve compliance

- Reached 100% compliance in monthly sign-offs and improved red amber green (RAG) ratings 100% by implementing series of controls to comply with SOX.

Strengthened team performance and operational reporting

- Designed and implemented cross coverage task list to ensure continuous workflow during key staff absences.

- Enhanced analytics of confidential data for CAO by creating HR metrics tools to track 200+ organizations by function, title, and group.

Continued

AMY GOLDBERG   773-531-3457 | amygoldberg@gmail.com | www.linkedin.com/in/agoldberg | Page 2 of 2

CLAYTON CAPITAL, New York, NY   Sep. 20xx–Dec. 20xx

INFORMATION TECHNOLOGY COO TEAM, Equities IT Division (Nov. 20xx– Dec. 20xx)

GLOBAL REAL ESTATE CONTROLLER, Corporate Real Estate, Finance (May 20xx–Oct. 20xx)

Scope: First team member on-boarded post Lester acquisition. Supported a 1,300+ global organization with $130M budget—emphasis on project costing. Managed all non-trading real estate and capital assets.

Developed tracking systems and reporting platforms to gain more efficiencies and insights

- Created first global tracking system for vendors to synthesize all assets and provide visibility to both legacy Lester contracts and Clayton.

- Unified previous disparate and regionalized view of £71M global budget by developing first global financial reporting platform for Corporate Real Estate Services (CRES).

Set stage for timely decision-making by improving reports

- Implemented efficiencies to release monthly business report 9 days earlier to month-end.

- Ensured smooth Clayton-Lester year-end transition by closing several legacy Clayton capital projects (asset value £31M+) within first 3 months of tenure.

LESTER AND SONS, New York, NY   May 20xx–Sep. 20xx

GLOBAL LONG-TERM LIQUIDITY MANAGER, New York (May 20xx–Sep. 20xx)

CAPITAL PLANNING | FIXED INCOME BUSINESS DECISION SUPPORT, Tokyo, Japan (May 20xx–May 20xx)

Scope: Initially hired at associate-level and promoted to assistant vice-president in just under 2 years. Oversaw India business outsourcing project. Communicated across functions up to C-level and externally to SEC. Managed 3 staff.

- Analyzed long-term uses and sources of funding by running model to calculate weekly one-year cash liquidity position (~$7B at Q2 20xx).

- Eliminated $416K in interest charges by identifying opportunity to reduce cash flow $131M from duplicated FIN46 gross ups.

EARLY CAREER

Gained insights into effective financial analysis & strategic planning, accounting, and reporting methods while working in dynamic financial roles at **University of Illinois, Outrage Games, and Sexton Financial Services.** Participated in the Japan Market Entry Competition (JMEC), known as the "Mini-MBA", where teams developed business plans for companies or products entering the Japanese market.

EDUCATION & PROFESSIONAL DEVELOPMENT

University of Michigan, Ann Arbor, MI – B.A. (Honors), International Studies and Spanish

McGill University, Tokyo, Japan – M.B.A. courses in Management Accounting, Statistics, and Marketing completed.

Professional Development: Know Your Client /Anti-Money Laundering Training; Internal Controls Training; Project Management Workshop; Communication Up, Down, and Across; Foundations of Supervision

SKILLS & AFFILIATIONS

SKILLS: Microsoft Office Suite (Excel, Word, PowerPoint, Outlook, Access); SAP; PeopleSoft Financials; Hyperion Essbase; Oracle Financial Analyzer; Business Objects; Conversational Spanish and Japanese.

AFFILIATIONS: Chicago Women in Finance; Professional Women's Club of Chicago (PWCC); Women in Insurance and Financial Services

Steve**Tripp**

stevetripp@gmail.com • Chicago, IL 60654
773-531-3457 • www.linkedin.com/in/stevetripp

CHANGE MANAGEMENT CONSULTANT

Connects with people quickly and understands technology to make large-scale change run smoothly

SUCCESS STRATEGIES FOR CHANGE MANAGEMENT

Resonate with all levels through clear communications: Boosted sales 200% by ensuring staff from C-level to individual contributor understood, approved, and executed recommended changes to new database product.

Develop employees to get results: Increased cost savings equivalent to $1M+ per year by training sales team on new RFP process to decrease lost opportunities.

Comprehend data to ease technology change: Helped client gain $4.7M in revenue by guiding implementation of new technology to change from mass marketing programs to customer-centric personalized communications.

Discover an organization's true needs: Synthesized large arrays of data to develop a solid strategy around merger of 4 internal offices with 4 distinct disciplines.

Transform business strategy to growth opportunities: Developed go-to-market strategy for business to break into retail industry, and implemented new sales methodology to move from product-focused to solution-focused company.

CERTIFICATIONS

PROSCI Change Management Methodology (ADKAR) • Palladium Kaplan-Norton Balanced Scorecard • Denison Culture Model

CHANGE MANAGEMENT EXPERIENCE

BUSINESS SOLUTIONS ARCHITECT, RETAIL PRACTICE • XEROX CORPORATION, Evanston, IL   20xx–20xx

Change Management Snapshot

Introduced new sales platform, Salesforce.com, to account team, leading to 20% increase in productivity and 13% higher close rates. Added initial $250K new revenue stream by re-launching organization into retail vertical with a new go-to-market strategy and rebranding initiative.

Scope: Provided industry analysis, insights, and positioning for product development team and served as thought leader and subject matter expert for retail arm of business.

Selected Achievements

> Gained 65% increase in new sales by implementing Solution Selling methodology and changing account reps' mindset to think about selling multiple products with services instead of only single products.

> Consulted on multimillion-dollar deal with Walmart—largest sale in 2013—to help migrate their e-commerce site to be more real-time, customer-centric, and global.

MARKETING DIRECTOR • LEO BURNETT, Chicago, IL   20xx–20xx

Change Management Snapshot

Helped Groupon gain $4.7M in revenue by guiding team through implementing new technology that allowed them to move from mass communications to customer-centric personalized marketing. Spearheaded large-scale merger of 4 internal offices as well as 4 disciplines to create a new loyalty and analytics entity of Leo Burnett network.

Scope: Managed teams up to 10 and directed strategy for new business development, agency positioning and product development for database marketing, analytics, and digital solutions areas of the agency.

Selected Achievements

> Grew Groupon account revenue more than 100% within first 6 months of relationship.

> Increased revenue more than 4% when industry average was down 10%.

> Played key role in landing multiple new business opportunities, including Sprint, Valspar, University of Chicago Hospitals, CVS, and Groupon.

STRATEGIC CONSULTANT • TRANSUNION, Chicago, IL   20xx–20xx

Change Management Snapshot

Guided major RFP change, moving business from multi-step constrained process to more streamlined process, equating to more than $1M annual savings in costs and lost opportunities. Conducted needs analysis and design of existing sales process and made improvements for a leaner, measurable enterprise sales process adopted by entire organization.

Scope: Quickly became most requested consultant to accompany account managers on sales calls because of superior ability to listen to clients, interface easily with C-level and IT, diagnose problems that needed to be solved, and present best solution to fit clients' needs.

Selected Achievements

➢ Won 8 accounts, including Vera Bradley and Service Master, with total contract value of $15M+, lifting win percentage 200% over previous year.

➢ Gained 200% sales increase for database solutions by recommending changes to data model, features, and reporting capabilities of flagship product.

DIRECTOR, CUSTOMER INTELLIGENCE GROUP • OGILVY & MATHER, Chicago, IL   20xx–20xx

Change Management Snapshot

Created business case for organization to change to outsourcing model for database marketing products and led migration, leading to $500K+ cost savings and higher quality solutions. Managed client migration of complex marketing automation tool on budget and within 3 months, including introducing never before used technology.

Scope: Headed agency's database practice. Directed project teams of 2-4 to design, develop, and implement marketing database and web-based marketing solutions. Selected to serve as member of agency's millennial segment practice.

Selected Achievements

➢ Lifted annual revenue $21M with 3% increase in average check and 7:1 ROI by leading strategy and execution of first-ever kid's club loyalty program for McDonald's.

➢ Championed complete CRM overhaul with new segmentation strategy, new metrics, and standardized data strategy and processes for Allegra Pharmaceuticals.

EARLY CAREER

Recognized thought leader and top "up and coming" consultant in database, data warehousing and data quality industry. As third employee of DeCosmo Consulting Group, grew firm 400% in 3 years leading to acquisition by Fair-Isaac.

EDUCATION

HARVARD BUSINESS SCHOOL, Harvard Executive Education—Managing an Interactive Future, Boston, MA

DEPAUL UNIVERSITY, Computer Career Program, Chicago, IL

NORTHERN ILLINOIS UNIVERSITY, Bachelor of Science in Economics, DeKalb, IL

OF NOTE

GUEST LECTURER – Topic: CRM and Database Marketing at Direct Marketing Days, Chicago Association of Direct Marketing, Northern Illinois University, DePaul University, and Loyola University Chicago MBA program.

ADDITIONAL TRAINING – Think, Inc. Strategic Negotiation Training (20xx); Holden Sales Method (20xx); Make Your Point Communication (20xx); Creative Business Idea (20xx).

RICK WATERS

Senior Executive • Business Development • Marketing • Operations • Finance

773.531.3457 • rickwaters@gmail.com • Northbrook, IL 60062 • www.linkedin.com/in/rickwaters

Intuitive leader who doubles growth and cuts costs up to 40% for organizations.

Leads 25% increase in conversion rates with innovative marketing techniques.

Streamlines processes to save 50%+ efficiencies.

- **Revenue Growth Accelerator**: Grew large financial services account 1,200% over 6 years.
- **Trusted Advisor**: As employee #4 of now 130-person firm, often sought out by founders to be "sounding board" for new ideas and "final eyes" on critical presentations.
- **Marketing Innovator**: Implemented first online multivariate testing and introduced new down-sell program.
- **Process Improver**: Eradicated duplicative technology and vendors in several areas to lower overall expenses ~20% and streamline workflow.

PROFESSIONAL EXPERIENCE

DATA POINTS ONLINE, Elgin, IL   20xx–Present

Leading digital marketing agency helping Fortune 500 brands earn more customers via multi-channel marketing programs.

Vice President Corporate Development & Corporate Secretary pro tem (20xx–Present)

$12M+ Revenue • $1.2M Operation Budget • 5 Direct Reports

Scope: Handle multiple corporate-level functions—legal, facilities, acquisition planning, and investor relations—to ensure business runs smoothly and efficiently. Head retail industry accounts.

Sales Performance

- Doubled retail business ($6M to $12M) in 3.5 years, equating to ~20% of overall business.

Operations / Facilities

- Reduced time and effort >50% on processes for extracting data from client invoicing systems.
- Negotiated multiple leases for facilities both local and remote and oversaw office renovations to accommodate employee growth, postponing a potential move for 5 years.

Cost Savings

- Cut general and administration expenses ~30% by improving travel expense tracking and identifying additional savings opportunities.
- Saved ~$20K/year by switching to new conference call and online meeting vendor.

Vice President Enterprise Operations (20xx–20xx) | **Vice President Client Services** (20xx–20xx)

Scope: Initially recruited by founder to manage large financial services client so company could expand into additional vertical markets. Assessed operations to create efficiencies and prepare for new hire to manage.

Sales Performance

- Grew top-line revenues by nearly 1,200% ($3.9M to $50M) over 6 years by implementing innovative marketing programs that generated >1.5M new customers for clients.
- Exceeded new customer unit, revenue, and contribution target nearly 30%.

Marketing

- Increased conversion rates 25% by introducing programs to align prospects with appropriate product.

Operations

- Lowered legal expenses 50% by consolidating services.

Client Snapshot: Anthem; American Express; Citibank; Charter; Commodity Cable; ITT; Total Cable

RICK WATERS   773.531.3457 • rickwaters@gmail.com • Page 2 of 2

METRIC MARKETING GROUP (Formerly The Hancock Group), Schaumburg, IL   19xx–20xx
Second-largest provider of roadside assistance in the country. Also offers membership-based consumer affinity programs.

Assistant Vice President Business Development (20xx)

Scope: Secured content and distribution partners for new Internet start-up division. Assessed M&A opportunities. Directed efforts to develop distribution strategies for B2B2C and B2B2E.

Marketing

- Lowered costs by reducing reliance on call centers by collaborating to develop first auto club website to move application process online.

Assistant Vice President Sales & Account Management (19xx–19xx)

Scope: Originally recruited from vendor relationship to expand oil industry presence. Managed $80M P&L. Supervised teams across business development, client relationship management, and marketing. Exceeded or met client profitability margins, budgeted revenue, and contribution targets.

Sales Performance

- Secured 6 new oil industry clients, 150% increase, bringing total share of oil industry market up to 80%.
- Increased marketing database access 312% over 4 years, providing clients bigger prospect universe.
- Expanded quantity of product and services under contract 650%, enabling business development goals to be achieved or surpassed.

Client Snapshot: AAA Oil; Bright Petroleum; Energy Fuel; Speedway; Texan Petroleum

VAULTCARD SERVICES, INC. Cheyenne, WY & Jacksonville, FL   19xx–19xx
Formerly publically held credit card insurer. 13M customers, $158M revenue and $22M in earnings in 19xx.

Director of Sales & Client Management

Scope: Managed account management, marketing, and operations team generating $60M+ revenue. Served on executive team that re-negotiated strategic multi-year $244M contract for company's largest client.

Innovation

- Surpassed response expectations by developing and producing new interactive sweepstakes program.

Client Snapshot: Experian, JC Penny

BOARD INVOLVEMENT

Business Marketing Association (BMA), Chicago, IL

- Board of Directors (20xx–20xx) – Collaborated on plan to reposition association for new growth. Led membership renewal program.
- Instructor for BMA Basic Course (20xx–Present); Speaker at Integrated Marketing Expo (20xx); Speaker at Marketing Days Conference (20xx)

EDUCATION

University of Iowa, Iowa City, IA

- Master of Business Administration in Finance and emphasis in Business Strategy
- Bachelor of Science in Business and Marketing

Professional Development

- GE Training – Greenbelt Quality – DMAIC, DMADV; Mergers & Acquisitions, Negotiating to Win; Strategic Communication, Executive Presentation, Managing Conflict

Patty Bain, M.A.

773-531-3457 ◆ pbain11@gmail.com ◆ Chicago, IL ◆ **Linked in**.

◆ Learning & Talent Management Professional ◆

Inspiring high-level change and impact in organizational culture by creating
out-of-the-box engaging and sustainable employee development programs.

Why you need Patty Bain on your training development team...

☑ EXPERIENCED COACH AND TRAINER skilled at understanding and assessing both individual's and organizations' strengths, challenges, and motivating them towards development.

☑ ENERGETIC PROBLEM SOLVER who isn't afraid to ask "why?" in order to discover the best solution.

☑ EFFECTIVE COMMUNICATOR AND RELATIONSHIP BUILDER adept at partnering cross-functionally with staff of all levels to achieve goals in human capital initiatives.

PROFESSIONAL EXPERIENCE

PATTY BAIN CONSULTING, Santa Monica, CA   20xx-Present

Training and Talent Development Consultant

ONBOARDING | TRAINING DESIGN | LEADERSHIP DEVELOPMENT | CURRICULUM DEVELOPMENT | TEAM BUILDING | CAREER MAPPING

Coach leaders on implementing new-hire onboarding training and team-building workshops to increase employee engagement and retention. Use MBTI and DISC assessments to guide individuals on career progression.

Challenge: ⟩ Provide talent development services to 30+ clients — start-ups, small businesses and individuals.

› Developing online documentation and 2-day job aid to facilitate new hire training and increase productivity.

› Coached client to pursue her passion to find a career path she loves by guiding her to pitch a project for her current employer, who accepted, and gain confidence to launch her business.

› Assessed talent of two clients, brothers, and recommended how tasks could be divided among them to launch new side business more efficiently.

CALIFORNIA WATER WORKS, Anaheim, CA   20xx-20xx

Leadership Development High Program Manager (20xx)

VENDOR MANAGEMENT | BUDGET | 360 ASSESSMENTS | INDIVIDUAL DEVELOPMENT PLANS (IDPs) | PROGRAM ANALYSIS

Managed high potential talent programs to build leadership capabilities of identified high-potential leaders. Served as lead analyst for enterprise-level development program using 360 assessments to create IDPs. Standardized and streamlined processes to institutionalize program knowledge.

Challenge: ⟩ Complete and execute two high potential talent programs for 60 participants in 8-month period.

› Turned around project budget from $30K over to $6K under by bringing facilities coordination in-house and moving to digital materials.

› Conducted post-session surveys and needs assessment using focus groups to tailor training content.

› Engaged with executives to gain program support, speak and serve as mentors for participants.

Challenge: ⟩ Design and facilitate "train the trainer" courses for organizational leaders on delivering 360 assessment results and creating IDPs for their subordinates.

› Facilitated training and coached leadership on scoring methodology and conducting developmental conversations with direct reports.

› Received 85% approval rating in post session evaluations and 95% of participants found the material enhanced their performance.

› Increased program retention by creating and managing job aids, resources and materials.

> "Patty not only possesses deep expertise in all things people, organizations and their development, but her adaptability and intellectual curiosity show that she is a forever learner, capable of accomplishing tasks outside of her direct experience."
>
> – Kevin Trent, colleague

Continued

Patty Bain, M.A.   773-531-3457 ♦ pbain11@gmail.com ♦ linkedin.com/in/pattybain ♦ Page 2 of 2

California Water Works Continued

Learning and Development Senior Analyst (20xx)

BLENDED LEARNING | MARKET RESEARCH | JOB ANALYSIS | SUCCESSION PLANNING | NEW HIRE TRAINING | STRATEGY ALIGNMENT

Supported introduction of first leadership program, for supervisor roles in the technical career path, affecting 2.5K employees. Sought partnership with learning analytics team to create cohesive analysis.

Challenge: Design sustainability program for leadership and technical training impacting 14K employees.

> **Reduced costs $20K per program** by moving paper-based system to electronic. Developed entire framework of electronic process and achieved 100% implementation.

> **Obtained stakeholder buy-in** to go forward with project that would streamline implementation of best practice training.

Challenge: Manage training for field leadership and turnaround culture to focus more on safety.

> **Designed and developed blended learning solutions** to reduce cycle time and increase work quality.

> **Provided learning evaluation and measurement consultation,** based on Kirkpatrick's model, for executive leaders and stakeholders to operationalize KPIs and develop improvement strategies.

CLEAR CONSULTING, Los Angeles, CA   20xx

Job Analysis Consultant

BEHAVIORAL INTERVIEWING | PERFORMANCE TESTING | SURVEY CREATION | JOB ANALYSIS

Internship completed with 3-person team. Analyzed and validated skills, tasks and job abilities of culinary contract positions by observing key staff job performance and conducting surveys with subject matter experts (SME).

> **Created performance tests, behavioral interview questions and knowledge, skills and abilities (KSAs)** that were implemented by organization.

PRIOR CAREER   20xx-20xx

Counselor | Coach, New York Hope, Manhattan, NY — Coached 35+ court-involved young adults and families in 6-month intensive program. Developed customized IDPs to strengthen critical skills and achieve future success.

> **Achieved 95% completion rate** by providing training using simulations, group discussions and role-playing methodologies.

Counselor | Coach, Brooklyn Psychology Clinic, Brooklyn, NY — Managed continuing education training for staff members by providing critical technical skills workshops. Counseled 50+ high-needs clients.

> **Initiated, implemented and led educational training for clinical staff** by utilizing the ADDIE process and developing monthly "train the trainer" modules to achieve higher performance and improve engagement.

EDUCATION & CERTIFICATION

The Chicago School of Professional Psychology, Los Angeles, CA

> Ph.D. in Business Psychology, specialization in Talent Development - Expected 20xx

> M.A. in Psychology - 20xx

California State University, Los Angeles, CA — B.A. - 20xx

MBTI Assessment Step I and Step II, The Myers & Briggs Foundation, License MBTI-20xx-xxxxxxx

SKILLS & AFFILIATIONS

SKILLS: Fluent in Hindi, Punjabi, and Urdu. DISC, Adobe Captivate, Articulate Storyline, Microsoft Office Suite

AFFILIATIONS: Member, Association for Talent Development (ATD); Member, Society for Industrial and Organizational Psychology (SIOP).

Joseph Tribbiani

Senior Multimedia Designer
Embraces new challenges to deliver cost-savings and improved brand engagement while complying with business objectives

📱 773-531-3457   ✉ joeytribbiani@gmail.com   📍 Palatine, IL 60060   in www.linkedin.com/in/joetribbiani

▶▶▶▶ Experience

SENIOR MULTIMEDIA DESIGNER | OWNER,
Friends Media, Palatine, IL, 19xx–Present

Scope: Design video, print, Websites, and presentations on periodic basis for small businesses.

- **Videography**: Reduced customer service calls by implementing assembly videos for complex furniture pieces.

- **Retail launch**: Spearheaded all marketing materials to promote new store opening. Drove customers to store via direct marketing and Facebook page and captured foot traffic by designing display window.

- **Visual presentations**: Improved PowerPoint deck readability and engagement to create clearer message.

MANAGER OF VIDEO SERVICES | MULTIMEDIA DESIGNER,
Acme Publishing, Deerfield, IL, 20xx–20xx

Scope: Brought in as senior graphic designer focused on print. Promoted after 2.5 years, taking on projects that included video and motion graphics. Managed one multimedia designer and budget up to $50K.

> *"I could count on Joe in the clutch to **go the extra mile to deliver the impossible**."*
> — Chris Campbell, managed Joe at Acme Publishing

BUSINESS INITIATIVES
- **Process improvement**: Streamlined video approval process by implementing new reviewing platform to capture all changes in one single place, whether remote or not.

- **Cost savings**: Cut software subscription spend more than 87% annually ($6K/yr.) by sourcing new vendors.

- **Revenue generation**: Filmed content for online course that exceeded first year revenue goals within 10 days of launch.

DESIGN INITIATIVES
- **Internal product launch**: Implemented first in-house video promotion for new research platform.

- **Quick turnaround**: Produced onsite testimonial and recap videos.

- **In-house production studio**: Collaborated with creative design manager to source build-out of internal production studio.

SR. GRAPHIC DESIGNER, Galileo Wines International, Lake Bluff, IL, 20xx–20xx

Scope: Designed 50+ projects annually for 40 different products.

- **Photo shoots**: Set up first internal studio and directed product shots.

▶▶▶▶ Education & Associations

B.F.A. in Graphic Design, Columbia College, Chicago, IL

National Association of Broadcasters, Member

Competencies

▶ Video Production

▶ Photography

▶ Audio Post Production

▶ Motion Graphics

▶ Non-linear Editing

▶ Graphic Design

Portfolio

Status Quo Acme
Earned double the views from previous videos.

2015 User Conference
3000+ views.

Technology

▶ Adobe Creative Suite (InDesign, Photoshop, Illustrator, Premiere, After Effects, Muse Lightroom, Audition)

▶ Final Cut Pro X

▶ Apple Keynote

▶ Microsoft PowerPoint

▶ Brightcove

▶ YouTube

▶ Wistia

AMY S. SMITH

"You have to win on the inside to win on the outside." — Amy S. Smith

Unlike most corporate communications professionals, Amy S. Smith is an expert in results-oriented engagement—both internally with employees and externally with customers. Beyond her talent for solving specific business issues with clear communication strategies, Amy measures the outcomes of her efforts in meaningful ways to help increase a company's top and bottom line.

With more than three decades of marketing, agency, public relations and corporate communications experience, Amy brings her multi-disciplined expertise to organizations that want to change the status quo.

Most recently, Amy was a key member of the Public Affairs leadership team at Baxalta, where she successfully helped launch the $18B biopharmaceutical spin-off of Baxter. There she developed an employee engagement program exceeding expectations, helping deliver a total return of 60% in the company's inaugural year.

As a result of her proposal to integrate internal and external communications across digital and social channels, Amy was asked to establish Baxalta's digital news center over a two-year period. Within just one year Amy had the digital news hub up and running, delivering measurable improvements in brand recognition and perception.

A natural overachiever, Amy also deployed global measurement standards—established by the Coalition for Public Relations Research Standards—for media reporting and web analytics in one year for Baxalta. With the assistance of measurement expert Katherine Miller, she consolidated redundant media monitoring across the global Public Affairs organization, leading to an annual cost-savings opportunity of $500K beginning in 2015.

Passionate about employee engagement, the internal communications program Amy developed at Baxter Nutrition was credited by the executive vice president as the single most influential factor in a margin improvement program that exceeded the annual goal by 22%. That same year, employee engagement measured greater than 90% and the division achieved its sales plan for the first time in six years.

Over her 16 years in an agency environment, beginning with The Herman Miller Company, Amy made public relations services a new revenue stream that outperformed advertising revenue after just two years. And, true to her ability to create communications that resonate with both employees and customers, at Didier Advertising & PR she conceived the campaign to announce the global merger of Pfizer Animal Health and Smith-Kline Beecham Animal Health, where the artwork was then adapted to Pfizer's brand communications and used for the next decade.

Amy earned her Bachelor of Arts degree in English at Northern University in DeKalb, IL. She was a recipient of the university's Outstanding Young Alumnus Award and is a past president of the Northern Club of Chicago.

Amy and her husband, John, an electrical contractor, live in Glenview, IL and have four 20-something children that help keep her in touch with the generation with the greatest economic impact in the U.S., Millennials. An avid NFL fan, September through January Amy spends more time than she should on her weekly pool picks and watching *ESPN Sunday Countdown, NFL Game Day* and *NFL Red Zone.*

RICK WATERS

Senior Executive • Business Development • Marketing • Operations • Finance

773.531.3457 • rickwaters@gmail.com • Northbrook, IL 60062 • www.linkedin.com/in/rickwaters

No one is more intuitive than Rick Waters about understanding business issues and the emotions of the stakeholders tied to it. Unlike most executive leaders, Rick goes the distance to ensure he has the right facts to base his decisions and recommendations for solving problems. Will it benefit the client? Is it going to be profitable? How will it affect the way we do business? It comes naturally to him to evaluate with a 360° view.

With more than two decades of management expertise spanning from business development to marketing to operations to finance, Rick is uniquely equipped to understand multiple areas of business. He is seeking to apply his knowledge to an Advisory Board position where he can provide guidance on growth strategies.

When he initially started as the fourth employee with Data Points Online, Rick grew top-line revenues by nearly 1,200% managing the account for a large financial services client. Today, Data Points Online serves multiple industries and has more than 130 full-time employees.

Now, Rick heads the retail industry accounts, nearly 20% of the overall business. In the last 3.5 years he has been able to double the size of the retail business. Previously, he led multiple corporate-level functions including acquisition planning and investor relations.

Rick's passion lies in providing the consumer with the best experience possible. On a recent trip to Guatemala, he visited several call centers to evaluate strategies on providing after hours and weekend support to clients' retail dealers.

Throughout his career he has been heavily involved in developing cutting edge strategies for multi-channel marketing, including off-line, online and mobile.

Prior to Data Points Online, Rick served as Assistant Vice President Sales & Account Management and later Business Development for Metric Marketing Group, formerly The Hancock Group. This is where he truly mastered his relationship building skills and grew new oil industry clients 150%, capturing 80% of the market, while expanding the quantity of products and services under contract 650%.

Proudly extending his leadership acuity to his professional associations, Rick served on the board of directors of the Business Marketing Association (BMA) for several years. During his tenure he collaborated with other board members to initiate the new positioning of the association in order to turn it around and increase growth. He also enjoys teaching the Interactive Marketing module of the BMA Basic Course, which he has done for the last 6 years, guiding young professionals in the art and science of direct response marketing.

Knowing that finance and marketing sometimes don't see eye to eye, Rick went back to earn his M.B.A. in Finance, and an emphasis in Business Strategy, from the University of Iowa in Iowa City, so he could learn better ways to make these groups relate. This is where he also completed his B.S. in Marketing.

His passions away from work include maintaining and riding vintage motorcycles, touring the back roads of the U.S.A. to the tune of 10,000 miles a year. Born in Japan and living there until he was 12, Rick appreciates different cultures. He resides in Northbrook, IL, and has two grown children, Jonathan, who lives and works in Chicago, IL and Christine, who lives and works in Brattleboro, VT.

Rachel Green

Tenacious, results-focused, consultative sales professional ► Healthcare, Medical Devices ► Seeking new opportunities

Summary

My name is Rachel Green, greenr@hotmail.com, and finding new ways to penetrate markets in the medical device and healthcare industries is what I do best.

"If you do what you've always done, you'll get what you've always gotten." --Tony Robbins

My whole sales philosophy ties in to this quote and it is the driver behind my success. I constantly strive to build upon wins and improve my sales process to gain even more traction in the marketplace.

CONSULTATIVE SALES APPROACH
The critical key to expanding into new markets is being able to act as a strategic partner to my accounts. Listening to their concerns helps me identify their educational needs and solutions that will improve their patient care. With this approach I exceeded my sales goals 20% in my first 9 months at Tec Health.

ENTREPRENEURIAL SPIRIT
Whether it's thinking of a new approach to create demand for a product or identifying implanting centers willing to embrace a new shared-care concept, I consistently make the extra effort to secure new sales and referral streams.

CONQUERING SALES GOALS
Throughout my career I have earned numerous awards for exceeding market share growth. At 2 different organizations I ranked in the top 5% of the sales force, nationwide. Most recently at Tec Health, surpassing my sales goals up to 24% and initiating the groundwork for the first shared patient care site in Illinois led to an unusual mid-year promotion.

Outside of work, I continue to feed my competitive spirit on the tennis court. Nothing beats a good match to renew my energy for when I am back in the office.

► HOW CAN I HELP YOUR COMPANY GROW?
If you seek a business development manager or sales consultant to help you penetrate new markets to expand your reach, I would welcome the opportunity to speak with you. I can be reached at: greenr@hotmail.com or 773-531-3457.

Specialties: Medical device sales, consultative selling, business development, market development, and change management.

Experience

Seeking Employment | Business Development Manager | Account Representative | Sales Professional at In Healthcare or Medical Device Company
20xx-present (6 months)
Description: I am seeking a Business Development role for a national healthcare or medical device company.

As a dedicated, energetic, results-oriented sales professional I have a history of ramping up fast to break into new markets and surpass sales goals.

SELECT ACCOMPLISHMENTS

☑Exceeded sales goals 20% after just 9 months in a new market.

☑Instrumental in developing first shared patient care site in Illinois for Tec Health to create opportunity to develop a referral stream.

☑Overcame programmatic changes affecting Iowa while covering vacant territory and opened 4 additional shared patient care sites.

☑Ranked in top 5% of sales force nationwide at 2 different organizations.

Sales Manager | Market Development Manager | Sales Consultant at Tec Health Corporation
20xx-20xx (4 years)
Initially hired to grow sales in a new market, Western Suburbs and Central Illinois, I analyzed the market and strategized how to best establish referral sources. Within my first 9 months on the job I exceeded my sales goals 20%. The following year I surpassed my goals by 24%, setting the pace for an unusual mid-year promotion where my territory was expanded.

ADDITIONAL ACCOMPLISHMENTS
☑Developed strategic plan to implement first shared patient care site in Illinois, creating a consistent referral stream from 30+ sites.

☑Contender for President's Advisory Board.

☑Ranked in top 20% of field sales, nationwide.

☑Contributed 30% revenue to bottom-line, achieving overall growth in 20xx.

☑Introduced heart device into new territory exceeding goals in 20xx-20xx.

Clinical Sales Representative | Account Manager | Business Development Manager at Brain Technologies
20xx-20xx (2 years)
Moving from pharmaceuticals to medical devices, this was my first role selling an orthotic device to pediatricians, neurosurgeons and craniofacial surgeons.

ACCOMPLISHMENTS
☑Secured 18 new accounts during tenure.

☑Achieved "100" Referral Club.

☑Exceeded monthly revenue goals for 4 consecutive months in 20xx.

Sales Representative | Account Manager | Account Executive at Mears & Company (formerly Shearing Point)
20xx-20xx (3 years)
Seeing the need for additional funding to make a more significant impact in a limited territory, I created a detailed proposal focused on ROI and highlighted the benefits of investing for key customers. As a result, I was granted $1K to execute my plan. Shearing Point was acquired by Mears & Company towards the end of my time there.

ADDITIONAL ACCOMPLISHMENTS
☑Ranked in top 5% of all U.S. sales team -- #55/1013.

☑Earned "Move the Needle Award" for exceeding market goals for Crestor 15%.

☑Awarded Crestor 49 Award for increasing market share with target physicians.

☑Increased goal attainment > 13 points for Crestor and > 23 points for Allegra.

☑Selected as district representative on Cardiovascular Advisory board in 20xx.

Professional Healthcare Representative | Account Executive | Sales Professional at Pfingston Corporation
20xx-20xx (7 years)
After 6 years as a speech and language pathologist I transitioned into pharmaceutical sales. I drove sales in women's healthcare, neurology, psychiatry, urology, long-term care, pharmacies and hospitals.

ACCOMPLISHMENTS

☑Surpassed quota 250% while promoting hormone replacement therapy during market collapse.

☑Achieved 114% sales quota by devising migraine Medicaid pull-through initiative.

☑Secured product on Southern Illinois University Health Services formulary by developing and executing strategic plan to educate end-users and drive sales.

☑Earned "Consistent Achiever's Award" 3 times during course of tenure for exceeding 100% market share.

☑Received "Winner Select Award" for achieving highest portfolio growth.

☑Won "Get After It Award" for achieving consistent market share growth for product.

☑Ranked in top 5% of national sales force and earned "President's Club Award" in 20xx.

Speech, Language Pathologist at Lutheran Hospital
19xx-20xx (3 years)
Evaluated, developed plan of care and treatment for patients in SNF, rehabilitation, out patient, acute and pediatrics.

Rick Waters

VP Corporate Development | Senior Executive | Relationship Builder | Marketing Innovator | Revenue Accelerator

Summary

GOOD INTUITION BUILDS GREAT RELATIONSHIPS

It is in my nature to be in tune with what is going on around me and how it affects whatever situation I am in – business or personal. I go the distance to ensure I've heard from all stakeholders and have the right facts to base my decision on the best solution for the business challenge.

As the fourth employee at Data Points Online I have contributed to its growth in a variety of ways over the past 15 years. Initially, I grew our largest account 1,200% in my first 6 years and most recently, doubled our retail business in just over 3 years.

While business development is still the core of my role, I am also involved in finance and operations, constantly assessing how we can do business faster and more cost effectively.

My passion lies in providing the consumer with the best experience possible. On a recent trip to Guatemala, I visited several clients' call centers to evaluate strategies on expanding support during non-work hours.

In addition to Data Points Online, I have extended my leadership acuity to professional associations like the Business Marketing Association (BMA). I served 3 years on the board of directors and collaborated to initiate a new position for the association to encourage more growth.

Outside of work, you'll find me riding my vintage BMW motorcycle across the back roads of the U.S.A. It's not only the ride I enjoy, but the planning of my trip and meeting all kinds of interesting people along the way.

▶ How Can I Help You?
Is your organization looking to increase your strategic edge and turn your data into new customers? Are you looking for an experienced executive to join your board of directors? Please contact me:
✉ rickwaters@gmail.com
✆ 773-531-3457

Experience

Vice President Corporate Development | Enterprise Operations | Client Services at Data Points Online
20xx-Present (14 years)

VP CORPORATE DEVELOPMENT (2008–Present) | DOUBLED RETAIL BUSINESS IN JUST OVER 3 YEARS

In this role I lead our retail industry accounts along with handling multiple corporate-level functions including legal, facilities, acquisition planning, and investor relations.

Recently, I oversaw the renovation of our current space to accommodate for our growing staff.

My negotiation and cost-cutting efforts resulted in a 30% savings in general and administration expenses. And by implementing a switch to a new online meeting vendor we realized an approximate $20K in annual savings.

VICE PRESIDENT ENTERPRISE OPERATIONS (20xx–20xx) | LOWERED OVERALL EXPENSES 20%

During this interim role, I laid the foundation for a dedicated full-time person to take over the operations part of the business. I spent the majority of my time assessing the systems we had in place and implementing ways to eliminate duplicative technology and create efficiencies. When I consolidated our legal vendors to just one, it lowered our expenses by 50%.

VICE PRESIDENT CLIENT SERVICES (20xx–20xx) | GREW TOP LINE REVENUES BY NEARLY 1,200% | GENERATED 1.5M CUSTOMERS FOR CLIENTS

I was recruited by the founder as employee #4 and managed the largest financial services client so he could turn his focus on developing additional vertical markets. In the course of my tenure in this role, I implemented innovative marketing programs that helped grow our revenue ~1,200% and generated 1.5M new customers for our clients.

With the explosion of new customers this also grew the products we offered – going from just one product to 12 for one single client.

Assistant Vice President | Business Development | Sales | Account Management at Metric Marketing Group (Formerly The Hancock Group)
19xx-20xx (5 years)

ASSISTANT VICE PRESIDENT BUSINESS DEVELOPMENT (20xx) | DEVELOPED STRATEGIES TO MOVE ONLINE

As someone who stays on top of trends in the marketplace, I moved into a new area of the business focused on bringing processes online to better serve our customers. I was able to reduce our reliance on call centers by collaborating to develop the first auto club website so the application process could move online.

ASSISTANT VICE PRESIDENT SALES & ACCOUNT MANAGEMENT (19xx–19xx) | INCREASED CLIENT BASE 150%

Initially recruited from a vendor relationship, I was tasked with expanding our presence in the oil industry. At the time I came on board we had about 3 clients in this market. I led the team in securing 6 more clients in the industry, bringing our total share of the oil industry market to 80%.

As a result of increasing these clients, we grew our marketing database 312% over 4 years, providing our clients with a bigger prospect universe. This also expanded the number of products and services we had under contract 650%.

Director of Sales & Client Management at VaultCard Services, Inc.
19xx-19xx (3 years)

RETAINED COMPANY'S LARGEST CLIENT | INTRODUCED NEW SWEEPSTAKES PROGRAM

As a member of the executive team, I helped re-negotiate a strategic multi-year $244M contract with our biggest client. I also developed and produced the first of its kind voice-activated sweepstakes program that exceeded response expectations.

This was all done while managing several teams – account management, marketing and operations – generating $60M+ revenue.

Chandler Bing

chandlerbing@gmail.com • 773-531-3457 • Glenview, IL 60026 • www.linkedin.com/in/chandlerbing

June 3, 20xx

Mr. Michael Scott
Bank of America
9 West 57th Street
New York, NY 10010

Dear Mr. Scott:

Success in sales is measured by results and building long-term trusted relationships drives those results. Inherent relationship building is my strength that has allowed me to carry over clients from position to position throughout my career. Now, I would like to bring this ability to Bank of America in the role of VP Sales Manager.

The keys to my sales success are rooted in the following strategies:

> **Persist with tact**: Offering alternative solutions allows me to grow current clients and secure new ones.

> **Listen well and learn quickly**: Moving from broadcast communications to the audio-visual industry I discovered needs and new channels fast, allowing me to continue to surpass my quota.

> **Adapt and change**: Growing up in the credit and collections area, I smoothly transitioned into sales using my financial background to make clients feel comfortable with decisions.

With my most recent consultant work, I realized I miss the comradery and dynamics of working for a corporation. As such, I am exploring new opportunities to contribute to your corporate sales strategy and build relationships from the inside, out. May we meet to explore your needs further and discuss what I can offer?

Sincerely,

Chandler Bing

Enclosure

ROSS GELLER

Portland, OR 97201 (Open for relocation) • rgeller@gmail.com
773-531-3457 • www.linkedin.com/in/rossgeller

November 21, 20xx

Mr. Sheldon Cooper
Director of Marketing
Chicago Sports Museum
835 North Michigan Avenue
Chicago, IL 60611

Dear Mr. Cooper,

When I respond to negative comments on social media, it's like using my keyboard to diffuse a bomb. I artfully craft my response in order for my organization to help turn a detractor into a promoter. This is just one way I have been successful managing social media, and would now like to bring those skills to the Chicago Sports Museum in the role of Social Media Manager.

Throughout my career, I have started new processes for organizations in web content, public relations, and social media. Highlights include:

* Initiated sending samples with press releases so media could test and review gear.

* Conducted first-ever live press event for Razor Motosports.

* Took initiative to introduce motorcycle sub-section for MillennialMen.com.

I am confident I can help the Chicago Sports Museum grow their social media presence and member base. I would like the opportunity to meet with you to further discuss your needs and other ways I can help. As a Chicago native, I am looking to relocate to the Midwest, and I can be reached at 773-531-3457. Thank you for your consideration.

Sincerely,

Ross Geller

Enclosure

RICK WATERS

Senior Executive • Business Development • Marketing • Operations • Finance

773.531.3457 • rickwaters@gmail.com • Northbrook, IL 60062 • www.linkedin.com/in/rickwaters

November 4, 20xx

Mr. Mark Radke
GoSite, Inc.
3110 Camino Del Rio S. #212
San Diego, CA 92108

Dear Mr. Radke:

Growing a company is hard, but rewarding work. As the fourth employee of a now 130+ organization, I've seen first-hand the good, the bad, and the ugly that comes with growing a business.

In my first six years at Data Points Online I grew our largest account 1,200%. My intuitiveness and innovative marketing programs helped our clients generate over 1.5M new customers.

With business development as the common thread of my tenure, my role expanded to operations and finance where I have effectively cut costs and streamlined processes, reducing efforts up to 50%.

This experience is what I bring to the table as an advisory board member at GoSite, Inc.

Interested? May we talk?

Sincerely,

Rick Waters

Enclosure

Cheryl Minnick, M.Ed., Ed.D, CCMC, NCRW
University of Montana – Academic Enrichment

Cheryl Minnick, M.Ed., Ed.D, CCMC, NCRW
University of Montana
406-243-4614
cminnick@mso.umt.edu

Passionate, lively and engaging, Dr. Cheryl Minnick is career counselor/internship coordinator at the University of Montana with nearly 30 years' experience in higher education, 20 of those in the area of career counseling. She holds both a masters and doctorate with specialization in career counseling. Trained by top industry experts, she is one of less than 50 Nationally Certified Résumé Writers in the country. Cheryl is a guest instructor with Career Thought Leaders, a think tank for the now, new, and next in careers; teaches webinars for the Career Academy; and sits on the NRWA Certification Board for resume writing certification. Over a three-year period, she partnered with the Montana Department of Labor to train employment professionals statewide on best practices in resume creation, cover letter writing, and applicant tracking systems.

Cheryl is a certified Academies Career Management Coach whose career advice has been featured on AOLJobs, Voice America radio, CareerSparx and Resume Writer's Digest . . . who has published career development research in the Journal of Academic Administration in Higher Education and The New Accountant . . . and, whose resumes and cover letters are published in books including, "Modernize Your Resume: Get Noticed—Get Hired;" "Designing the Perfect Résumé," "How to Pop your Résumé," Gallery of Best Cover Letters," "The Twitter Job Search Guide" and "101 Job Seeking Tips for Recent College Grads." If not on campus working with students, she can be found helping mid-level to senior managers through her boutique career consulting business, The Paper Trail. Cheryl has successfully helped hundreds of students and professionals successfully navigate careers and achieve professional success.

Colin Smith

U.S. Citizen
Helena, Montana
Cell Phone: (406) 465-1023
Email: Colinsmith@gmail.com

June 1, 20xx

U.S. Department of the Interior
U.S. Fish and Wildlife Service
Albuquerque, New Mexico

      RE: **Fish Biologist position (GS-0482-09)**
                Job Announcement # R2-13-955510-CL-DEU

Dear Recruiting Team:

"Working outside in remote locations, hiking with heavy packs and climbing steep slopes, rocky stream beds and rugged trails in extreme weather conditions to perform fishery investigations" … is my dream career! My skill in fishery sample techniques, identification, seining, electrofishing, experimental gill and trammel netting and marking techniques, including PIT and VIE tagging, were gained as a fisheries field tech intern with both the U.S. Fish and Wildlife Services and the Montana Fish and Wildlife and Parks.

A new University of Montana honors graduate with a bachelor of science in biology (fish ecology), I am excited to enter the field as a fish biologist and am prepared through:

    Lab study: allowed me to conduct sampling methods using differing techniques, monitor fish populations, operate field equipment and prepare detailed records using statistical software.

    Classwork: in limnology, ichthyology, fish culture, oceanography, aquatic botany and fauna taught me to plan and perform fish culture techniques and collect and analyze fishery field data.

    Field study: taught me to become safety-focused when operating and maintaining university, state and federally-owned vehicles, field equipment and research facilities.

It is evident that I offer additional qualifications than most new graduates which will allow me to make immediate, valuable contributions to your field research team. I am eager to put my experience and education to work for the New Mexico Fish and Wildlife Conservation.

You will find me sincerely dedicated to improving conservation and sustainable management, as well as protecting and preserving fishery resources and aquatic ecosystems. If you seek a motivated young professional who loves to learn, works well in teams and offers the personal drive and confidence to succeed, I would welcome an interview. Thank you for your time and consideration. I look forward to speaking with you.

Best regards,

Colin Smith
Enclosure: résumé

SUZIE SUCCESS

Los Angeles, California ☐ (816) 222-3333 ☐ Suzie.Success@gmail.com

Uniquely qualified for position as

STUDENT SUCCESS COORDINATOR

Passionate **HEALTHCARE PROFESSIONAL** with experience developing, implementing and coordinating lifestyle change programs. Dedicated to empowering students to reach their full potential in school and personally through one-on-one coaching, mentoring and teaching. Hold three years' experience working across campus with multiple constituents, including faculty, staff and administrators to design, facilitate and <u>implement educational</u> programs. Skilled in:

Health and Wellness Education – Project Management – Group Workshop Facilitation
Wellness Coaching – Assessment and Measurement – HIPAA Patient Charting – Motivational Interviewing
FERPA Confidentiality – Workshop Design and Implementation – Behavioral Change Theory

HIGHER EDUCATION LEADERSHIP RECOGNITION

Student Health Ambassadors' Committee Board Member
National Association of Student Affairs Professionals General Assembly participant
National Award Recognition for Outstanding Preventative Program, "Tobacco Free Campus"

PROFESSIONAL EXPERIENCE

WELLNESS CENTER, Health Coach – CARE Coordinator – SMART Counselor
UNIVERSITY OF LOS ANGELES, Downey, California, September 20xx –June 20xx

Develop, deliver and assess healthy behavior support services for 16,000 student campus, including sleep improvement, stress and time management, sex education, tobacco quit support, exercise guidance and nutritional coaching.

- ☐ **Conducted needs assessment** to identify students' current conditions and/or behaviors compared to desired conditions or healthier behaviors to develop and offer remediation programs, services and workshops.
- ☐ **Developed marketing campaign** targeting specific students in need of assistance and/or academic, personal, financial, relationship building and/or social-emotional support to foster greater academic and personal success.
- ☐ **Collaborated with campus clubs**, student affairs programs, academic affairs departments, faculty, staff and peers to build awareness of campus programs and services and provide referrals to supportive community resources.
- ☐ **Coached and mentored students** on developing and implementing SMART goals into their personal lives to improve positive physical, social, emotional and mental health and gain greater academic and career success.
- ☐ **Taught health education workshops** to groups of 25˚ undergraduate students. Prepared and delivered curriculum using Blackboard and Moodle learning platforms and Microsoft Office Word, Excel and PowerPoint.
- ☐ **Offered students one-on-one coaching** to help overcome barriers preventing them from achieving and excelling academically, socially, emotionally and physically; helped students self-identify focus areas for CARE.

EDUCATION & CERTIFICATIONS

UNIVERSITY OF LOS ANGELES, Downey, California, June 20xx

Bachelor of Science, Health and Human Performance – Community Health Education
CPR / AED, American Heart Association BLS for Healthcare Providers, renewal December 20xx
CPR / ECC, Emergency Care & Safety Institute – Emergency Medical Responder, renewal December 20xx

NANCY NURSE

1234 Twin Creek Drive
Missoula, Montana 59803

Cell: (406) 123-4567
Nancynurse@gmail.com

December 6, 20xx

Providence Medical Group
Rock Creek Family Medicine Clinic
4321 Bear Tracks Lane, Suite 201
Missoula, Montana 59808

Re: RN Care Coordinator

Dear Recruiting Team:

Next week, I graduate with a BS in Nursing from Montana State University's accredited School of Nursing, and in January will sit for state licensure. As an entry-level nurse, I am excited to serve on a healthcare team to help families receive the best health outcomes through comprehensive, personalized care. My educational goal has always been to work in a family medicine clinic to provide routine, urgent and preventative care on a small team led by primary care providers. Rock Creek Clinic's reputation for providing quality, compassionate care is notable, so when I learned of your RN Care Coordinator opening, I could not wait to apply!

My nursing education has well-prepared me to deliver support to healthcare teams in assessing, planning, implementing and evaluating patients' individual nursing care needs. During my internship at Western Family Healthcare Center and three clinical rotations with Benefis Health Systems, I gained experience using the collaborative nursing process approach with patients, family members and healthcare providers. I am especially proud of the praise I received from supervisors for delivery of compassionate, gentle healthcare to vulnerable populations, seniors and patients with disabilities. I look forward to continuing to serve, learn and expand my nursing skills as I contribute to our community's health needs.

You will find me to be equally dedicated, ethical and respectful– a new nurse who will use clinical skills to support Providence Medical Group's commitment to distinctive patient healthcare focused on trust, respect, communication and teamwork. Confident my credentials match your required qualifications, I welcome an opportunity to interview with you to more fully reveal my experience and sincere interest. I look forward to meeting your team, and thank you for your consideration.

Sincerely,

NANCY NURSE
Enclosure: résumé

Jim VENUE

Relocating to Los Angeles
(123) 456-7890 | jimvenue@gmail.com

VENUE MANAGEMENT – EVENT PRODUCTION

Deliver positive entertainment and lasting memories, whether in the spotlight or behind the scenes. Worked live entertainment and concert events, including Paul McCartney, Blue Man Group, Rascal Flatts and Clint Black. Thrive in high-pressured events where fiery ambition and sharp hustle are required.

♦ Graphic and Poster Design	♦ Risk Mitigation	♦ Ticketing / Will Call
♦ Social Media and SEO	♦ Event Ideation / Execution	♦ Equipment Management
♦ Sponsorship Outreach	♦ SWOT Analysis	♦ Contract Negotiations
♦ VIP and Artist Management	♦ Event Reconciliation	♦ Post-event Debriefs
♦ Brand Promotion	♦ Stage Management	♦ Budget Management

ENTERTAINMENT EXPERIENCE

Event Production – Intern
COLLEGE PRODUCTIONS, City, State, August 20xx – May 20xx

Student-run, student-funded organization bringing the community top-quality entertainment– jazz to modern dance, blues to ballet, comedy to gospel music and Broadway plays to opera.

- Polished event management skills working under tight time constraints, managing stress with ease and taking initiative to independently identify and complete tasks.
- Box Office (**Kip Moore** and **Joan Baez**); Usher (sold-out **Old Crow Medicine Show**); Crowd control (**Dierks Bentley**); Two-day build (**Blue Man Group**); Show assistant (sold-out **Rascal Flatts**).
- Ushered patrons and managed seat conflicts while simultaneously serving as artists' runner.
- Managed equipment load-in/load-out and built stages under direction of artists' stage managers, production teams and crew members.

Venue Management – Volunteer
THE BIG CITY THEATER, City, State, May 20xx – September 20xx

Live entertainment 1100-seat proscenium style venue staging rock, county, hip-hop, electronic concerts, stand-up comedy shows, burlesque troupes, ballets, symphonies and private events.

- Shadowed control booth manager at **Phil Vassar** concert operating sound/lighting equipment; and managed sales, inventory and reconciliations for **Neal McCoy** concert merchandising table.
- Worked weekend and evening Box Office operations to assist patrons with ticket and parking permit purchase using AXS Ticket software to process payments.
- Succeeded in fast-paced environment as **Jason DeShaw** concert usher; NPC Big Sky Championship set-up crew; and **Buddy DeFranco** Jazz Festival marshal drawing 1500+ junior high students.
- Presented superb communication skills and professional appearance as runner and greenroom manager for **Clint Black** concert and load-in/load-out assistant for stand-up comedian **Brian Regan**.

EDUCATION

B.S., Business Entertainment Management, University of Northern, City, State, May 20xx
Venue Management –Class Project, August 20-27, 20xx

Paul McCartney "Out There" Tour - Stage Crew
Assisted 9 entertainment engineers with 175 semi-truck load-out and week-long build; 23 ground support engineers with roof and event stage system, rigging, module staging and barricades; 10 production crew with event production that drew 25,000 fans– a touchstone moment for the city and the largest concert in state history.

Ken Quarterback

Cell: 406-123-4567
Kenquaterback@gmail.com
Pullman, Washington

CAREER GOAL: FINANCIAL ANALYST

Professionally-driven college senior with first-rate leadership and communication skills. Raised on a family cattle ranch, learned as a boy to work hard for success. High school and college athlete possessing well-defined skills in time management, problem solving, detail organization and strategic analysis that will lead to employer and client satisfaction. *Seeking career-start entry-level role in financial analysis. Open to relocation and travel.*

> *"Ken works extremely hard. Coming from an eight-man high school football program, he's in a key role, making the calls on our front line and leading the team. He's smart, trustworthy, hard working and anchors our team."*
>
> *WSU Head Coach, Mike Leach*

EDUCATION

B.S., Accounting and Finance - GPA 3.82 - Washington State University, May 20xx
Graduated with **4.0 GPA** from Colfax High School in Colfax, Washington, 20xx

NCAA Pac-12 Football: Four-year full-ride scholar, two-year starter, Pac 12 All-Conference honors and All-Academic selection. Played in 3 nationally-televised championship games.

Confident: With fierce competitive drive and tenacious spirit, honed a "can do" attitude and ability to remain positive. Always strive to improve, contemplate and take risks.

Self-Motivated: Face difficult situations, handle error and adversity with fervor, evaluating performance and working to improve results after each athletic game and academic exam.

Competitive: Owing to hard work, drive for success and commitment, earned solid grades while concurrently succeeding on the playing field, at championship games and in class.

Mentally Tough: While traveling to games, juggled competing school and sport deadlines, extracurricular leadership activities and community volunteer service.

LEADERSHIP AND VOLUNTEER EXPERIENCE

Field Experience - WSU Ambassador, *Corporate Marketing course, summer 20xx*
— Elected to represent WSU in a highly-competitive summer field experience class. Traveled across the Northwest meeting Microsoft, Edelman, WONGDOODY, R2C Group and NIKE executives. Exposed to corporate culture to practice networking strategies and represent the Business School.

Teacher Assistant - Intern, *Pullman Christian School, Pullman, Washington, spring 20xx*
— Participated in weekly noon hour games to stress the value of a healthy lifestyle, story circle to talk with K-3 graders about being a good student and Tutor Time to help 9-12 graders master algebra and calculus.

Youth Mentor - Volunteer, *Sunnyside Elementary School, Pullman, Washington, fall 20xx*
— Coordinated, setup and ran Carnival Night games ensuring students an extraordinary time as they moved from game to game. Represented Cougar football while interfacing with students as a fun, encouraging male role model.

Community Engagement - Fundraiser, *Walk a Mile in her Shoes, springs 20xx – 20xx*
— Walked 1 mile with teammates around Campus Square to kick-off each football season wearing football jersey and high heels (yes, size 14) to bring attention to campus and community programs that work to prevent rape, sexual assault and gender violence against women.

COACH DODGE JACKSON

P.O. Box 123456
Two Dot, Montana

Cell: (406)123-4567
coachjackson@gmail.com

PHYSICAL EDUCATION TEACHER

Student-Focused ▪ Innovative ▪ Resourceful ▪ Collaborative

Dedicated teacher who strives to help students transform marginal grades into exceptional ones by creating learning environments built on mutual respect and open communication that facilitate social and intellectual growth. Caring, educator able to work collaboratively and constructively with students, parents, colleagues and administrators. Eagle Scout who holds strong belief in the power of sport, sportsmanship and team spirit to advance learning, socialization, positive behaviors and lifelong physical fitness. *Sports coaching and teaching areas include: football, basketball, track and field, tennis, volleyball, water polo, fencing, weight lifting, and archery.*

"Committed to Creating Positive Learning Environments and Making a Difference in the Lives of Students"

EDUCATION

UNIVERSITY OF MONTANA, Missoula, Montana, 20xx
State of Montana Teaching Certification – P.E. and Health Endorsement, #123321
Bachelor of Science, Health and Human Performance – Health Enhancement, GPA 3.98
National Association for Sport & Physical Fitness Education Health Enhancement Student of the Year, 20xx
Mortar Board Most Outstanding Senior Award, 20xx

— ▪ ▪ ▪ —

Emergency Medical Technician, April 20xx
Nonviolent Crisis Intervention Training, Crisis Prevention Institute, 20xx
Adult and Child First Aid, CPR and AED, American Heart Association, 20xx

TEACHING EXPERIENCE

Grades 1-12 P.E. and Health Enhancement, Guidance and Title I Reading Teacher (substitute)
TWO DOT PUBLIC SCHOOLS, Two Dot, Montana, August 20xx – present

At a school boasting student body of 35 taught by 10 teachers and 1 Para-professional, juggle roles as teacher, track, volleyball and basketball coach, referee, test coordinator, class and honor society advisor and occasional bus driver.

- Welcome high parental involvement as Class C coach for girls varsity volleyball, girls varsity basketball and grades 5-12 track programs and referee junior high volleyball and basketball.

- In accordance with Montana state teaching standards, design, teach and evaluate health enhancement lesson plans instilling in students appreciation for lifetime health and fitness through team, group, and individual sport.

- Direct state/national test administration of CRT, ACT, PSAT and Smarter Balanced tests to ensure grade levels are aligned, academic standards implemented, and students graduate with college and workforce readiness skills.

Lila Livingston

Chicago, Illinois — (123) 456-7890 — lila.livingston@gmail.com

April 22, 20xx

Ms. Please Hierme
Campus Sourcing Manager
PricewaterhouseCoopers
805 Southwest Broadway
Portland, Oregon 97205

Re: Elevate Leadership Program

Dear Ms. Hierme:

Eager to begin my career at the forefront of the professional service industry, I am drawn to PwC's reputation and commitment to recruiting and developing young leaders. University of Chicago's Business School has many talented students who have participated in your Elevate program, and speak highly of the experiences. I have been encouraged by alumni, seniors, faculty, and a current PwC associate to supplement my academics with the leadership and industry experience Elevate offers. I hold unique skills and experiences that have prepared me for the opportunity, including:

Commendable academic performance achieved through a drive for excellence, passion for personal growth, and eagerness to succeed in the global business market.

— Earned a cumulative 3.98 GPA while juggling full-time employment and a demanding campus leadership role, gaining excellent communication, organization, time management, and social skills.

Strong interpersonal and consultative skills obtained through professional, high-end customer-facing roles at the Waldorf Astoria New York, J. Crew in Los Angeles, and Trump International headquarters.

— Received recognition by Delta Nu Sorority as their top fundraiser by securing $50,000 in donations in three months, showcasing strategic-relationship and partnership-building skills.

Proven analytical and problem-solving abilities mastered from experience in campus leadership positions and employment in collaborative company settings.

— Strengthened ability to solve problems, analyze warning signs, and discover solutions in team-oriented environments, resulting in increased productivity and efficiency.

A high-achieving information systems major, I am interested in the professional service industry and will bring my skills and experiences to the Elevate program. Beginning my career at PwC through your competitive and prestigious leadership program will allow me to further develop business skills, interact with seasoned professionals, and test myself in a dynamic industry. Doing so will build a strong foundation for a successful, lasting career for me at PwC.

My résumé displays a solid dedication to academics and professional drive for success; I am confident that my unique attributes, skills, and potential will be positive additions to your Elevate program and PwC team. Thank you for your time and strong consideration. I look forward to hearing from you.

Sincerely,

Lila Livingston

Enclosure: résumé

Jessica Holbrook Hernandez,
Certified Social Branding Analyst
President/CEO of Great Resumes Fast

Jessica Holbrook Hernandez
President/CEO of Great Resumes Fast
www.greatresumesfast.com   1.800.991.5187
www.linkedin.com/in/jessicaholbrook
www.twitter.com/greatresume
www.facebook.com/GreatResumesFastLLC

I started Great Resumes Fast more than 7 years ago with the mission of using my 12+ years of human resources, recruiting, and hiring experience to create interview-winning resumes for job seekers who really didn't know what a resume should look or "sound" like. My desire—and the heart of my business—is for everyone here to use his or her expertise and experience within the "hiring sphere" to assist job seekers who do not have the time, experience, or expertise to create interview-worthy resumes.

We operate on the principle of The Golden Rule (Luke 6:31) and always strive to treat our clients the way we would like to be treated.

I hand-select exceptionally talented, credentialed, and ambitious writers who are laser-focused on putting client needs first and creating unique resumes, cover letters and LinkedIn profiles that make our clients outshine their competition. Our exclusive resume consultation and collaboration process is the secret behind our success—and the reason we can guarantee our clients interviews within 60 days or less.

Our success has earned us a 5-star rating from three independent resume writer-review websites, much praise from our highly satisfied clients (check out my LinkedIn recommendations) and 10+ independent "Best Resume Writer" awards.

In addition to 12+ years of experience as a hiring manager, recruiter, and human resources manager directing the hiring and talent acquisition of thousands of job seekers, I employ writers with similar experience and documented credentials.

A nationally recognized resume expert, Jessica Holbrook Hernandez is President/CEO of Great Resumes Fast and a former human resources manager and recruiter. Leveraging more than ten years' experience directing hiring practices for Fortune 500 companies, Jessica has developed proprietary, innovative, and success-proven resume development and personal branding strategies that generate powerful results for the clients of Great Resumes Fast. As a global resume authority and trusted media source, Jessica has been featured and quoted numerous times throughout CNN.com, Monster.com, Job Talk America radio, SmartBrief, International Business Times, and more. Jessica also has her Bachelor of Science degree in Communications/Public Relations from the University of North Florida.

JOHN SMITH

info@greatresumesfast.com | 800-991-5187 | www.linkedin.com/in/jessicaholbrook

CHIEF INFORMATION OFFICER

Protecting and growing organizations by merging business-driven technology leadership with military discipline, advanced training, and experience in security, counterterrorism, and intelligence

Respected technology executive with 15+ years as an IT leader, strategist, and consultant for global organizations and 22+ years in the military—demonstrating deep knowledge of business, P&L, IT operations, security (including threats to systems, information, and critical infrastructures), mobile/application development, and system optimization. Engaging public speaker.

LEADERSHIP STRENGTHS

- Strategic Planning & Execution
- Business & Technology Alignment
- Team Building & Leadership
- System Security & Business Continuity
- Solution Architecture & Design
- Organizational Change Management
- Budgeting, P&L & Cost Savings
- Project Planning & Launch
- Performance Improvement

SELECT CREDENTIALS

MBA in Management Information Systems

PhD Candidate (ABD) in Strategic Security – Intelligence, Counterterrorism & Protection

Project Management Professional (PMP)

Secret Security Clearance (SSC)

MILITARY EXPERIENCE

United States Armed Forces | 19xx to 20xx

Senior Key Leader / Lieutenant Colonel

Earned promotions and recognition during successful career with the U.S. Armed Forces. For the past 9 years (four years in Baghdad), provided leadership and expertise to international governments and organizations through training, advisory services, and high-stakes projects. Led diverse teams. Expertly allocated resources. Made decisions quickly, accurately, and thoughtfully.

- **Provided critical services to 1.5M people** by planning and executing major improvements to water, sewer, garbage, and electricity services in Baghdad, Iraq. In one project, overhauled processes and operations in a power plant facility to dramatically improve productivity and efficiency.
- **Built relationships with senior executives and government officials** (to the president and prime minister levels).
- **Received a Commendable Honor Award from the U.S. Department of State** for major contributions to improving utilities (water, sewer, electricity, garbage, and other services) and the overall infrastructure in Baghdad.

TECHNOLOGY CAREER HIGHLIGHTS

ABC Department of Transportation (ADT) | 20xx to Present

Vice President Resolution Strategies / Deputy CIO

ADT provides technical solutions to ensure safe, reliable, and high-performing assets and operations on a global scale. The company has 8,500 employees in 60 countries.

Provide vision for IT and business operations in current role. Pioneer strategies and initiatives to boost competitive position and influence growth. Lead IT departments in several countries (55 employees). Control $35M annual budget. Partner with executives to align technology and organizational strategies. Manage global projects. Define and track KSIs and SEHs. Deliver presentations to the board of directors.

JOHN H. SMITH, RPh, PharmD, BCPS

800-991-5187 | info@greatresumesfast.com | Callahan, FL
LinkedIn: John H. Smith

CLINICAL PHARMACIST

In-depth knowledge of disease states, drug interactions, and dosing
Commitment to safety and excellence in patient care

Forward-thinking pharmacist with a history of providing safe, accurate, and efficient care to patients in hospital and retail pharmacy environments. Unique career combines advanced education and board certification with 20+ years of experience including **inpatient pharmacy, oncology, pediatrics, dosing/monitoring, and IV room.**

Lifelong learner and team builder dedicated to improving patient outcomes by serving as a drug specialist, tireless researcher, and advocate for **evidence-based medication therapy.** Trustworthy and completely reliable.

AREAS OF EXPERTISE

- Pharmacy Operations
- Medication Use in Hospital Setting
- Team Building & Collaboration
- Improving Patient Outcomes
- Patient Care & Support
- Exceptional Communication Skills
- Anticoagulation Dosing
- Training & Instruction
- Hospital & Retail Experience

EDUCATION

Doctor of Pharmacy (PharmD) | Golden State University

Bachelor of Science (BS) in Pharmacy | Cambridge University School of Pharmacy

Board Certified Pharmacotherapy Specialist (BCPS)

Leadership Development Training • Basic Life Support (BLS) Certified

---

CAREER HIGHLIGHTS

Sloatsburg Regional Medical Center • Callahan, FL • 20xx to Present
Clinical Pharmacist

Provide safe, accurate, and efficient care to patients. Collaborate with providers and other hospital staff to maximize medication effectiveness and minimize adverse drug effects. Counsel patients on prescription and OTC medications. Manage renal dosing/monitoring and anticoagulation dosing. Lead and motivate pharmacy and support staff. Ensure 100% compliance.

Select contributions:

- Proposed and gained approval from the medical executive committee to allow pharmacists to order renal function labs on patients to ensure safe and effective dosing, expanding pharmacists' role in patient care.
- Educated and informed the health care team on renal function assessment and medication dosing.
- Performed extensive review of anticoagulation INR values and identified a trend of elevated values in heart failure patients—informed the pharmacy director and assisted in enhancing staff education.
- Improved patient care: Performed MIU and reduced use of ketorolac.

JOHN H SMITH

info@greatresumesfast.com • 800.991.5187
Callahan, Florida
Linked **in**

CONSULTING & LEADERSHIP PROFILE

Highly driven leader, innovator, and project manager with the expertise and tenacity to solve real-world business problems by leveraging MBA education and 20+ years of hands-on experience.

- ❏ Develop **clear, actionable strategies** as part of a **global solutions management team** responsible for targeting revenue-generating opportunities and coaching the sales force to target **$80M in new business** opportunities.

- ❏ Demonstrate a **cutting-edge approach to problem solving** by consulting with decision makers and delivering complex solutions that precisely align with each client's vision, budget, and priorities.

- ❏ **Played integral role in turning around underperforming projects**—and provided strong, cross-discipline leadership to achieve **on-time, within-budget outcomes**.

- ❏ Broad knowledge of business operations including **sales and marketing, team building, strategic planning, performance analysis, and full-scale project management**.

AREAS OF EMPHASIS

Client Relations & Communication | Needs Analysis | Project Planning & Execution | Process Redesign | Systems Analysis & Optimization | Team Building | Change Management | Strategic Planning & Execution | Business Development | International Experience (Cross-Cultural Leadership & Coordination) | Technical & Engineering Background

CAREER HISTORY

ABC ENGINEERS – Callahan, FL
Strategic Alliance Head Leader • 20xx to Present

Rehired by former employer to create and execute a business development strategy for North America targeting untapped opportunities in the process-safety space. Drove the **$80M growth strategy** by transitioning the sales organization from product to solution sales. Provided sales and business support. Realigned sales and engineering processes.

- **As key leader of the worldwide resolution lead team,** coordinated activities between international engineering and sales organizations to drive profitability for the process safety business.

- **Consulted with the sales organization** to identify competitive markets and establish customized solutions to capture the attention and close deals with specific customers. Developed and participated in client presentations to increase impact and close deals.

- **Initiated market sector analysis** designed to improve market segmentation (based on customer buying behavior) and responsiveness (based on customer needs).

- **Recognized as subject matter expert** by internal teams and prospective customers—bold presentations and skillful client relations paved the way for new accounts with Sysco, ACME, and Houston Regional Utilities.

STONEWALL BASICS – Callahan, FL
Operational Management – Lead Project Manager • 20xx to 20xx

Initially hired as project manager and earned **promotion to a leadership role** for a key safety project within the Sysco program. Then, provided cross-discipline leadership for additional projects (totaling $7.0M) to eliminate inefficiencies and guide all projects to achieve on-time, within-budget results. Supervised six team members.

- **Enabled growth into new market segments** by reviewing marketing documents for new product offerings.

- **Received two ENG Awards for contributions as a leader and problem solver**—including delivering one of the first technical integrations for a fire and gas system replacement project.

- **Managed and strengthened client relationships.**

STARLET RESOLUTIONS INC (formerly ACN Network) – Callahan, FL and Tokyo, Japan
Lead Project Engineer • 20xx to 20xx

JOHN H. SMITH

info@greatresumesfast.com • 800-991-5187 • Callahan, FL
www.linkedin.com/in/jessicaholbrook

LEADER + TEAM BUILDER

— Driving profitability and productivity through operations, procurement, and project leadership —

Forward-thinking leader with the ability to manage people, projects, and daily operations to influence growth and streamline processes in highly competitive, regulated, rapidly changing industries

Hands-on experience and education in health care and environmental sectors—with the commitment, focus, and enthusiasm to take a company, project, or team to the next level of performance. Proficient in targeting and closing public- and private-sector accounts and cultivating relationships with key decision makers to boost loyalty and satisfaction. Fast learner with a tenacious work ethic and a relentless concentration on company growth and success.

— AREAS OF EMPHASIS —

- Team Development & Leadership
- New Business Development & Procurement
- Client Relations & Communications
- Project Definition, Planning & Implementation
- Compliance Management
- Process Redesign & Improvement
- Time-Sensitive Documentation & Reporting
- Proactive & Effective Issue Resolution

CAREER HIGHLIGHTS

Victory Health Associates, Inc., Callahan, FL • August 20xx to Present

SENIOR LEADER / SENIOR PROJECT MANAGER

Initially hired as project administrator and earned two fast-paced promotions with wide-ranging accountability for operations, business development and procurement, nationwide project leadership, and relationship management.

Provide leadership to build strong teams, streamline processes, and develop new business while delivering medical programs for national accounts. Negotiate federal, state, local, and private contracts. Forge relationships with physicians, clinical laboratories, and clients. Coordinate logistics, resolve project-related issues, and ensure compliance with regulatory and industry standards. Lead projects with concurrent deadlines and changing priorities. Oversee business and office operations.

Select contributions and milestones:
- ✓ Trained and **supervised 15 employees** in administrative, clinical, and project-driven roles and provided motivation and guidance for on-time, on-target completion all deliverables in multiple, simultaneous projects.
- ✓ **Developed 25+ winning proposals** leading to public- and private-sector contract awards.
- ✓ Recently closed the company's largest account—a **$15M contract**—and initiated plans to manage the four-year engagement.
- ✓ Provided **project, business, and relationship management** to achieve approximately **$4M in annual revenue.**
- ✓ **Increased customer satisfaction** by representing the company as a **senior leader and trusted point of contact** for operational, medical, and compliance matters.
- ✓ Co-landed the **company's second-largest account**—the resulting project yielded **over $600K annually.**
- ✓ Expertly managed relationships with clinical laboratories and **4,500+ health care providers nationwide.**
- ✓ Performed **scientific and clinical research** on toxins, organic compounds, and specific diseases to support medical consulting and litigation projects.

ABC Marketing Systems, Hope, FL • June to August 20xx

MARKETING COORDINATOR / INTERN

JOHN SMITH
Objective: **Facilities Manager / Engineer**

800-991-5187 · info@greatresumesfast.com
Callahan, FL
LinkedIn: John Smith

QUALIFICATIONS PROFILE
— Dedicated to the growth and success of ABC Network —

Loyal and team-oriented professional with 25 years of experience driving efficiency and profitability by managing engineering, capital equipment, and process improvement projects. Natural leader with the ability to coordinate and inspire teams, suppliers, and contractors to meet deadlines and exceed quality standards. Drive SMART goals and continuous improvements.

AREAS OF EMPHASIS

- Team Building & Leadership
- Project Management
- Manufacturing Engineering
- Process Redesign & Improvement
- Budgeting & Cost Estimating
- Customer & Supplier Relations
- Lean Manufacturing
- Time & Resource Management
- Proactive Problem Solving

Our maintenance department has been without a full-time facilities manager for many years. I believe that I can lead, motivate, and strengthen the team to improve cooperation and achieve our company goals at the same time.

PROFESSIONAL EXPERIENCE

ABC NETWORK – Callahan, FL
Manufacturing Engineer · 19xx to Present
Manage engineering and equipment projects to boost performance in ABC Network's Engineered Core facility. Lead and expedite the project life cycle for customer-driven initiatives. Oversee safety, quality, budgets, timelines, and ever-changing priorities.
Select contributions:

- ► Supported the organization's growth and expansion by performing **engineering and facility improvement projects** simultaneously, including highly technical projects for some of ABC Network's most valuable customers.

- ► Directed the purchase and installation of **ABC Network Newark's first autoclave**—a project that required **strong leadership** and problem-solving abilities. Oversaw and coordinated the activities of 45 different companies (about **95 people**) and **worked closely with the maintenance department** to execute the successful project in 2.2 years.

- ► **Managed the capital request system** to justify and obtain funds, and oversaw the research, purchase, installation, and operation of six large ovens for processing composite parts since 20xx; recently purchased a seventh oven.

- ► Developed and **enhanced production processes** using Lean Manufacturing techniques.

MEYER TECHNOLOGY – Hope, FL
R&D Engineer · 19xx to 19xx
Consulted with customers regarding snowboard designs. Researched materials and processes, and built necessary tooling for quality product development and streamlined production.
Select contributions:

- ► Promoted the company's **quality and production goals** while developing **new customer product designs** that met manufacturing and scheduling requirements.

- ► **Researched, tested, and implemented materials** for use on new products.

EDUCATION

Bachelor of Science in Industrial Technology (19xx) · Florida State University

Training & Development: Layup Training · Process Safety Boot Camp · CTIS V4 Training: Surface Design, Manufacturing, Advanced Modeling, Energy DTE, Numerical Quality Manufacturing, Introduction to Modeling · Extensive Safety Training

JOHN SMITH

800-991-5187 • info@greatresumesfast.com • Callahan, FL
LinkedIn: John Smith

EXCELLENCE IN OPERATIONS & CUSTOMER CARE

Improving performance by engaging and developing a company's greatest assets —its customers and employees

Hands-on, people-oriented executive with 15+ years of experience introducing practical, real-world strategies to increase profitability and productivity. Proficient in building strong teams, processes, and infrastructures through operations leadership and skillful relationship management. Proven expertise in business, finance, and marketing is grounded in the knowledge that *authentic customer and employee relationships are critical to company success.*

EXECUTIVE CORE STRENGTHS

- Operations Management
- Customer Relations & Loyalty
- Performance Improvement
- Marketing & Business Development
- Process Redesign & Change Management
- Team Building & Leadership
- Budgeting & Forecasting
- Operational Effectiveness
- Project Management

Driving *rapid and sustained growth* by cultivating relationships at all levels, from the CEO to production staff.

Identifying and capitalizing on *revenue-generating opportunities*.

Pinpointing needs and executing customized projects that yield tangible value—*profitability, productivity, and efficiency*—through **loyal relationships**, leading-edge engineering technologies, and operating procedures.

CAREER HIGHLIGHTS

ACME NETWORK SYSTEM TECHNOLOGIES, Callahan, FL

Senior Director – Operations, Business Development, and Customer Care | 20xx to Present

Provide vision and direction for an engineering and marketing consulting practice. Oversee operations, sales, client services, financial management, and infrastructure optimization services for industrial and corporate clients. Lead teams of engineers, partners, and subcontractors to plan and execute projects with efficiency and precision—while focusing on client satisfaction.

BUSINESS LEADERSHIP & GROWTH

- Developed the operating model, client services approach, multi-level consulting methodology, and sales and marketing strategy to boost profits and performance in a competitive marketplace.
- Increased profits by targeting >80% of consulting services for both highly efficient and reliable advanced technologies.
- Identified and capitalized on advanced HVAC systems targeted for the custom residential market.

RELATIONSHIP MANAGEMENT

- Nurtured relationships with medium- to large-sized organizations to build trust, improve loyalty, and ensure customer satisfaction while planning and implementing efficient, reliable systems.
- Created a network of commercial and industrial prospect by leveraging personalized relationship-building strategies.
- Partnered with other organizations to expand capabilities and further drive revenue growth.

TECHNOLOGY & ENGINEERING INNOVATION

JOHN SMITH

800-991-5187 • info@greatresumesfast.com • Callahan, FL

SENIOR TECHNOLOGY LEADER IN BUSINESS DEVELOPMENT, PARTNER MANAGEMENT AND MARKETING

Strategic leader with 25+ years of experience in leadership across *business development, partner management, marketing, evangelism, product management and sales.*

Consistently selected for high-stakes projects and new business initiatives for leading technology companies and start-ups. Proven experience in *Cloud Services (IISS, KapS, MiceeS), Internet Security* and *Technology Infrastructure* markets. Proficient in working with IEVs, AudioChannel, Enterprise Customers and Service Providers. Track record of delivering rapid, impactful results by directing global teams from diverse functional areas.

PROFESSIONAL EXPERIENCE

CORE SYSTEMS INTERNATIONAL

Director Business Development – CSI Systems (Cloud Business) • 10/20xx to Present

Provide leadership and direction in *driving strategic alliances* and *building partner ecosystem* with IEVs for CSI cloud. Drove CCFE deal for KapS and supported E&S to expand product portfolio. The role expanded to include product management for a new cloud service – CSI Systems Managed Private Cloud. Nominated as a *High-Potential Director at CSI (top 5% globally).*

- *Led the CCFE deal with intel Systems* for KapS, which resulted in acquisition by CSI to form the core component of CSI Systems Development Platform. *SE lead for KapS E&S strategy.*

- *Drove alliance efforts* with CloudSys, ACME, Paxon, Sysco, Officenet, Prell, Runwright Systems, GE Cloud, Excel Systems, CFG. Led partner and resell agreement negotiations, enhanced sales and channel enablement and executed demand-generation campaigns for ISS solutions to drive partnership success.

- *Conceptualized and built the partner ecosystem* to increase visibility and revenue for Officenet based CSI Cloud. Defined strategy, value proposition and technology alignment and executed CUSYS. Recruited 185+ IEV partners, exceeding revenue goals and influencing *over 75% of total CSI revenue* within 15 months of inception.

- Additionally responsible (since June 20xx) for *product management and product marketing for CSI Systems Managed Private Cloud* with Officenet based compute, storage and networking services and iCloud based KapS. Drove CCFS development, value proposition, business model, competitive and gap analysis, messaging and sales readiness content to the *launch of Beta at CSI Inside Systems 20xx in Paris.*

SYSCO INTERNATIONAL CORPORATION

Director, Emerging Business Team • 2/20xx to 10/20xx

Led Sysco's International, a global technology adoption and marketing program for Windows iCloud, Windows Phone 8a and Windows 10. *Selected a worldwide portfolio of 65+ start-up companies.* Accelerated their growth through co-marketing, channel enablement, mentoring, engineering support and a community of incubators, investors and advisors.

- Drove product adoption amongst portfolio companies and marketed evidence through Videos, success stories, presentations at events and other product marketing channels. Improved portfolio satisfaction rating by 5 points. *Sysco adoption by over 55% of the portfolio.*

- *Influenced the Windows icloud direction* to add KapS service to then existing ISS services, through strong input to Sysco International leadership from Windows iCloud portfolio companies.

CELL NETWORK SYSTEMS INC.

Director Cloud Alliances and Start-up Marketing • 1/20xx to 2/20xx

Developed new markets for Cell's Startup Marketing Business Unit, with additional responsibility for business development for iCloud. *Managed $5M+ annual marketing budget* and led a team of 25 direct reports.

John Smith

Callahan, FL (Metro)   800.991.5187 | info@greatresumesfast.com | <u>LinkedIn Profile</u>

Senior-Level Executive

Industrial & Manufacturing Design

Concept Engineering | Change Management | Client Satisfaction | Business Leadership
Strategic Development & Execution | Continuous Improvement | Timely & Cost-Effective Solutions

Executive-level industrial engineer with distinguished record **of pioneering multimillion-dollar revenue-producing product lines** for 30+ years.

⇨ Builds and maintains strong, trusting, and long-term client relations through "Hear the Customer" approach that ensures customer requirements are acknowledged in product-development initiatives.
⇨ Provides leadership, vision, and direction to industrial-design teams to start, plan, execute, control, and close complex process and system improvement projects.

50+ patents. *Open to relocation.*

Career Chronology

ACME Company, Callahan, FL   20xx–Present
Hired for this 2nd-largest American office-furniture manufacturer based on previous successes in change management and concept engineering. Restructured product development and manufacturing processes around customer-centric methodologies that became **universal standards across corporation.**

Director of Healthcare Markets (20xx–Present)
Sales | Marketing | Contracts | Product Development | Senior Leadership. Assumed this newly created position in 20xx, after **leading successful 20xx entry** of company into healthcare-furniture business market.
⇨ Directed product development activities including:
- In-depth healthcare market analysis research on business and market trends.
- Direction of cross-functional teams that adapted "Hear the Customer" methodologies.
- Creation of business buying models and practical product solutions.
- Development of key channel partner network.
⇨ Launched in 20xx as **$40M** line with **annual revenues growing to $75M** (projected) through 20xx, based partially on expansion into patient-care facility market.

Director of Concept Development (20xx–20xx)
Established Concept Development Team comprising industrial designers and model makers based on determining customer needs *before* production and *not afterwards.*
⇨ **Positioned company as holistic, 1-stop supplier** for all office-furniture products and trusted advisor role through "Hear the Customer" methodologies.
⇨ Mentored and coached team to adopt broad, cross-functional approach used to scope, interview, process, and create viable product and process concepts for commercialization.
⇨ Introduced and implemented repeatable HTL process for product development that included:
- Tollgate review process and creation of Executive PMA (Project Management Action) monthly reviews to ensure all project steps were completed according to pre-defined success metrics.
⇨ **Propelled company into education-market leadership position** with introduction of EduLINK education line, which **generated sales of $35M+** over 5 years.
- **Process was adopted companywide as product-development foundation** after successful implementation in school furniture market.

JOHN H. SMITH

800-991-5187 • info@greatresumesfast.com • Callahan, FL • LinkedIn: John H Smith

SENIOR EHS LEADERSHIP

Eliminating injuries and workers compensation costs / Reducing risk at local and global levels

- ❑ **30 years of international experience** developing and implementing environmental health and safety (EHS) programs to improve performance in high-risk environments.

- ❑ **Expert in analyzing root causes, defining metrics to control risks, and tracking outcomes.** Developed strong teams and productive relationships with business and regulatory stakeholders. **Management systems and organizational behavior approach**. Drive for **continuous improvement.**

- ❑ **Successful career** began as a civil and safety engineer in heavy construction with extensive contract administration. Advanced to include infrastructure, logistics, and industrial operations in diverse fields—utilities, energy, and aviation.

SELECT CONTRIBUTIONS

Reduced lost-time injuries 80% in first 6 months
… largest decrease for any Armed Forces industrial organization or command worldwide.
Decreased workers compensation cases by an additional 45%

Eliminated fatalities from four per year to ZERO
… at another organization with high-risk activities and 65,000 personnel. **Eliminated** permanently disabling injuries to **ZERO. Decreased lost-time injuries 60%** through management systems analysis, root cause analysis, and innovative program execution.

Developed and directed EHS programs for high-risk work processes in the U.S. and overseas
…involving environmental hazards, industrial processes, energized utilities, hazardous energy and GO/MO, radiation, fall protection, underground and confined space entry, material handling, transportation, maintenance, cranes and powered industrial vehicles, heavy construction, contract management, fire prevention, Life Safety Code, ventilation, elevated work platforms, and ergonomics.

CAREER HIGHLIGHTS

Recent timeline overview: Traveled extensively throughout the Middle East and returned to the U.S. to resume a career in EHS leadership by stepping into temporary, contract roles.

REYNOLD CONTROL SERVICES – Baghdad, Iraq

Safety Engineer • 20xx to 20xx

Provided technical expertise for an environmental health and safety (EHS) consulting firm changing the work culture in an environment that attributes many on-the-job fatalities to "fate."

Select contributions:

- ✓ **Advised on** safety and occupational health training to meet **OSHA standards.** Developed curriculum tor the United Kingdom Association (UKA) to train companies poised to obtain **ISO 200H, ISO 8591, and OSHA 5461 certifications.**

- ✓ **Inspected industrial facilities and construction operations**. Proposed solutions to **mitigate** safety and fire hazards, and control risks.

JOHN SMITH

800-991-5187 • info@greatresumesfast.com • Callahan, FL
LinkedIn: John Smith

EXCELLENCE IN OPERATIONS & CUSTOMER CARE

Improving performance by engaging and developing a company's greatest assets—its customers and employees

Date

Name
Title
Company
Address
City, State Zip

Dear (NAME):

As a seasoned operations and customer service executive, I am able to inspire teams and influence customers for maximum revenue and profitability.

For more than a decade, my efforts have significantly increased the top and bottom lines through people-focused leadership, growth planning, and relationship management—and I am confident that I will add effective and long-lasting value to your team at (COMPANY NAME).

Highlights of my qualifications include:

- ❏ *15+ years of experience* as a leader and problem solver with proven expertise in sales and business development, customer care, operations, and financial management.

- ❏ Talent for *cultivating relationships with key decision makers at all levels of an organization*—from the CEO to the production floor—to execute key initiatives and launch sustainable sales and profit performance.

- ❏ History of achieving business goals by instilling a culture of teamwork, accountability, and service excellence—resulting in *immediate and lasting performance growth*.

Please review my résumé, visit my LinkedIn Profile, and contact me at 800-991-5187 to discuss how my background will help achieve your vision and goals—from my first day on the job. I hope to hear from you soon to schedule an interview.

Sincerely,

John Smith

P.S. My unique career combines all aspects of operations including marketing, sales, team building, finance, and the latest in technology innovations. For this reason, I can offer a fresh perspective and wide-ranging expertise to your team.

JOHN SMITH

800-991-5187 ▪ info@greatresumesfast.com ▪ Callahan, FL

SENIOR TECHNOLOGY LEADER IN BUSINESS DEVELOPMENT, PARTNER MANAGEMENT AND MARKETING

Date

Name
Title
Company
Address
City, State ZIP

Dear (NAME):

I am a senior executive with 25+ years of experience in leadership roles across **business development, partner management, marketing, evangelism, product management and sales.**

Throughout my career, my efforts have **substantially improved revenue and market positioning for large and small organizations — including ACME Systems, HP Networks and Quad Core Systems.**

I am currently seeking my next career opportunity and would appreciate if you could consider my résumé for senior leadership roles in the Buck County area.

Should you want additional details about my skills and experiences, I can be reached at 800-991-5187 or info@greatresumesfast.com.

Sincerely,

John Smith

JOHN H. SMITH, RPh, PharmD, BCPS

800-991-5187 | info@greatresumesfast.com | Callahan, FL
LinkedIn: John H Smith

CLINICAL PHARMACIST

In-depth knowledge of disease states, drug interactions, and dosing
Commitment to safety and excellence in patient care

Date

Name
Title
Hospital or Health System
Address
City, State Zip

Dear (NAME):

It is with genuine interest and enthusiasm that I am contacting you at this time. Currently, I am seeking an opportunity to join a leading-edge, patient-focused pharmacy team, and I am confident that I will add significant and lasting value to your organization.

My background includes **advanced education, board certification, and 20+ years of experience as a dependable and knowledgable pharmacist in hospital and retail settings**. I am passionate about my work and driven to provide unparalleled service and support to patients through counseling and safe, efficient, and accurate prescription processing, compounding, and dispensing.

Throughout my career, I have developed a reputation for innovation and excellence in central pharmacy, oncology, pedriatics, NICU, and IV room patient services. I am diligent in reviewing medication orders, ensuring accuracy and appropriateness, and improving patient outcomes.

Please review my résumé for an overview of my education and career history, and then contact me at 800-991-5187 or info@greatresumesfast.com to schedule an interview. I look forward to learning more about your requirements and providing additional information and insights into my unique background.

Thank you for your kind consideration.

Sincerely,

John H. Smith, RPh, PharmD, BCPS

P.S. (NOTE: Include this P.S. when targeting Orange Regional Medical Care ONLY. Remove it for your recruiter distribution and when targeting other organizations.) **Through personal experience, I am aware of your commitment to** world-class patient care at Orange Regional Medical Care, and I feel strongly that I will meet or exceed your high standards of excellence.

John H. Smith
Cover letter template for email (e-note)

Suggested E-note Subject Lines:

Re: Position Name and Posting # (if applying for a specific position posted online)
Or
Re: Career Opportunities I Clinical Pharmacist

Add to Subject Line
Referred by (Name) *(if contacting the company based on a referral)*

E-note Content:

Dear Mr. / Ms. (Last Name):
(If last name is known. Otherwise avoid salutation line altogether. That's better than using the generic "Dear Sir or Madam" or "To Whom It May Concern.")

(Name of referral) suggested I contact you regarding (insert position or opportunity). *(If using a referral. Otherwise, don't use this line.)*

It is with genuine interest and enthusiasm that I am contacting you at this time. Currently, I am seeking an opportunity to join a leading-edge, patient-focused pharmacy team, and I am confident that I will add significant and lasting value to one of your client organizations.

My background includes **advanced education, board certification, and 25+ years of experience as a dependable and knowledgable pharmacist in hospital and retail settings**. I am passionate about my work and driven to provide unparalleled service and support to patients through counseling and safe, efficient, and accurate prescription processing, compounding, and dispensing.

I have developed a reputation for innovation and excellence in central pharmacy, oncology, pedriatics, NICU, and IV room patient services. Plus, I am diligent in reviewing medication orders, ensuring accuracy and appropriateness, and improving patient outcomes.

May we schedule a time to talk? Please contact me at 800-991-5187 or info@greatresumesfast.com to arrange a meeting.

Sincerely,

John H. Smith, RPh, PharmD, BCPS
* * * * * *
800-991-5187
info@greatresumesfast.com
LinkedIn: John H. Smith

JOHN H SMITH

info@greatresumesfast.com • 800.991.5187
Callahan, Florida
Linked in

CONSULTING & LEADERSHIP PROFILE

Highly driven leader, innovator, and project manager with the expertise and tenacity to solve real-world business problems by leveraging MBA education and 20+ years of hands-on experience.

Date

Name
Title
Company
Address
City, State Zip

Dear (NAME):

I am genuinely pleased to contact you about the (INSERT TITLE) opportunity with (COMPANY NAME). With my advanced education and solid experience in project management, engineering, and business development, I am confident that I will add measurable value to your organization and for your clients.

In addition to an analytical mindset and creative problem-solving talents, I bring a great deal of energy and commitment to my work. Whether I am consulting with clients, executing projects, or uncovering new revenue-generating opportunities, I am able to deliver **leading-edge solutions on target, on time, and within budget**.

My qualifications include:

- ❏ MBA in progress (I will complete the program in January 2017) with 20+ years of experience as a project manager and innovator for Fortune 500 and other clients.

- ❏ Broad-based background in engineering leadership that is balanced with responsibilities in business development, budgeting, P&L, and international project management.

- ❏ Proven capacity to translate a client's vision and needs into concrete solutions that improve business operations, meet technical requirements, and support growth.

Please review my resume and contact me at 800-991-5187 to schedule an interview. I look forward to speaking with you.

Sincerely,

John H. Smith

P.S. Every time I step into a new situation, I am able to use my past experience and skills in a new way. Plus, I am a tenacious and focused leader and fast learner with the ability to make sound decisions with speed, accuracy, and accountability.

JOHN H. SMITH

John H. Smith
Cover letter template for email (e-note)

Suggested E-note Subject Lines:

Re: Position Name and Posting # (if applying for a specific position posted online)
Or
Re: Career Opportunities I Clinical Pharmacist

Add to Subject Line
Referred by (Name) *(if contacting the company based on a referral)*

E-note Content:

Dear Mr. / Ms. (Last Name):
(If last name is known. Otherwise avoid salutation line altogether. That's better than using the generic "Dear Sir or Madam" or "To Whom It May Concern.")

(Name of referral) suggested I contact you regarding (insert position or opportunity). *(If using a referral. Otherwise, don't use this line.)*

It is with genuine interest and enthusiasm that I am contacting you at this time. Currently, I am seeking an opportunity to join a leading-edge, patient-focused pharmacy team, and I am confident that I will add significant and lasting value to one of your client organizations.

My background includes **advanced education, board certification, and 25+ years of experience as a dependable and knowledgable pharmacist in hospital and retail settings**. I am passionate about my work and driven to provide unparalleled service and support to patients through counseling and safe, efficient, and accurate prescription processing, compounding, and dispensing.

I have developed a reputation for innovation and excellence in central pharmacy, oncology, pedriatics, NICU, and IV room patient services. Plus, I am diligent in reviewing medication orders, ensuring accuracy and appropriateness, and improving patient outcomes.

May we schedule a time to talk? Please contact me at 800-991-5187 or info@greatresumesfast.com to arrange a meeting.

Sincerely,

John H. Smith, RPh, PharmD, BCPS
* * * * * * *
800-991-5187
info@greatresumesfast.com
LinkedIn: John H. Smith

https://www.LinkedIn.com/in/jessicaholbrook

LEADER + TEAM BUILDER

— Driving profitability and productivity through operations, procurement, and project leadership —

> **Forward-thinking leader with the ability to manage people, projects, and daily operations to influence growth and streamline processes in highly competitive, regulated, rapidly changing industries**

Date

Name
Title
Company
Address
City, State Zip

Dear (NAME):

As a dedicated and driven professional, I am able to streamline processes, close profitable accounts, and inspire superior performance. Drawing on my real-world experience and education in health care, business, marketing, and environmental policy, I am confident that I will be a valuable addition to your leadership team.

I offer the following qualifications:

- ✓ Bachelor's degree in Marketing and Environmental Policy combined with ten years of on-the-job experience as a leader, consultant, and project manager.

- ✓ Unique ability to solve problems while directing multiple projects, meeting the needs of numerous high-profile clients, and managing relationships with over 4,500 medical facilities nationwide.

- ✓ Proven expertise developing new business with government and commercial clients.

- ✓ Demonstrated success developing, inspiring, and coordinating cross-functional teams responsible for business administration, clinical operations, and project execution.

Please review my resume for more details about my background, and contact me for an interview at your convenience. I look forward to speaking with you.

Sincerely,

John H. Smith
P.S. I am committed, tirelessly, to *doing what it takes* to meet every deadline, exceed client expectations, and pave the way for my company to succeed.

JOHN H. SMITH, RPh, PharmD, BCPS
Hospital & Health Care
Callahan, FL

HEADLINE

Clinical Pharmacist | Hospital Pharmacy | Knowledge of Drug Interactions & Dosing | Improving Safety & Patient Outcomes

SUMMARY

I have been a pharmacist for many years—providing world-class service in both retail and hospital environments.

My commitment to lifelong learning and unwavering focus on safety and excellence in patient care inspired me to return to school to advance my education and expertise in the health care field. In 20xx, I added the following credentials to my list of qualifications:

Doctor of Pharmacy (PharmD)
Board Certified Pharmacotherapy Specialist (BCPS)

For 22+ years, I have provided safe, accurate, and efficient care to patients including inpatient pharmacy, oncology, pediatrics, NICU, dosing/monitoring, and IV room. I am diligent in reviewing medication orders, verifying renal levels when appropriate, and providing the best possible evidence-based medication therapy.

At the same time, I am a dedicated and inspired team player who is trustworthy, accountable, and completely reliable.

To me, patients are always my priority. I have been known to call or visit patients in their rooms to verify information and overall health. I have also introduced new processes or training programs to enhance safety and accuracy—and avoid dangerous drug interactions.

Specialties include:
-- Pharmacy Operations
-- Medication Use in Hospital Setting
-- Team Building & Collaboration
-- Improving Patient Outcomes
-- Patient Care & Support
-- Exceptional Communication Skills
-- Anticoagulation Dosing
-- Training & Instruction
-- IV Admixtures
-- Chemotherapy
-- Hyperalimentation Solutions
-- Renal Dosing & Monitoring

EXPERIENCE

Sloatsburg Regional Medical Center • Callahan, FL
Clinical Pharmacist
20xx to Present

I joined this medical center in 20xx to provide safe, accurate, and efficient pharmacy services to patients. I collaborate with providers and other hospital staff to maximize medication effectiveness and minimize adverse drug effects.

My work involves reviewing medication orders, renal dosing/monitoring, and anticoagulation dosing to protect patients and the hospital. I counsel patients on prescription and OTC medications. I supervise and coordinate pharmacy and support staff and ensure 100% compliance with requirements, standards, and safety protocols.

-- Performed extensive review of anticoagulation INR values and identified a trend of elevated values in conjunctive heart failure patients—informed the pharmacy director and assisted in enhancing staff education.
-- Proposed and gained approval from the medical executive committee to allow pharmacists to order renal function labs on patients to ensure safe and effective dosing; expanding pharmacists' role in patient care. This project was in conjunction with my PharmD training.
-- Improved patient pare by performing MIU and reducing the use of ketorolac.

Orange Regional Medical Care Center • Callahan, FL
Clinical Pharmacist and Pharmacist Trainer
20xx to 20xx

I was rehired by my former employer to provide accurate, appropriate medication to patients in the central pharmacy, IV room, and oncology satellite of Orange Regional Medical Care Center.

I was responsible for reviewing medication orders, renal dosing and monitoring, compounding special dosage forms, IV admixtures, chemotherapy, and other essential tasks in a hospital setting.

Expanding upon my work in pharmacy services and patient care, I trained and coached new pharmacists and collaborated with providers and other hospital staff to improve medication therapy management.

ABC Pharmacy • Hope, FL
Relief Pharmacist
20xx to 20xx

In this hands-on pharmacist position—in a privately held retail pharmacy—I supervised teams to boost productivity and enhance patient relations, satisfaction, and loyalty.

In addition, I managed pharmacy operations and services including processing, compounding, and dispensing prescriptions, and counseling patients on prescription and OTC drugs.

Regional Medical Center • Callahan, FL

Staff Pharmacist
19xx to 20xx / 19xx to 19xx

I originally joined Regional Medical Center earlier in my career (before my military experience), and they rehired me in 19xx. In this staff pharmacy position, I provided consistent and accurate pharmacy services in the central pharmacy (including internal medicine and cardiology patients), IV room, pediatrics satellite, NICU, and oncology satellite.

My work involved all of the typical aspects of medical center pharmacy services—reviewing medication orders for accuracy and appropriateness, counseling patients, and safely processing/dispensing medications.

When the pharmacy was short-staffed, I volunteered to work nights for three months to fill an urgent staffing need.

State Regional Medical Department of USA • Tokyo, Japan and Texas
19xx to 19xx
Director of Pharmacy Services / Director of Outpatient Pharmacy / Quality Assurance Program Manager

During my career with the U.S. Armed Forces, I was often selected for new and additional roles and responsibilities—including taking on new departments and teams without having had prior experience in those areas.

My tasks included directing pharmacy, X-ray, and laboratory operations to offer uninterrupted, quality care to patients. I also managed outpatient pharmacy staff (25 personnel) to accurately dispense an average of 4,500 prescriptions daily.

As a leader and pharmacist, I prepared staff schedules, oversaw inventory, counseled patients, streamlined processes, and resolved patient concerns. I also performed as quality assurance program manager for my attention to detail and commitment to 100% compliance.

* * *

I established the foundation for a successful career in a prior position with CVS Pharmacy. I started as Intern and Staff Pharmacist, and was promoted to Pharmacy Manager within 6 months of employment. In this retail pharmacy position, I oversaw staffing, inventory, customer service, prescription processing, and dispensing.

EDUCATION

Doctor of Pharmacy (PharmD)
Golden State University

Bachelor of Science (BS) in Pharmacy
Cambridge University School of Pharmacy

CERTIFICATIONS

Board Certified Pharmacotherapy Specialist (BCPS)

Basic Life Support (BLS) Certified

COURSES

Leadership Development, United States Armed Forces

ORGANIZATIONS

American Regional Medical Center of Pharmacists (ARMC)
Member

Florida State Pharmacy Association
Member

Buck County Aging Services Association
Expert Presenter on Medications and Fall Risk

VOLUNTEERING

Brown Junior High School
Former Reading/Math Mentor

West Elm Elementary School
Former Reading/Math Mentor

SKILLS

Pharmacy Operations
Pharmacy Services
Hospital Pharmacy
Medication Use
Improving Patient Outcomes
Prescription Processing
Anticoagulation Dosing
Renal Dosing
Renal Monitoring
IV Admixtures
Chemotherapy
Hyperalimentation Solutions
Clinical Drug Consultations
Evidence-Based Medication Therapy
Staff Supervision
Team Building
Training
Patient Counseling
Patient Relations
Prescription Drugs
Prescription Dispensing
Quality Assurance

Safety
OTC Drugs
Quality Assurance Manager
Collaboration
Communication
Technology Systems
Process Improvement
Compliance Management
Documentation
Reporting

Cheryl Lynch Simpson,
CMRW, ACRW, COPNS

Cheryl Lynch Simpson
ExecutiveResumeRescue.com
info@executiveresumerescue.com
614.891.9043

Cheryl Lynch Simpson is a Career, Job Search, and LinkedIn Coach and 30-year veteran of the career management industry. As a 21-time global award-winning Master Resume Writer, she specializes in serving mid-career to senior executives in more than 30 different industries. Cheryl blends expertise in job search strategies with her proprietary job search program and elite career branding to hone in on her client's WhyBuyROI – the reason employers should hire them and the quantifiable impact their hire has had on employers in their past. Known for her skill in visual branding, she has earned multiple Toast of the Resume Industry (TORI) awards for her stunning resume designs and innovative layouts.

MARIELLE N. HAWTHORNE

SENIOR GLOBAL HEALTHCARE MARKETING EXECUTIVE

Medical Devices | Pharmaceuticals | Biotech

I AM A ...

❖ Senior Global Marketing and Business Development Executive who fuels achievement of stretch business goals and catalyzes multimillion-dollar revenue growth.

❖ Product development and acquisition expert who excels at analyzing competitor strategies, trends, and market landscapes to uncover and seize product opportunities.

❖ Strategic planner who leads the evolution, establishment, and execution of upstream global marketing in alignment with overall business and product portfolio goals.

In short, I'm a brand champion who propels product lines to next-level performance. *Achievement snapshot:*

- **SANSCRIT:** Initialized a $100M, 5-year revenue pipeline, directing start-up commercialization for 3 biotech products.

- **REVERSA:** Surpassed $265M sales goal and pushed share growth 11% YOY. Revamped global marketing operations.

- **PMI INTERNATIONAL:** Penetrated 3 new markets, produced $50M in sales, and drove $6M in new business.

WITH 13+ YEARS OF EXPERIENCE IN ...

CAREER TIMELINE

TARGETING ...

❖ Senior global marketing roles in healthcare, pharmaceutical, or biotech companies.

❖ Mid- to large-size organizations with micromanagement-free cultures that value high potential talent, are open to calculated risk-taking, and expect accountability.

❖ Open to US relocation, particularly in FL, SC, GA, PA, IL, or Washington DC.

OFFERING EXPERTISE IN:

BOTTOM-LINE ORIENTATION

Deliver rapid results by leveraging self-awareness, ethics, and values to align with and realize corporate results. Employ a custom coaching style to guide talent to peak performance.

UPSTREAM + DOWNSTREAM MARKETING

Pair upstream and downstream marketing strengths and new business development skills to drive revenue in all market cycles.

HEALTHCARE BRAND MANAGEMENT

Catalyzed >$100M in career revenue with start-up to multinational organizations in pharmaceutical and biotech industries.

89455 17th Street West, #1202 • San Francisco, CA 65752 • 573.257.9614 • mnhawthorne@gmail.com

MARK W. TIBBETTS

C-SUITE EXECUTIVE: CEO IPRESIDENT I CHIEF COMMERCIAL OFFICER

Mark Tibbett's is a global business executive who specializes in commercializing intellectual property. With a record of influencing more than $120M in revenue throughout his career, he possesses a blend of marketing, branding, and product management expertise that enables him to over-deliver on revenue, growth, expansion, and brand recognition targets.

After long tenure and a series of increasingly responsible senior leadership roles with Standard & Poor's, Mark joined Electrolite in a key C-level position spanning business and marketing oversight of a mission-critical product line producing hundreds of millions of dollars in revenue. As the organization's digital marketing and product digitization expert, he facilitated Electrolite's shift from print to digitized product lines while driving a marketing overhaul organization-wide.

EARLY CAREER

Mark launched his career as a **Credit Analyst** with IBM. Quickly promoted through sales roles to **Regional International Sales Manager**, he subsequently worked for Dell as **Global Strategic Account Manager**. His first true marketing role was **Manager of Strategic Marketing** for Xerox.

HOOVERS, 19XX – 20XX

Recruited to Hoovers in 19XX as **Director of Structured Finance Product Management**, he helped drive a new analytic software product from $500K to $15M in revenue. Mark revamped the business model and product group while expanding the client base 20 times over. Promoted in 2005 to **VP of Product Management Services for Ratings Market Development**, he spearheaded a product line turnaround that pushed revenue 16% and jumpstarted revenue growth for 2 previously stalled lines by $8M combined. In addition to relaunching 2 lines with restructured sales plans he championed Hoovers' transition to digital media as key designer of business, launch, and marketing strategies for licensed products.

Appointed in 20XX to **VP of Ratings Operations**, Mark led an organizational realignment leveraging Lean process improvement practices. By redesigning and rolling out new governance, marketing, and product sales initiatives he was able to increase profits 32% and client base 18% despite being in a tightly regulated industry in the midst of a credit ratings crisis.

MARKETING & PRODUCT MANAGEMENT AWARDS

Silver Bulldog Media Relations Award for Excellence in Media & Publicity Campaigns
20XX

Sabre Award for Best Global/ Multi-Market PR Campaign
20XX

Silver Anvil Award of Excellence for Reputation/ Brand Management
20XX

Hoovers Chairman's Award for Excellence in Marketing & Analytical Expertise
20XX

Hoovers Chairman's Award for Excellence in Marketing & Product Management
20XX

INSTITUTE OF ELECTRICAL & ELECTRONICS ENGINEERS, 20XX – PRESENT

Tapped to serve as **Chief Marketing Officer** for Electrolite in 20XX in a role equivalent to that of a Chief Commercial Officer, Group President, or EVP, Mark holds global P&L accountability for this professional organization's single largest revenue stream ($220M). He leads strategic planning, marketing promotions, and licensing for Electrolite's intellectual property in more than 80 countries.

Mark's tenure with Electrolite is marked by a dramatic rise in revenue (+65%) and new customers (+48%) as well as these achievements:

- ↗ Revitalized Electrolite's primary products, expanded the corporate market 18%, and boosted sales up to 9% year-over-year. Instilled value pricing mindset and sustained key market retention despite competitors' lost share.

- ↗ Catalyzed +90% customer retention by building the business case for an innovative client service management role.

- ↗ Spearheaded the $30M drive to digitize Electrolite's main product line and launched 15 new products.

- ↗ Honored with industry awards for global, multimarket public relations and reputation/brand management. Formalized and upgraded Electrolite's corporate marketing, elevated master brand, and unified sub-brands.

Mark earned a **BA in Business Administration** from Stanford University and completed leadership coursework at Columbia Business School. He presently sits on the **Board of Directors** of Hoovers' Federal Credit Union. Known as an "innovative leader who has a strong knack for getting things done", Mark Tibbetts guides teams to peak performance by leveraging high EQ to cultivate emerging leaders.

KRISTINE A. KOWALSKI

SENIOR BANKING EXECUTIVE

Driving sustainable results in the financial services secto

Date

Name of Company Contact
Title
Name of Company
Address
City, State Zip

Dear Name of Contact:

In the dynamic financial services market, I have a track record of growing revenues +15%, outperforming volume goals +112%, and revitalizing teams in senior mortgage, credit services/control, underwriting, loan sales, and finance field operations roles.

If you have a need, I can deliver similar results for your company. Specifically, I can:

- **Reengineer financial services operations** and drive up closing volumes (106% in less than 4 months).

- **Pave the way for multimillion-dollar revenue increases** ($76M for JP Morgan Chase).

- **Tighten Sarbanes-Oxley and Basel regulatory compliance** (restructured lending audit processes for 13 North/South American credit operations).

- **Over-produce on year-over-year sales targets** with no increase in staff (personal record is a 67% loan sales boost).

- **Rollout start-up field operations with out-of-the-ballpark performance** (achieved a zero credit-loss record for 8 straight years).

With deep knowledge of the financial services industry (credit, consumer lending, and mortgage, private, and corporate banking) gained through extensive tenure with JP Morgan Chase, I offer exceptional operations management skills and the proven ability to fuel growth and improve performance. The result is a tightly run, highly efficient team that consistently attains corporate targets.

May we meet to discuss your needs and the value I would bring to your company?

Sincerely,

Kristine A. Kowalski

Enclosure

LINKEDIN TEMPLATE

I. NAME

Art Mayhew

II. TITLE/TAGLINE

Senior Sales & Operations Executive

III. SUMMARY

ABOUT FORD
At Ford, we're passionate about designing, building, and selling the world's best vehicles with the world's best employees – 198K of them in 212 facilities on 7 continents.

ABOUT ME
I love people and it shows in everything I do, from the way I lead my team to the way I communicate change and overachieve goals. I sincerely believe people are the reason for our stunning success in recent years, and I'm proud to have played a big part in Ford's turnaround by generating >$431B in sales for 3 divisions.

SALES & REVENUE GROWTH
✔ Led automotive industry sales 3 times and drove record-breaking revenues for 4 market-leading brands.
✔ Drove Ford fleet & commercial sales to #1 industry ranking in 2012.

OPERATIONAL EXCELLENCE
✔ Launched the Ford XX's leading-edge technology.
✔ Forged innovative promotional partnerships with Major League Baseball, Football, and Basketball.

PERFORMANCE REVERSALS
✔ Initialized the first-time Ford market dominance in 19 years and the best US Camaro sales in 70 years.

The secret to my success is EMPLOYEE ENGAGEMENT. In 2012, my team scored 16 points higher on our year-over-year employee engagement survey – the highest scores in all of Ford's sales and marketing divisions.

But, in the end, it's not about survey results. It's about what we do every day and how we treat people. Because let's face it, engaged teams produce better business results.

IV. EXPERIENCE

Title: US VP – Commercial Sales [Fleet & Commercial Operations I Marketing/PR/Promotions]
Company Name: Ford
Employment Dates: 20XX-Present
Job Description: Surpassed $13B revenue benchmark by $250M versus 2010. Lead 156-member team to produce 21% of US sales.

Title: General Sales Manager [Dealer Network Management I Residual Development I Sales]
Company Name: Ford

CEO | PRESIDENT | BOARD MEMBER

Catalyzed >$6.7B in Revenue + $3B in Profits Career-Long

Date

Name of Recruiter
Title
Name of Organization
Street Address
City, State Zip

Dear Name of or Recruiter:

As a performance turnaround executive with more than 12 years of C-level leadership and M&A-fueled growth for market leaders such as Coca-Cola, Delta, and Smith Wesson, I excel at delivering +20% sales and +15% profitability gains. If you have a client company in search of an articulate results driver, perhaps we should talk.

Recognized repeatedly for producing in excess of $560M in savings and synergies, I have proven my ability to optimize sales, distributions, and supply chain operations.

EXPERIENCE PROFILE:

CAREER TRAJECTORY:	Rose into senior sales, marketing, operations & distribution roles with COCA-COLA before joining VASCO as **President of Manufacturing, Distribution & Supply** and **President/CEO**. Served DELTA as **Executive Group VP of Operations** and was subsequently recruited as **President/CEO/Board Member** for SMITH WESSON SUPPLY.
LEADERSHIP STRENGTHS:	Visioning & Strategic Planning I P&L Maximization I Sales Operations Management I Supply Chain Optimization I Purchasing I Cost Containment I M&A Strategies & Integrations I Technology Integration I Profit & Market Value Growth I Continuous Process Improvement I Board Governance
BOARD EXPERIENCE:	Currently a Board Member of Smith Wesson Supply A Previously served on the boards of Ben & Jerry's I Advent Medical I Van Camp Dealer Association I Wendover Beverage
CREDENTIALS:	**MBA I BS in Business Administration** A University of Colorado

My objective is a C-level leadership or board role within the food service, supply chain logistics, or multi-channel distribution industries. I am open to relocation and my total salary expectation is in the mid-7-figure range.

I am available to interview with any clients you may be working with at your convenience, and appreciate both your time and consideration. Thank you.

Respectfully,

Karla Noriano
ENC: Résumé

LINKEDIN PROFILE

Contact Info:

Name: Eric J. Peters

Headline: Award-winning sales and operations executive and green marketing Subject Matter Expert

Summary: With a passion for sales generation, people leadership, and green marketing, I have earned a record of year-over-year profit gains and cost containment with a major US auto maker, while winning repeated promotions into progressively responsible executive roles. My contributions to ABC Cars' dramatic 2009 performance reversal include:

LEADERSHIP STYLE: Pushed US sales from 45.7 to 71.2% of ABC's business, embracing stretch targets and energizing teams with a compelling vision.

BEST-IN-CLASS MARKETING: Recognized by *Automotive News* for social blogging outreach as Top 10 major marketing move of 2010.

SALES & MARKETING RESULTS: Strengthened cash flow by slashing advertising budget 41% and lowering company vehicle inventory 47.3%. Restructured divisional headcount 17% and lowered promotional spending 47% for 2009.

GREEN MARKETING: Produced more fuel solutions than any other auto brand and designed symbols for 5 alternative fuel pathways later adopted globally.

"Great communicator. Great team-builder. Great leader in the eyes of dealers and wholesale teams."
[John Weiring, VP of North American Sales & Marketing, ABC Cars]

Specialties: Breakthrough Sales Attainment | Green Marketing | Market Share Penetration | Revenue Generation | Digital Lead Management | Retail Sales Generation | Dealer Performance Maximization | Profit Turn Arounds

Experience:

Title: North American Vice President
Company Name: ABC Car Corporation
Industry: Automotive
Employment Dates: 20XX – Present
Job Description: Promoted to reverse declining sales growth and propel sales, marketing, advertising, PR, sales promotion, and product development to next-level performance for this division with $35 billion in annual revenue. Achievement highlights:

MARKET SHARE PENETRATION:
>> Propelled 2010 market share from 8.4% to 12.7%, the largest industry mid-car segment rise and pushed sales to 31% total market share through the launch of best-in-class marketing campaign.

CRITICAL REVENUE GENERATION:
>> Increased car revenue 25% from $12 billion to $15 billion CYTD through brand-level margin success, aggressive cost containment, decreased spending, and strategic incentive management.

MEDIA & DIGITAL LEAD MANAGEMENT:
>> Drove "superlative" media share of voice to #1 industry-wide by investing leadership and presence in up to 30 constituent, media, and social networking interviews daily to promote award-winning products.

Title: Division General Manager
Company Name: ABC Car Corporation
Industry: Automotive

PRABU PARTIL

SOCIALLY CONSCIOUS VISIONARY WHO CULTIVATED $215B IN GLOBAL BUSINESS OPPORTUNITIES

▪ SENIOR IT, TELECOM & CLOUD BUSINESS DEVELOPMENT EXECUTIVE ▪

CAREER BRAND: High-octane revenue rainmaker with an unwavering focus on driving profit growth, client retention, and corporate revenue. Talented utility player with a passion for emerging and disruptive technologies.

LEADERSHIP PEDIGREE: Networking dynamo proficient in 5 languages. Inclusive executive who champions and role models legendary relationship management.

BUSINESS DEVELOPMENT ROI: Articulate business development strategist and stakeholder engagement master who positioned >$215B in revenue career long:

- Generated $175M+ in new business and closed ~ $750M in new deals, exceeding corporate quotas up to 246% for 10 consecutive years.
- Enabled STEALTH server Ethernet switching solutions to reach more than 450 companies across 33 industry segments.
- Solidified partnership with $100B Asian industrial conglomerate serving 420M subscribers that propelled Verizon into Chinese market.

$595B IN ALLIANCES

$981M IN DEALS

$838M IN SALES

UP TO 253% OVER QUOTA

UP TO 156% YOY GROWTH

"PRABU POSSESSES THE 'OPEN SESAME' MAGIC NEEDED TO PENETRATE EMERGING MARKETS." – JT WILSON | APPLE

CHANNEL PARTNER MANAGEMENT ▪ GLOBAL ENTERPRISE SALES ▪ C-LEVEL SALES & MARKETING ▪ GO-TO-MARKET PLANNING ▪ PROFIT DELIVERY ▪ GLOBAL BRAND & PRODUCT POSITIONING ▪ STRATEGIC MARKETING ▪ DEAL ACQUISITION, NEGOTIATIONS & CLOSING

BUSINESS DEVELOPMENT EXPERIENCE & ACHIEVEMENTS

XUAJEI TELECOM | NEW YORK, NY | 20XX – Present
Chinese $100B global telecom & technology firm with 100K+ employees.

SVP OF GLOBAL BUSINESS DEVELOPMENT

Recruited to direct technology commercialization, localization, and democratization spanning the newly realigned consumer retail, and mobile ecosystems of the company. Preside over an executive team of 12 and a $125M P&L.

Jumpstarted $135M in Technology Deals & >$5.95B in Key Alliances with Industry-Leading Partners

- **STRATEGIC ALLIANCE-BUILDING:** Forged high-profile strategic alliances with key industry leaders to access best-in-class technologies on behalf of Xuajei's 250M subscribers. Select alliances include:
  - Proposed $2.7B project with China's largest social media network to initiate the nation's largest private and public sector Greenfield data center and renewable energy opportunity.
  - Secured, incubated, grew, and led lucrative partnership with Apple to propel potential $3B+ business opportunity and commercialize next-generation computing system throughout the Xuajei global enterprise.
  - Won $70M+ deal to initiate joint venture and expand CDN media and security products/solutions access.
  - Orchestrated strategic collaboration with Amazon to launch $180M+ expansion of film/television streaming services.
- **TECHNOLOGY DEAL DEVELOPMENT, NEGOTIATIONS & CLOSING:** Closed and spearheaded service rollout for a $67M transit, data center, business continuity, and disaster recovery deal as part of a $6B global network services engagement.
  - Set vision, strategized, and guided a potential $450M alliance spanning 4 business lines with Cisco. Led a team of 40 through build-out of +$68M, M2M platform design, consulting, and installation services.

STEALTH NETWORK TECHNOLOGIES | NEW YORK, NY | 20XX – 20XX
Leading supplier of Gigabit & 10G Ethernet network infrastructure solutions with $550M in sales.

VP OF US SALES

Built next-generation network revenue from zero to $22M in 4 months by penetrating 3 new markets. Drove US market expansion that boosted sales 6X in 3 years. Oversaw $144M P&L; laid foundation that won $380M in major contracts with Microsoft and Apple.

NEW YORK, NY | 176.556.2428 | PPARTIL@GMAIL.COM

RAND MICHAEL PAULSON, JR.

Fueled >$2B in New Revenue Growth & Catalyzed 100+ Global JVs/Alliances Valued at +$4B

Conceptualized 65+ New Brands & 2K New Products/Extensions

Consumer Products | Packaged Foods & Beverages | Consumer Technology

Turnaround executive who infuses stagnant companies with energy, focus, and international dynamism. Expert in forging businesses from white space by aligning internal assets with strategic vision and market opportunities. Insatiably curious and passionate leader who builds consensus and fosters internal and external collaboration. Bottom-line-driven C-level leader with broad-based commercial and business skills gained through early career Universal Studios tenure and global exposure (US | Europe | Mexico | Australia | Asia).

u   Built-Out Tingret US Operations, Turned Around Asian Business Unit & Paved the Way for +18% Expansion

u   Captured $970M in Revenue for Universal Studios & Jumpstarted +37% Profit Gains for 2 Consecutive Years

EXECUTIVE PEDIGREE
MBA • Harvard Business School | **BS in Global Management** • Oxford University

EXECUTIVE EXPERIENCE

GLOBAL PRESIDENT • TINGRET TECHNOLOGY – New York, NY   20XX–20XX

Drove 50% growth and double-digit expansion, spearheading a major culture shift and business improvement initiative for this VC-backed leader in virtual reality software. Directed a multimillion-dollar P&L with a team of 140 on 5 continents.

u   **Launched US operation from the ground up.** Negotiated and closed key +$50M, C-level anchor deals that earned the company unprecedented national publicity and business development credibility.

— Captured $150M in recurring revenue for the first time in the company's 12-year history, overcoming inherited focus on one-off transactional deals. Gained "halo" marketing effect through elite deals with Wendy's and Topps Trading Cards.

— Instituted first-ever business disciplines and protocols to leverage operational efficiencies and drive profitability.

u   **Reversed Asia-Pacific business unit performance from a decline to +18% growth.** Reorganized unit to align with objectives set with core customers and resellers; rebuilt unit senior leadership.

CEO • NITRAFIT – New York, NY   20XX–20XX

Recruited to unify and right-size operations in the aftermath of 5 non-integrated acquisitions for this $370M consumer products and technologies company. Presided over a 450-member team; reported to CEO of corporate holding company.

u   **Delivered double-digit CAGR** through acquisition consolidation and corporate restructuring. Streamlined administration, aligned business goals, rebuilt senior leadership team, and revamped vision.

u   **Trimmed $140M in expenses** while instituting best practices, positioning the business for expansion, and leveraging core creative, development, and supply capabilities. Merged 5 disparate entities into 1 streamlined global company.

u   **Positioned +$825M in annualized 3-year sales** by expanding footprint to penetrate new market segments. Negotiated complex deals with Taco Bell, Pentel, and Build-A-Bear Workshop Asia.

> *Rand is the most dynamic leader you'll ever meet. His charisma charms everyone he meets and is paralleled only by his financial & business acumen.*
> Telly Palmerston – CEO, VIVEK INTERNATIONAL

SENIOR TECHNOLOGY SALES MANAGER

ACHIEVED 16 STRAIGHT YEARS OF DOUBLE-DIGIT YOY SALES

LEADERSHIP STYLE:

- Drove unprecedented triple-percentage sales gains, catapulting US sales from 28% to 76% of HP's business. Fueled above-and-beyond team performance by harnessing talent and empowering emerging leaders.

BEST-IN-CLASS MARKETING:

- Capitalized on new marketing initiatives to catalyze +12% profits, +13% market share, and +24% consumer awareness.
- Pioneered social blogging outreach recognized by *Computing Magazine* for boosting brand visibility 53%.

SALES & MARKETING RESULTS:

- Strengthened cash flow by slashing advertising budget $143M (44%) and lowering company inventory 52%.
- Restructured divisional field structure to trim headcount 23%; lowered promotional spending from $212M.

OUT-PACED SALES GOALS UP TO 130%			
YEAR	TARGET	SALES	% TO PLAN
2014	$184M	$214M	130%
2013	$172M	$201M	128%
2012	$156M	$198M	125%
2011	$76M	$97M	123%
2010	$58M	$69M	120%
2009	$22M	$27M	118%

CORE COMPETENCIES:

ATTAINING BREAKTHROUGH SALES	SUSTAINING MARKET SHARE	OVER-PRODUCING REVENUE TARGETS
DOMINATING RETAIL CHANNELS	TURNING AROUND PROFITABILITY	INCREASING DIGITAL LEADS
MAXIMIZING VERTICAL SALES	REBUILDING SALES TEAMS	REVAMPING SALES COMP PLANS

SENIOR SALES LEADERSHIP EXPERIENCE

HEWLETT PACKARD   19XX – Present
NORTH AMERICAN VP OF SALES [20XX – Present]

Promoted to reverse declining national sales growth, rebuild product development, and regain market dominance. Direct $46M divisional P&L with 325 staff, 300 agency personnel, and 4.2K US channel partners. Lead $27M in domestic advertising.

TURNED AROUND US SALES:

- Halted hemorrhaging sales, regained growth, and pushed revenue from $28M to $46M. Revamped national sales team and compensation strategies around rebranded products.
- Improved printer revenue 28% ($21M) by deepening brand-level margins. Cut costs $14M and decreased spending 19%.

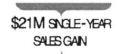

$21M SINGLE-YEAR SALES GAIN

REVITALIZED PRODUCT DEVELOPMENT:

- Championed "test and learn" strategy to reinvigorate innovation, restructured talent development, and revamped product line leadership. Streamlined new product rollout cycle from 18 to 3 months.
- Transformed product positioning through realignment of brands with profit targets. Consolidated 12 product lines to 3 and rewrote web marketing playbook while strengthening channel partner training and product knowledge.

GEORGE L. PARKER

SENIOR OPERATIONS EXECUTIVE

Natural Leader + Process Improver Who Drives +17% Top- + Bottom-Line Performance

Proven Leadership in High-Stakes, High-Pressure Environments

Senior efficiency and strategic planning expert with enterprise experience spanning supply chain management, operations, finance, and HR. Cross-functional track record gained through multidisciplinary education, international experience in Europe, Asia, and Africa, and a highly decorated military career encompassing operations, logistics, and training. Current Top Secret Clearance.

Frank Multicultural Communicator + Consensus-Builder with an Inclusive Leadership Style that Cultivates Accountability

Executive MBA in Progress with an Emphasis on Innovation, Strategy Design + Organizational Leadership

SELECT CAREER ACHIEVEMENTS

SUPPLY CHAIN MANAGEMENT	Led employment of thousands of assets spanning 8 major and 31+ smaller global locations.
BUSINESS OPERATIONS	Saved $45M, leading crisis planning to enable in-operation refueling after base decertification.
FINANCE	Administered $3.7B supply chain; built business case for $630M DOD investment.
HUMAN RESOURCES	Possess >13 years' experience in leadership development; led thousands of indirect personnel.

LEADERSHIP STRENGTHS

GLOBAL OPERATIONS LEADERSHIP w CRISIS MANAGEMENT w STRATEGIC PLANNING w BUSINESS PROCESS REENGINEERING
DECISION CHAIN INFLUENCER w PROJECT MANAGEMENT w COST CONTAINMENT w EXECUTIVE COMMUNICATIONS
TALENT + LEADERSHIP DEVELOPMENT w STAKEHOLDER RELATIONSHIP MANAGEMENT

SENIOR LEADERSHIP ACHIEVEMENTS

US NAVY – SAN DIEGO, CA   2000 – PRESENT

EXECUTIVE DIRECTOR – STRATEGIC PLANNING [20XX – PRESENT]

Instrumental in steering the development and rollout of the Navy's first internal PhD-level strategic planning training program from the ground up with zero budget, requirements, structure, or curriculum in place. Led build-out of budget, candidate screening process, and curriculum from scratch. Roadmapped 5-year budget growth from $1700K to $5M as program matures.

- **Screened, selected, and oversaw an initial pool of 30 Ph.D. candidates at 15 US universities** in preparation for expansion to 90 in 6 years. Positioned to carve out Army-wide savings on the hire of external strategic planning consultants.

CHIEF OF AIR OPERATIONS – AFGHANISTAN [20XX – 20XX]

Drove air operations for US naval forces in Afghanistan impacting >4K assets. Defined and articulated $3B in contract aviation, personnel, and supply chain logistics.

- **Generated +$45M in aviation fuel savings** by establishing aircraft/staging operations and aerial refueling within Afghanistan to eliminate twice-daily round trips to prior staging locations.

- **Optimized fleet safety**, authoring point paper for Department of the Navy Congressional testimony on sequestration effects. Saved $420M detailing maintenance reset and correlated accident rates.

CHIEF OF OPERATIONS – SAN DIEGO, CA [20XX – 20XX]

Presided over leadership development/education operations with >5K employees and a $325M budget. Directed semi-annual adult learning conference for 250 officers. Nailed down $25M+ FY14 savings through the redesign of cost and structure strategies.

CHIEF OF AVIATION OPERATIONS – CHARLESTON, VA [20XX – 20XX]

Tapped lead aviation operations for the US Navy Central Command in support of Operations Iraqi/Enduring Freedom.

- **Tightened interoperability with US forces and NATO partners** as a key advisor. Coached and demonstrated a formal problem-solving methodology for large enterprises impacting HR, operations, logistics, strategic planning, and intelligence.

- **Standardized interface with USAF and increased ground crew safety.** Mapped integration plan and established operational best practices to optimize cross-functional communications and performance.

KENNETH COOPERMAN

CEO | PRESIDENT ~ PAYMENT SERVICES | E-COMMERCE | PRIVATE EQUITY

PIONEER OF MARKET-DISRUPTIVE TECHNOLOGY THAT SPAWNED $12B IN REVENUE
Out-Performed Investor Expectations 10x | Captured + Sustained #1 Market Position since Inception

Financial services technology visionary who drove $22B in sales via 40K online stores delivering goods and services in >179 countries. Chief sculptor and advocate of an award-winning, Gen 2.0 online business platform that set new e-commerce global benchmark and decimated competitors. Conceive bold business dreams and champion realization by empowering excellence.

BUSINESS + PERSONAL HONORS

Best E-Commerce Solution ~ SMALL BUSINESS COMPUTING | **Best Customer Service** ~ THE NEW YORK TIMES
100 Brilliant Companies ~ ENTREPRENEUR | **Best Overall Company** ~ WALL STREET JOURNAL
INC 500 ~ INC MAGAZINE | **Entrepreneur of the Year** ~ ERNST & YOUNG

ACADEMIC PEDIGREE

MBA ~ THE WHARTON SCHOOL OF BUSINESS | **MIS** ~ NEW YORK UNIVERSITY
Executive Development ~ HARVARD BUSINESS SCHOOL + CAMBRIDGE UNIVERSITY

SELECT VOLUSION ACHIEVEMENTS

- Built the world's most innovative, payment services platform, revolutionizing small business e-commerce.
- Out-positioned competitors by raising >$5B in annual funding and investing in proprietary technology.
- Transformed technology platform from a single to a multi-market, multi-product, and multi-channel growth engine.

EXECUTIVE LEADERSHIP EXPERIENCE

CEO | VOLUSION | New York, NY | 20XX–20XX

Recruited to seize technology and market leadership in the midst of stalled profits. Built and launched market-leading technology solutions and led C-level executive team of 6. Delivered above-market returns across multiple growth stages, economic cycles and shifting competitive landscapes.

TRANSITIONED VOLUSION FROM START-UP TO DOMINANT MARKET LEADER

Set vision, crafted strategy, built internal/external consensus, and restructured business plan pivoting from ($800k)/month burn to positive cash flow and profitability in <90 days. Attracted new capital and established steep-growth trajectory.

- **Attained 85%+ market share as largest payment services provider to small businesses.** Out-innovated traditional providers, road-blocked competition, and fueled company expansion from $32M to $1.8B in annual revenue.

JOSEPH STUDENT

(406) 123-4567   joestudent@gmail.com   Missoula, Montana

PROFESSIONAL REFERENCES

Mr. George Timothy Clooney   **Main Office: (913) 222-3333**
Company President and Internship Supervisor
Ocean Twenty Film Company
12345 East Hollywood Avenue
Hollywood, California 90260
GTC@ocean20.com

Mr. William Bradley Pitt   **Cell Phone: (801) 111-2222**
Co-President and Producer
Plan B Entertainment
9150 Wilshire Boulevard, Suite 350
Beverly Hills, California 90212
WBP@PlanBEntertainment.org

PERSONAL REFERENCE

Coach Mick Delaney   **Office: (406) 243-1111**
Head Football Coach
Intercollegiate Athletics
University of Montana
Hoyt Athletic Complex 208
Missoula, Montana 59812
Michael.Delaney@umontana.edu

ACADEMIC REFERENCE

Dr. Entertainment Professor   **Office: (406) 243-1234**
Management and Marketing Department
School of Business Administration
University of Montana
Gallagher Business Building #ABC
Missoula, Montana 59812
Entertainment.professor@umontana.edu

SUZIE SMITH

➤ • • ◄

| Cell: (406) 123-4567 | Missoula, Montana | suziesmith@gmail.com |

PROFESSIONAL REFERENCES

George Timothy Clooney
Company President and Internship Supervisor
Ocean Twenty Film Company
12345 East Hollywood Avenue
Hollywood, California 90260
Main Office: (913) 222-3333

*Direct supervisor for film editing internship on "By the Sea" to be released April 2015.

William Bradley Pitt
Co-President and Producer
Plan B Entertainment
9150 Wilshire Boulevard, Suite 350
Beverly Hills, California 90212
Cell Phone: (123) 456-7891

*Direct supervisor for summer 2014 internship working in content distribution promoting film shorts.

➤ • • ◄

ACADEMIC REFERENCE

Dr. Entertainment Professor
Management and Marketing Department
School of Business Administration
University of Montana
Gallagher Business Building, Room 123
Missoula, Montana 59812
Private Office: (406) 243-1234

*Served as Dr. Professor's teacher assistant supporting his senior-level Entertainment Management courses.

JOHN SMITH

Relocating to Scottsdale, Arizona | 406-555-4444 | johnsmith@gmail.com

PROFESSIONAL REFERENCES

Justin Greene   **Cell: (406) 123-4567**
ENTERTAINMENT VENUE OWNER
Big Venue Somewhere
123 Main Street
Las Vegas, Nevada 12345

"John is the most diligent, driven marketing coordinator (intern) I've worked with in my twenty years in entertainment. He is completely focused on brand building, revenue generation, artist engagement, community outreach and delivery of exceptional entertainment. I'd hire him again in a heartbeat!" ~ Justin Greene

Jeremy Sauterson   **Cell: (123) 456-7890**
FORMER SENIOR VICE PRESIDENT
Creative Advertising
Paramount Pictures
Los Angeles, California 12345

"His strong internship experience with talent, venue management and social media puts him way ahead of students who have only studied such ideas in abstract." ~ Jeremy Sauterson

Dr. Jim Johnson   **Cell: (111) 222-3333**
ANIMATION PROFESSOR
University of Montana
Media Arts Department
McGill Hall, Room 123
Missoula, Montana 59801

"An exceptional student in the classroom, John has been successful in internships in digital media and film editing. His four years' experience in event production and marketing, coupled with his academic studies, presents a strong candidate. He is one of our finest graduates, and I recommend him without hesitation." ~ Dr. Johnson

JOSEPH SIMONSTAN

(406) 123-4567   joesimonstan@gmail.com   Missoula, Montana

PROFESSIONAL REFERENCE

George Timothy Clooney   **Main Office: (913) 222-3333**
Company President and Internship Supervisor
Ocean Twenty Film Company
12345 East Hollywood Avenue
Hollywood, California 90260
GTC@ocean20.com

Mr. Clooney can speak from firsthand knowledge regarding my achievement in video editing and quality control for external distribution, post-production routing and coordination, as I was his direct report during a highly competitive summer internship.

PERSONAL REFERENCE

Mick Delaney   **Office: (406) 243-1111**
Head Football Coach
Intercollegiate Athletics
University of Montana
Hoyt Athletic Complex 208
Missoula, Montana 59812
Michael.Delaney@umontana.edu

Coach Delaney can speak to my performance as a student-athlete in and out of the classroom, as I was starting quarterback for three seasons for NCAA Division I football and won the highly competitive All-Conference Academic Award under his guidance.

ACADEMIC REFERENCE

Entertainment Professor   **Office: (406) 243-1234**
Management and Marketing Department
School of Business Administration
University of Montana
Gallagher Business Building 123
Missoula, Montana 59812
Entertainment.professor@umontana.edu

Dr. Professor served as my advisor, mentor and upper-core supervisor. Under his three-year guidance, I helped coordinate Entertainment Management classes and assignments and was honored with the SoBA "STAR Award" for superior achievement which is given to 10 of 3,000 business majors each year.

Suzie Smith
MARKETING ASSISTANT

CONTACT DATA

406.123.4567

SSmith@gmail.com

Linkedin.com/SuzieS

PROFESSIONAL REFERENCES

JIM BROWN
Regional Marketing Manager
NIKE
1 Bowerman Drive
Beaverton, Oregon 97005
503.671.6453

JAMES WHITE
Merchandise Marketing Manager
Nordstrom
500 Pine Street
Seattle, Washington 98101
206.628.2111

JAMESON BLACK
Executive Team Lead
Target
1000 Nicollet Mall
Minneapolis, Minnesota
612.304.6073

CHERIE NEWTON

PO Box 123 • Rural Town, Montana
Cell: 406.123.4567 • Email: cnewton@gmail.com

PROFESSIONAL REFERENCES

Credentials available from University of Montana Career Services: 406.243.2022

James Addison
Second Grade Teacher
St. Peter Clever Elementary School
123 Central Main West
St. Paul, Minnesota 55104

651.123.4567
jamesadd@frontiernet.net

Dr. Jennifer Smith
Professor of Education
St. Catherine University
2004 Randolph Avenue
St. Paul, Minnesota 55105

651.456.7890
jennifersmith@stcat.edu

Walter Disney
Superintendent / Principal
Seeley Lake Elementary
200 School Lane; PO Box 840
Seeley Lake, Montana 59868

406.123.4567
waltdisney@blackfoot.net

Suzie Sweet
Second Grade Teacher
Seeley Lake Elementary
200 School Lane; PO Box 840
Seeley Lake, Montana 59868

406.444.5555 ext.123
suziesweet@blackfoot.net

Amy L. Adler
MBA, MA, CMRW, CCMC

Amy L. Adler, MBA, MA, CMRW, CCMC
www.linkedin.com/in/amyladler
fivestrengths.com
everydayresumes.com
twitter.com/AmyLAdler
(801) 810-5627

As an executive resume writer and career coach, Amy L. Adler, MBA, MA, CMRW, CCMC has the privilege of meeting the most amazing people every day and telling their stories. Each new executive with whom she works has contributed something amazing, but often they don't see it, so she translates what is in their heads into language that hiring executives understand, appreciate, and act on. Thus, she works one-on-one with demanding executive job seekers to uncover, deconstruct, and rebuild their career histories into powerful demonstrations of talents, accomplishments, and professional branding. She captures executive job seekers' career histories using their unique career goals as the lens to focus their talents and expertise, ensuring the hiring executives learn exactly what they need to know, via their executive resume, LinkedIn profile, cover letter, and strategic career coaching.

A Certified Master Resume Writer, Amy has written hundreds of resumes for C-level executives and professionals around the world. Amy has won two TORI Awards for Best Executive Resume and has been nominated the TORI's Best Career Re-Entry Resume, plus she has been invited to serve as a TORI judge. She holds an MBA from Boston College, a Master of Arts from New York University, and a Bachelor of Arts from Franklin and Marshall College. Amy can be reached via the Five Strengths Career Transition Experts website at http://fivestrengths. com or by calling (801) 810-5627.

EXECUTIVE LEADER: TECHNOLOGY, STRATEGY, VISION, AND EXECUTION

Sir or Madam:

If you are currently sourcing a strategic and INNOVATIVE TECHNOLOGY LEADER for a prime client, then we should speak about the leadership and experience I deliver. While I am happy to refer candidates your way as well, I hope you'll keep my credentials in mind as you work with your clients seeking strategic leadership in IT.

It's hard to imagine now that, at one time, a major global publisher did not have the means to sell and distribute its content online. With vision and deep experience, I architected, built, and scaled the enterprise ecommerce platform to support our multifaceted ecommerce strategy. By 20XX, the ecommerce platform supported 29% of our revenue, making it one of our most efficient IT investments to date. Moreover, I have also led development, QA, product, and support organizations to achieve our business goals. With an eye to innovation and creation of a culture of disruption, I guide my teams to focus on our customers' needs as served through business and technology solutions.

As a business leader, my reputation is for building, inspiring, and mentoring global IT developer teams. More crucial to my company's success, I coach my teams to work across business units when executing on technology roadmaps. Inevitably, my team's work directly influences revenues, as my experiences with International and Legal Publishers both clearly prove (see attached résumé for additional details). I look forward to bringing this expertise to a top organization.

Once again, I hope that we will speak about possible positions in IT strategic leadership, particularly if one of your clients is seeking an executive IT expert. If so, please reach out to me to explore my career history. At the same time, as I mentioned, I'm happy to provide referrals within the industry as well. You can reach me in confidence at the above telephone number or email address; I look forward to hearing from you.

With best regards,

George Thom
Enclosure: Résumé

SCOTT BANKS

123 Anystreet, Anycity, ST 55555 | (801) 810-5627 |sbanks@fivestrengths.com

QUALIFIED FOR:

VICE PRESIDENT, B2B ENTERPRISE SALES

AWARD-WINNING SALES OPERATIONS EXECUTIVE

Supported $45M+ incremental sales revenue in <6 years.
Builds, designs, and executes profitable sales strategies for distributed teams.
Leads large sales organization of 130+, advancing its expertise to match corporate buying economy.
Plans for and produces sales wins in untapped spaces.
Maximizes customer lifetime values and deepens market penetration.
Develops and delivers sales training for maximum revenue growth and business impact.
Data-driven analytics, projects, and sales strategy that maximizes sales to Fortune 500–50 business clients.

EXECUTIVE EXPERIENCE

Director, Sales Development & Operations   20XX–Present
Bringheart Corporation, Trenton, NJ

As executive sales operations leader, refreshed approach to sales pipeline, providing new avenues for sales automation for this nearly 100-year-old company providing technology and strategy to support employee recognition programs in Fortune 500 companies. Directed all aspects of sales, including pipeline development, sales strategy, team training, sales collateral development, and more, for outstanding sales performance year over year.

LED SALES TEAM AND PROCESS AT EXECUTIVE LEVEL

- Managed team through radical structural change beginning 20XX; encouraged all to grow into new structure.
- Provided quality team leadership and recognition, as emblematic of corporate core values. Engaged all individuals at their levels, ensuring communication of value of their efforts. Encouraged team to grow their careers, sometimes assisting them in transferring throughout company.
- Proponent of management by walking around strategy, refreshing connections daily with current and former team members, to strengthen sense of team and improve morale to highest level within company.
- In 20XX, was selected as part of executive team to certify as Arbinger trainer and to train entire company on best practices around teamwork. Improved priorities, minimized push-back, and increased trust as strategy changed.
- Initiated Intranet site for sales team, and, ultimately, company; converted all materials to robust online site, cutting printing budget to $0. Evolved site to serve as significant resource to sales team.
- Evolved onboarding process and mentored new sales team members.

PLANNED AND EXECUTED SALES STRATEGY AND OPERATIONS

- Led first determination of customer retention rate, proving 92% retention on 1,550 parent accounts each valued at $29K+, on 4,500+ total customers.
  - Worked with SAP developers to combine data from disparate sources to determine official customer retention metrics by corporate view, sales area, and 60 regional sales offices globally.
- Accurately assessed value of accounts and regions with data generated from Salesforce.com, in first data-driven approach to evaluating pipeline; yielded deeper regional penetration with increased staffing.
  - Aligned data to opportunities within each geographic area, which supported sales team growth from 79 to 129 sales professionals, at significant but worthwhile investment to company.
  - For example, in San Francisco, anecdotal reporting of opportunity supported 1 sales team member for 30 years; new data supported recruitment of 3 additional sales team members, initiated in January 20XX.
  - Realigned and apportioned sales regions according to new information, assigning sales hunters to effectively generate new accounts and client retention teams to expand existing accounts.
- Directly engaged in technology sales role and technology sales training.

GEORGE THOM

801-810-5627 | gwaltham@fivestrengths.com

EXECUTIVE LEADERSHIP FOR TECHNOLOGY
STRATEGY—VISION—EXECUTION

MAXIMIZING REVENUE WITH INNOVATIVE TECHNOLOGY SOLUTIONS
BUILDING MULTISITE TECHNOLOGY TEAMS FOR CULTURE OF INNOVATION AND DISRUPTION

**Collaborating with business units for revenue growth | Creating and executing strategic vision and roadmap
Leading large onshore and offshore developer teams | Developing products. | Focusing on user experience**

Executive Leadership | Entrepreneurship | Revenue Models | Business Growth | Cross-Functional Collaboration
Ecommerce | Architecture | Infrastructure | Agile Development | Software Development Lifecycle | Global Teams

EXECUTIVE EXPERIENCE

Senior Director of Engineering, Ecommerce (International Publishers Education)
Director, Ecommerce and Analytics (International Publishers –Higher Ed)
Lead Architect / Technical Lead
International Publishers, New York, NY 20XX–Present

As head of engineering team for ecommerce, delivered entrepreneurial vision, roadmap, and execution for ecommerce platform architecture, development, and rollout. Focused development and quality assurance teams on broad business vision, which was company's first enterprise ecommerce solution. Achieved broad support for information technology solutions driving business goals. Identified and invested in revenue-focused technologies. Dissected user requirements and root needs, envisioned solutions, and designed efficient solutions. Known for collaborative approach; regularly invited contributions from all to promote best outcomes.

Strategic Information Technology / Ecommerce Leadership

- Established and executed on strategy for ecommerce channel, which supported $210M revenue (29% of all revenue growth by 20XX); system grew from 890 users in 20XX to 5.8M users (5700 concurrent) in 20XX, directly increasing higher education sales 28% YOY 20XX–20XX and more beyond.
- Architected complete ecommerce platform, strategizing and supplying vision for overall infrastructure and strategic plan since 20XX. Proved experience and expertise in infrastructure design.
- Instituted rapid release model for monthly releases using Agile software development to speed response to business environment.
  - Influenced and gained trust of internal and external business partners to accept managed risks to achieve software update goals quickly.
  - Achieved 0% downtime in deployments, each transparent to customers, mitigating risk to revenue.
  - Responded more quickly with rapid release program to failures and to marketplace.
  - Supported Amazon Reseller Program and enabled timely introduction of trial access program.

- Served as institutional resource to sales and marketing team; suggested technology plans to support marketing and sales vision, adding intelligence and experience to product design strategies. For example, recommended methods to support sales team needing CRM tracking of instructors' use of products.

Technology Team Leadership

- Earned promotion to overall ecommerce leadership, to oversee all of International Publishers' ecommerce solutions, building on initial platform designed for higher education group, and to double team size.
- Built teams from ground up, selecting and combining top technology talent across multiple locations and building culture of innovation and disruption.

Susan Williams

801-810-5627 | susanwilliams@fivestrengths.com | linkedin.com/in/susanwilliams | twitter.com/susanw

Brand Strategy and Multi-Platform Marketing Executive

Brand Builder | P&L Leadership | Revenue Growth
Influences and Captures Mind Share and Wallet Share of Women, Millennial, and Multicultural Consumers

Chief marketing executive inspires *love of* and *loyalty to* brands.
Penetrates new markets for Fortune 500 consumer and packaged goods, luxury brands, television, music, and digital products.
Stewards brand proposition and delivers on value to customers and clients to yield top-line revenue and year-over-year growth.
Strategizes cross-functionally with R&D, research, sales, operations, finance, creative, and more to meet corporate objectives.
Rallies spirited, loyal teams with individual connections and devotion to common goals.
Experienced in agency and in-house marketing.

EXECUTIVE EXPERIENCE

Marketing and Business Consultant | 20XX–Present
SW Consulting, Chicago, IL

Consulted with small businesses to grow acquisitions and engagement.
- For startup Ouchie app developed multiplatform B2B and consumer marketing plans with an e-commerce program, was recruited to create subscriber acquisition plan and social CRM program to drive unique experience, with goal of launching with 150K subscribers in year 1.
- At Leap Innovations, where technology meets education, was tapped to consult on social media and branding.

Adjunct Instructor | 20XX–Present
Booth School of Business, University of Chicago, Chicago, IL

Lectured at graduate level in business communication program, teaching students from position of experienced industry executive.
- Recruited for expertise and talented presentation style; coached students on persuasion and communication styles.
- Taught Business Communication class (Fall 20XX) with plans to teach Crisis Communications in Spring 20XX in highly focused one-on-one student engagement model.

Managing Partner and Chief Marketing Strategist | 20XX–20XX
Powerhouse Marketing Agency, Chicago, IL

Recruited by and reported to CEO to lead agency's approach to media planning and buying, analyze and evolve social currencies for agency's largest account, and build expertise in luxury female categories to pitch for new business.
- Sold Powerhouse Planning to 3 clients, generating incremental revenue and shifts in media dollars from traditional vehicles to more relevant digital and social platforms.
- Using proprietary psychographic model, incorporated new consumer insights, augmented demographic segmentation methodology, and analyzed traditional and social CRM, ultimately created differentiated customer experience, enhanced knowledge of customer bases, and influenced radical shift in agency's second largest client's digital media spend from 12% of $345M U.S. media mix to unprecedented 33%.
- Evaluated social currency model, reviewing, analyzing, and adjusting mechanisms for social media to build and enhance conversation about customer brands. Enhanced conversation between 12% and 25% for 3 $100M+ clients.
- Mobilized CPG client to market to millennial audiences with fresh perspective, supporting unique audience's approaches to engagement with cleaning products over those of prior generations.
- Participated in business development process, acquiring 2 new clients.
- Clients/businesses worked on included NBC Universal, L'Oreal, SC Johnson, Welch's, Pandora, and Arm & Hammer.

Executive Vice President and Chief Marketing Officer | 20XX–20XX
Major Cable Provider, Topeka, KS

Recruited by CEO to generate revenue and revive brand, which was losing ratings to competition and loyalty of core viewers, spending resources on media without clear ROI, experiencing declining ad revenue, and flat digital growth. Reversed downward trend with 3-year strategic plan, and laid groundwork to position organization financially to buy company back from majority shareholder, Comcast.
- Led 22-person team, strategically transitioning marketing from on-air promotion shop to an integrated function, combining creative services, content development, digital media, strategic marketing and branding, integrated and partnership marketing to reach core audiences.
- Elevated brand's overall digital sophistication with modern user experience and improved web/digital strategy.

Grew Bottom Line with Brand Makeover	
+27	New advertisers.
+10.8%	Revenue.
+9%	EBITDA.

Kimberly Robb Baker
NCRW, CJSS, CMRW

Kimberly Robb Baker
This Little Brand
twitter.com/thislittlebrand
linkedin.com/in/kimberlyrobbbaker
facebook.com/kimmohiuddin
movinonupresumes.com/samples
kim@movingonupresumes.com

Kimberly Robb Baker, career story coach and writer, uses the process of resume writing to help her clients define their unique value. Together, they review work and life experience and identify trends to uncover brand qualities that are a perfect match for their next role. The deep exploration helps them define, internalize, and embody that value whether they are in an interview or in line at the store.

Ms. Baker's visually appealing, highly branded resumes, cover letters, and LinkedIn profiles instantly communicate how each client can contribute in their new environment. Executives, entrepreneurs, and rising stars reach out to have her tell their career stories. While Ms. Baker is a multi-credentialed and multi-award-winning resume writer, former certification chair of the National Resume Writers' Association, and trusted resource to the media, she is most proud of one accomplishment: more than 70% of her business is with repeat and referred clients.

You can connect with Ms. Baker at ThisLittleBrand.com.

TARA PRICE

Enterprising... Decisive... Effective

High-Value Outside Sales Executive

Waukegan, IL 60085 • 847.555.5555 • TPrice874@me.com

Poised to Apply Unflinching Tenacity and Proven Strategies to Achieve Ambitious B2B Sales Goals

~ Expected Mailing Date ~

<<FullName>>
<<Title>>
<<BusName>>
<<Street>>
<<CSZ>>

Dear Hiring Team:

Do you need a sales rep who's not afraid to take her knocks and use lessons learned to outperform expectations? Then we should talk, because my greatest successes have started as failures.

There was the time I was on the Board of the Junior League of Waukegan and we ended up with 10,000 surplus cookbooks because a distribution deal fell through. The alliances I made with junior leagues across the country, local businesses, and even the US Navy not only got us back in the black, but ended up being valuable connections for the league and for my business.

By turning failure around, learning from it, and just plain moving forward without fear of, it I h

Junior League Waukegan Fundraise Revenue in $K

- Multiplied sales, frequently gaining double- or triple-digit year-over-year increases
- Made long-lasting connections with influential people and organizations
- Helped my clients fulfill their most important goals

The well-known musician and outdoorsman Ted Nugent said of me, "Tara knew what she wanted. The stakes were high and she was willing to fail." That willingness has enabled me to take the calculated risks that have led to the successes you see in the attached resume.

iOrganize Waukegan Revenue in $K

My primary focus now is finding a way to exceed your most challenging sales goals. May we speak in person so I can learn more about your needs? I guarantee that the meeting will be worth your while.

Thank you for taking the time to consider my candidacy.

Sincerely,

TaraPrice

Tara Price

Maria M. Erin

407-555-5555 • Orlando, FL
MariaMErin@icloud.com

READY TO APPLY BUSINESS AND FINANCE SUCCESS AS A
FULL SERVICE REGISTERED REPRESENTATIVE
BUSINESS DEVELOPMENT | RESEARCH | ANALYSIS | SALES

> **"Obstacles are those frightful things you see when you take your eyes off your goal."** —Henry Ford

Business and sales thought leader with a reputation for spotting opportunities—and red flags—others miss. Offer meticulous research and compliance skills paired with fresh strategies. Quickly gain product and market knowledge and deliver top sales and customer service in sophisticated, highly regulated industries. Known for:

- **Achieving double- and triple-digit YOY growth with top-1% sales performance.**
- **Building high retention and referral rates** among loyal body of customers.
- **Developing and delivering compelling programs to educate** clients as well as colleagues and team members.
- **Bringing honest, ethical approach** to strategic planning and problem resolution.

Offer degree in Economics and Marketing, experience building and leading businesses with up to $1.9B in annual sales, and a win-win outlook that has added hundreds of millions in revenue—even when my role was primarily that of an individual contributor.

> "From the first time I met Maria, I felt completely at ease and comfortable talking with her... She always has my best interests at heart and intuitively knows how best to meet my requests."
>
> "Honest, professional, impeccable integrity and always available. These are the words that describe Maria Erin."
>
> *- 9-Year Clients*
> *Lynne & Dale Dommel*

FINANCE, BUSINESS, & SALES CONTRIBUTIONS

DISNEY COMPANY, DISNEY VACATION DEVELOPMENT, Orlando, FL   20XX–20XX
$500M Disney-owned vacation ownership and real estate firm offering members lifelong access to 500+ global destinations.
Senior Sales Guide & Licensed Realtor: **High-Value Sales • Regulatory Compliance • Compelling Presentations • Financial Projections**

Hired to sell vacation ownership onsite at Walt Disney World, earning rapid promotions. As one of only 14 on the elite cruise team, partner with colleagues sign new clients. Make high-impact presentations to large groups and meet individually with couples to counsel them on fulfilling their dreams within their budget. In sales and training capacities, traveled extensively to the Mediterranean, Mexico, the Caribbean, Japan, and to New York and Los Angeles. Delivered 1K+ presentations.

SALES VS. GOAL

2013	210%
2012	180%
2011	175%

Takeaways for full-service trading: Growing book of business, performing custom break-even analysis for clients, client retention, helping clients hedge against inflation, savings and spending planning, asset equity assessment, and selling product that is anticipated to grow in value.

Growing $17M Gross Revenue Business (20XX) & Advancing Organization.

- **Ranked in top 1% of agents every year of tenure, generating $17M in 2013.** Broke gross and net sales records 6 years running.
- **Maintained #1 closing ratio in firm and ranked in top 1% in industry since 2006.**
- **Enabled $180M+ in additional revenue since 2013. Conceived idea and gained buy-in from senior managers to developed and implement cruise-specific channel.**
- **Exceeded projections 200% on special 8-week assignment as sole sales trainer for new Japan-based office.** Ran training initiatives in New York and Los Angeles as well.
- **Built referral programs that account for 50% of business from existing customers.**

50+ Awards & Honors, Including: Leadership Circle—Every Year
Voted Team Captain 4 X
Named to Top-Performer Team
Ranked in top 1%

Only agent to achieve "Leading the Way" designation (2013) for exceptional performers who exceed goals, engage teams across channels and functions, act as role models, identify key opportunities, communicate effectively, and uphold the Disney brand and culture.

Played Key Role in Doubling Cruise Channel to 8 Figures for Projected 200% Growth by 20XX.

Situation: Recognized opportunity for improved operational and sales performance by creating dedicated team for cruise channel. At the time, teams were split between cruise- and land-based sales.

Approach and Results: Won buy-in from senior management and led development of strategy, scripts, SOP, and training. Joined dedicated selling team.

- Grew channel 60% in first year, from $50M in 2012 to $80M in 2013.
- Generated $100M+ 2014 sales YTD.

CRUISE CHANNEL SALES

2014 (P)	$150M
2013	$80M
2012	$50M

See next page for entrepreneurial success, building and managing $1.9B global business, and academic qualifications.

Maria M. Erin

"Your customer doesn't care how much you know until they know how much you care."– Damon Richards

FINANCE, BUSINESS, & SALES CONTRIBUTIONS, CONTINUED

JACK O'GRADY'S CHOP HOUSE, Jacksonville Beach, FL   20XX–20XX

Fine dining establishment serving loyal customer base of high-net-worth families and prominent businesses.

VP of Finance / Co-Owner: **New Business Launch • High-Net-Worth Clients • PR • Market Cultivation • Market Segmentation**

Steered financial strategy and back-office operations for fine dining startup from site purchase to profitable sale. Oversaw hiring, payroll, banking relationships, cash-flow management, and marketing. Played key role in site selection, remodel, branding, and market definition.

Takeaways for full-service trading: Fiscal planning, high-value negotiations, outreach to high-net-worth families, leveraging media to establish reputation in a new industry.

> **"And a good time was had by all...**
> It looks like it could have started life as a Prohibition Era speakeasy: dark wood balustrades, chandeliers with cut glass lampshades, gilt-framed mirrors... Sounds of table conversation that flows when people are having a good time."
> - *Times-Union*

From Startup to 7-Figure Business and Profitable Sale in 4 Years.

- **Built $3.5M business—at 28% profit margin—from ground-up.**
- **Gained media coverage and built relationships** with companies and elite families.
- **Sold business for high multiple** based on profitable operations and brand equity.

CORPORATE EXPRESS DELIVERY SYSTEMS, Washington, DC   19XX–20XX

One of the world's largest express delivery and global logistics companies.

Director of Sales, Worldwide Logistics: **M&A Integration • Growth Strategies • Team Building • Sales Operations • Global Markets**

Hired as Global, promoted to develop nascent global logistics channel. Built team of 250+ account managers, sales reps, and corporate account managers globally. Reported to and collaborated with C-suite executives.

Takeaways for full-service trading: Strategic innovation, client education, sales operations for complex product, high-growth sales and operations strategies, and M&A insights and integration.

Establishing Global Sales Organization. Running Sales & Operations in Support of 4X Growth.

- **Boosted sales 4X from $420M to $1.9B** and grew team from 70 to 250 as Director of Sales. Spurred organic growth and serviced growth resulting from several acquisitions.
- **Centralized training program** in support of transition from many small, globally dispersed delivery companies into a unified organization with a shared vision, skillset, sales and operations language, and goals.
- **Earned company's highest award 3 years straight** and signed clients like GM, ITT, Baxter, Apple, Medtronics, Bank of America, and ADP as Global Account Manager.

EDUCATION, PROFESSIONAL DEVELOPMENT, & COMMUNITY INVOLVEMENT

Bachelor of Science, **Economics & Marketing**, Miami University, Oxford, OH—*ADPi Sorority, Aisec Miami, AMA, MMA*

Selling and Leadership Courses: IBM, Wilson Learning, Dale Carnegie Training, and the Walt Disney Company

Hold FL Real Estate License (since 20XX)

Completed Studies for Series 7 License—pending sponsorship

Active with Komen Foundation and Pug Rescue of Central Florida. Head the Architect Review Board of the Philips Cove Community Association

Oscar Clement

OClement@gmail.com
Los Angeles, CA 90001 • (213) 555-5555

Business Leader: Finance • Marketing • Operations/Supply Chain

Corporate Finance:

☑ P&L Accountability
☑ Budget Management
☑ Financial Projections
☑ Fiscal Analysis
☑ Financial Operations
☑ Risk Analysis
☑ Data Management

Marketing & Business Development:

☑ Retail Channels
☑ Wholesale Channels
☑ B2B & B2C Sales
☑ Market Segmentation
☑ Value Creation
☑ Product Creation
☑ Product Management
☑ Contract Management
☑ Strategic Partnerships
☑ Customer Acquisition
☑ CRM

Operations & Supply Chain Management:

☑ Organizational Design
☑ Site Analysis
☑ Warehousing
☑ Distribution Centers
☑ Offshore Sourcing
☑ Ethical Oversight
☑ Overseas Shipping
☑ Vendor Management
☑ Technology Management

"Collaborate to form the best plan, then get your hands dirty and get it done."

MBA candidate with real-world experience, ready to learn and contribute in equal measure. Bring leadership history that has led to double- and triple-digit growth in diverse industries.

CAREER SNAPSHOT

Founder, Sweet Bean
20XX–Present
Shifted preconceptions about coffee franchises by adding high-end cakes to struggling locations.

	Industry Average	Sweetest Buzz
Startup Costs/Site	$300K to $500K	**$50K**
Time to Profitability	18 Months	**4 Months**
Turnkey Operations		**Future administrative transfer to franchise management firm**

Founder, Wholesale Cake Deco
20XX–20XX
Recognized demand for high-quality cake accessories in underserved market segments. Established ecommerce platform and international supply chain.

Wholesale Cake Deco Stats	
Supply Chain	2,200 SKUs from 3 countries
Customer Shipping	Two S. CA fulfillment centers
Online Business	Innovative ecommerce platform
Business Dev.	50,000 B2B customers
Turnkey Operations	Absentee business in 3 years
Exit	Sold for profit in 2012

Sales/Ops Manager, Nice Cake
20XX–20XX
Transitioned company from losses to 30% net annual profits. Targeted customer segments based on business units' core competencies. Created corp. strategy to build sustained competitive advantage.

Nice Cake Lines	2002	2011
All Business	7 % Net Loss	30% Net Profit (~$500K/year)
Weddings	17% GPM	65% GPM
Children's Birthday	8% GPM	32% GPM
Adult All-Occasion	22% GPM	82% GPM

Sales Engineer, Acme & Sil Valley Systems, 19XX–20XX
Promoted from customer support to sales engineer for largest account and helped grow it from $35M to $100M. Gained access to 50 labs in 6 countries to prove viability of new SAN solution.

Annual Sales

$35M $100M

EDUCATION

Executive MBA, University of Southern California, Los Angeles, CA; Anticipated May 20XX
Enhanced real-world experience through study of leading-edge company valuation methods and M&A strategy. Created case studies and projects around present-day corporate M&A transactions, effects of high growth on company culture, leadership change, market segmentation, domestic and international strategy, influencing company culture, sustaining competitive advantage, value creation, cost accounting, capital structure and maximizing shareholder value, and utilizing debt and equity markets.

BS, Operation Management Information Systems, Santa Clara University, Santa Clara, CA; 19XX
Excelled in blended technology/business program, a core component of which was full-time, relevant work experience. Mastered hands-on IT skills and business concepts, progressing from personally installing physical layer telco equipment to running design, execution, and administration of campus-wide phone/data build-out encompassing 8 buildings and ~16,000 data and phone connections.

Built reputation for devising elegant solutions to complex problems. This "problem solving" mindset established groundwork for positioning products as the solution to clients' most pressing needs.

PHILOSOPHY: "No matter what field you're playing on, value is the key. Whether in technology or cakes, I have made an impact by breaking everything into segments, defining each offering's unique value, and putting it all back together in a more elegant, profitable form that speaks directly to its intended audience."

212.555.5555
New York, NY 10458
RFisk@gmail.com
linkedin.com/in/bobfisk
bobfisk.com

Robert Fisk

You already know about brand management.
This is different.

"Bob is an exceptional strategic thinker who brings passion and energy to all aspects of his role…I consider Bob to be a thought leader in emerging communication and media trends with a deep clinical and technical aptitude."
— Chris Tama, Then-President at Ogilvy CommonHealth Worldwide

BRAND & MARKETING COMMUNICATIONS EXECUTIVE

"There's no exact title for what I do. I'm a scientist, a sales strategist, and a storyteller. My goal in any situation is to spot trends and find opportunity. I gather data creatively and use it to our advantage."

Servant leader who approaches problems with the philosophy that there are no "best" practices. They can always be improved. Land and grow major clients, earning trust by meeting their growth needs innovatively and on terms they can say yes to. Consistently achieved double-digit business growth throughout 20 years, holding leadership positions and winning awards at Ferguson, Ogilvy, Grey, IPG, Torre Lazur, and Pfizer.

Make massive leaps by appropriately sharing information across divisions and companies. Build world-class teams and coach them to top performance, leading by example and listening with an open mind.

Emotidata at a Glance

Business Development & Social
4+ New Fortune 100 Clients Each Year
90% of Meetings Moved to Proposal
Twitter Chat with 3M+ Impressions
"Top Contributor" — LinkedIn Consumer Insights Group (53K+ members)

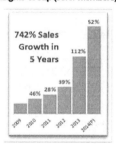

742% Sales Growth in 5 Years

EXECUTIVE LEADERSHIP IN BRANDING AND COMMUNICATIONS

Emotidata, New York, NY, 20XX to Present
Leading brand management firm specializing in measuring emotional responses to every aspect of brands and their messages.

Managing Director, Brand Engagement—Head 14-member team of medical directors, methodology advisors, technology officers, and multidisciplinary technical experts. Remove guesswork from brand management by developing multiple protocols for quantifying consumer emotions and engagement. Build on the work of Dr. Paul Ekman, using out-of-the box and custom tools to strengthen brands and messaging for clients.

- **Drove double-digit YOY growth** by developing uniquely relevant brand engagement products. Produced **the most user-friendly data analysis** in the industry.
- **Captured business from much larger competitors,** including Nielsen, Millward Brown, and Innerscope. Generated industry buzz to attract clients with a pull marketing strategy.
- **Enabled multilayered, custom coding with ease** by inventing remote-controlled network LED TTL transmitters that seamlessly mark the beginning and ending of specific coding cycles.
- **Democratized key technology by lowering the cost of entry for eye trackers.** Developed units from out-of-the-box and open-source elements that cost $100 to $1000 total compared to existing equipment on the market for ~$50K per unit. In January of 2014, launched Analabs to teach researchers and students how to build these and other emotional coding tools. **Gained immediate trust from potential clients in a field where no other competitor manufactured eye trackers.**

Product & IP Development

Brand Emotion Profile
Pupil Reactivity Index
Facial Action Coding System (FACS)
Remote-Controlled Coding Markers
"Hacked" Eye Trackers
Program Pursued by $3B SaaS Co.

Sample Brand Emotion Profile
- Anger
- Contempt
- Disgust
- Fear
- Happiness
- Sadness
- Surprise

Representative Case Study: Revealing the Best Concept

Situation: Client was developing a new creative campaign, and they needed to know which concept was the most emotionally engaging. They had hired a market research firm that delivered inconclusive, verbatim data from physicians and stated that each concept was "equally positive." Emotidata was hired to perform a retrospective analysis of the interview tapes.

Approach & Results: Quantified nonverbal behavior of physician interviewees using the Facial Action Coding System (FACS). Behaviors included speech patterns, emotion, and body language. Coders identified contradictions between verbatim statements and nonverbal behavior, revealing predictive insights into how the concepts would work in the marketplace.

- Client identified clear, winning concept substantiated with data.
- Emotidata earned an RFP for future work 2 days after final presentation.

Partial Client List
L'Oreal, Hershey, Pepsi, Merck,
Bausch + Lomb, Frito Lay,
Procter and Gamble,
Hershey, Victoria's Secret

Olivia Johnson

ofjohnson@gmail.com ♦ 214.555.5555

Marketing & Event Management

"Companies need connections to their markets to create long-term loyalty." - *Groundswell*

Connecting with markets through: **Brand Management · Traditional Marketing · Experiential Marketing · Event Planning**

Strategic thinker and creative executer delivering communications and live experiences that engage clients and lay a foundation for long-term brand relationships. Masters-prepared professional whose background in business and finance bring a structured, ROI-conscious approach to creative campaigns. Trusted counselor to senior executives, providing actionable risk/reward analysis of marketing decisions. Humanize communications, inspiring meaningful contributions across all levels and functions.

- √ **Build lasting brand loyalists while generating leads to fuel current sales goals.**
- √ **Inspire internal stakeholders to collaborative, brand-conscious action with communications that are clear, compelling, and personal.**
- √ **Evangelize corporate mission through marketing collateral, media mentions, and integrated advertising.**
- √ **Mine excellent presentation skills and consultative approach to create compelling, branded sales collateral.**
- √ **Harness technology to amplify messaging, with fluency in Microsoft Office, PowerPoint, and Visio and working knowledge of Photoshop, Photoshop Touch, and Final Cut Pro. Passionate instigator of social media conversations.**

Marketing & Event Planning Impact

BUSINESS DEVELOPMENT & MARKETING ASSOCIATE, **Capstone Partners**, Dallas, TX; OCT. 20XX–Present
Fast-growth private equity fundraising firm that supports clients in marketing private equity opportunities from offices worldwide.

Recruited for creative outlook and understanding of finance. Hired into client-side project management, overseeing creation of marketing collateral. Quickly earned promotion into business development team, collaborating with VP of business development to launch dedicated Marketing Group. Manage graphics and marketing vendors. Maintain company website and coordinate print advertising. Head swag creation, end-to-end event planning, and event budgets up to $50K.

Took Marketing & PR Efforts to the Next Level

- **Upgraded marketing collateral.** Freshened up language and graphics to align with corporate brand as a leading-edge, authority in private equity funding and marketing. Tightened up language and incorporated graphics.

- **Improved effectiveness of business development team** by collaborating with them to translate their sales strategies into proposals with engaging copy and visual elements.

- **Helped build brand credibility and reach out to untapped market.** Partnered with Business Development to create high-demand offering proposal for clients who already have a full portfolio of investors.

- **Doubled interviews in industry publications** with targeted PR outreach.

> **Personal Social Media Project**
> Created *Deliciously Dallas*
> **Facebook** and **Twitter** outlets.
> Present unique local
> entertainment opportunities
> to **3,200 followers, reaching
> 10K per week.** Co-produced
> and hosted **videos that
> amplified reach.**

Contributed to Collaborative Culture and Made Marketing a Priority

- **Unified disparate input from local managing partners and European partners.** Developed mission statement consensus.

- **Made marketing a priority at the firm.** Established shared timeline and engaged support of extremely busy cross-functional stakeholders, despite having no direct reporting relationship. Created culture of personal connection, incorporating phone calls and face-to-face interaction in an environment with a heavy bias towards email communications.

Created Local Pilot Event that Expanded into National Branding / Experiential Marketing Campaign

- **Increased attendee engagement at annual Dallas conference.** Rebranded Capstone's gathering from formal estate dinner to more relaxed brewery event—complete with swag gift beer mug—that met with enthusiastic feedback and started many business conversations.

- **Enabled Capstone to "share the stage" on a national level with larger firms.** Parlayed success of Dallas event into San Francisco and New York gatherings which have resulted in an expanded network of clients and contacts.

NANCY RILEY, MBA

Boston, MA 02201 • 617.555.5555 • nriley123@hotmail.com

MANAGED 9-FIGURE P&L • OPTIMIZED MARKETING SPEND — FROM SHOESTRING TO 8-FIGURE • GREW BUSINESS ACROSS GLOBAL MARKETS & SUPPLY CHAINS
EMPOWERED TEAMS TO ADD MILLIONS IN SALES • ENGAGED RETAILERS AND PARTNERS IN WIN/WIN ALLIANCES

MARKETING EXECUTIVE / GENERAL MANAGER
• • • Translating Trends and Consumer Insights into Brand Strategies that Drive Top- and Bottom-Line Growth • • •

Multi-award-winning business and marketing leader with 17+ years' experience launching and turning around domestic and global brands. Combine analytics, instinct, and team resources to arrive at novel, effective strategies.

Provide cross-functional teams with the stability and knowledge base to support game-changing innovation. Offer global outlook born from business and personal travel to 40 countries. Experience in FMCG, Specialty Retail, Online/Direct and Franchise Field Consulting. Win trusted insider status with franchisees.

Awards
Procter & Gamble Personal Leadership Award
Herbalife Marketing Excellence Team Award
Pfizer AG Equal Opportunity Award
McNeil Marketing Excellence Award
Judge: Effie Awards

CAREER SNAPSHOT

BATH & BODY WORKS Grew net sales $25M and brought post-reorg employee engagement to 100%.

PROCTER & GAMBLE Added $10M in incremental sales, bringing luxury experience to mass market and salvaging endangered retail relationships. Made double-digit sales and profit improvements by reaching 1st- and 2nd-generation Latinos.

HERBALIFE Renewed brand health of $440M Cell-U-Loss after 3 years of decline with "Zip Up Your Hunger" campaign. Partnered with *People* magazine and Levi Strauss.

PFIZER AG Won Marketer of the Year for successful launch of 40+ SKUs in 8 months. Designed 1st-of-their kind initiatives to connect with gay consumers (raising sales 9%) and reach key influencers (#1 pharmacist recommended).

FORD Boosted Ford Motor Sales regional franchisee annual revenues 7% by establishing the trust needed to implement effective marketing and operational strategies.

EXECUTIVE CONTRIBUTIONS

BATH & BODY WORKS (BBW), Director, Product Strategy & Development — South Deerfield, MA; 20XX to Present

Hired into VP-equivalent role to elevate product strategy for $876M business from reactive fast-follower to proactive consumer-centric approach. Executive responsibility increased from 3 US categories to total global responsibility for all brands and divisions, driving $276M in new product sales. Lead team of 15.

Adding Millions in New Product Sales and Improving Profit Margins through Change Management and Team Empowerment

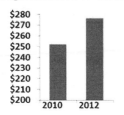

Net Sales in Millions

"She establishes where the team is going and makes sure they all have the same sense of urgency that she has. Nancy will also shift the direction of the team if there is a key business case for doing so.
Nancy plain and simple knows how to make money!"
— Manager Comments on Annual Review

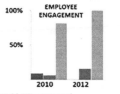

EMPLOYEE ENGAGEMENT

■ % Disengaged
■ % Highly Engaged
■ % Engaged or Highly Engaged

Situation: Inherited newly formed team of people who had been re-assigned through corporate reorganization. Bath & Body Works needed new consumers, but was hindered by Product Development's focus on execution rather than development of growth strategies.

Approach: Created professional development plan and processes. Established and delivered formal training program. Mentored team in identifying wide-space opportunities, validating them, and bringing them to market. Championed product lifecycle management system to support unified approach, creating a cross-functional view of projects and automating non-value-added work. Partnered with Consumer Insights group to create consumer segmentation study that formed the basis of product positioning and roadmaps.

- Grew new product sales 8.7% to $276M, with 50 bps margin expansion. Attracted new consumers by shifting culture from reacting to competitor innovations and vendor proposals to leading the way in fulfilling unmet market needs.
- Boosted employee engagement score 1870 bps in 12 months, a result of increased confidence and effectiveness of team.
- Accelerated speed to market by giving teams the tools to focus on value-added work.

Wendi Weiner
JD, NCRW, CPRW, CCTC, CCM

Wendi Weiner
The Writing Guru
www.linkedin.com/in/thewritingguru
www.facebook.com/thewritingguru
twitter.com/writing_guru
(888) 285-9982

Wendi Weiner, creatively known as The Writing Guru, is an accomplished attorney, former college writing professor, 4X certified executive resume writer and career transition coach, and global career expert. She is a member of the prestigious Forbes Coaches Council and a board member for The National Resume Writers' Association.

Wendi has been featured for her top-notch expertise in national radio broadcasts, Forbes, The Huffington Post, Fortune, Business News Daily, Monster, Careerealism, and CareerBuilder. She is the owner of The Writing Guru, a top-ranked resume service firm based in Miami, Florida, with national and international clientele served in more than 30 industries. Wendi is also a dedicated philanthropist and active leader for the Jewish Federation of Broward County.

GOLDIE NORMAN

785 Ocean Parkway, Brooklyn, New York, 11230 • (212) 932-8567 • goldienorman@gmail.com

CREATIVE DESIGN SPECIALIST

Leveraging passion for the arts with a knack for building relationships and employing creative analysis.

Talented and detail-oriented certified interior designer with over 15 years of experience in conceptual design, project management and retail sales. Stellar academic credentials, including honors, from top-ranking liberal arts college. Resourceful consultative approach and superior communication skills which have fostered long-term client relationships. High-ranking sales throughout career with exceptional customer service, comprehensive knowledge and proven reputation for improving operations, executing innovative solutions and delivering superior results.

SPECIALIZED KNOWLEDGE & ACHIEVEMENTS

❖ **Relationship Building & Client Relations**: Achieved highest rate of repeat clientele and lowest rate of return. Built long-lasting relationships with clients via consultation and education on the merits of design plans which resulted in consistently being ranked in the top 5% for sales.

❖ **Sales Execution & Marketing Design**: Performed over 750 in-home design consultations and closed at 95%. Achieved "Rookie of the Year" and twice received "Local Service of Excellence" in recognition of outstanding sales at Ethan Allen. Created marketing collateral for Go-To-Market Solutions which encompassed preparing and designing websites, logos, business cards, brochures, postcards, mailings and presentations.

❖ **Project Management & Control**: Displayed tenacious dedication to deadlines and commitments. Performed superior project completion utilizing unique and imaginative organizational and space planning solutions. Oversaw design process from conception through consultation and down to the finished product within budget constraints and deadlines, including ordering, delivery and coordination of skilled-trade workers.

❖ **Creative & Technical Writing**: Selected by New York Design Preservation League to mentor new guides for engaging Art Deco Tours as a result of successful writing and facilitating tour scripts. Drafted and created attractive and compelling lengthy 80-page presentations on sales and marketing analysis. Authored 65-page guidebook, "The Locals Guide to New York City," covering New York history, architecture, restaurants and entertainment. Successfully wrote and researched grants for "The Talking Information Center," a radio reading service for visually impaired.

PROFESSIONAL EXPERIENCE

MARKETING AND RESEARCH SUPPORT CONSULTANT | **Creative Solutions Inc.**, NY, NY (2009–Present)

Researched and synthesized data from printed sources, websites and on-site visits for healthcare consulting company. Re-wrote and edited all content for printed materials and presentations. Worked independently and utilized strong problem-solving skills to manage variable projects and challenges.

CERTIFIED INTERIOR DESIGNER & DESIGN SERVICES DIRECTOR | **Pottery Barn**, NY, NY (2000–2009)

Provided clients with interior design solutions to best serve their individual needs through creating functional and aesthetically pleasing spaces. Executed designer referral service of high-end clientele with $250K annual revenue.
- Recognized for excellent project management and customer service, including ranking in top 5% of sales.
- Oversaw 20 designers in the program and broadened scope of available price points and design styles.
- Implemented consulting and buying service for visitors shopping for specific items which resulted in assisting 10 shoppers in a day and increasing revenue for this program by 15%.

EDUCATION, CERTIFICATIONS, & ADVANCED SKILLS

B.A., Geology with Art History concentration – Skidmore College • Saratoga Springs, NY

Interior Design Certificate with high honors – Massachusetts Bay College • Wellesley, MA

Interior Design Society (IDS) Certification – Council for Qualification of Residential Interior Designers (CQRID)
MS Office Suite • MapPoint • MAC iWork Suite • POS Systems • Sketch Up • Interior Design Software • Web Development

GOLDIE NORMAN

785 Ocean Parkway, Brooklyn, New York, 11230 • (212) 932-8567 • goldienorman@gmail.com

IT MANAGEMENT EXECUTIVE | BUSINESS CHANGE AGENT

Proven Ability to Align Business Needs with Technical Solutions and Superior Business Acumen

Passionate, driven, and dynamic senior level technology professional with Master of Science in Computer Information Systems and 19+ years of broad-based experience in IT education and training. Dedicated self-starter with superior technical skills and proven emphasis on team leadership and collaboration. Team-based management style with demonstrated record of identifying potential issues and offering solutions to align business objectives with organizational needs.

- 10+ years' experience in **web development and design** using JavaScript, CSS, Visual Studio, ASP.NET, C#, ADO.NET, Visual Studio.NET and Web Services
- Trusted advisor in leading **mid-size IT and business development projects** through curriculum development and distance education-related training.
- Recognized for **successful project management expertise** in scope development, project tracking, application testing, and application implementation.
- Proven track record of experience in **multimedia and web design technologies**, including video conferencing/ webinar technologies.

CORE SKILLS & KNOWLEDGE

Infrastructure Strategy • Network Security & Support • Testing & Troubleshooting • Project Management & Coaching • Staff Training & Supervision • Team Building & Leadership • Ethics • Conflict Resolution • Quality Assurance • Process Improvement • Budget Planning • Programming Languages • Database Design & Integration

Technical Proficiencies

Microsoft SharePoint 2010/2013, Microsoft .NET Framework (ASP.NET, C#, Visual Studio.NET, ADO.NET), Microsoft Content Management Server 2002, ASP, HTML, CSS, JavaScript, XML, MS Internet Information Server, MS SQL Server (2000, 2005,2008), Telerik RADControls, Webtrends, Visual SourceSafe, Lotus Notes/Domino (6, 6.5), , MS Office (2010,2013), MS FrontPage, MS Project (2002, 2010), MS Visio (2007,2010)

CAREER PROGRESSION

CAMPBELL'S SOUP COMPANY, New York City, NY   2000- 2015
Senior Systems & Business Analyst
- **Strategic Business Leadership**: Served as liaison between business and development teams with demonstrated excellence in documentation and communication skills. Partnered with other developers to ensure timely and efficient production of Intranet and Internet content.
- **Application Management**: Developed applications to successfully deliver customer solutions, product expansion, performance improvement, and infrastructure, including security and administration. Led web application development team projects for multi-unit eBusiness technologies and solution teams. Implemented and maintained multi-tiered Internet, Extranet and Intranet applications using Microsoft .NET technologies. Utilized web services, workflow and connectivity to internal and external data sources.
- **Troubleshooting & Support**: Handled root-cause analysis and troubleshooting applications issues, developing test plans and test cases in support of Unit and End User testing

Key Accomplishments & Achievements:
- Received CEO Award for Business Excellence (2013), CEO Award for Safety Excellence (2014), and Achieve Award
- Developed online procurement system using SharePoint 2013 resulting in $7MM company savings.
- Managed project with $1.5 MM budget where 20+ internally-hosted SharePoint websites were redesigned in Adobe AEM and moved to Amazon Web Services resulting in annual savings of $80K in maintenance and administration costs.
- Trained 900 users for enterprise-wide corporate social media application.

GOLDIE NORMAN

785 Ocean Parkway • Brooklyn, New York 11230
(212) 932-8567 • goldienorman@gmail.com

OPERATIONS MANAGEMENT EXECUTIVE

Proven Track Record of Leading and Improving Operations While Executing Innovative Solutions

High-impact, charismatic, and results-oriented senior operations executive with over 13 years of experience in quality control and business management. Fiscal champion of high-performing teams and recognized for streamlining operations, driving processes, and optimizing productivity. Exceptional business acumen with comprehensive knowledge of developing training programs and proven reputation for delivering superior results.

- Inventory Control
- Reports
- Relationship Management
- Quality Assurance
- Conflict Resolution
- Training & Supervision
- Systems & Control
- Project Management
- Database Management
- Logistics
- Cost Reduction Measures
- Risk Management

PROFESSIONAL EXPERIENCE

RILEY ENTERPRISES, New York, NY, 2012–Present
Director of Operations • Logistics Manager
Oversee and supervise logistics department, develop and execute onboarding procedures, and establish and manage staff training program.
- Increased 450 customers, 16 direct reports, and 14 routes to 1300+ customers, 29+ direct reports, and 24 routes.
- Implemented fuel tracking program resulting in hiring to date savings of over $250,000.
- Overhauled standard operating procedures resulting in insurance policy cost-savings of $40,000.
- Launched company's drug free workplace (DFW) program resulting in additional 5% insurance policy savings.

WENDELE ENTERPRISES, INC, New York, NY, 2006–2012
Field Operations Manager
Managed 75 direct reports and 15 indirect reports. Oversaw scheduling, performance, and payroll. Directed quality control, corrective action, conflict resolution, hiring, training, and termination.
- Implemented comprehensive quality assurance program that met and exceeded company standards.
- Executed training program to include classroom presentations, field education, and training videos.
- Managed and coordinated all inbound and outbound sales programs and professional development.

GASWIRTH NATIONAL LEASE CORP., New York, NY, 1998–2005
Terminal Manager
Directly supervised 19 commercial tractor-trailer drivers and managed interstate and intrastate dispatch of 30 to 50 commercial drivers for load tracking and emergency response. Administered new hire training, safety inspections, driver surveillance, scheduling, payroll, and oversaw security concerns for 18 locations.
- Received "Top Performance" awards for 5 consecutive years (2000–2005).
- Reduced security costs by over 65%. Increased employee performance standards by 41%.

THE SECURITY CORP., New York, NY, 1992–1996
Custom Protection Officer & Supervisor
Handled armed security and supervision of security officer teams for public schools, international airports, state and federal courts, and high-security non-government and government offices.
- Awarded recognition for consistent superior performance and team improvement.
- Lowered security costs by 53% in public sector and 27% in private sector.

EDUCATION

Bachelor of Science in Business Management – **FIVE TOWNS COLLEGE**, Nassau County, NY

GOLDIE NORMAN

785 Ocean Parkway, Brooklyn, New York, 11230 • (212) 932-8567 • goldienorman@gmail.com

SENIOR COUNSEL
Leveraging Comprehensive Knowledge and Experience in Complex Commercial and Securities Litigation

Tenacious, accomplished, and results-driven senior litigation attorney with exceptional academic credentials from top-ranked law school. Demonstrated **10+ years** of multi-faceted experience encompassing dispute resolution, federal appeals, and complex commercial litigation, including practice at **Am Law 100 and Am Law 200 firms**. Admitted to practice before all New York state and New York Federal Courts, and Second Circuit Court of Appeals.

- ♦ Hands-on knowledge in leading cases from inception through final disposition in both state and federal court.
- ♦ Solid negotiations management, superior courtroom presence, and strong research and writing skills.
- ♦ Trusted advisor and advocate in directing litigation and discovery teams to deliver superior case results.
- ♦ Demonstrated capacity to expand practice groups, reinforce client retention, and increase overall percentage of commercial matters.

CORE SKILLS & SECTOR KNOWLEDGE

Business & Contract Disputes • Partnerships & LLCs • Fraud & Breach of Fiduciary Duty • Corporate Governance • Business Torts • Antitrust • Insurance Disputes • Regulatory & Internal Investigations • Class Action Defense • Federal Civil Rights

PROFESSIONAL EXPERIENCE

ATTICUS FINCH LLP, New York, NY   2005–Present
Senior Counsel and Practice Chair, Commercial and Securities Litigation Department
Oversee all cases, attorneys, and staff in practice group. Evaluate, investigate, and determine strategy in trials, oral arguments, appellate matters, motions, discovery matters, client communications and counseling, and court submissions. Enhance team members' professional development and performance by providing continuous training and mentoring.

Representative Engagements:
- Led $280 million contract and trade secret misappropriation action against pharmaceutical contract manufacturer for unlawful competition in marketplace.
- Obtained $11.6 million judgment against issuer of promissory notes in breach of contract action involving real estate development projects.
- Directed $54 million action against investment manager for participating in fraudulent scheme to manipulate IPO price and corporate valuation of online social networking company.
- Steered counsel in $78 million action against major ophthalmic manufacturer for breach of contract and mismanagement claims related to failed development of cutting edge intra-ocular lenses.
- Served as lead counsel for plaintiff in federal Section 1983 litigation against municipal police officers and federal agent for excessive force and retaliation.

EDUCATION

Juris Doctor – NEW YORK UNIVERSITY SCHOOL OF LAW, New York, NY
Merit Scholar • Editor, NYU Law Review • Member, Trial Team

Bachelor of Arts, *cum laude*, History – COLUMBIA UNIVERSITY, New York, NY
Alpha Epsilon Pi Fraternity • Phi Betta Kappa • Golden Key Honor Society

---

National Institute of Trial Advocacy (NITA) Deposition Seminar • Trial Advocacy Seminar • Alternative Dispute Resolution Seminar • Negotiation Seminar

Goldie Norman's quest for improving the quality of life for her clients began as a mission for answers while on her own health journey. As a young child, Goldie suffered from extreme stomach issues which were unable to be resolved by modern medicine. By age 20, her dream of becoming a mother continued to deteriorate due to increasing hormonal imbalances, gut issues and kidney problems.

After studying law, psychology and family counseling in Russia, Goldie attended Novosibirsk State University to learn more about holistic healing methods. After undergoing extensive detoxification of her body based on traditional healing methods and herbalogy she learned at the Novosibirsk State University, she was able to conceive naturally with identical twin girls. However, her immunity and GI tract were compromised which resulted in her daughters being born with severe allergies, gut issues, sleep disturbances and neurological problems.

Desperate for real answers and a cure for her daughters, Goldie moved to the United States and enrolled at the prestigious Institute for Integrative Nutrition. By implementing nutrition and lifestyle changes, she regained control of her own health and the health of her family. As a result, she granted her family the biggest gift of all - radiant health!

Today, Goldie's mission as a licensed health coach is to help everyone - from pregnant mothers, to young athletes, to people with compromised GI tracts and hormonal imbalances, and to those simply wanting to lose a few pounds. She seeks to help all clients look and feel their best and to regain their health through the balance of holistic living. Goldie's strong belief is that everyone has an absolute right and the power to be radiantly healthy. As a certified health coach, she possesses top-notch skills and knowledge on cutting-edge research in health and wellness. She uses that knowledge to provide the tools for helping her clients regain their health.

Let Goldie accompany you into your dream state of wellness by synchronizing all parts of your life.

If you can imagine it, you can achieve it. If you can dream it, you can become it." – William Arthur Ward

GOLDIE NORMAN

785 Ocean Parkway, Brooklyn, New York, 11230 • (212) 932-8567 • goldienorman@gmail.com

---

June 1, 2016

To Whom It May Concern:

I am writing to express my interest in obtaining the trial attorney position with the Department of Justice Office Boards and Divisions in its New York City office. As a talented and tenacious attorney with a zest for helping others, I firmly believe that my academic credentials, practical experience in handling fraud matters, stellar writing skills, and vivacious personality make me an excellent candidate for this position and for the Department.

My legal career has been marked by a selection of challenging work due to my reputation for getting things done with a proactive style and inspiring team performance. I have acquired and concentrated my experience in multi-faceted areas of the law, with extensive focus in civil and criminal insurance fraud litigation. My strong litigation background has simultaneously provided a solid foundation for my transition from the private sector into the public sector. This exposure in conjunction with my expertise in academia and devoted knack for public speaking have also aided in this smooth transition.

As a collaborative team-player who is focused on building relationships in all aspects of professional development, I believe I am uniquely qualified for this specific position as it is identical to the work I have successfully impacted for the past 15 years in the private sector and 5 years in the public sector. Enclosed please find a copy of my resume for your review. I welcome the opportunity to meet with you and to further discuss my credentials. Thank you for your consideration, and I look forward to hearing from you in the near future.

Very truly yours,

Goldie Norman

Eric Glass

Luxury Watch Buyer and Sales Consultant at WatchUWant.com ◆ "Knowing what my customers want and what makes them tick!

Summary

Are you a passionate watch enthusiast? Are you looking for one-on-one personalized service that exceeds your expectations?

Honesty. Loyalty. Trust. Passion. Professionalism.

Those are 5 adjectives that accurately describe WHO I am and WHAT I stand for in the luxury watch business.

I am a relationship builder with a proven record of success in providing superior client and customer service. More than 50% of my clients become repeat clients - they send me pictures of their large collections and I work hard to provide them with the best value in buying, selling or trading their watches.

I am a business visionary with more than 15 years of experience in hospitality, sales, and management. I am also a strong problem-solver who focuses on the ever-changing market trends and watch cost analysis.

When it comes to personalized service, top quality and transparency in client relations, I am the go-to person for my clients.

BUY, SELL, or TRADE your luxury watch!
Panerai, AP, IWC, Roger Dubuis, Franck Muller, Rolex, Cartier, Breitling, Patek Philippe, Ulysse-Nardin and Bell & Ross.

✉ E-MAIL: eric@watchuwant.com
☎ DIRECT PHONE LINE: (954) 449-7205
Instagram: @ericluxurywatches

Luxury Watch Buyer
watchuwant.com
April 2014 – Present (2 years 3 months) Hollywood, Florida

WUW is the #1 buyer, seller, and trader of new and pre-owned luxury watches. For over 15 years, WUW has been the gold standard and most respected name in the pre-owned luxury watch business. Our clients include Fortune 50 to 500 CEOS, high-ranking executives, entrepreneurs, business owners, athletes, celebrities, and billionaires.

WHY choose me for your next watch sale?

✔ I provide superior professional service in buying, selling or trading experience for YOUR luxury timepiece.
✔ I consistently hit and exceed monthly goals/quotas due to providing the ultimate client experience and top notch customer service.
✔ I maintain knowledge of current marketing trends in luxury watches, including watch specs, historical pricing, condition details and watch nuances.

Here are excerpts from REAL TESTIMONIALS from some of my clients as published on the WUW website:

Bob Janitz, NCRW

Bob Janitz
www.linkedin.com/in/bobjanitz
jganitz@yahoo.com
www.janitz.com
817.253.6533

Bob Janitz is a Nationally Certified Résumé Writer accredited by The National Résumé Writer's Association (The NRWA) in the Dallas-Fort Worth, Texas Metroplex. He has 23 years of experience creating custom documents for entry-level to executive job seekers in sales, marketing, finance, legal, information technology, education, project management, operations, product management, and healthcare.

Bob wrote his first resume in 1993, while employed by Procter & Gamble. The resume was for a co-worker who got the interview, landed the job, and started advertising Bob to others in the Company.

In 2008, Bob joined The National Résumé Writers' Association and became a full-time resume writer. Through education in The NRWA and experience, he achieved the Nationally Certified Résumé Writer status in 2014. In 2014, Bob was the President of The NRWA.

Jim Schwartz, CPA

Dallas, Texas ◆ 214.555.1212 ◆ jim_schwartz@gmail.com

Chief Financial Officer ~ Chief Operating Officer

Certified Public Accountant and business executive with more than with 20 years' experience in corporate accounting/finance leading companies through change and challenge to profitable growth. Bottom-line operations and business manager with extensive knowledge of complex operations and broad comprehension of corporate structure, compliance issues, and strategy.

Core Knowledge and Skills

Strategic Financial Planning & Execution • Financial Management & Reporting • Financial Analysis
Internal & External Auditing • Budget Development & Oversight • Mergers & Acquisitions
SOX/Regulatory Compliance • Risk Management • Project Management • Operations Management

Professional Experience And Accomplishments

JONES & JONES MANUFACTURING-Fort Worth, Texas   6/2013–1/2016
Chief Financial Officer

Member of the Executive Management Team, reporting directly to the CEO. Directed all accounting and treasury functions including financial planning; financial reporting; internal auditing; tax planning, compliance, and reporting; capital budgeting; SEC regulatory filings; corporate finance including bank relationships; debt financing and equity raises; and mergers, acquisitions, and divestiture activities.

- Transformed retail distribution business in significant decline, losing ~50 million in sales from 2012–2013 to an E-Commerce technology and service solutions business, shipping over $1.5 billion in annual gross merchandise value (GMV).

- Achieved explosive sales growth: $55 million in 2013; $107 million in 2014; and $120 million in 2015.

- Completed multiple public and private placement equity raises including investor presentations, due diligence, and drafting sessions:

  - ✓ Oct 2013 Public Offering; $21.8 million.

  - ✓ Jun 2014 Private Offering; preferred shares-$10 million.

  - ✓ Apr 2015 Public Offering warrants attached; $5 million.

- Conducted due diligence during the $75 million acquisition of two competitors.

- Realized 5% annual savings by negotiating major shipping contract.

- Oversaw company move from Minneapolis to Fort Worth. Expanded and/or relocated all facilities to prepare for growth; hired and trained new accounting and finance staff.

- Negotiated banking agreements and amendments and other significant contracts.

- Integrated prior acquisition; divested legacy business and completed two additional acquisitions.

- Converted and integrated accounting systems and oversaw re-engineering of operating processes.

Michael Andrews

Sherburne, New York 13460 ◆ 315.555.1212 ◆ mike_andrews@gmail.com

Operations Director • Logistics Management

Collaborative Business Leader Focused on People, Process, & Profit

Strategic senior manager with 16 years' experience leading cross-functional supply chain teams focused on developing logistics processes to improve efficiency and service performance. Exceptional knowledge of logistics operations including routing, warehousing, inventory control, and customer service. Collaborative leader with a motivational style that propels performance and sustains accelerated growth.

✓ Strategic Planning & Execution
✓ Multi-Site DC Operations
✓ Integrated Logistics
✓ P&L/Budget Management
✓ Business Development
✓ Project Management
✓ Training & Development

Professional Experience And Accomplishments

LOGISTICS COMPANY-Euless, Texas   6/2012–4/2016
Regional Director of Operations | $11 million annual revenue | 12 direct reports

Directed 10 site operations in 5 states, providing third-party logistics services to grocery and general merchandise distribution industry leaders. Managed operational budgets, P&L performance, business development, safety, customer service, and professional training and development.

- Delivered 260% increase to 2015 budget in existing services revenue through efficient labor scheduling and improved operational efficiencies.

- Captured more than $1 million in new service agreements by negotiating contracts.

- Realized 20% net margin on revenue after winning a customer auditing service agreement.

- Created KPIs and metrics to monitor individual productivity and create analytical-based solutions.

WORLD INDUSTRIES-Dallas, Texas   3/2009–6/2012
Regional Logistics Manager | $6 million annual revenue | 10 direct reports

Managed warehouse, delivery, customer service, and third-party logistics operations for five locations in the western United States. Controlled operational budgets, contracts, real estate leases, and inventory. Collaborated with the sales team to anticipate demand and exceed customer expectations.

- Decreased cost per unit 19% by executing sound logistics practices and lean processes that reduced waste and operating costs in Distribution Centers in Des Moines, Iowa and Seattle, Washington.

- Reduced operating costs 14% after streamlining processes and renegotiating service contracts.

- Boosted on-time delivery to 86% from 77% and service levels to 93% from 89% by training dispatchers on optimal routes and coordinating product sourcing with production managers.

- Increased warehouse employee productivity by implementing visual management systems designed to maintain compliance with standard work.

Education

STATE UNIVERSITY OF NEW YORK AT ALBANY   M.B.A., Management
NEW YORK UNIVERSITY   B.A., Sociology and Psychology

Rod Lawrence

Dallas, TX ◆ 214.555.1212 ◆ rod.lawrence@gmail.com

SENIOR VICE PRESIDENT OF SALES

Growth Catalyst | Turnaround Architect | Value Creator

Customer-focused sales executive and business development authority recognized for driving revenues and profits in exploding and contracting economies. Exceptional influencer and mentor of top-performing sales organizations with a motivational style that propels employee performance and sustains accelerated growth.

- ✓ Strategic Planning & Execution
- ✓ Profit and Loss Accountability
- ✓ Mergers & Acquisitions
- ✓ Business Analysis and Development
- ✓ Sales and Key Account Management
- ✓ Leadership Development

EXECUTIVE BENCHMARKS AND MILESTONES

- Increased revenue to $1.2 billion from $714 million in large account segment.
- Negotiated $60 million net incremental revenue deal to become an authorized commercial reseller.
- Grew Amazon revenue to $40 million from zero in 4 years.
- Led $700 million business acquisition and integration into sales organization.
- Achieved $10 million profit and 600 basis point gain, reversing $5 million operating loss.

Professional Experience and Accomplishments

ABC COMPANY-Austin, TX   *7/2012–6/2016*
Executive Vice President

Brought onboard to lead the transition from a small local/regional distributor of office supplies to a national authorized reseller partners with $100 million in annual sales.

- Captured $10 million reseller contract supplying large commercial customers.
- Negotiated $60 million net incremental revenue contract to become an authorized commercial paper products reseller.

CUSTOMER SERVICES GROUP, Chicago, IL   *1/2007–7/2012*
Group Vice President

Handpicked by CEO to design, develop, and implement the strategic planning, P&L, and operating leadership of the sales organization's turnaround and reorganization.

Strategic Planning and Execution:

- Terminated $95 million in non-strategic and unprofitable relationships by redefining go-to-market strategy, driving profitable growth in core strategic applications.
- Transformed sales organization from an operationally focused support team to a customer focused, sales driven revenue generating business unit.
- Realigned sales team into a Business Development team and a Client Solutions group. Deployment strategy involved close team selling between these two groups.

Revenue and Profit Growth:

- Realized $120 million annual core business sales by capturing multi-year contracts with Major clients including WellPoint, Expedia, Verizon, Tribune Companies, UPS, New York Times, and Humana.
- Restored company to profitability with year over year quarterly comparatives of 20%.

Tina Kashlak Nicolai, PHR, CPBA, CARW
Lominger Certified (Interview Architect)

Resume Writers' Ink
tina@resumewritersink.com
407-578-1697

Resume Writers' Ink was founded in 2010 by Tina Kashlak Nicolai. She offers her clients a strategic, trifecta approach by combining her unique background weaving together pragmatic client results with creative marketing.

Tina's trifecta approach comes from having a tenured career as a:

- Hiring leader for several Fortune 100 companies (including Disney World)
- Full cycle recruiter (20+ years and currently working in talent acquisition)
- Journalist and Marketing expertise

Resume Writers' Ink, LLC is known for it's distinct ability to write classic, contemporary, and creative (infographic) resumes for executives and professionals. Tina's clients seek her out for her expertise in writing for:

C-suite Executives, Sr. Executives, IT Professionals, Engineers, Project Managers and career-focused professionals (all industries)

Additionally, Tina is sought out on an ongoing basis by leading industry career journalists and media where she contributes best practices, tips, and advice in major media streams, including but not limited to:

Business Insider Careers

Forbes Careers

Careers in Government (blogger)

International radio groups

Monster Careers

She's been featured in numerous book publications as well as sought out for keynote speaking and career motivation talks.

Tina took her start-up business from unknown to making Forbes' "TOP 75 BEST CAREER WEBSITES" competition in 2012. She achieved this distinction during Forbes' inaugural year and named again in FORBES 2013 list of Best Career Websites. FORBES retired the BEST CAREER WEBSITE list after two years.

Tina holds two degrees from Duquesne University in Pittsburgh, PA; BA Journalism and BA Media Communications. Additionally, she is certified in:

- Certified Behavioral Coach, CPBA
- Lominger/Korn Ferry Certification
- Certified Advanced Resume Writer, CARW
- PHR SHRM

In her spare time, Tina enjoys competing in triathlons, caring for lost and stray pets, geocaching, and scuba diving. She and her husband reside in Orlando, Florida.

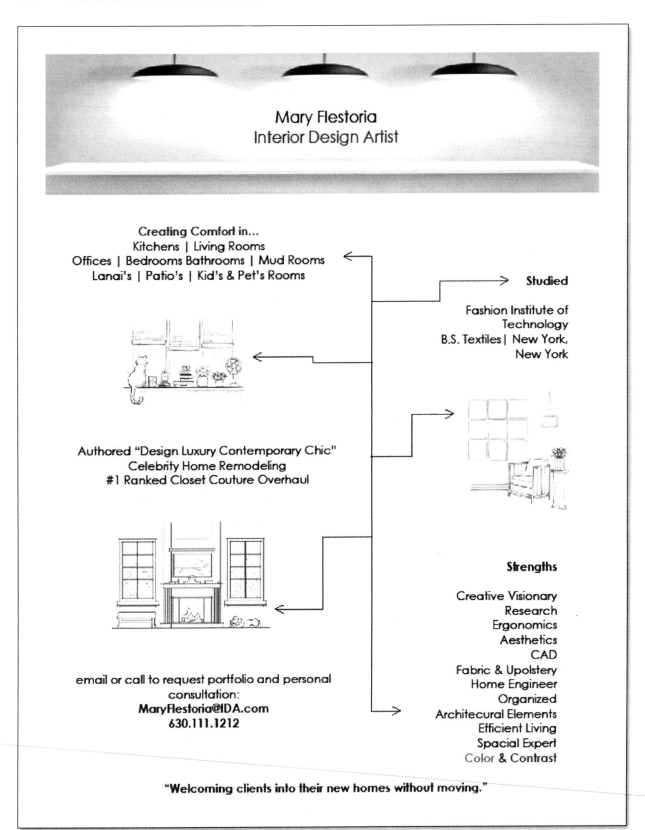

Mary Flestoria
Interior Design Artist

Creating Comfort in...
Kitchens | Living Rooms
Offices | Bedrooms Bathrooms | Mud Rooms
Lanai's | Patio's | Kid's & Pet's Rooms

Studied

Fashion Institute of
Technology
B.S. Textiles | New York,
New York

Authored "Design Luxury Contemporary Chic"
Celebrity Home Remodeling
#1 Ranked Closet Couture Overhaul

Strengths

Creative Visionary
Research
Ergonomics
Aesthetics
CAD
Fabric & Upolstery
Home Engineer
Organized
Architecural Elements
Efficient Living
Spacial Expert
Color & Contrast

email or call to request portfolio and personal
consultation:
MaryFlestoria@IDA.com
630.111.1212

"Welcoming clients into their new homes without moving."

Michael Lainic
Sr. Systems Engineer

P: 407-113-2222
Orlando, Florida
mikeLainic@hire.me

About Me...

Systems Engineer specializing in requirement analysis, system design, and system testing.

Languages...

English 100% French 50% German 100%

Interests...

Robotics &&&&&
Volunteering &&&&&
Computer Aided Design (CAD) &&&&
5K's &&&
Travel &&&&&
STEM Mentor &&&&&

Professional History...

AeroDyna Systems / Sr. Systems Engineer 2012-Present

- Created and updated ongoing presentations for client briefings and status reporting.
- Knowledgeable in ALIS warfighters and considered "go to" team member for expertise and trouble-shooting.
- Keenly assessed technical errors and accurately articulated to customer.

Lockstep Technological / Systems Engineer 2009 – 2012

- ALIS expert proficient in system modeling and testing.
- Secret Clearance.
- Working experience of system integration and tests with U.S. Navy assets.

Skills...

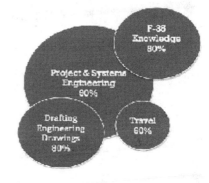

Education...

- **University of Central Florida | Orlando, Fl**
  - Bachelor's Computer Engineer
  - Graduated 4.0

International Project Work...

Susan Cashnick

  407.222.1111

 susiecash@me.com

 savisue.com

*for traditional resume

Socially skilled and engaged in the success of telling business stories. Fuses competitive market research with custom business niche. Expands reach and skyrockets online presence.

Corporate Footprint

- **Global Research | Director, Story Telling | 2014 – Present**
- **Helping Hands | Executive Marketing Director | 2009 – 2014**
- **AlphaOmega Marketing | Founder & CEO | 2004 - 2009**

Achievements...

Social Metrics   **Shorty Award**   **ANA Genius Award**

"What they say..."

Susan is a social genius & leader in corporate Story Telling! ~ Andy G. | Global Research, CEO

Best Leader and mentor! ~ Cassie K. | Helping Hands, Marketing Manager

Fluent...

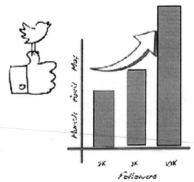

Hello!   *Bonjour!*   *Ciao!*

 **Seton Hill** UNIVERSITY

M.B.A Entrepreneurship
B.A. Marketing

best known for... Innovation Leading Teams

Inspiring Individualization strategic mapping

analytical *Creative Rule Breaking*

Social Engagement Navigating Ambiguity

Social Architecture Compelling CONTENT

<u>driving Change</u> **ahead of the curve**

Contact

T.J. "DJ" Young

P. 615-555-1212

"talented & entertaining!"
~Boss Martin

On-Air Personality
Contemporary Hit Radio ✻ Country ✻ Rock
Recipient of ACM On-Air Personality Nomination

☑ *Established presence as morning on-air personality on FM radio targeting the 18 - 34 year old demographic. Versed in country, contemporary, and rock music, culture, events, and social media.*

☑ *Turned around struggling country station through bootstrap on-air personality while enthusiastically engaging listeners and fans at public appearances, fundraising commitments, professional sporting events, and community related events.*

☑ *Contributed to station revenue increase of 24% through delivering compelling contests, celebrity interviews, trending news, and authentic rapport with listening audience.*

Radio Morning Host:

KKLQ, Birmingham, AL 2014-Present
KTWX, Danville, MS 2013-2014
WTOP, Erie, PA 2011-2013

Television Appearances:

Host, Country Weekend Jam Telethon
Host, Educators in Action Telethon
Host, CMA Afternoon Rock Commercials

Education:

BA Media Communications
University of Dayton, OH

Results: Increased listening audience by 40% in 6 months and improved station ranking from 38 to 32 in both country and contemporary markets.

Celebrity Interviews:
Utilized industry network of peers to secure celebrity participation in "Celebrity Softball Challenge for Kids."

Results: Locked in contracts with country music artists Mel Morris, Kat Jay Dee, and Rocket Fuel for annual softball charity event raising $500K.

Public Appearances / Events

Rock'n Rodeo Raffle
Grand Ole Oprey Mission
Celebrity Softball Challenge for Kids
Chili Cook-Off, Ole Miss
Miss Tennessee Charm Pageant
Super Saturday Auction
"Rock Rhythm" Fashion Show for Gen Y

Social Media & Contests:
Captured new listeners through mainstream social media sites by working with promotions manager, marketing director, and program director.

Results: Hyped contests, chat, and presence on Twitter.com and Facebook.com targeting Gen Y audience. Blasted "In It to Win It" winners on the web and on the air. Social media fans increased 500% in 3 months.

T.M. Joseph

703.888.3323 | tmjoseph@hireme.com

Special Projects | **International Store Openings**

Hallo! Ciao! Hola! Bonjour! Hello!
80% travel - global

Where I studied:
B.S. Business Management, International Studies

Where I worked:
Runway Couture | District Sales Manager (2012 – Present)
RJK Design Haus | District Sales Manager (2009 – 2012)
Fashion Cut-outs | District Trainer (2006 – 2009)

❝ T.M. is an incredible leader, creative problem solver, risk taker, and fearless. Her energy and exciting personality draw people to her. A breath of fresh air to work with.
~James Latham, Runway Couture, Director of Operations

How I achieve results...

Engaging Others
Leadership
Story Telling
Team Motivation
Transparency
Goal Setting
Planning
Forecasting
Social Media
Marketing
Recruiting Top
Talent
Accountability
Contests

←----My passion

Wall of Awards; KPI's

#1 Sales District out of 55

.9% Shrink

#1 Sales Conversion in Company

Krista Kash

407-555-5555 | Orlando, Florida

Lifestyle Health & Wellness Professional *known for infusing holistic approach with clean eating for people and their pets.*

4	99	98
Step Approach to health and healing	Percent Client Approval Rating	Out of 100 customers referred friends based on results

Creates custom plans to suit individual needs of people and their pets targeting. Balanced approach in natural environment.

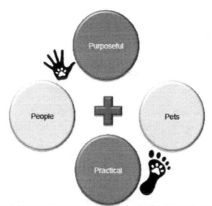

Purposeful

People

Pets

Practical

(human & pet)

Expertise in:

Behavioral Modification
Diet & Exercise | Client Support & Motivation
Individual & Group Workshops | Health & Well Being
Muscular & Skeletal Functions | Individual & Family
Surgical Recovery Therapy

Education

B.S. Nutritionist
B.S. Sports & Fitness
University of Central Florida
Orlando, FL

A.S. Vet Tech
Valencia College
Orlando, FL

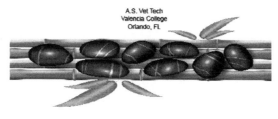

Appendix

More of "What the Pros Say" Resumes

As a resume writer, what is your definition of a resume?

A resume is a future-oriented personal marketing document that should be written to convey that you understand the employers' needs, have the proven ability to meet them, and that you will do so in a way that produces a higher return on the employer's investment in hiring you (ROI) than your competitors will.

Michelle Dumas, NCRW, CPRW

A resume is a written communication of your brand, value proposition, experience, and accomplishments. It doesn't just tell readers what you've done, it tells them what to think about what you've done and why it's relevant in their environment.

Kimberly Robb Baker, NCRW, CJSS, CMRW

When you begin composing a resume (blank computer screen), what thoughts or writing philosophies are in your mind?

When I begin on a new resume, there are two main things that I try to keep in mind and these are the first facts that I capture on paper, because it is from these that the rest of the document flows. First, what is the focus of the resume? Understanding the focus helps me to understand who the audience is for the resume. To be truly effective, a resume should be written to show how the candidate will solve the needs and problems of the audience. Without a clear understanding of the focus and audience for a resume, I am unable to write another word. I write this at the very top of the page to keep me on track as I write.

My second concern is related to discovering and capturing the client's "unique value proposition" or "personal brand." Most clients have no clue what it is that truly differentiates them and makes them uniquely valuable in the workplace. I help them uncover and identify this through the process of writing their resume. To do this, I begin the body of the resume by looking for the storyline. I jot down notes about the challenges they have faced in each position, the actions they have taken, they key results they generated, and the overall lasting impact on each employing organization that the client produced. Through this process, I begin to see threads of similarities in my client's accomplishments. Themes begin to emerge. These themes almost always point to and provide clues about the client's personal brand.

Michelle Dumas, NCRW, CPRW

As I begin composing a resume, I think about the experience the job seeker brings to the table and which elements/keywords of that experience support the target for the next phase in the job seeker's work life—be it a progression in the same career, initial entrance or reentry to the workforce, or a career change.

Beate Hait, CPRW, CRW

In your opinion, is it important to have a brand (either a branding statement or branding words) on a resume? Please briefly explain.

It is critical to have a (portable) brand statement with keywords and proof points artfully strung together with active verbs to bring credibility and life to the brand message. Whether those proof points are within a one-line branding statement, three- to five-line branding summary, bulleted quantified accomplishments (years in the industry, awards won, sales goals, etc.) or testimonials (tidbits from letters of recommendation or client commentaries) all written with a problem-solution-results oriented focus. I do this by weaving together keywords / key messages and supporting them with proof points all tailored and targeted toward a specific job or industry.

Cheryl Minnick, M.Ed., Ed.D, CCMC, NCRW

Personal branding is an often overlooked but very critical piece of your resume. It's the key to showing the employer how you're different from other similar candidates and how you'll be a benefit to the organization.

Jessica Hernandez, Certified Social Branding Analyst

Provided that you advocate for branding on a resume, what do you have your client think about to give you information to formulate the brand?

I have them take two assessments, StrengthsFinder 2.0 and the Fascination Advantage by Sally Hogshead. This gives me, and my client, insight into their innate strengths, what they do best, and some insight on how others perceive them. Once I have this information we talk about each strength and find examples when they've used that strength in their career. We also develop an anthem, which is a tagline for your personality. This comes from the Fascination Advantage assessment. Once I have the anthem I make sure that I pull out achievements in the resume that demonstrate this. The actual anthem may or may not show up in the actual resume.

Michelle Robin, NCRW, CPRW

I provide my clients with a brief questionnaire prior to our information-gathering consultation; their answers will help me to establish an agenda for the consultation. The following questions provide me with some insight about the reoccurring themes in the client's career and how to position him/her (formulate a brand):

1. How do you want to be perceived by your target audience?
2. What problems are you best at solving?
3. What words do your peers, staff, and external partners use to describe you?
4. If there were only 3 things you could share with an employer about your knowledge, skills, abilities, talents and background, what would they be?
5. What do you believe sets you apart from other professionals with similar skills and background?

Norine Dagliano, BA, NCRW, CFRW/CC

I have my clients brainstorm how they're similar to other candidates with the same experience/expertise and also how they're different than those same candidates. The differences usually represent their values and passions and are what will set them apart from their competition.

Jessica Hernandez, Certified Social Branding Analyst

I ask my clients many questions that help me uncover and formulate their brand, but the questions that are most helpful to me are those designed to help draw out their "story." I ask them to explain to me why they were hired or promoted into each position. What were the problems, challenges, or goals that they were brought in to help solve, overcome, or achieve? Then I ask them about their lasting impact on each employing organization. How was that company better off for having had you as an employee?

The themes that emerge from exploring the "story" of my client's career often help me identify their brand.

A second line of questioning helps me to focus in on how the client is the "same" (What are the baseline qualifications that you have, that most of your peers and competitors for this type of job also have?) and "different" (Now explain to me the qualifications you have that are different from most of your peers?). I often get some very brand-revealing answers with these questions.

Michelle Dumas, NCRW, CPRW

What is your resume writing philosophy about listing or mentioning transferable skills (e.g., communication skills, time management, etc.) on a resume?

Transferable skills and the branding message should align, and should further align with the job or industry. Listing skills (hard skills—financial analysis, not soft skills—time management) gives recruiters a taste of what the client offers and provides a "hook" to stimulate interest and garner an interview. It's the charge of a resume writer to help clients (students) develop brand messaging, to infuse their resume (and interviews) with excitement, energy, potential, and possibility so as to "hook" the recruiter. A random skills list that does not speak to the job or industry is useless.

Cheryl Minnick, M.Ed., Ed.D, CCMC, NCRW

Transferable skills are important, but to make sure they're relevant, you might need to explain to the reader what they mean to them. So, a person with a customer service background going into sales has transferable "communications" skills, but they are much more relevant if they're framed in relation to negotiating, needs assessments, and presentations.

Kimberly Robb Baker, NCRW, CJSS, CMRW

Such skills are very important in almost any job. However, we must be careful in that we don't fill the resume with "fluff"—things anybody could say. Anyone can say that they have good communication skills—back it up with a concrete example of communicating with teams, presenting to clients, leading meetings, etc. Anyone can say they are a hard worker—give a specific example of when you went above and beyond to achieve a positive result—did you deliver a project ahead of schedule? Did you take on an extra responsibility and excel at it? Quantify when possible.

Nelly Grinfeld, MBA, NCRW, CEIC

While it's vital to do this, it is critical that it be done in a way that caters to both human and non-human (database) readers. Some hiring executives might like to see a listing of skills, for example, but computers are programmed to place a higher value on keywords used in sentences, so I try to do both. That way whoever reads the resume will be more likely to find what they are looking for where they expect to find it.

Cheryl Lynch Simpson, CMRW, ACRW, COPNS

Can you, as a resume writer, create a level of differentiation by mentioning professional qualities on a resume (e.g., work ethic, honesty, etc.)?

Yes, but mostly by showing rather than telling. Just saying that someone has a great work ethic, for example, is a fairly worthless and unprovable statement. But if I instead include a brief story about how this person stayed all night at work during a hurricane to ensure a critical IT system didn't fail, I don't have to say they have a strong work ethic because it will be self-evident. Using over-utilized adjectives in a resume isn't a powerful approach to communicating someone's brand. I believe it's necessary to craft powerful language and/or leverage unique stories and achievements to help the reader come to the conclusion you want them to reach.

Cheryl Lynch Simpson, CMRW, ACRW, COPNS

Yes, within limits. Any professional quality on a resume should be substantiated by a parallel work experience. I often use quotes from others on a resume to convey these kinds of soft skills. Those types of statements just have more credibility when they come from someone else.

Kimberly Robb Baker, NCRW, CJSS, CMRW

Brand differentiation can be created by noting professional qualities (industry hard and soft skills) as a sales pitch in headlines, taglines, branding statements, branding summaries and bullets. However, persuasive brand differentiation messages should be simple and brief, yet convey critical information. Let's be honest, the goal of a resume is to get through an Applicant Tracking System with a score high enough to get noticed, read and remembered in the 6.25 seconds it takes a recruiter to make a yes/no decision about a resume.

Cheryl Minnick, M.Ed., Ed.D, CCMC, NCRW

Do you still need a resume if you have a LinkedIn profile?

Yes, definitely. Your LinkedIn profile is your online persona, and it's not customized for the position you are applying for. Plus, your profile should not just be a resume dump. It needs to complement your resume. Therefore you need a resume to present yourself to an employer in a targeted fashion. And in an interview, at least an in-person one, the interviewer is not going to be reading off a screen. It seems very impersonal.

Michelle Robin, NCRW, CPRW

Yes, a LinkedIn profile has not eliminated the need for a resume. The #1 reason a job seeker needs a resume is that most—if not all—companies still require submission of a resume as the first step in the hiring process.

Beate Hait, CPRW, NCRW

Yes, you do—resumes are the currency by which human resources departments differentiate and evaluate potential candidates. Your LinkedIn profile is where they'll go once they've decided that your candidacy is worth researching further. Both are complementary but equally vital to your job search.

Jessica Hernandez, Certified Social Branding Analyst

Studies have repeatedly shown that employers spend between five to twenty seconds when first looking at a resume. As a resume writer, how do you create a resume to capitalize on such a brief period of time?

I focus the majority of my attention to crafting a headline and summary for the resume that will make someone take notice. The top third of your resume is crucial to get readers to read on. When I speak on resume writing, I ask my audience to picture the top third of their resume lying on the ground. Would someone picking it up be able to tell who you are, what type of position you want, and the value you uniquely bring to the table? Then would that person be looking for the rest of your resume?

Michelle Robin, NCRW, CPRW

I use the top 1/3 of the first page to capture the reader's attention, keep their interest, and visually set the job seeker apart from the competition. This includes a header, a strong branding statement, and a short summary paragraph that spells out talent, skill, and experience to catch interest.

I pack the rest of the resume with strong accomplishment statements and front-load them with impressive, relevant, quantifiable information.

Nelly Grinfeld, MBA, NCRW, CEIC

Ask yourself what a hiring manager in your market would want to know in order to call you in for an interview. Make sure that information is on the top half of the first page. That means that if you have experience or a degree that otherwise wouldn't be revealed until the second page, find a way to mention it in your opening profile or in a list of career highlights.

Kimberly Robb Baker, NCRW, CJSS, CMRW

Using color, as in a border line or table to separate sections, has been said to add three to four seconds to the time a reader spends on a resume. Bold text, used appropriately, also makes a difference.

Bob Janitz, NCRW

Should a resume be written or revised for each position a job seeker pursues?

A resume needs to be targeted for the desired position so the hiring person doesn't have to guess why this resume was presented. Especially in that top one-third of the resume, every element needs to support the job goal and convey the talents and value the person would bring to the table in that role.

If a job seeker does not have a clear target job direction in mind, I will advise that person to do some research, find the types of jobs that would be appealing, and share those job postings with me. Only then will I be able to craft an effective resume. I need to have a target in mind in order to be able to hit that target!

Beate Hait, CPRW, NCRW

Ideally—yes. Since we don't live in an ideal world, I realize it is often not feasible for job seekers to revise their resume for each submission they make. For this reason, some job seekers may benefit from two resume versions, if their job-search goals have two different paths. For all job seekers, I suggest that the best place to customize their candidacy is in the cover letter. The cover letter gives an opportunity to spell out exactly how they are qualified for this job, and to show genuine interest in, and suitability for, this specific job.

Nelly Grinfeld, MBA, NCRW, CEIC

The use of keywords is important on a resume. What would you consider are the more important kinds of information that lead to keywords?

I am an expert in resume writing. My client is an expert in his or her industry and profession. I listen carefully to the words and jargon my clients use in describing their work, as these are often the keywords and key phrases I will need to use in the resume. I also do a lot of research on the Internet, reading industry-specific websites and very frequently reading job announcements. The words and phrases used in job announcements are almost always important, and in my final check of a resume, I always read through it to make sure I have used as many of the keywords as possible within the body of the resume. A separate keyword section isn't necessary. You just need to make sure they are used, as naturally as possible, in the resume text.

Michelle Dumas, NCRW, CPRW

You don't want to just have a list of keywords in a core competencies section to game the ATS. You need to incorporate the words into your resume. For example, cross-functional team is a popular term. Instead of just listing that somewhere on your resume, put it into context. Something like, "Led cross-functional team across 3 departments to implement new ERP system with little to no downtime at point of transition," gets the term in there and shows your impact.

Michelle Robin, NCRW, CPRW

The job description's "required qualification" and "preferred qualification", as well as "education" sections will have the key qualification that your resume should attend to. When reading a job posting, if a key skill is repeated in the required, preferred and introductory section, it's probably pretty important.

Cheryl Minnick, M.Ed., Ed.D, CCMC, NCRW

What is your opinion regarding the use of a reverse Chronological resume?

Standard resumes are reverse chronological and I use them 95 percent of the time for my clients as they paint a great picture of the job seeker's career history.

Wendi Weiner, JD, NCRW, CPRW, CCTC, CCM

It does serve the majority of job seekers and it is what recruiters and hiring managers want to see. The disadvantage is it will highlight any gaps in employment or short-term jobs.

Michelle Robin, NCRW, CPRW

The typical format for a resume is a reverse chronological style since that shows a person's most recent experience first, and a potential employer will expect to see a trail of increasing responsibility with each job/position culminating with the highest level achieved to that point. If that describes a person's career trajectory and supports the target for the next job, the reverse chronological style is the one to use. It is also the style that most employers prefer to see.

Beate Hait, CPRW, NCRW

What is your opinion regarding the use of a Functional resume?

Never use it. Functional resumes are most often viewed as hiding gaps in employment.

Bob Janitz, NCRW

It is rare that I use this format. However in the case when someone is coming back to the workforce after a long period of time, it does a great job of highlighting relevant skills and accomplishments. I do warn anyone using this format though that they will not be finding a job through traditional methods. The functional format lends itself best to finding jobs through your network. You need to be all on board with that idea before going forward with this format.

Michelle Robin, NCRW, CPRW

What is your opinion regarding the use of a Dateless resume?

Stay away from a resume that eliminates all dates. Recruiters and HR gatekeepers are trained to weed out these resumes as they represent red flags or indicate the candidate is trying to hide issues.

Jessica Hernandez, Certified Social Branding Analyst

I can think of only two clients in the past twenty years for whom I created a dateless resume. In one case the client had dramatic gaps in her work history due to following her military spouse as he moved from place to place. In the other, she was returning to the workforce after nearly twenty years away while raising her family. In both cases, the resume was highly effective and successful for the client. But, I would not advocate this approach unless the circumstances truly called for it.

Michelle Dumas, NCRW, CPRW

You're going to have a hard time using a dateless resume because people want to know how current your experience is. This is especially true if you are targeting a large corporation who is more traditional in their hiring methods. A resume without dates will get thrown out.

Michelle Robin, NCRW, CPRW

Is it important to have a title on a resume?

It is important. It immediately tells the reader who you are.

Bob Janitz, NCRW

Titles are absolutely important! The person reading the resume has to know why it is in their hands.

Kimberly Robb Baker, NCRW, CJSS, CMRW

Yes. I believe a title takes the place of a traditional objective statement on a resume. When you have the title you're targeting at the top of your resume, it serves two purposes. One, it helps with keywords and two, it's easy to see at a quick glance what you're aiming to do.

Michelle Robin, NCRW, CPRW

What is your opinion regarding the use of an Objective Statement?

They died out with the dinosaurs. Nobody cares what a candidate "wants," they care what a candidate can "do."

Cheryl Minnick, M.Ed., Ed.D, CCMC, NCRW

Résumés are about the employers' needs and how you as a job seeker can meet them. Objectives are about your needs and desires as a job seeker. That is an important difference to understand. I don't remember the last time I wrote an objective statement on a resume. It has really been that long.

Michelle Dumas, NCRW, CPRW

I never use an objective statement on my resumes, even for recent grads. A traditional objective statement is all about the candidate's wants, not the employer's needs. These days employers don't care what the candidate wants. They want to know what the candidate can do for them. Sometimes on a young professional's resume I'll put the word "target" in front of the title they are aiming to get. That is subtle and short enough to get the point across.

Michelle Robin, NCRW, CPRW

As a resume writer, what do you want to achieve with a Summary section?

Profiles are critical—they are above the fold, they anchor the resume, and they entice the reader. The best, most effective profiles provide an easy-to-read overview of your brand, your value, and your impact and provide proof of your performance by summarizing your accomplishments and results that will have the greatest meaning and value for your target.

Michelle Dumas, NCRW, CPRW

I want to give the employer a brief snapshot of how my client can add value, be a benefit and solve the biggest problems the company is facing. Ultimately, employers are looking for someone who can meet a particular need. The job seeker's job is to know what that need is and then make the connection between their experience/expertise and how it can meet the need of the employer.

Jessica Hernandez, Certified Social Branding Analyst

My goal is to create a unique and digestible set of data points that specifically reflect the candidate. In fact, if the recruiter or hiring manager reads only the first third of the first page, they will have all the high-level information they need about the candidate's capability, history, and potential.

Amy Adler, MBA, MA, CMRW, CCMC

How do you go about formulating a Summary paragraph or Summary statements?

To decide what to include in the Summary section, I look at job postings to determine what an employer is looking for in a candidate for a specific position. I then review my notes on the job seeker's performance record, education, training and also soft skills, since these are often mentioned in job postings, and select those elements that pertain to both the job seeker and the employer's search criteria.

Beate Hait, CPRW, NCRW

I summarize the candidate's value for the job in three to five lines as tightly as possible, getting to the core of what he offers the employer for the particular job for which they are applying. I review the job posting, company mission statement, any employee's LinkedIn profile at that company (hopefully, the same job) and complete a Google search of the company to find news articles and get a fuller understanding of what the company does, what the job "is" and what the "pain points" might be.

Cheryl Minnick, M.Ed., Ed.D, CCMC, NCRW

Summary statements should be brief, pithy, and branded. Avoid paragraphs of more than two to three lines. Consider organizing the summary by category or with a short list of accomplishments that each represent a core component of your value in the market.

Kimberly Robb Baker, NCRW, CJSS, CMRW

Do you find it important, as a resume writer, to list Core Competencies/Skills somewhere on a resume?

Yes, it's a place that's easy to scan for key competencies and is best placed right where the eye will naturally fall. These core skills can also be matching keywords to gain a greater score in an Applicant Tracking System.

Cheryl Minnick, M.Ed., Ed.D, CCMC, NCRW

These skills can be highlighted specifically in a list, but they should naturally appear in the descriptions of the individual's accomplishments.

Amy L. Adler, MBA, MA, CMRW, CCMC

I always list these immediately after the summary statement.

Bob Janitz, NCRW

When you create the employment history section of a resume, what is your approach? What are you thinking?

The best résumés are a reflection of a person, NOT just a collection of words on a piece of paper. Instead they tell a memorable story that illustrates the unique promise of value that you bring to the workplace. Your resume is not about job duties and responsibilities. Instead, it should be strategically and thoughtfully written to promote you as a solution to an employer's needs and to prove your ability to deliver ROI.

Probably, the single most important thing I do when writing the body of the resume is to focus on CAR statements. Remember that an achievement has three parts—the challenge faced, the actions you took, and the results of your action (CAR). Overall, readers will be most interested in your results, and these should be the focus of the document, but all three parts are important. The reader needs to know about your challenges to place your achievements in context. What challenges have you faced? What did you do to meet these challenges? How did this benefit your employers? The final piece of this equation is the strategic impact. The big picture of how the client had a lasting impact on the organization. I write the narrative of the resume to succinctly tell the "story" behind each position, demonstrating to the reader that the client has the ability to solve problems, fulfill goals, and meet challenges.

Michelle Dumas, NCRW, CPRW

I cut down the person's responsibilities to the absolute bare minimum. And what is in there for the scope of the job, I try to frame as much like an accomplishment as I can. I like to use data points to illustrate things like budget, revenue and direct reports.
I am on a personal mission to remove the words "responsible for" from everyone's resume. No one cares what you were responsible for. They want to know what you can do for them.

Michelle Robin, NCRW, CPRW

The employment history should include the candidate's relevant experience. If the work history is longer than ten to fifteen years, I create a section called "early work experience" and briefly list older positions there.

Nelly Grinfeld, MBA, NCRW, CEIC

There are commentators that state you need only to emphasize the last fifteen years of experience (since it is the most recent and relevant) on a resume. What is your opinion?

This depends on the job seeker and the job search goals. If the older experience is relevant to what the job seeker wants to do next, then by all means include it and describe it briefly.

Nelly Grinfeld, MBA, NCRW, CEIC

That's usually true. When making that decision, ask yourself if there is anything of value in the earlier history. I almost always include a brief paragraph about early career, usually without dates. It's a part of branding a candidate. Most people are strongly influenced by their first professional experiences, and that influence is a part of what defines someone's professional brand.

Kimberly Robb Baker, NCRW, CJSS, CMRW

How important is it to quantify accomplishments on a resume? Please briefly explain.

Metrics are undeniable proof of success. Metrics in the context of challenges, actions, and results compel the hiring manager to understand the job seeker's ability to interpret and act on difficult situations.

Amy L. Adler, MBA, MA, CMRW, CCMC

A common misconception is that resumes should describe what you do in your current job and what you did in your past jobs. Actually, the most effective resumes are written from a future perspective. A resume should be full of achievements and accomplishments, and just copying a list of your job duties does not tell the reader what you actually achieved.

The strongest accomplishment statements are quantified, meaning they are measured and expressed numerically. Include measurable results in your resume; include numbers as often as possible.

Don't just say you tutored students; say how many and by how much their grades improved. Don't say you were successful; tell us exactly what results you achieved. Don't just say "increased"; tell us by what percentage. The reader will imply that you can produce similar results for them.

Nelly Grinfeld, MBA, NCRW, CEIC

Just telling the reader that my client has achievements isn't very effective unless they are presented in terms of the results and benefits they have produced for past employers. I always try to think in terms of the "so what" of the achievement. What did my client improve, save, increase, enhance, etc.? What impact did the work the client did have on the companies? I work hard to communicate the impact and ROI of my client's performance. Whenever I can, I use numbers to illustrate results (dollar figures, percentages, raw numbers, etc.), but even when I am unable to quantify achievements, the emphasis is still placed on the results and benefits of the client's work.

Michelle Dumas, NCRW, CPRW

Should a resume be written in the first person?

A resume is usually written in implied first person (first person with no personal pronouns). Some executive recruiters are used to seeing third person in the summary portion, making it more akin to an executive bio. Either is okay. Just be consistent.

Kimberly Robb Baker, NCRW, CJSS, CMRW

The resume should be written in implied first person, without using the word I. Also, omit a, the, an. Instead of saying "I led a team of 6 employees . . . " say "Led team of six . . . "—short, concise, to the point.

Nelly Grinfeld, MBA, NCRW, CEIC

Do you have any unique techniques in writing the Education section?

Often, I will use a "Focus" to match a keyword in the job posting or to illustrate to the recruiter an area of additional or focused study. For instance, "Master of Education in Educational Counseling, Supervision and Leadership (Career Counseling focus). If a job calls for a master's degree, yet the candidate has not completed the degree, I might use: Master of Business Administration in progress (54 of 60 credits completed).

Cheryl Minnick, M.Ed., Ed.D, CCMC, NCRW

There is a variety of additional information that can be included on a resume, such as: affiliations/associations, memberships, appointments (appointed positions), non-career related awards and honors, languages, and licenses, among others. How do you treat this information on a resume?

If the additional information is relevant and supports the focus of the resume, I include it. If not, I exclude it. However, if I exclude it, I will often create an "addendum" document that the client can include with the resume, or use as a leave-behind at interviews, if he or she thinks it is especially relevant for a specific position.

Michelle Dumas, NCRW, CPRW

Additional information such as those mentioned above can be listed either in its own section or included in the Summary section; it all depends on how relevant that information is to the target position and the space available in the resume. If it would serve the job seeker best to highlight certain information under a separate heading, that would be the best course of action. However, if that separate section happens to be on a new page as the only item on that page, then it's best to rethink that strategy and reformat the resume.

Beate Hait, CPRW, NCRW

If the client provides this data, it supports the job seeker's brand, and there is space for it, then I will include it. Often these kinds of information elements will help document someone's leadership skills, readiness for management roles, or career brand.

Cheryl Lynch Simpson, CMRW, ACRW, COPNS

What is your opinion about including recommendations on a resume?

I think it makes your resume stand out by using one to three quotes on a resume. It saves the recruiter time from having to go to LinkedIn to read them, or can entice a recruiter to go to LinkedIn to read more. Also, I believe it's stronger to have someone else say how great you are vs. you saying how great you are.

Michelle Robin, NCRW, CPRW

A short, impressive quote sometimes has its place on a resume; it validates the candidate, and shows the reader an "outsider's" perspective on the candidate. However, a recommendation should not be used instead of strong accomplishment statements.

Nelly Grinfeld, MBA, NCRW, CEIC

Including "pull quotes" from letters of reference or from performance reviews is a great strategy to use so others can "sing the praises of the job seeker" before the potential employer even asks for a reference. Including a link to the job seeker's LinkedIn profile—especially if that profile contains several impressive recommendations—is also a good strategy.

Beate Hait, CPRW, NCRW

What is your opinion about adding a QR code on a resume?

For a brief period of time we were using these a lot. But we also used tracking so we could tell how often the code was scanned, and the answer was: almost never. Accordingly, we don't often include them anymore unless we have a good reason to do so.

Michelle Dumas, NCRW, CPRW

For social media resumes, great—they will disappear in an ATS. The key is really what does the QR Code point the recruiter to, and why is that information not on the resume? Is it a video, a website?

Cheryl Minnick, M.Ed., Ed.D, CCMC, NCRW

Depending on what a QR code links to would determine the advisability of including that on a resume. Does it link to a website that shows the job seeker's portfolio of work, the person's LinkedIn profile or just to a website that displays the resume?

Beate Hait, CPRW, NCRW

How do you deal with employment gaps on a resume?

One strategy to minimize attention to gaps in employment is to move the dates closer to other text rather than drawing attention to dates if they are right-aligned on the page. Depending on the job seeker's circumstances, one could also briefly note what the job seeker did during the "gap" years (i.e., attending to a family member with health challenges; a sabbatical year; time devoted to professional development; stay-at-home parent). In anticipation of the question, the circumstance could also be briefly explained in the accompanying cover letter.

Beate Hait, CPRW, NCRW

Most often it's just using full years instead of the month and the year. However, when a client has a more significant gap, it depends on the reason for the gap. If they took some years off to take care of small kids, I may have a single line about that, and focus on what the person did volunteer-wise during that time.

Luckily, these days a gap is not so much an automatic red flag. Employers are more understanding. Just be honest about it. Some people even appreciate the risk you took to go out on your own for a while. I think as long as you can show you weren't stagnate and kept up with technology a gap is not a detrimental thing.

Michelle Robin, NCRW, CPRW

I have used "Personal Travel Sabbatical," and make sure to include a travel section; or I will use "Educational Sabbatical" and insert a certification or training that covers the gap; or insert a volunteer position (especially for stay-at-home parents returning to the workforce) that explains the time gap, "Teacher Assistant-Volunteer, Roosevelt Elementary School."

Cheryl Minnick, M.Ed., Ed.D, CCMC, NCRW

What is your opinion or philosophy regarding the use of color on a resume?

For most job seekers, their next career move will most likely come from a recommendation or via a networking opportunity—not through a blind online application. For this reason, it is best to create two resume versions: a "plain" version you will use to apply online, and a "fancy" version (with color, design elements, and any appropriate graphical representations) that you will use to network with. Remember that a resume with color, graphics, and fancy fonts should only be used to network with.

Nelly Grinfeld, MBA, NCRW, CEIC

My thoughts on using color on résumés has evolved over the past few years, especially now that résumés are almost always electronically submitted and viewed on screen. We are living in a culture of distraction in which we are constantly bombarded with content and information. Like it or not, people's attention spans are getting shorter. Color, when used in very selective, strategic ways, especially when you combine it with charts, graphs, and graphics that help to quickly convey complex information in easy-to-read and grasp ways, can be highly effective.

Five years ago I almost never used color because it was so unusual to see on a resume that it seemed almost jarring and flashy, in a not very flattering way. Almost like you were raising your hand and shouting "look at me, look at me" while jumping up and down. Today, I use touches of color on almost every resume, although I still tend to use muted color schemes and apply them in subtle and sophisticated ways. At the same time, I still provide my client with the same resume in a grayscale, for those situations when they think a more traditional approach would be better. But fewer of my clients are using the grayscale version. They all prefer the color.

Michelle Dumas, NCRW, CPRW

When you visually look over a resume, what are you looking at or looking for that confirms in your mind that you have written "a good one?"

I want to bring that candidate in for an interview. I can imagine meeting them and smiling. It is visually balanced with plenty of white space. I like to put the document at about 50 percent and just look at the visual balance.

Kimberly Robb Baker, NCRW, CJSS, CMRW

If the key points can be attained with a ten-second read and viewed on an iPhone—I feel it is good to go.

Virginia Franco, NCRW, CPRW

What is your opinion about the use of an infographic resume?

I think an infographic resume is best suited to job seekers in creative fields such as the arts, graphic design, visual merchandising, social media, marketing/advertising, publishing, or photography.

Beate Hait, CPRW, NCRW

I'm all for it, if it makes sense for the candidate. Someone in a traditional industry, like financial services, may get thrown out for having an infographic resume. If you do use one, you need to make sure it is clear and tells the right story. If people can't figure out the graphic, or it takes too long to connect the dots, so to speak, you're better off with a traditional resume.

Michelle Robin, NCRW, CPRW

Infographic Resume

As an infographic resume writer, when you start creating a resume for a job seeker, what are you thinking?

All clients go through a behavior-based scientific profile analysis plus a personal branding assessment. These help me understand who my client is in terms of leadership strengths and also what their brand represents. Once I have this information, I start to think about my client in images. Once I capture these images, I extract the key "must haves" and incorporate them into the document. Show personal branding/personality, metrics of some sort, languages, results, etc., recommendations from others, employment footprint, photo or caricature, and overall marketing message. I think of my client having a giant billboard on the highway and car driving by at 70 mph with a few seconds to be wowed! Every detail is meticulously thought through and each word is carefully selected. Telling a story in images is an art and when coupled with key ingredients, a powerful message is conveyed. I also think about appealing the document to both pragmatic and creative interviewers. There must be information/images for both the right and left brain.

Tina Kashlak Nicolai, PHR, CPBA, CARW
Lominger Certified (Interview Architect)

Can a CEO submit an infographic resume?

Sure . . . if he/she is trying to make a splash with an open and innovative culture. In the case of a CEO submitting a portfolio, I recommend an introduction document, an infographic, traditional line item resume, and a biography. There are also individual nuances that can be added to the CEO portfolio, but these are the basic must haves.

Tina Kashlak Nicolai, PHR, CPBA, CARW
Lominger Certified (Interview Architect)

LinkedIn

What is your opinion about the name a client should use on their LinkedIn profile? Should they use their birth name, the name they go by, or their birth name with the name they go by in quotation marks?

I recommend the name they go by in professional circles and by which their colleagues will recognize them. This should be the name they use on their resume, as well. If they wish, their birth name can be included in the summary section.

Michelle Dumas, NCRW, CPRW

LinkedIn is not a legal document, nor is your resume for that matter, so you are not required to use your legal name. I recommend clients use the name they preferred to be called as long as that coincides with what most people know them as. However, if you have a common name like Chris that can be shortened from a variety of other names, I would suggest you put your full name in quotes in the name field. They can also put a line in the summary that says "also known as" or "common misspellings" and list it there. That helps when people are searching.

Michelle Robin, NCRW, CPRW

What is your opinion about including one or two professional designations in the last name box of a LinkedIn profile?

If they are supportive of my client's career focus and goals, we include them. Like everything, I justify my choice by thinking strategically and thoughtfully about my client's career goals.

Michelle Dumas, NCRW, CPRW

How do you view the Headline section? What is your thinking when you formulate the Headline?

Be specific and use keywords that directly reflect the position you're pursuing. If you do not include specific keywords it will default to you current job title. Separate these keywords with symbols. For example:

Executive Resume Writer | C-Level Resume Writer | LinkedIn Profile Writer

Or you could create a one-line personal branding statement that clearly articulates what you do:

"I create visually engaging and interview-winning executive resumes and LinkedIn profiles for busy top-tier executives."

Jessica Hernandez, Certified Social Branding Analyst

120 characters matter. Make the most of them. Your headline should not be your job tile. Instead, it should be similar to your resume branding statement to serve as a pitch to your own personal news story.

Wendi Weiner, JD, NCRW, CPRW, CCTC, CCM

I view the headline section as a short version of the client's WhyBuyROI. If the client is unemployed, then I use the headline to showcase a key result or two. If the client is employed and looking for work passively, I use the headline to underscore their current role and achievements. For job seekers in active search mode I try to weave in industry-specific keywords along with the client's #1 preferred geographic location.

Cheryl Lynch Simpson, CMRW, ACRW, COPNS

What is your strategy regarding the use and location of keywords in a LinkedIn profile?

Relevant keywords should be found throughout all sections of your LinkedIn profile—in the headline, summary, skills, education, memberships, etc. Headline and summary are the most vital places for this. Recruiters search for keywords to find candidates on LinkedIn, so the more your profile is populated with keywords, the better your chances of being found by recruiters.

Nelly Grinfeld, MBA, NCRW, CEIC

Keywords definitely matter. I recommend utilizing them creatively and weaving them throughout the summary and headline as those are what stand out the most and are scanned by the human eye first. Consider having your own core skills section within the confines of your LinkedIn profile in the summary section.

Wendi Weiner, JD, NCRW, CPRW, CCTC, CCM

We go to great lengths to make sure the client's profile is keyword rich. While this is true of the entire profile, and I don't have any technical validation for this next statement, I've found that the keywords in the summary section, headline statement, job title fields, and the most recent one or two job description fields seem to be weighted more heavily.

Michelle Dumas, NCRW, CPRW

How do you approach or what strategy do you use when writing the Summary section to a LinkedIn profile? And, how does it differ from the Summary section of a resume?

In the summary section you have 2,000 characters to create a compelling story that demonstrates your value and sells your unique expertise. Instead of having one huge block of text, consider breaking up the information into a sub-headline, short paragraphs, and perhaps a keyword list at the end.

Your summary section should be engaging and original: Take the opportunity to showcase who you are as a professional and what makes you interesting, memorable, and extraordinary.

It should be written in the first person: LinkedIn is a place to communicate with others. When you write the summary in the first person, visitors to your profile will easily imagine what it would be like to have a conversation with you.

It should be angled toward the specific people you care about the most: Before writing a single word, you must determine who you are talking to. Recruiters? Hiring managers? Potential clients? What will this audience want to know about you? How will you capture their attention?

It should be clear on what you want the reader to do next: You must spell out to the reader what you're looking to accomplish, and what you'd like for them to do next. Give them a call to action. Even if you're a stealth job seeker, you can still be pretty clear on what you'd like to happen next, without outing yourself.

Nelly Grinfeld, MBA, NCRW, CEIC

The original purpose of LinkedIn is to cultivate connections and relationships, and to aid in networking. While the LinkedIn summary needs to have messaging and branding that is consistent with the resume, I rewrite the summary to be more personal and conversational in tone. The summary section for the LinkedIn profile is often written to reveal a bit more of the client's "story" in a more personal way than the summary section of the resume.

Michelle Dumas, NCRW, CPRW

What is your strategy and approach when drafting the Job Experience section?

Unlike a lot of LinkedIn profile writers, I believe this section should be brief based on research done into how recruiters and hiring managers read profiles. As a result,

I present a one- to two-sentence overview of each role followed by their strongest achievement. I also include a brief skills section to insert relevant keywords.

Cheryl Lynch Simpson, CMRW, ACRW, COPNS

It is important that the details (job titles, companies, dates, etc.) are consistent with the resume and it is also important that the overall message and the story that we focus on is consistent with the storyline, brand, and message of the resume. It is just as important that the LinkedIn profile tells a compelling and enticing story of challenges faced, actions taken, results produced, and strategic impact, as it is in the resume. However, I usually rewrite the resume text for the LinkedIn profile, to tell the story in a more conversational tone. Sometimes I will also remove whole numbers from quantified accomplishments or tone down the story of a company in turmoil, to make it more appropriate for a wider audience. For example, telling the story of a company that was in chaos and failing, then "saved" by my client could be insulting to others who were involved in that situation. While the chaos and failure may be the absolute truth, less controversial language is called for on LinkedIn.

Michelle Dumas, NCRW, CPRW

Cover Letters

Do you employ a formula or strategy when crafting a cover letter for a client? If so, what?

I have no formula. As with everything I do, my letter-writing strategies are very tailored to the unique needs of my client. However, I will note here one of the biggest mistakes that I see job seekers make, and even other resume writers: not understanding and tailoring the letter to the audience. There are many different situations in which you might need a cover letter during your job search. For example, introducing yourself to a recruiting firm, reaching out to people in your network, responding to job announcements, or asking for an informational interview. In each of these cases, the focus of the letter and the points emphasized will be slightly different, to address the concerns of the audience. There is no such thing as one letter that is appropriate for every audience. I often write a portfolio of letters for my clients, to make sure they have a good model to use as a starting point for every situation they may encounter.

Michelle Dumas, NCRW, CPRW

A great cover letter must be short, it must address an actual person, it must be explicit in what you're applying for and why you want the job, and it must briefly summarize the value you will bring to the organization. It must help the reader connect the dots by using three to five bullet points to outline exactly how you are the best fit for the position.

Nelly Grinfeld, MBA, NCRW, CEIC

A cover letter needs to be short and to the point and yet be a customized self-marketing document for a specific position. Usually three paragraphs will suffice: intro, why the person qualifies for this position and call to action.

Beate Hait, CPRW, NCRW

First, I make sure that the cover letter presents my client's WhyBuyROI in a way that aligns with the content of the other documents I am creating for them. Second, I also align the letter with their primary job-search strategies. That is, if they plan to pursue jobs via job boards I'll write a different kind of letter than if they plan to do a lot of networking or company targeting. Third, I try to identify brand assets the client has that I can leverage in some way—testimonials about their work, articles they've written, awards they've won, unique achievements, and so on. Selecting one or two of these elements to showcase in a short cover letter can help their candidacy to stand out.

Cheryl Lynch Simpson, CMRW, ACRW, COPNS

The shorter the cover letter the better! I write an e-note style cover letter as my take on the traditional cover letter is that it's now obsolete. Think about a brief email you'd write to the employer that states your interest in the position and how/why you're a great fit. The points you use to address your fit for a role should be tied to the needs of the organization. Brief + Why + Need = the perfect e-note.

Jessica Hernandez, Certified Social Branding Analyst

What technique do you use to quickly capture the attention of the reader of a cover letter?

I front load key skills—example: a lawyer who worked for an Am Law 100 firm or graduated from a top-five law school should advise that from the outset of the cover letter to capture the reader's attention. It is all about the art of persuasion when it comes to crafting a cover letter and selecting which key traits or accomplishments stand out.

Wendi Weiner, JD, NCRW, CPRW, CCTC, CCM

You must include a customized cover letter about who you are and what unique, relevant contribution you would bring to that company. Don't send a generic cover letter: make it customized, interesting, and relevant, but keep it brief. A good cover letter is your opportunity to show genuine interest and to prove that you are qualified for the job.

Nelly Grinfeld, MBA, NCRW, CEIC

Open the letter by promising a benefit, identifying a need, illustrating industry/company insight, sharing an accomplishment or revealing your passions. Then go on to explain that this is why you are writing and expressing your interest in company Y/position X.

Norine Dagliano, BA, NCRW, CFRW/CC

What makes a cover letter persuasive or impactful?

When you speak directly to the pains of an organization and how you have solved similar pains in the past, that is what will be persuasive.

Michelle Robin, NCRW, CPRW

Statistics show that only 30 percent of cover letters are read. You want a cover letter that is not cookie cutter and instead impacts the reader by making him/her say, "Wow! This is someone who has the skills and really wants the job!"

Wendi Weiner, JD, NCRW, CPRW, CCTC, CCM

What tricks-of-the-trade do you use when writing a cover letter?

First, cover letters are trending shorter these days, so it's imperative to say more with fewer words. This can be accomplished through succinct writing that gets to the point through the use of clear language and action verbs. Second, I try to write in my client's voice. I use their language and phrasing whenever possible so the letter sounds like them rather than me (trying to sound like them). Third, I allow the client's brand and achievements to speak for themselves by getting out of their way. I view a cover letter as a brief summary of a client's career and as such this very short document must quickly hone in on what sets the client's experience apart from that of other candidates. Above all, the letter must convey why this person should be interviewed or hired rather than the next person.

Cheryl Lynch Simpson, CMRW, ACRW, COPNS

What suggestions would you pass along about writing a post-interview thank-you letter?

It's best to write a post-interview thank-you letter (or email) as soon as possible after the interview. Write one for each person on the interview team, noting an impression from the day or a follow-up comment to what was discussed, and express your continued interest in the position. Writing a short thank-you note to the receptionist would also make a great impression, since the receptionist is likely to mention the job seeker's thoughtfulness to the hiring authority.

Beate Hait, CPRW, NCRW